IBN 'ARABI AND THE CONTEMPORARY WEST

Comparative Islamic Studies
Series Editor: Brannon Wheeler, US Naval Academy

This book series, like its companion journal of the same title, publishes work that integrates Islamic studies into the contemporary study of religion, thus providing an opportunity for expert scholars of Islam to demonstrate the more general significance of their research both to comparatavists and to specialists working in other areas. Attention to Islamic materials from outside the central Arabic lands is of special interest, as are comparisons that stress the diversity of Islam as it interacts with changing human conditions.

Published

Orientalists, Islamists and the Global Public Sphere: A Genealogy of the Modern Essentialist Image of Islam
Dietrich Jung

Earth, Empire and Sacred Text: Muslims and Christians as Trustees of Creation
David L. Johnston

Ibn 'Arabi and the Contemporary West: Beshara and the Ibn 'Arabi Society
Isobel Jeffery-Street

Notes from the Fortune-Telling Parrot: Islam and the Struggle for Religious Pluralism in Pakistan
David Pinault

Prolegomena to a History of Islamicate Manichaeism
John C. Reeves

IBN 'ARABI AND THE CONTEMPORARY WEST

BESHARA AND THE IBN 'ARABI SOCIETY

ISOBEL JEFFERY-STREET

SHEFFIELD UK   BRISTOL CT

Published by Equinox Publishing Ltd.

UK: Office 415, The Workstation, 15 Paternoster Row, Sheffield S1 2BX
USA: ISD, Suite 2, 70 Enterprise Drive, Bristol, CT 06010

www.equinoxpub.com

First published 2012

© Isobel Jeffery-Street 2012

All rights reserved. No part of this publication may be reproduced or transmitted in any form or by any means, electronic or mechanical, including photocopying, recording or any information storage or retrieval system, without prior permission in writing from the publishers.

Library of Congress Cataloguing-in-Publication Data
Jeffery-Street, Isobel.
  Ibn Arabi and the contemporary West : Beshara and the Ibn Arabi Society / Isobel Jeffery-street.
     p. cm. -- (Comparative Islamic studies)
  Includes bibliographical references and index.
  ISBN 978-1-84553-670-1 (hb) -- ISBN 978-1-84553-671-8 (pb) 1. Ibn al-'Arabi, 1165-1240. 2. Ibn al-'Arabi, 1165-1240--Influence. 3. Beshara Trust. 4. Muhyiddin Ibn 'Arabi Society. 5. Philosophy, Islamic. 6. Mysticism--Islam. I. Title.
  B753.I24J44 2010
  181'.92--dc22
                   2009026245

ISBN   978-1-84553-670-1 (hardback)
       978-1-84553-671-8 (paperback)
       978-1-84553-818-7 (eBook)

Typeset and edited by Forthcoming Publications Ltd
www.forthcomingpublications.com

Contents

Acknowledgments	ix
INTRODUCTION	1
The Life of Ibn 'Arabi in Brief	2
Ibn 'Arabi's Influence in the West Today	5
Further Studies of Western Sufi Movements	14
Disciplinary and Methodological Approach to the Study	18
Religious Experience and Mysticism	20
Problems with the 'Language' of Mysticism	23
Universality and Particularity in Religion	25
Research Methods and Data	26
Structure and Contents of the Chapters	31
Note on Transliteration and Transcription	34
1 BULENT RAUF	35
Early Life	35
Bulent Rauf and Ibn 'Arabi	36
The Beginnings of Beshara	42
Bulent Rauf's Writings and Translations	46
Bulent Rauf and the 'Hidden Saints'	46
Posterity	51
Conclusion	53
2 THE BESHARA TRUST: EARLY YEARS	54
Bulent Rauf and the Origins of Beshara	54
Swyre Farm	58
The Twenty-Nine Pages: Teaching Ibn 'Arabi at Swyre Farm	60
Early Students of Beshara and Swyre Farm	63
Bulent Rauf in Residence at Swyre Farm	65
The *Blue Fusûs* and Titus Burckhardt	66
J.G. Bennett and the Beshara School	68

3 CHISHOLME AND SHERBORNE: THE INTRODUCTION OF STRUCTURED, RESIDENTIAL COURSES   74

The Acquisition of Chisholme and Sherborne   74
The Introduction and Purpose of a Structured
    Residential Course   77
Course Schedule   79
Basic Rules of Behaviour   86
Course Supervision   86
Organisation and Funding   87
Conclusion   88

4 AN INTRODUCTION TO THE TEXTS AND TEACHINGS OF IBN 'ARABI USED FOR STUDY BY THE BESHARA SCHOOL   89

The Twenty-Nine Pages: An Introduction
    to Muhyiddin Ibn 'Arabi's Metaphysics of Unity   90
Ontology and Cosmology   92
Doctrine of the Logos   99
Epistemology   102
Mystical and Metaphysical Psychology   104
Mysticism   106
Religion, Ethics and Aesthetics   108
The Figure of Jesus and the 'Seal of Sainthood'   111
Ibn 'Arabi and the Feminine Dimension in the Divine   114
Other Texts Used on Beshara Courses   116
Conclusion   126

5 RECENT BESHARA EDUCATION: THE COURSES AND THEIR AIMS   128

The Meanings of 'Beshara' as Understood
    by Some Participants   128
Beshara as a Global Manifestation   130
Ibn 'Arabi and the 'Seal of Sainthood'
    as a 'Meaning' (Spiritual Reality)   132
The Aims of the Beshara Courses   135
What is an 'Esoteric Education'?   139
Conclusion   141

6 STUDENT EXPERIENCES DURING AND FOLLOWING THE COURSES   142

Motivations for Taking the Intensive
    Six-month Introductory Course   143

	'Second-generation' Students	145
	Some Students' Experiences of the Courses	147
	Life After a Beshara Course:	
	Applying Course Experience to Everyday Life	160
	Conclusion	175
7	**THE PILGRIMAGE THROUGH TURKEY**	176
	The Purpose of the Pilgrimage	176
	The Influence of Ibn 'Arabi and its	
	Relevance to the Journey	178
	The Shrines Visited and their Connection with Ibn 'Arabi	181
	Other Islamic, Christian and Hellenistic Sites Visited	
	and their Connection with Ibn 'Arabi	182
	The Travellers	183
	Itinerary of the Journey	185
	Visitation (*ziyâra*) of the Shrines of Muslim Saints	186
	The Travellers' Reactions to the Visits	192
	Conclusion	202
8	**OUTREACH**	205
	Publications and Publicity	205
	Communication and Outreach	217
	Other Methods of Outreach and Communication	
	Continuing into the 1980s	220
	International Expansion	223
	Beshara Today	226
9	**THE MUHYIDDIN IBN 'ARABI SOCIETY**	231
	Introduction	231
	Foundation Period	234
	Early Days: The Library at Concordia House	237
	The Development of the *Journal*	240
	1984 Onwards: The First Annual Symposium	243
	The Evolution of the Society through the 1980s	
	to the Early 1990s	248
	The Society through the 1990s to the New Millennium	254
	The Global Expansion of Knowledge of Ibn 'Arabi	258
	Conclusion	261
	Bibliography	267
	Index	277

ACKNOWLEDGMENTS

I would like to express my gratitude to my supervisor, Professor James Morris, for all his help and guidance to me through the duration of this study; also to Professor Alexander Knysh who set me on the path of this research. To the students of the Beshara School and the members of the Muhyiddin Ibn 'Arabi Society who have been so freely and kindly prepared to co-operate with me in many aspects of data collection. In particular I would like to thank the chairman of the Muhyiddin Ibn 'Arabi Society, Grenville Collins, for his ongoing encouragement and support; Richard and Cecilia Twinch for putting up with my perpetual onslaught of enquiries; Martin and Caroline Notcutt; Jane Clark, her late husband Robert[1] and Stephen Hirtenstein all who provided invaluable advice and guidance. The Principal of the Beshara School at Chisholme, Peter Young, was a continuous source of help, information and enlightenment and I would not have made much progress without the gracious assistance of Peter Yiangou and his wife Alison. There are numerous other people to whom I feel deep appreciation for their particular help during my research. These include Abraham and Lesley Abadi; Christina Hill; Sara Hirtenstein; Daniel Hirtenstein; Francis and Christopher Ryan; Stuart and Rahima Kenner; Narda Dalgliesh; Adam Dupré; and Meral Arim. It also was a very great privilege to have met and to have had lively and informative discussion with Angela Culme-Seymore, wife of the late Bulent Rauf. Another particularly supportive figure has been Mhairi Macmillan. I would also like to express profound appreciation to Professor Ralph Austin whose fascinating themes of conversation during the Annual British Muhyiddin Ibn 'Arabi Society Symposium, held to celebrate the millennium in 2000 at Chisholme House, included startlingly accurate prophesies. A special mention must go to Paul Auchterlanie, head librarian at the University of Exeter, without whose help and steerage this work would never have got off the ground and who has provided ongoing support throughout.

1. Sadly, Robert Clark died on the 1 January 2003.

There are countless more students and participants of both the Beshara School and the Muhyiddin Ibn 'Arabi Society who were infinitely generous in providing data via interviews and other means whom I would like to thank by name but who wished to remain anonymous.

My thanks go to the Spalding Trust, the Bulent Rauf Scholarship Trust and a third fundmaking Trust, which requested anonymity, for so generously providing financial assistance.

I am indebted to my mother and father, my children Beej and Becky and grandson Kalum, my siblings and their off spring and my husband for their patience and support during the my long course of study and especially to my father for his generous proof-reading efforts. Special thanks also to Tona and Morag for their help with troublesome computers.

INTRODUCTION

For eight centuries since his death in 1240 CE, Muhyiddin Ibn 'Arabi was a leading inspiration for Islamic religious thought from Morocco to China and Indonesia, providing profound justification for the diverse creative, intellectual and artistic currents of Islamic civilisation prior to the colonial era. In the past century there has been an increasing interest in his ideas in the non-Muslim world that is beginning to reflect and parallel this previous influence. His emphasis on the spiritual realities and metaphysical unity underlying religious and cultural diversity helps to explain his remarkable intellectual and religious appeal to modern thinkers and students from the most diverse religious and cultural backgrounds. At the same time, his ideas find ready practical application for contemporary global concerns ranging from artistic and literary creation to ecological, psychological and scientific thought.

This study investigates one recent aspect of the wider spread and creative reception of Ibn 'Arabi's ideas in the contemporary West. It focuses on a particularly active and influential group of individuals, largely based in the UK, some of whom were among the first to translate and disseminate the writings of Ibn 'Arabi and his commentators into English.[1] This group, which eventually developed a 'school for the study of esoteric education' under the name of Beshara, began to study and translate Ibn 'Arabi's works in the early 1970s, around the pivotal figure of a Turkish teacher by the name of Bulent Rauf. Their intention from the start has been to use the ideas of Ibn 'Arabi experientially to promote a deeper spiritual and practical realisation of his teachings, above all through their wider creative and active expression in all areas of life.

---

1. Earlier English translations included those of R.A. Nicholson such as the *Tarjumân al-ashwâq* (London: Royal Asiatic Society, 1911); *Studies in Islamic Mysticism* (Cambridge: Cambridge University Press, 1921); 'The Lives of Umar Ibnul Farid and Muhyiddin Ibn 'Arabi', *Journal of the Royal Asiatic Society* NS 38.4 (1906), pp. 797-824; *The Mystics of Islam* (London, 1914); *The Mathnawî of Jâlâl 'uddin Rûmî, Books I–VI* (London: E.J.W. Gibb Memorial Trust, 1926, 1930, 1934; latest repr. 1982) and R.W.J. Austin, *Sufis of Andalusia* (*The Rûh al-quds and al-Durrat al-fâkhirah of Ibn 'Arabi*) (London: Alan & Unwin, 1971).

Whilst the Beshara School was developing, a more scholarly aspect of the group's work gradually emerged, beginning in 1976, in the form of the Muhyiddin Ibn 'Arabi Society. The purpose of that Society was to encourage the translation, interpretation and dissemination of the works of Ibn 'Arabi and his followers in order to expand knowledge of his teachings on a global scale. The Society's most influential activities have included the organisation of annual international symposia in England and the USA, and the publication of a biannual academic journal devoted to Ibn 'Arabi's works and wider influences. The Society also houses its own expanding library collection in Oxford.

The central focus of this study is to demonstrate how the Beshara School interprets and utilises Ibn 'Arabi's concepts in its courses of esoteric education, and how the students of the school and the school's other activities have encouraged an expanding network of influences in an increasingly global setting. The study also surveys the emergence of the Muhyiddin Ibn 'Arabi Society and its subsequent expansion into a transnational organisation involving academic and creative contributors to its symposia and journals from countries around the world.

THE LIFE OF IBN 'ARABI IN BRIEF[2]

Ibn 'Arabi, whose full name was Abu Abd Allah Muhammad ibn al-'Arabi at-Tâ'î al-Hâtimî, eventually became known as Muhyi ad-Din, meaning 'The Revivifier of the Religion'. He also later became familiarly referred to as al-Sheikh al-Akbar, 'The Greatest Sheikh'. He was born in 1165 in Murcia, Andalusia, now Spain. His father 'Ali was employed by Muhammad ibn Sa'id ibn Mardanîsh the ruler of the city. In 1172 'Ali moved his family to Seville following the conquest of Murcia by the Almohad dynasty. Ibn'Arabi grew up in the environment of the court and later completed military training. As a young adult he was employed in an official capacity to the governor of Seville and later married a woman named Maryan. In his teens he underwent a spiritual experience which led to a vision of God. Prior to this he had lived a life typical of a lively and sociable young man. This profound experience, though, influenced

---

2. Probably the most comprehensive and detailed biographical study of Ibn 'Arabi to date is Claude Addas's *Quest for the Red Sulphur: The Life of Ibn 'Arabi* (trans. Peter Kingsley; Cambridge: The Islamic Text Society, 1993). Previous to this Miguel Asín Palacios offered detailed biographical details early on in his book *El Islam Cristianizado* (Madrid: Plutarco, 1931) and a book that traces Ibn 'Arabi's historic life along with his spiritual development is Stephen Hirtenstein's *The Unlimited Mercifier: The Spiritual Life and Thought of Ibn 'Arabi* (Oxford: Anqa, 1999).

his thinking and writing for the rest of his life. Following the experience, he had numerous visions of Jesus whom he refers to as his first guide on the path to God. As a consequence of the changes to his son, Ibn 'Arabi's father introduced him to his friend, the philosopher and judge Averroes (Ibn Rushd). The result of the meeting highlighted the chasm that Ibn 'Arabi perceived existing between knowledge acquired through the approach of rational thinkers and those of the 'gnostics' to whom knowledge is gradually unveiled and who acquire true insight into the nature of things. It was not until he was nineteen years old that Ibn 'Arabi underwent formal training as a Sufi after which he dedicated his life to the spiritual path. He studied with many Sufi sheikhs as well as with masters of other Islamic sciences such as the Quran, *hadith*, recitation and jurisprudence. Among his many spiritual teachers were two elderly women. The first was Shams of Marchena and the other Fatima of Cordova. This is interesting because female Sufis were rare at this time.[3] At the age of thirty Ibn 'Arabi left Andalusia for the first time and travelled to Tunis. In 1200, he was required through a vision to travel East. He performed the Hajj in 1202. It was whilst residing in Mecca that he had two meetings of significance. The first was with a young woman named Nizam who inspired one of his greatest poems, *The Interpreter of Desires* (*Tarjumân al-ashwâq*). He was forced to compose a commentary explaining the inner meaning of the poem because of accusations that the words he wrote were too erotic for pious sensibilities; he wrote 'All our poems are related to divine truths in various forms…'[4] Also whilst in Mecca he had two visions, the first of a meeting with the eternal or divine youth who represented the 'fusion of opposites, the *coincidentia oppositorum* in whose wholeness all things are resolved'.[5] The second vision was confirmation of his status as the Seal of Muhammadan Sainthood, i.e., he believed that he was the last saint in the line of the Prophet Muhammad. It was also during his first visit to Mecca that he began to compose his magnum opus *The Meccan Revelations* (*al-Futûhât*

---

3. For more details of Ibn 'Arabi's relationship with these women, particularly Fatima, see Austin's translation of Ibn 'Arabi's, *Sufi's of Andalusia*, pp. 142-43.

4. *Al-Futûhât al-Makkiyya* (4 vols.; Cairo, 1911; repr. Beirut: Dâr Sadir, n.d.; partial critical edn by O. Yahia; Cairo: al-Hay'at al-Misriyyat al-Amma li'l Kitab, 1972), III, p. 562. In his work *The Bezels of Wisdom* (The complete translation of the *Fusûs al-Hikam*) (New York: Paulist, 1980), p. 7, Ralph Austin suggests that: 'One suspects that the relationship between Ibn 'Arabi and this young woman had something of the quality of that between Dante and Beatrice, and it serves to illustrate a strong appreciation of the feminine in him, at least in its spiritual aspect'.

5. As explained by Austin, *The Bezels of Wisdom*, p. 8.

al-Makkiyyah) which included a compendium of subjects from metaphysics, cosmology, jurisprudence, psychology to spiritual anthropology.

Following this visit Ibn 'Arabi then travelled widely through Anatolia with a scholar that he met in Malatya named Majd ad-Dîn Ishaq. They stopped for a time in Mosal where he was invested with the kirqua, the initiatory cloak, by Ibn al-Jamî, who had himself received it allegedly from the immortal spiritual guide Khidr who had had mysterious meetings with Moses (Q. 18:65-82). Ibn 'Arabi was himself to have many significant meetings with Khidr particularly during his earlier spiritual ascent.[6]

For several years Ibn 'Arabi continued to travel in the East visiting major cities in Turkey, Syria and Egypt as well as Mecca and Medina for the second time. He became well acquainted with the Sultan of Konya, Kay Kaus, even writing him a letter of advice on the proper treatment of Christians. This letter serves to illustrate that whilst Sufis were beyond law and doctrine in their inner search for the divine Reality, they recognised the importance of law and doctrine for the benefit of the community. It is as a result of spiritual contacts that he made in Konya that Ibn 'Arabi's influence in Sufi circles has become so dominant right down to the present day.

As well as the Sultan Kay Kaus, he had other aristocratic and intellectual contacts including Malik az-Zahir (1186–1218), a son of Saladin. He was also teacher to the Ayyabid ruler of Damascus, Muzaffar ad-Dîn (d. 1238). Some accounts claim that after the death of Majd ad-Dîn, Ibn 'Arabi married his widow and brought up his son Sadruddîn al-Qûnawî (d. 1274). Qûnawî, having become a leading disciple of Ibn 'Arabi, wrote numerous important books and trained many famous scholars.

In 1223 Ibn 'Arabi settled in Damascus where he wrote and taught. It was here that he completed his great work *Meccan Revelations*, his major collection of poetry the *Dîwân* and most relevantly the synopsis of all his

---

6. The mysterious Prophet Khidr has been linked with such nature deities as the Green Man and Pan. According to William Anderson (an associate of the Beshara School), Muslims have identified St. George with Khidr and 'there are legends of him in which, like Osiris, he is dismembered and reborn; and prophecies connecting him, like the Green Man, to the end of time. His name means the Green One or the Verdant One, he is the voice of inspiration of the true aspirant and committed artist. He can come as a white light or the gleam on a blade of green grass, but more often as an inner mood. The sign of his presence is the ability to work or to experience with timeless enthusiasm beyond one's normal capacities', *Green Man: The Archetype of Our Oneness with the Earth* (London: HarperCollins, 1990), pp. 29, 75. Ibn 'Arabi usually experienced Khidr as a man with extraordinary abilities such as that of walking on water.

teachings *The Bezels of Wisdom*. Here in Damascus he was surrounded and served by a group of disciples, including Qûnawî, until his death in 1240.

Ibn 'Arabi's ideas tended to court controversy from the nascent stages of his career onwards. For example, early in his travels to the East he visited Cairo, where his teachings were denounced by the traditional Islamic interpreters. This kind of antagonism continues to the present day in certain Muslim circles, because the expressions used for mystical experience are usually abhorrent to the minds of those limited to traditional religious doctrine.[7]

However, it is undeniable that the works of Ibn 'Arabi culminate in a feast of spiritual and intellectual disciplines that he attempts to merge into a system of thought that in addition to its enormity and universality also encompasses issues central to human experience. As Ralph Austin proposes, Ibn 'Arabi lived during the culmination of a significant phase in Islamic development because only eighteen years after his death the Mongols invaded the Fertile Crescent dealing a terminal blow to Islamic civilisation in the East

> so that in a sense, the great gathering together of Islamic spiritual learning in the written works of Ibn 'Arabi, before the storm of political, social and cultural upheaval, becomes for later, less secure, generations an invaluable source of spiritual inspiration. Ibn 'Arabi represents a culmination not only of Sufi exposition but also, in a very significant way, of Islamic intellectual expression.[8]

IBN 'ARABI'S INFLUENCE IN THE WEST TODAY

This study is set within the contextual framework of Ibn 'Arabi's influence in the contemporary West. Prior to setting out this framework it is important to point out how his expanding influence today reflects the historical influence of his ideas in the Muslim world in the centuries following his death. Ibn 'Arabi wrote at least 350 works of varying lengths.[9] These writings constitute a synthesis of Islamic scriptures, science and previously oral teachings whose eventual spread throughout the Muslim world deeply influenced spiritual teachings and their wider cultural expressions in each region. His works were already distributed in

---

7. See further on this below, pp. 20-25.
8. Austin, *Bezels of Wisdom*, p. 14
9. Osman Yahia in his *Histoire et classification de l'oeuvre d'Ibn 'Arabi* (2 vols.; Damascus: Institut Français de Damas, 1964), lists some 700 written works, but many of these are apocryphal.

his lifetime, during which they were rigorously copied and read in his presence before being disseminated to an ever-expanding audience. Two of his most influential disciples were his own step-son, Sadruddîn al-Qûnawî, and Ibn Sawdakîn who systematically read his magnum opus *Meccan Revelations* (*al-Futûhât al-Makkiyya*) with Ibn 'Arabi himself and who continued to teach that work after Ibn 'Arabi's death in 1240 CE. After Ibn Sawdakîn's death in Aleppo in 1248 CE, when al-Qûnawî settled permanently in Konya, the centre of focus of Ibn Arabi's disciples moved to Anatolia, from which Ibn 'Arabi's influence began to expand much more widely. Qûnawî was also to become sheikh to Qutb al-Dîn al-Shîrâzîand and Fakhr al-Dîn al-Irâqî, who were both substantial contributors to Oriental Sufism. He was a friend of Jalâl al-Dîn Rûmî (d.1273), whose *Mathnawî* encouraged the flourishing of Sufism in Iran and further afield.[10] Ibn 'Arabi himself had been in contact with both 'Umar Shihab al-Din al-Suhrawardi,[11] who was himself a significant influence in Sufi circles, and with Ibn al-Farid (1182–1235), who has been described as the greatest mystical poet of Arab Islam. Soon after his death Ibn 'Arabi's influence was also being felt in the West through Abu al-Hasan al-Shadili (1196–1258) and his order, which was soon to inspire the rise of other Sufi orders in North Africa and the Middle East.

It is not only in the Islamic but also in the Christian world that Ibn 'Arabi's early influence was experienced. In his book *Islam and the Divine Comedy*, Asín Palacios attempts to demonstrate that there are elements of the influence of Ibn 'Arabi in the works of Dante.[12] This is not so surprising as the influence of Muslim Spain in Europe at this time was considerable. Some of the writings of the German mystic Meister Eckhart also bear a significant resemblance to Ibn 'Arabi' monistic approach, and like Ibn 'Arabi, Ekhart also fell victim of the religious authorities of his day.[13]

It was at around this time that Konya, a place of refuge from the Mongol invasions, was the cultural capital of the Seljuk realms and of much of the Eastern Islamic world, and it was through a line of teachers and poets emerging from there that Ibn 'Arabi's ideas were spread throughout the Muslim world.

10. See n. 1 above.
11. Of the Suhrawardiyya Order.
12. Miguel Asín Palacios, *Islam and the Divine Comedy* (trans. Harold Sunderland; London: J. Murray, 1926).
13. Ibn 'Arabi constructed a complex Neo-Platonic Gnostic system that stressed the underlying unity of all beings (*Wahdud al-Wujûd*) and their common origin in the unique and indivisible Godhead.

This past historic process is now being reflected in many ways in the modern world. For example, a central protagonist in the emergence of Beshara and the Ibn 'Arabi Society was a Turk of noble Ottoman heritage, Bulent Rauf. This process is also reflected in the wide international contemporary influence of another Turkish teacher, Shaykh Muzaffer Ozak (1919–1986), who introduced the Khalwati-Jerrahi Sufi Order to America beginning in 1980. This order also applied Ibn 'Arabi's concepts in its teachings, and is now active in translating and publishing his work, paralleling many of the activities of the Beshara School and the Ibn 'Arabi Society discussed below. Similarly, in several fascinating articles, Victoria Holbrook has related the *Melamî* Sufi Order of Turkey to Ibn 'Arabi, from his lifetime to today.[14] This supra-order of the Ottoman spiritual elite placed special emphasis on the central role of the 'invisible' creative focus of spiritual influence throughout all dimensions of human life. Thus it corresponds with the ethos of the 'Jelveti' Sufis of the Ottoman world, who also promoted the need for active spiritual engagement in the world, a theme which is central to the ethos of the Beshara School.[15]

Western interest in the works of Ibn 'Arabi really originated in the early part of the twentieth century, initially through French and Spanish translations which included parts of the *Bezels of Wisdom* (*Fusûs al-Hikam*) and *Meccan Illuminations* (*al-Futûhât al-Makkiyya*). This was the first time that Ibn 'Arabi's ideas became available to wider (non-academic) audiences.[16] A number of early students of his ideas belonged to a school of religious thought for whom the first leading exponent was

14. Victoria Holbrook, 'Ibn 'Arabi and the Ottoman Dervish Traditions: The Melamî Supra Order', Part 1, *JMIAS* IX (1991), pp. 18-35; and Part 2, *JMIAS* XII (1992), pp. 15-33.

15. The *Melamî* ethos will be explored in more detail in Chapter 1 below.

16. Probably the first apparent work of Ibn 'Arabi to be translated in the West was actually the work of the thirteenth-century Sufi, Awhad al-Din Balyânî, known as *The Treatise on Divine Unicity*, translated into English in 1909 by T.H. Weir. It was reprinted as *Whoso Knoweth Himself* (Gloucestershire: Beshara, 1976) and translated into French by Michel Chodkiewicz as *Épître sur L'unicité Absolue* (Paris: Les Deux Océans, 1982). Other early English translations of writings of and scholarly information about Ibn 'Arabi include the works of Nicolson, including *Studies in Islamic Mysticism*, the *Tarjumân al-ashwâq*, 'The Lives of Umar Ibnul Farid and Muhyiddin Ibn 'Arabi' and *Mystics of Islam*. Early European translations included Asín Palacios' Spanish study of Ibn 'Arabi's life, *El Islam cristianzado* and *La escatologia musulmana en la Divina Comedia* (Madrid: Granada, 1923), and also H.S. Nyberg's German study, *Kleinere Schriften des Ibn al-'Arabi nach Handschriften in Uppsala und Berlin zum ersten Mal hrsg. Und mit Einleitung und Kommentar von H.S. Nyberg* (Leiden: Brill, 1919).

René Guénon.[17] Guénon and his equally influential follower, Frithjof Schuon, had initiatic connections with the North African Shadhili Sufi tariqa in Egypt and with the Algerian Shaykh al-'Alawî.[18] Ibn Arabi's influence has long been widespread among many North African and Arab Sufi traditions, and these early translations were strongly influenced by the traditional Sufi approaches in these areas.[19] Although Guénon and those European readers influenced by him pursued diverse fields of activity and expression, what they all had in common was the advocacy of the transcendent unity of all revealed religious traditions. Schuon,[20] in particular, applied the central ideas of Ibn 'Arabi to articulating this perspective.[21] This approach provided an influential contribution to

17. In his recent book *Against the Modern World: Traditionalism and the Secret Intellectual History of the Twentieth Century* (Oxford: Oxford University Press, 2004), pp. 77 and 135, Mark Sedgwick suggests that the work of Guénon was not founded on Ibn 'Arabi. Although Guénon was very interested in Ibn 'Arabi's theories he probably did not read Arabic and wrote to one of his followers in Paris who knew Ibn 'Arabi well for references on his works. Sedgwick also argues that evidence in Guénon's library also revealed that he was far more interested in Hinduism than Islam.

18. The well-known Algerian Sufi sheikh who was the inspiration of Martin Lings' book *A Sufi Saint of the Twentieth Century: Shaykh Ahmad al-'Alawî* (London: Allen & Unwin, 1971).

19. Alexander Knysh points out in *Islamic Mysticism: A Short History* (Boston: Brill, 1999), pp. 251-52, that there is a 'pervasive influence of Ibn 'Arabi's teachings on the leaders of African Sufism. Whether by direct reading of Ibn 'Arabi's works or filtered through secondary renditions of his ideas, such as those by 'Abd al-Wahhâb al-Sha'rânî (d. 936/1565) and 'Abd al-Ghanîal-Nâbulusî (d. 1143/1731), his teachings gained wide currency among many African Sufis'.

20. As pointed out by Sedgwick, *Against the Modern World*, p. 151, Schoun was influenced by a number of slightly obscure religious perspectives as well as having become a Muslim with a Sufi initiation from the Alawiyya. He was also prone to visions and had been appointed as a sheikh in a Sufi order in a vision, but as Sedgwick explains 'he was also a universalist with a primordial initiation from the Sioux (native Americans) and was appointed to a universal mission by the Virgin Mary in another vision'.

21. As demonstrated in his book *The Transcendent Unity of Religion* (London: Faber & Faber, 1965). Other major works by Schoun include *From the Divine to the Human: Survey of Metaphysics and Epistemology* (Bloomington, Ind.: Library of Traditional Wisdom, 1983); *The Play of Masks* (Bloomington, Ind.: The Library of Traditional Wisdom, 1992). Other younger exponents include S.H. Nasr whose works include 'Ibn 'Arabi in the Persian Speaking World', in *Al-Kitâb al-tidhkâri: muhyî Ibn Arabî fi dhikrâ al-mi'awiyya al-thâmina li-mîlâdih 1165–1240* (Cairo: alHay'a al-Misriyya al-'Amma li 'L-kitâb, 1969), pp. 257-63 and Huston Smith, *The World's Religions: Our Great Wisdom Traditions* (San Francisco: Harper, 1991).

efforts to foster a pluralistic perspective within the comparative study of religions through its suggestion of the possibility of mutual understanding and co-operation between adherents of different historical traditions. The way in which this early process occurred through the activities of Guénon and his followers reflects the situation following Ibn 'Arabi's death and the remarkable way that his ideas were appropriated and assimilated to justify and encourage the extraordinary cultural diversities and creativity that typified the rapidly expanding post-Mongol Islamic world.[22] Other well-known representatives of this school of thought that was to become known as the 'Traditionalist' or 'Perennialist' school included Titus Burckhardt[23] and Martin Lings,[24] who were regular

---

22. For some of the most important recent works that illustrate this historical diffusion, see Leonard Lewisohn, *Classical Persian Sufism from its Origins to Rumi* (New York: Khaniqahi Nimatullahi, 1994) and *The Heritage of Sufism*, vol. 2 (Oxford: One World, 1999); Sachiko Murata, *Chinese Gleams of Sufi Light: Wang Tai-yü's Great Learning of the Pure and Real and Liu Chih's Displaying the Concealment of the Real Realm* (Albany: SUNY Press, 2000); Alexander Knysh, *Ibn 'Arabi in the Later Islamic Tradition: The Making of a Polemical Image in Medieval Islam* (Albany: SUNY Press, 1999); James W. Morris, 'Ibn 'Arabi and His Interpreters', Part I, *Journal of the American Oriental Society* 106 (1986), pp. 539-51; Part II, 106 (1986), pp. 733-56; Part III, 107 (1987), pp. 101-19 (and an updated and significantly more detailed version is available on the Muhyiddin Ibn 'Arabi Society's website at ibnarabisociety.org); Holbrook, 'Ibn 'Arabi and the Ottoman Dervish Traditions'; Michel Chodkiewicz, 'The Diffusion of Ibn 'Arabi's Doctrine', *JMIAS* IX (1991), pp. 36-57; Hamid Algar, 'Reflections of Ibn 'Arabi in Early Naqshbandî Tradition', *JMIAS* X (1991), pp. 45-56; Alexander Kynsh, 'Ibn 'Arabi in Yemen: His Admirers and Detractors', *JMIAS* XI (1992), pp. 38-61; James W. Morris, '"...Except His Face": The Political and Aesthetic Dimensions of Ibn 'Arabi's Legacy', *JMIAS* XXIII (1998), pp. 19-31; Mustafa Tahrali, 'A General Outline of the Influence of Ibn 'Arabi on the Ottoman Era', *JMIAS* XXVI (1999), pp. 43-54; Omar Benäissa, 'The Diffusian of Akbarian Teaching in Iran During the 13th and 14th Centuries', *JMIAS* XXVI (1999), pp. 89-109; Mahmud Erol Kiliç, '"The Ibn 'Arabi of the Ottomans": 'Abdullah Salâhaddîn al-'Ushshâqî (1705–82)', *JMIAS* XXVI (1999), pp. 110-20; James W. Morris, 'Ibn 'Arabi in the "Far West"', *JMIAS* XXIX (2001), pp. 87-121.

23. Titus Burckhardt, *Mystical Astrology According to Ibn 'Arabi* (Eng. trans.; Gloucestershire: Beshara, 1977); *Introduction aux Doctrines Esoteriques de L'Islam* (Paris: Dervy-Livres, 1969); *Principes et methodes de L'art Sacré* (Lyons: Derain, 1958); *Alchémie: Sinn und Weltbild* (trans. from English edn by Madame J.P. Gervy; Basle: Foundation Keimer, 1974; Milan: Archè, 1979). See Chapters 2 and 4 for more details about Burckhardt and the relationship between his work and the Beshara School.

24. Martin Lings, *The Book of Certainty* (London: Rider & Co., 1952); *Symbol and Archetype: A Study of the Meaning of Existence* (Cambridge: Quinta Essentia,

contributors to the journals *Etudes traditionnelles* and *Studies in Comparative Religion*.

Another major contribution to the expansion of influence of Ibn 'Arabi in the West in the last century occurred through the attractions of what Henry Corbin has called Ibn 'Arabi's 'metaphysics of the imagination'.[25] Through this approach, the ideas of Ibn 'Arabi have been freely adopted by artists, writers and especially Jungian psychologists to support their own creative activities and spiritual points of view. This influence was channelled through the writings of Henry Corbin,[26] Toshihiko Izutzu[27] and other members of the Eranos circle, a group of scholars, psychologists and artists such as the English poet Kathleen Raine and her *Temenos* associates,[28] who tended to apply the Jungian psychological approach to their various scholarly and creative theories. Henry Corbin, in particular, lived for decades and had long-term academic contacts in Iran, where Ibn 'Arabi has had so much lasting influence on many areas of culture, particularly Sufi poetry and the Islamic arts. More recently S. Wasserstrom has pointed out that Corbin's thought had deeply influenced his close friend Mircea Eliade and some of the other influential scholars of the study of religions in the second half of the twentieth century, in ways that also reflect the continuing influences of Ibn 'Arabi.[29]

In the artistic realm, Ibn 'Arabi's ideas have influenced a wide range of creative and artistic activities in the West today in much the same way that they once did the key Muslim commentators, for example the poetry of Rûmî (1207–1273)[30] and Ibn al-Fârid (1181–1235).[31] His insights are

1991); *What is Sufism?* (London: Allen & Unwin, 1975); *A Sufi Saint of the Twentieth Century*.

25. Morris, 'Ibn 'Arabi in the "Far West"', p. 107.

26. His works available in English on Ibn 'Arabi and his Muslim interpreters include *Alone with the Alone: Creative Imagination in the Sufism of Ibn 'Arabi* (trans. from the French by Ralph Manheim; Princeton: Princeton University Press, 1998) and *Spiritual Body and Celestial Earth: From Mazdean Iran to Shi'ite Iran* (trans. Nancy Pearson; London: I.B. Tauris & Co., 1990).

27. Izutzu's major work on Ibn 'Arabi was *Sufism and Taoism: A Comparative Study of Key Philosophical Concepts* (Berkeley: University of California Press, 1983).

28. Kathleen Raine, who died in 2003, was editor of *Temenos*, a review devoted to the imaginative arts.

29. S.M. Wasserstrom, *Religion after Religion: Gershom Scholem, Mircea Eliade, and Henry Corbin at Eranos* (Princeton: Princeton University Press, 1999).

30. Through his poetry, Rûmî demonstrates 'universal Sufism', as pointed out in the work of Geaves (see below).

31. For examples of some of these commentators, see Annemarie Schimmel's *Mystical Dimensions of Islam* (Chapel Hill: University of North Carolina Press,

today still helpful in illuminating such creative activities as architecture, fine art, poetry and literature, as will be demonstrated in the study. His influences, though, particularly in various forms of spiritual discipline or therapy are not always widely realised or explicitly acknowledged—and this too closely parallels the earlier Islamic historical situation. Historically, Muslim scholars and writers have often applied Ibn 'Arabi's ideas in their teachings without formal acknowledgment in contexts in which only readers familiar with his work would discern his ideas.[32]

Regarding Ibn 'Arabi's standing in relation to the numerous Sufi movements active in the contemporary West, it cannot be disputed that in most of those movements his ideas play some role, whether openly acknowledged or not. This is because almost all historical forms of Sufism since his lifetime were influenced by his ideas in some respects. A common feature of these contemporary Sufi groups, as in the past, as Hermansen[33] and Geaves[34] point out, is that they have all emerged around the figure of a living guide or sheikh. This sheikh would initially be surrounded by a small group of students who have often provided a primary readership and audience for the initial popular translations and studies of Ibn 'Arabi. These recent Sufi teachers in the West have come from diverse parts of the Islamic world, as already in the earlier cases of Guénon and Schuon, providing their students with the initial means of transplanting Ibn Arabi's ideas into a non-Islamic setting.[35] As in the case of this study, those pioneering Western guides have usually been themselves initially of Muslim cultural origin, and it appears that generally this primary spiritual process is private and historically virtually imperceptible at first.

Not surprisingly, the personalities through which Ibn 'Arabi's ideas were initially transmitted to the West tended to have their origins in Sufi

---

1975), pp. 259-86; Morris, 'Ibn 'Arabi and His Interpreters'; Fakhruddin Iraqi, *Divine Flashes* (trans. Peter Lamborne Wilson, J. Morris and William Chittick; New York: Paulist, 1982); 'The Continuing Relevance of Qaysari's Thought: Divine Imagination and the Foundation of Natural Spirituality', in *Papers of the International Symposium on Islamic Thought in the XIIIth and XIVth Centuries and Daud al-Qaysari* (ed. T. Koç; Ankara, 1998), pp. 161-71. Many other relevant sources are included in n. 22 above.

32. See particularly Michel Chodkiewicz's *An Ocean Without Shore: Ibn 'Arabi, the Book and the Law* (trans. David Streight; Albany: SUNY Press, 1989).

33. Marcia Hermansen, 'Hybrid Identity Formations in Muslim America: The Case for American Sufi Movements', *The Muslim World* 90 (2000), pp. 158-97.

34. Ron Geaves, *The Sufis of Britain: An Exploration of Muslim Identity* (Cardiff: Cardiff Academic Press, 2000).

35. Morris, 'Ibn 'Arabi and the "Far West"', pp. 103-7.

groups from the same parts of the Islamic world where his teachings were most widely transmitted, including Turkey and Egypt (former Ottoman realms), South Asia and Iran. Historically and even today, the cosmopolitan Ottoman cultural elite was especially active in transmitting those concepts, and Bulent Rauf, the central figure in the development of the Beshara School and the early Ibn 'Arabi Society, came from that spiritual and cultural tradition. The activities of another originally Ottoman order mentioned above, the Khalwati-Jerrahi tariqa, were also developed in America under the charismatic leadership of the Turkish Shaykh Muzaffer Ozak.[36] Members of this order have been active in translating and transmitting the works of Ibn 'Arabi in the Americas. Ibn 'Arabi's influence has also been historically central in South Asia,[37] and the earliest influential Sufi sheikh in the West, Hazrat Inayat Khan (1880–1927), was an Indian Chishti musician and spiritual teacher. In 1910 he departed for Europe to teach Sufism and in 1923 he founded the Sufi movement. Following his death, his son Pir Vilayat Khan established the 'Sufi Order in the West', which thrives in the US, Canada, Britain and Europe. The Sufi Movement is still active in Holland, run by Vilayat's brother Hidayat Khan. In the work of Inayat Khan there are important teachings and practical approaches visibly reflecting themes from Ibn 'Arabi's thought that were widely spread through the Sufi traditions of the Caucasus, Central and South Asia.[38] It was from there that he drew the complex Sufi teachings he first introduced and communicated in Europe and the Americas.[39]

36. Many editions, translations and commentaries of Ibn 'Arabi's works have been undertaken by American members of this order, including, from the East coast, translations by T. Bayrak and R.T. Harris. See. e.g., R.T. Harris' translation, *Journey to the Lord of Power: A Sufi Manual on Retreat by Muhyiddin Ibn 'Arabi* (Rochester, Vt.: Inter Traditions International, 1990). On the West coast, psychologists and members of the order, R. Frager and J. Fadiman, have published books relating Ibn 'Arabi's ideas and other Sufi concepts to psychology, therapy and counselling. They are, for example, joint editors of *Essential Sufism* (San Francisco: Harper San Francisco, 1997). Some of the books are published by Pir Press, a publishing house which is connected to the New York branch of this order.

37. Reflected in, for example, the symbolism in the Islamic architecture of the Taj Mahal.

38. Morris, 'Ibn 'Arabi in the "Far West"', p. 114.

39. Pir Vilayat Inayat Khan has written and edited a number of works on Sufism including *That Which Transpires Behind that Which Appears: The Experience of Sufism* (New York: Omega, 1994).

Further South Asian Sufi guides who were instrumental in the spread of Ibn 'Arabi's ideas in the West[40] include Bawa Muhaiyaddeen (late 1800s–1986)[41] who was from Sri Lanka, and Meher Baba (1894–1969)[42] who was born in India of Persian (Iranian) descent. They both creatively applied Ibn 'Arabi's ideas in the ways that they had been transmitted in the multi-religious cultural context of India, and adapted them to suit the new contemporary American and European context for medicine, psychology, spiritual guidance as well as more imaginative and artistic disciplines.[43]

An even earlier major influence in introducing esoteric Sufi teachings into Europe and America was the Russian Georgei Ivanovitch Gurdjieff (1877–1949).[44] He had travelled extensively in Central Asia and the Middle East, spending some years in contact with Sufi teachers of Iran and Central Asia. He introduced a form of spiritual exercise into the West based on a distinctive method of self-exploration which involved music and sacred dance. His chief disciple was Peter Ouspensky (1878–1947) who set up his own esoteric school in London and whose book *In Search of the Miraculous* provides the most vivid accounts of his

---

40. According to Alexander Knysh in *Islamic Mysticism*, p. 284, apart from the Naqshbandiyya, most Indian tariqas adhered to the doctrine of the Oneness of Being (*wahdat al-wujûd*) which they trace back to Ibn 'Arabi and his commentators. The Naqshbandiyya held a negative approach to other religions, rejecting Ibn 'Arabi's theory of *wahdat al-wujûd* as conducive to religious pluralism.

41. Bawa Muhaiyaddeen was the author of over twenty books including *A Book of God's Love* (Pennsylvania: Fellowship Press, 1976) and *Islam and World Peace: Explanations of a Sufi* (Pennsylvania: Bawa Muhaiyaddeen Fellowship, 1987). He had a universalistic approach to Sufism, not insisting on conversion to Islam for his disciples, he believed that 'truth has no limits, boundaries or compartments'. See further 'The Bawa Muhaiyaddeen Fellowship', www.bmf.org.

42. Meher Baba's many writings include *Discourses* (London: Victor Gillancz, 1955) and *God Speaks* (New York: Dodd Mead, 1976). A quote from a synopsis of Baba's book *God Speaks* on 'The Meher Baba Association' website (www.meherbaba.co.uk) includes evidence of the influence of Ibn 'Arabi's emphasis on *wuhdat al-wujûd* (Oneness of Being): 'the goal of life is conscious realization of the Absolute Oneness of God inherent in all animate and inanimate beings and things'.

43. Bawa Muhaiyaddeen's disciple, the poet Coleman Barks, played a key role in the popular spread of Rûmî's poetry and ideas in North America.

44. Gurdjieff's major works include: *Meetings with Remarkable Men* (New York: Dutton, 1969); *Beelzebub's Tales to His Grandson: An Objectively Impartial Criticism of the Life of Man* (New York: Dutton, 1978); and *Life is Real Only Then, When 'I Am'* (New York: Dutton, 1982).

teachings.[45] A dedicated disciple of both these men was J.G. Bennett, who based his own teachings on their practical and philosophical approaches. Bennett had strong connections with the Beshara School in its earliest days, first through lecturing to the nascent school, and second through the fact that the extensive country mansion which he used as his academy for esoteric study, Sherborne House, was purchased by the Beshara Trust after his death to use for their courses.[46]

In addition to the recent Iranian influences of Ibn 'Arabi already mentioned above, there have been many publications and seminars on Ibn 'Arabi's works sponsored by the branch of the Iranian Ni'matullahi Sufi Order that was widely established in America and Britain by Dr. Javad Nurbakhsh, along with other Sufi and spiritual groups of Iranian origin.

Following on from the above initial 'transmissions' figures, a further wave of expansion of influence, both visible and invisible, can begin to be witnessed through the 'ripple effect' of those creative figures who have been connected to the above-mentioned spiritual groups and Sufi orders. A particularly noticeable example of such influences are the translations of the works of Rûmî by the celebrated poets Robert Bly (Ni'matullahi) and Coleman Barks (Bawa Muhaiyaddeen), which have become best sellers in the United States and Canada.

As the above evidence shows, Ibn 'Arabi's influence is undoubtedly spreading in various forms throughout the Western world today, and the contribution of this study should be considered within that wider historical and cultural context. To underpin this context it is appropriate at this point to discuss the present expansion and study of Sufism in the West in relation to the Beshara School and the Muhyiddin Ibn 'Arabi Society.

FURTHER STUDIES OF WESTERN SUFI MOVEMENTS

The phenomenological and comparative study of religion is a relatively new academic discipline, and the serious study of Islam within this wider discipline is even more recent. In the past century there has been increas-

---

45. Ouspensky's most important works are *In Search of the Miraculous: Fragments of an Unknown Teaching* (New York: Harcourt, Brace, 1949) and *A New Model of the Universe* (New York: Random House, 1971).

46. John G. Bennett was Principal of an esoteric school, the International Academy for Continuous Education, at Sherborne House. Following his death the property was purchased by the Beshara Trust. His major works include: *Christian Mysticism and Subud* (London: Institute for the Comparative Study of History, Philosophy and the Sciences, 1961); *Intimations: Talks with J.G. Bennett at Beshara* (Gloucestershire: Beshara, 1975); and *Witness: The Story of a Search* (New Mexico: Bennett Books, 1997).

ing interest in 'Eastern' religions in the once predominantly Christian West. Many of these traditions have recently been transported, transposed and assimilated into a Western setting. A common term for these developments is 'new religious movements', but as Moojan Momen points out in his recent survey of the discipline,[47] Christianity, Islam and Buddhism all began as 'new religious movements' within other established religious systems. He makes an interesting suggestion which actually coincides in some ways with a recent paper presented by Peter Young,[48] suggesting that 'we today could be witnessing among the new religious movements, the next major world religion about to emerge in the same way that Christianity emerged from the religious turmoil of the Roman Empire'.[49] Momen applies several classifications to the term 'new religious movements', but the one most relevant to this study refers to the way in which some religious traditions have been adopted and assimilated recently into the West. He describes how these 'new' spiritual movements are typically appropriated from existing religious traditions, explaining that even if they diverge from certain largely dominant forms of the tradition, they are, however, adequately similar to be considered part of the wider tradition of these established religions. Some examples he cites include Jehovah's Witnesses, ISKCON (International Society for Krishna Consciousness), The Friends of the Western Buddhist Order, and a variety of Sufi groups that have all recently arisen in the West. This last point has a particular bearing on this study in that, as we shall see, the participants of the Beshara School, whilst insisting that they are not a Sufi order and are open to people of all backgrounds, do, in fact, use a preponderance of Islamic and Sufi texts as well as quietly adapted practices in their teaching. Therefore the Beshara School may be included, along with the other recently Westernised Sufi groups already mentioned, as a prime example of the way in which central spiritual aspects of Sufi teaching are being more widely adapted and assimilated into various Western settings.

In a recent article[50] in which she illustrates how Sufism has recently been creatively assimilated into many domains of American culture,

---

47. Moojan Momen, *The Phenomenon of Religion: A Thematic Approach* (Oxford: Oneworld, 1999), p. 65.

48. Peter Young is the present Principal of the Beshara School, and he made a similar suggestion in a paper that he presented at the 1999, annual symposium of the Muhyiddin Ibn 'Arabi Society, entitled 'Ibn 'Arabi: Towards a Universal Point of View'.

49. Momen, *The Phenomenon of Religion*, p. 508.

50. Hermansen, 'Hybrid Identity', pp. 158-97.

Marcia Hermansen refers to an earlier paper[51] in which she applied the garden metaphor of 'hybrid' and 'perennial' movements. She suggested that whilst 'hybrids' melded the practice of traditional local cultural forms of Islam with at least some concession to the American context, the 'perennial' movements stressed the unity of religions and consequently did not always require the formal profession of Islam by participants.[52] Hermansen's 'perennial' model somewhat resembles the Beshara example and closely echoes Guénon's 'traditionalist' school of thought. (Although Guénon himself in later life did personally advocate observance of the basic Islamic rituals, not all participants of the 'perennial' movements insist on that requirement for all of their participants.) Hermansen lists a broad spectrum of active Sufi movements in North America illustrating the great diversity and multiplicity of these movements, and their expression and development, which itself mirrors the historical spread of Sufism and Islam in the past. Of particular relevance to this study is how each of these groups of both variations tended to form around a particular 'charismatic' Muslim leader, reflecting the way in which the Beshara School formed around the figure of Bulent Rauf.

As part of his comprehensive study about Sufism and popular Islamic spirituality in Britain,[53] Ron Geaves examines the adaptation and assimilation of Sufism into sections of British society in a similar way to Hermansen. He shows how a significant percentage of the ritually observant Muslim population in Britain have active links with traditional Sufi tariqas. He also highlights another form of Sufism in Britain, frequently adopted in the past century, which he terms 'universal Sufism', broadly corresponding with Hermansen's 'perennials'. He briefly discusses how Sufism was introduced into European cultures in the late nineteenth and early twentieth centuries, providing useful biographical outlines of those individuals who were most instrumental in this activity. Those initial formative figures possessed the qualities mentioned above, that is, of being 'charismatic' Muslim leaders, although the forms of Sufism that they developed in Britain did not always require a formal 'conversion' to Islam. Those early leaders included Idries Shah (1924–1996), who had a

---

51. Hermansen, 'In the Garden of American Sufi Movements: Hybrids and Perennials', in *New Trends and Developments in the World of Islam* (ed. Peter B. Clark; London: Luzac, 1997), pp. 155-78.

52. Hermansen, 'Hybrid Identity', p. 159.

53. Geaves, *The Sufis of Britain*. Geaves's primary area of study has been the migration of Muslim communities from South Asia to Britain, with particular emphasis on various forms of Sufism, understood broadly as 'popular' religion and devotional life within these communities.

Pakistani father and a Scottish mother. He was very active in introducing Sufism to the West, lecturing and writing over thirty-five books. Geaves suggests that Shah particularly advocated the *Malamati*[54] school of mysticism, which coincides with Ibn 'Arabi's esoteric teaching and certain emphases of the Beshara School. According to this spiritual ideal, adherents of this approach do not demonstrate their spiritual life and practice in a publicly external manner, such as their form of dress, but live ordinary lives striving quietly for perfection and genuine spiritual influence in whatever direction they are guided.[55]

The other early figures listed by Geaves, who introduced a universal type of Sufism to the West, include individuals already discussed above, including Georgei Gurdjieff, Peter Ouspensky, J.G. Bennett and Hazrat Inayat Khan. Geaves also discusses a range of other more recent Sufi movements that have attracted a large British following, but do insist on formal religious conversion, such as the Haqqani Naqshbandis branch, which has roots in Turkey and Syria, under the present leadership of the Turkish Cypriot Shaykh Nâzim.[56]

The Beshara School, however, does not fit comfortably within any of the categories mentioned above, since it shares important qualities of *both* of Hermansen's models ('hybrid' and 'perennial'), as well as Geaves's 'universals'. In any case, as both authors openly admit, such typologies are necessarily superficial and problematic, as can readily be seen when applied to earlier historical cognate religious movements, for example, the considerable number of comparable popular spiritual groups in earlier Christian contexts such as Unitarians, Christian Scientists, Quakers and Mormons. Typically it is the relevant cultural and political context that determines where each such movement ends up. In any case, the Beshara School does insist that it is not explicitly an exclusively Sufi

---

54. Holbrook, 'Ibn 'Arabi and the Ottoman Dervish Traditions'.

55. This restraint of outward spiritual expressionism finds parallels in such Christian offshoots as the Society of Friends (Quakers) and Friends of God.

56. Shaykh Nâzim al-Qubrusî al-Haqqânî (b. 1922) is the current leader of the Naqshabandi Sufis who trace their antecedents to central Asia. Nâzim's particular tariqa has its roots in the eastern parts of the Ottoman Empire. Shaykh Nâzim was sent to London by his Shayhk, Abdullah al-Dagestani, in 1970 to establish a tariqa in the West. He now has one of the largest Western Sufi followings with centres in North America, Britain, Western Europe, the Middle East, South and South East Asia. This tariqa has had considerable success in attracting converts from amongst educated people outside Islam and from within the Muslim world. Shaykh Nâzim has produced numerous publications including: *The Fruit of Perfect Practising and Real Belief is Peace* (Birmingham: Zero, 1988); *Don't Waste* (Sri Lanka: Zero, 1989); *Power Oceans of Love* (London: Zero, 1993).

movement and that it does not have a sheikh. Many observers would argue though that Bulent Rauf was its original sheikh, as he shared virtually all the typical characteristics of a charismatic Sufi teacher, whilst rigorously refusing the official title.

DISCIPLINARY AND METHODOLOGICAL APPROACH TO THE STUDY

This study is situated within the academic discipline of the study of religion and applies the 'phenomenological' approach to its theory and methodology. The study of religion is a relatively new academic discipline which has rapidly expanded in the late twentieth century as a result of the sweeping changes and newly emerging global patterns of life,[57] reflecting the worldwide spread of all the major religious traditions under these new world-historical conditions. Moojan Momen[58] suggests that in its wider meaning the earlier nineteenth-century discipline of the 'history of religions' merges imperceptibly with the phenomenology of religion, but the former approach tended to be textually and historically based, whereas the modern discipline integrates that with the more immediate contemporary testimony of the observed or interviewed subject, including relevant contributions from all the related disciplines of the humanities and social science. Momen explains the phenomenological approach as follows:

> The 'phenomenology of religion' is not so much a theory of religion as an approach to the study of religion. It is, however, based on the assumption that humanity's religious life is an entity in its own right and does not need to be reduced to sociological or psychological explanations. It is best understood as a 'neutral' description and emphatic attempt to get inside the experience itself.[59]

This description is historically connected to the original concepts of *philosophical* phenomenology as initiated by Edmund Husserl (1859–1938). This approach opposes reductionist and scientistic models of earlier approaches, because it considers reducing religious phenomena to social, anthropological, psychological or other definitions a misleading over-simplification. It also countered those earlier positivists who applied an evolutionary scheme to religious history, because any such scheme relies on extraneous value judgments. According to this theory, the most

---

57. This discipline was originally and more commonly known as 'Comparative Religion' or 'History of Religion'.
58. Momen, *The Phenomenon of Religion*, p. 65.
59. Ibid., p. 66.

effective way of understanding the complexity of the phenomenon of religion is to try to get inside the religious experience itself in order to understand the 'intentionality' (actual inner meaning) of phenomena.[60]

A key tool of Husserl's method is 'bracketing' or the phenomenological *epoché*. According to this view the external world must be held in suspension or 'bracketed'. The researcher must suspend his or her beliefs and judgments as to the truth, value or existence of particular religious phenomena. Instead their attention should focus on the experience itself as an impartial observer. The other key tool is *einfuhlung*, which involves procuring an emphatic understanding of the religious experience of others. Through the use of these tools, the researcher may gain insight into either the religious phenomenon or the essential structures of the religious tradition being studied. These structures may be identified through the 'eidetic vision', a term coined by Husserl, which means the intuitive apprehension of the '*eidos* (form) of a phenomenon'. He believed that the *eidos* of a phenomenon could only be comprehended by means of intuition and insight, not by experience or rational thought. According to Momen, one particular application of these methods by phenomenologists is to accumulate a body of source material about a particular phenomenon and then to search for its essential core meaning.[61]

One of the early formative examples of phenomenological interpretation was the approach of Rudolf Otto (1869–1937) in his book *The Idea of the Holy*.[62] Another even more lastingly influential founder of this approach was Mircea Eliade (1907–1986). Eliade extended phenomenology from being a methodological tool to the very basis for a science of religion. His approach differed from Otto's in that he focused not so narrowly on religious experience as an encounter with the 'numinous' or sacred, as on religious symbols and ritual as mediators between humans and the sacred. Recently the concepts of phenomenology have continually evolved and altered through the influence of the thousands of scholars and researchers worldwide now involved in this rapidly expanding discipline. For example, Ninian Smart[63] developed the concept of *epoché* into what he terms 'methodological agnosticism', meaning that the researcher should conduct his or her enquiries in such a way that they presuppose neither acceptance nor denial of the truth of particular claims about the

60. Ibid., p. 67.
61. Ibid.
62. Rudolf Otto, *The Idea of the Holy* (trans. J.W. Harvey; London: Oxford University Press, 1923; original German ed. 1917).
63. Works include *Concept and Empathy* (London: Macmillan, 1986) and *The Philosophy of Religion* (Oxford: Oxford University Press, 1979).

ultimate reality. Wilfred Cantwell-Smith[64] emphasised the other principal trajectory within phenomenology, which is the need to achieve empathy and understanding of what it is like to belong to a particular religious tradition by observing the universe through perspectives from within the confines of that particular worldview. In the view of the Islamacist, Richard C. Martin,

> The achievement of phenomenology was important for theorising about religion generally, but of little long-range consequence for methodology. Many phenomenologists have opted for methodological pluralism, combining whatever approaches in historical, linguistic, and social-scientific studies that would seem to throw light on the religious phenomena under investigation. Especially from the vast collections of field data made by social anthropologists, the diverse expressions of human religious behaviour have been culled and refined in search of common patterns—the universals of human religiousness.[65]

Martin's remarks on this wider discipline accurately reflect the characteristic procedures of this study, combining historical contexts and phenomenological and participant observation. However, I also agree with his suggestion that the phenomenological methodological approach on its own may not do full justice to analysis and interpretation within the study of religious phenomenology, which could benefit from additional methodological tools, particularly, as in the case of this study, those of the psychologist.

RELIGIOUS EXPERIENCE AND MYSTICISM

In spite of the fact that the phenomenological approach to methodology was utilized in this study, it is important also to highlight some issues related to religious experience and the 'language' of mysticism. This is because it is necessary to illustrate and emphasise that religious and mystical experiences are *real* for the person experiencing them and have been attested to cross-culturally and historically for time immemorial.

It was the American philosopher and psychologist William James (1842–1910), who in one of the most famous early studies investigated the intense 'religious experiences' of a few exceptional individuals during their times of solitude. (Later studies involved whole populations

---

64. Wilfred Cantwell-Smith, 'Comparative Religion: Whither—and Why?', in *The History of Religions: Essays in Methodology* (ed. Mircea Eliade and Joseph Kitagawa; Chicago: University of Chicago Press, 1959), pp. 31-58.

65. Richard C. Martin, 'Islam and Religious Studies', in *Approaches to Islam in Religious Studies* (ed. Richard C. Martin; Tempe: University of California Press, 1980), pp. 7-8.

in non-solitary circumstances.) James concluded that there are a number of 'varieties of religious experience' but that they may have a common core.[66] There are many ways of assessing religious experience (REs), the most commonly used being a specially drafted question. The version used in British surveys is the one developed by the Alister Hardy Research Centre in Oxford: 'Have you ever been aware of or influenced by a presence or power, whether you call it God or not, which is different from your everyday self?' Another approach is to obtain descriptions of the accounts of the experiences and then analyse the contents. Several authorities have compiled lists of religious experiences from various religions, cultures and historical periods but probably the most widely used is that of W.T. Stace.[67] Common to religious experiences are all or some of these descriptions:

> Unifying vision, all things are one part of a whole.
> Timeless and spaceless.
> Sense of reality, not subjective but a valid source of knowledge.
> Blessedness, joy, peace and happiness.
> Feeling of the holy, sacred and divine.
> Paradoxical, defies logic.
> Ineffable, cannot be described in words
> Loss of sense of self.

Stace omitted from his list visions, voices, trances and ecstasies believing that these did not belong to the universal core experience.

In their well-known work,[68] psychologists Benjamin Beit-Hallahmi and Michael Argyle suggest two important divisions within 'religious experiences'. The first is of being in contact with a transcendent being experienced as outside oneself, of awe and dependence. Rudolf Otto described this as the numinous experience.[69] The second division, sometimes described as mystical, is the immanent unity of all things. The two aspects can manifest in union and are found described in major religious writings as, for example, 'a feeling of unity with God, fear, awe and reverence, dependence, a journey inwards and upwards, love and marriage, the goal of union with the divine'.[70]

---

66. William James, *The Varieties of Religious Experience: A Study in Human Nature* (2nd ed.; New York: Longmans Green, 1902).

67. W.T. Stace, *Mysticism and Philosophy* (Philadelphia: Lippincott, 1960), p. 79.

68. Benjamin Beit-Hallahmi and Michael Argyle, *The Psychology of Religious Behaviour, Belief and Experience* (London: Routledge, 1997), pp. 74-75.

69. Otto, *The Idea of the Holy, passim* (see esp. pp. 5-11).

70. C.B. Smith and S. Ghose, 'Religious Experience', *Encylopedia Britannica* 26 (1989), pp. 624-37, quoted in Beit-Hallahmi and Argyle, *Psychology of Religious Behaviour*, p. 75.

Although the most solidly defining factor seems to be that these experiences are both universal and historical, some of them may not be interpreted as religious at all. Certain accounts have described feelings of unity with other people in a crowd and states of ecstasy that can be secularly induced, for example, by music, sex or nature. However, many of the categories listed could well be recognised by Beshara students.

Psychologists have proposed numerous explanations for the possible triggers of the inducement of religious experiences; for example, some could be the result of the effects of certain drugs such as mescaline found in the cactus peyote, marihuana and LSD. These drugs may cause similar experiences as those described above as well as others such as hallucinations. Students of Beshara do not imbibe any form of drug including alcohol, so this could not account for any of their experiences described in later chapters of this study.[71] Beit-Hallahmi and Argyle investigated the backgrounds of people prone to religious experiences and found that such experiences were more common among religious people. Regarding cognitive structures, those who had religious experiences had higher scores on the Repression-Sensitization scale which is intended to measure openness to unusual, reality threatening aspects of experience.[72] There are other psychological hypotheses the phenomena, such as the disposition towards schizophrenia or a mild form of the ailment schizotypy.[73] Another very common suggestion for the phenomena, particularly classic mystical examples such as those of the conversion of St. Paul on the road to Damascus and the visions of the sixteenth-century mystic St. Teresa of Avila, is the argument for temporal lobe epilepsy. This could account for fainting, seeing bright lights, feeling possessed and experiencing auditory and visual hallucinations. It also transpires that many non-religious epileptics become religious after such episodes. Scott Atran supports this suggestion adding that autism could also produce religious experience type symptoms.[74] Michael Persinger, in *The Neuropsychological Bases of God Beliefs*, suggests that 'God experiences and religious rituals are evolutionary consequences of neural organisation'[75] and that the neural substrate of religious experience is available to everyone. Atran offers an

---

71. Chapters 6 and 7.
72. Beit-Hallahmi and Argyle, *Psychology of Religious Behaviour*, p. 91.
73. A personality dimension indicating a disposition to have schizophrenia described by G. Claridge, *Origins of Mental Illness* (Oxford: Blackwell, 1985).
74. Scott Atran, *In Gods we Trust: The Evolutionary Landscape of Religion* (Oxford: Oxford University Press, 2002), pp. 188-89.
75. Michael Persinger, *The Neuropsychological Bases of God Beliefs* (New York: Praeger, 1987), p. 137.

extremely interesting conclusion to his discussion of the possibilities of neuropsychological causes of religious experiences as follows:

> None of the religious pathologies that I have summarised—temporal lobe epilepsy, schizophrenia, autism—implies a localised neural substrate for extreme religious experiences in the temporal lobe (or anywhere else in the brain). More significant, neither is there any evidence that less extreme, more 'routine' religious experiences have some characteristic brain activation pattern.[76]

In other words it appears that from the perspective of a neuropsychologist there is no physical cause to explain religious experiences.

PROBLEMS WITH THE 'LANGUAGE' OF MYSTICISM

A central and widely experienced problem involving religious experiences, and particularly mysticism, which is normally categorised within the wider definitions of the religious experience, is how to describe the experiences, since the experiences themselves defy language structures, being usually ineffable or indescribable.[77] This surfaced as a familiar problem during research for this study.

William James[78] proposes four qualities that differentiate mystical experiences from other religious experiences. These are:

Ineffability: That the experience 'defies expression, that no adequate report on the contents can be given in words'.

Noetic quality: 'Although so similar to states of feeling, mystical states seem to those who experience them to also be states of knowledge… They are illuminations, revelations, full of significance and importance, all inarticulate though they remain, and as a rule carry with them a curious sense of authority…'

Transiency: 'Mystical states cannot be sustained for long, except for rare instances. Often, when faded, their quality can but imperfectly be reproduced in memory; but when they recur it is recognised; and from one recurrence to another, it is sustainable of continuous development in what is felt as inner richness and importance'.

Passivity: 'Although the oncoming of mystical states may be facilitated by preliminary voluntary operations as by fixing the attention… Yet when the characteristic sort of consciousness has set in, the mystic feels as if his own will were in abeyance and indeed sometimes as if he were grasped and held by a superior power'.

---

76. Atran, *In Gods we Trust*, p. 195.
77. See Stace's list, p. 21 above.
78. James, *Varieties*, p. 380.

In his book *Mystical Languages of Unsaying*, Michael Sells discusses not only problems of describing mystical experience but of the difficulties encountered when attempting to speak of the transcendent. For example, in the Introduction to his book he proposes:

> That mode of discourse begins with the *aporia*—the irresolvable dilemma—of transcendence. The transcendent must be beyond names, ineffable. In order to claim that the transcendent is beyond names, however, I must give it a name 'the transcendent'. Any statement of ineffability, 'X is beyond names' generates the *aporia* that the subject of the statement must be named (as X) in order to affirm that it is beyond names...[79]

On the other hand, not all scholars of religion support the view that mystical experience (and talk of the transcendent) is ineffable. In his article 'Mystical Experience, Mystical Doctrine, Mystical Technique'[80] Peter Moore argues against the claim by many philosophers that mystical experiences are not accessible to rational enquiry on account of their ineffability. He argues that if the experiences are so ineffable, why do the mystics write so much about them? Other complex arguments circumvent the problem of mysticism and the subject of the universal and particular in religion.[81] A common claim amongst scholars of religion is that mysticism is a universal and cross-cultural experience. In his article 'Language, Epistemology and Mysticism'[82] Steven Katz remarks upon Stace's claim for a 'common universal core' across the world's religious spectrum.[83] He suggests though that Stace and others who hold this view are misguided, as they are

> being misled by the surface grammar of the mystical reports they study. That is to say, what appear to be similar sounding descriptions are not similar descriptions and do not indicate the same experience. They do not because language is itself contextual and words 'mean' only in context.[84]

---

79. Michael Sells, *Mystical Languages of Unsaying* (Chicago: University of Chicago Press, 1994), p. 2.

80. Peter Moore, 'Mystical Experience, Mystical Doctrine, Mystical Technique', in *Mysticism and Philosophical Analysis* (ed. Steven T. Katz; New York: Oxford University Press, 1978), pp. 101-33.

81. See below, p. 25.

82. Steven Katz, 'Language, Epistemology and Mysticism', in Katz, ed., *Mysticism and Philosophical Analysis*, pp. 22-75.

83. Stace, *Mysticism and Philosophy*, pp. 106-7.

84. Stace, *Mysticism and Philosophy*, pp. 46-47.

Katz also argues that James's models are not necessarily universal as, for example, his definition of ineffability is 'not the basis on which one can compare experience...'[85]

So it becomes apparent that even scholars of religion are in conflict of agreement in terms of the arguments surrounding the problems of ineffability and the mystical experience.

UNIVERSALITY AND PARTICULARITY IN RELIGION

As will be explored in more detail in Chapter 5 below, the Beshara School claims that it is non-creedal and beyond institutionalised religion and that its aim is to assist its students to 'taste' or have experience of Ultimate Reality (which is their own ultimate reality) face to face. This claim then begs the question, that if this is so why is there such a preponderance of Islamic material and practice used by the school relative to material from other religious sources?

The problem of pluralism or the universal versus the particular in religion has been rigorously addressed from a Christian perspective although some of the classic arguments would equally apply to Islam or any other religion. One of the most articulate exponents of the pluralist argument has been the theologian John Hick, but as may be observed in the footnote below, issues related to pluralism versus exclusivism or the universal and particular in religion are not straightforward, particularly where the problems of truth claims arise.[86]

85. Katz, 'Language, Epistemology and Mysticism', p. 48.
86. In 1972 Hick proposed a 'Copernican revolution in Theology' concerning Christianity's place amongst world religions 'Copernican Revolution of Theology' in *God and the Universe of Faiths: Essays in the Philosophy of Religion* (New York: St Martin's Press, 1973), pp. 120-32. As discussed in Wolfgang Pannenburg's 'Religious Pluralism and Conflicting Truth Claims: The Problem of a Theology of the World Religions' in *Christian Uniqueness Reconsidered: The Myth of a Pluralistic Theology of Religions* (ed. Gavin D'Costa; Maryknoll, N.Y.: Orbis, 1990), pp. 96-106, Hick pleaded for a vision where all the various religions would be considered alike as planets circling around one absolute Truth. He has, though, been criticised for ignoring the question of truth in his proposal for a theology of religious pluralism and especially for reducing the significance of the fact that different religions make conflicting truth claims. He does not deny that there are disagreements on several levels between people of various religions regarding issues of historical belief as well as concerning doctrine (for example on reincarnation and on different ways of conceiving and experiencing the ultimate reality as personal or non-personal). However, he holds that the issues where the conflicting truth claims of the different traditions occur are not of great religious, i.e., soteriological importance though he admits their metaphysical significance. In 'The Jordan, the Tiber, and the Ganges:

In order to clarify briefly the way in which the Beshara School understands its situation within the argument, two recent quotes from its website are provided below:

> Religion often means binding oneself to a dogma or a set of rules expounded by leaders who are seen to be superior in wisdom. In fact, they are intermediaries between the worshipper and the Almighty. Beshara is the way of no intermediaries and so one's religion becomes a private matter.[87]

> The knowledge that Beshara brings is tied to all religions and not fixed to any one; texts studied from all the major religions and various practices used at the school are also drawn from them. However, these do not define the student in the way a religion might; rather, each person must find their own place according to themselves. This education is inclusive and seeks to extend rather than limit how we see ourselves in the context of this world.[88]

However, a senior supervisor and original participant of the school did explain recently that the prevalence of Islamic material and texts used by the school was not, as has been sometimes suggested, because it is a contemporary Westernised Sufi movement but simply because Bulent Rauf, who was involved with the school from its beginnings, was Turkish and he introduced the original adherents to Ibn 'Arabi who was Muslim. It has also been suggested that the resonance of the Arabic language is conducive to opening the consciousness to an exalted state, particularly during *zikrs*.

RESEARCH METHODS AND DATA

For this study I utilised both textual sources and data acquired through field research. Consultation of written sources was necessary to provide a wider historical context for the emergence and expansion of the Beshara Trust and the Muhyiddin Ibn 'Arabi Society. This written data was obtained through careful scrutiny of the Society's unpublished internal archives and documentation as well as the external publications of both organisations. These included the public literature and records of the Beshara School and the Muhyiddin Ibn 'Arabi Society dating from the

---

Three Kairological Moments of Christian Self Consciousness' in *The Myth of Christian Uniqueness* (ed. John Hick and Paul Knitter; Maryknoll, N.Y.: Orbis, 1987), pp. 89-116 (103) Raimundo Pannikka counters Hick's proposal from a Christian Exclusivist angle explicitly denying that there can be an ultimate reduction of the phenomenal plurality into an all-encompassing new systematization and asserts that the incommensurability of ultimate systems may be unbridgeable.

87. Online: beshara.org/essentials/faq.html (accessed 12 October 2008).
88. Online: beshara.org/essentials/faq.html (accessed 12 October 2008).

beginnings to the present day, such as newsletters, minutes of meetings, magazines, journals and symposia proceedings, and more recently, public websites. A wide range of readily available secondary sources (all in English), dealing with related works on Ibn 'Arabi, including biographies, translations and interpretations, allowed me to enhance my own understanding of his life, historical background and mystical philosophy.

The chapters interweave straightforward historical narratives concerning the evolution of the two organisations based on readily accessible written and verbal sources with more phenomenologically based data. However, there is increased emphasis on the historical narrative in the first four and final two chapters, with the main phenomenological focus in Chapters 5, 6 and 7.

The field research was conducted through the standard anthropological methods of collecting data, including structured and informal interviews and discussions, as well as participant observation on an ongoing basis between 1998 and 2002. My interviewees and discussants were all participants, in one way or another, in the activities of the Beshara School and in the annual symposia, or subscribers to the journal or newsletter of the Muhyiddin Ibn 'Arabi Society. The interviews and discussions were undertaken during periods of participant observation, at conferences or lectures, at specifically arranged meetings, on social occasions or through extended telephone conversations. I also obtained some original material through letters replying to a standard set of written questions.

The interview process began through the method of structured interviews, involving a specific set of questions recorded with a tape-recorder. The tape-recorder, I was told during the first round of interviews, was unwelcome, so from then on I used a reporter's notebook. Also during this first round of interviews, it became apparent that the use of a structured set of questions was not very helpful and that a conversational type of longer, less structured interview, incorporating all the required questions, was more effective for this type of research. This was because this approach provided a more relaxed setting, therefore allowing the possibility to resume and continue conversations at a later date. The informal relaxed approach was also required because a substantial proportion of the interview material dealt with religious phenomenology, involving private, intimate religious experiences of the interviewees. As a researcher I was privileged to be the recipient of some of these experiences and this was another important reason why I chose the phenomenological approach for this part of my research.

My 'participant observational' periods of data collection included attending a nine-day residential course at Chisholme, the Beshara

School's current premises in Scotland, in November 1998, a study seminar on Ibn 'Arabi in August 1999 and the Muhyiddin Ibn 'Arabi Society's annual symposium in August 2000, both held at Chisholme, as well as the Oxford symposia in 1998, 1999, 2001 and 2002. I also joined the annual two-week pilgrimage to Turkey, which is open to all interested parties, in December 2000.

My purpose in using these anthropological methods of collecting data was to enable myself to develop an accurate, in-depth understanding of those individuals who helped to create the Beshara School and the Ibn 'Arabi Society, and of those who continue to be attracted to attending Beshara courses. I wanted to know of any previous spiritual education or experience, how the students had heard about the school and what they hoped to gain from the courses. Most importantly, I wanted to know how the courses had affected them and how what they had learned, experienced or realised was manifested in their daily lives over a longer period of time. It quickly became apparent, for example, that there were some core experiences that appeared to be common to all those interviewed, whilst there were also individual interpretations which were generally dependent on the particular participant's work, occupation or life situation. For example, the way in which a psychologist manifests what he or she has realised on a Beshara course will not be quite the same as that of the artist, although the base understanding is similar. This is because of the way in which the teachings of Ibn 'Arabi, as interpreted through the school, become a reality for the students during the courses. Most of my interviewees expressed the wish to remain anonymous, and in order to respect this requirement, I have consistently used pseudonyms for all interview data, but not for publicly published written sources.

As already stated, the gathering of accurately reflective data through these prescribed methods was a delicate process, hence my choice of the phenomenologist's approach. In my role as a participant observer, particularly on the nine-day course and the pilgrimage to Turkey, I discovered that having gained the trust and co-operation of my fellow participants, my greatest challenge was the need to combine the anthropologist's objective distance with the necessarily empathic approach of the religious phenomenologist. There were times when this process was difficult, but even these occasions provided valuable insights into the spiritual and emotional ambience generated by the ethos and teachings of the school and the spiritual atmosphere at certain sites in Turkey.

The total number of participants interviewed breaks down as follows:
- Formal and informal interviews with participants of the Beshara School—44
- Female—27

- Male—17
- First generation participants—28
- Second generation participants (children of original students)—5
- Current students on the intensive residential six–month course—5 (I also had informal discussions with 20 current students of both the intensive and advanced six-month courses on the pilgrimage to Turkey.)
- Participants from the American branch—4
- Interviewees with strong associations with the school or Society, but who were never students of the school—4.

My interviewees were principally English speaking, university educated, middle class and nominally Christian by birth, although there were some from Jewish backgrounds. Since the instigation of the long residential courses in the mid-1970s until 2000, there have been approximately twelve Muslim participants predominantly from Turkey. In 2000, two nine-day courses were held in Jakarta Indonesia, comprising thirty participants overall. Ninety-five percent of these were Muslim. A further course is scheduled to take place in Indonesia in June 2003 upon which forty potential students have reserved bookings. Again, the majority of these students are Muslim, twenty of whom took part in one or other of the previous courses held in that country.[89]

The national origin of my interviewees included most English-speaking countries, as well as the Middle East, Russia, and several countries in the European Community. Thirty of these people have been cited under pseudonyms in the thesis and there were many more associates of the school with whom I had conversations but whose names I have not recorded. These conversations contributed to a wider general understanding of the ethos of the school and Society.

There are at least three hundred former students of the Beshara School's long residential (six-month) courses worldwide, and many hundreds (or several thousand) more people have participated in the past thirty years in the wide range of other activities that the school has to offer, including short courses, seminars and retreats.[90] I did attempt to acquire more specific statistical data related to the Beshara School courses, for example, enrolment numbers since the school's establishment, the volume of inquiries and fluctuation of interest. However, the Principal informed me that such data are not available at present.

89. Discussion with Peter Young, the present Principal of the Beshara School, May 2003. (During revision of this manuscript in 2008/9 I learnt from Peter Young that this course is now held annually in Indonesia.)
90. Phone conversation/interview with The Principal (2002).

My approach to the aspects of this study which involved field work and the problems that arose out of it are similar to those recounted by many anthropological students of religions, including Francine Jeanne Daner.[91] Although her study was on the Hare Krishna movement in the United States, her main approach to data collection was through participant observation and interviews, during which she had to gain the confidence of her interviewees, which was a delicate and gradual process. She then had to attempt to empathetically immerse herself in the activities of the movement, whilst also trying to maintain a scholarly distance. During her similar research into Sufism in modern Egypt, Valerie J. Hoffmann describes the necessity of becoming, as the observer, as much a part of the ambient society as possible.[92] To enable this to occur, she had to adopt the locally routine Islamic dress and behaviour as much as possible. Katherine Pratt Ewing also makes some very interesting points regarding her own attempts and failures at maintaining complete scholarly detachment and distance during her research into sainthood in Pakistan.[93] One of her revealing failures involved a dream experience in which she seemed to be visited by a saint and her inability to provide a purely psychological explanation for its contents.[94] Another example was when she seemed to be overcome almost hypnotically and subconsciously against her will by the power of a *Pir*.[95] I likewise encountered some difficulty in maintaining an objective stance during much of my data collecting. Although I am not a long-term participant in the activities of the school (apart from time spent at Chisholme and elsewhere as a participant observer), I am significantly sympathetic to the approaches and methods applied as I have previous extensive personal involvement with somewhat similar 'esoteric' groups. This added to the fact that I have a propensity for spontaneous 'religious' and/or mystical experiences, further contributed to the difficulty in maintaining scholarly distance and detachment.[96] I found myself at times being 'drawn into' or 'overcome by' an activity such as meditation or *zikr* at the school, or

---

91. Francine Jeanne Daner, *The American Children of Krishna: A Study of the Hare Krishna Movement* (New York: Holt, Rinehart & Winston, 1976), pp. 1-5.

92. Valerie J. Hoffmann, *Sufism, Mystics, and Saints in Modern Egypt* (Colombia: University of South Carolina Press, 1995), p. 27.

93. Katherine Pratt Ewing, *Arguing Sainthood: Modernity, Psychoanalysis and Islam* (Durham: Duke University Press, 1997).

94. Ibid., pp. 160-62.

95. Ibid., pp. 190-95.

96. I have always been susceptible to these 'experiences' but was diagnosed with 'petit mal' (minor epilepsy) recently, so perhaps this would account for them. See above pp. 22-23.

'overwhelmed' by what is difficult not to describe, for example, as a 'powerful presence' at the shrine of a saint in Turkey. My tactic in dealing with these problems was to try to observe my experience in a detached way, as if it was happening to a third party or interviewee.

Other scholars of Islamic studies within the study of religion (or related areas of anthropology) whose methodological approaches contributed to and influenced my understanding of my methods, particularly because they involved the phenomenological approach to studying related dimensions of contemporary Islam, include Reinhold Loeffler, Louis Brenner, Carl Ernst, Dale F. Eickelman, Clifford Geertz and Michael Gilsenan.[97]

STRUCTURE AND CONTENTS OF THE CHAPTERS

This study is divided into nine chapters. The early chapters (1–4) provide a necessary historical (and with less stress, phenomenological) descriptive context for understanding the genesis, growth and increasing influence of the two organisations. Chapters 5, 6 and 7 focus more closely on the phenomenological dimension of the participants' actual experience of the courses and the lasting effects on their lives and professional activities. Chapter 8 explores the way in which the school has developed its wider programme of 'outreach' and networks for the broad practical cultural and social expression of its teachings, whilst the final chapter focuses on the Muhyiddin Ibn 'Arabi Society.

Chapter 1 provides a brief biographical account of Bulent Rauf. Rauf was a sophisticated and highly educated Ottoman aristocrat who settled in England in the late 1960s. At the time of the establishment of the Trust in 1971, he was surrounded by a group of young intellectuals (from Ireland, Europe, the United States, Australia, the Middle East and Israel) who were interested in a wide range of spiritual matters. These people were, together with Rauf, co-founders and co-ordinators of the Trust at its beginnings; many of them are still involved with guiding and managing the Trust's various activities today. Although never putting himself forward in a position of official leader or 'master' of the Beshara School,

---

97. Reinhold Loeffler, *Islam in Practice: Religious Beliefs in a Persian Village* (Albany: SUNY Press, 1988); Louis Brenner, *West African Sufi: The Religious Heritage and Spiritual Search of Cerno Boker Saalif Taal* (Berkeley: University of California Press, 1984); Carl Ernst, *Eternal Garden: Mysticism, History, and Politics at a South Asian Sufi Center* (Albany: SUNY Press, 1992); Dale F. Eickelman, *The Middle East: An Anthropological Approach* (New Jersey: New York University Press, 1989); Clifford Geertz, *Islam Observed: Religious Development in Morocco and Indonesia* (Chicago: University of Chicago Press, 1968).

Rauf was undoubtedly the common focus of its establishment and that of the Ibn 'Arabi Society, and without him neither organisation would have emerged. The emphasis of this chapter is on Rauf's traditional family and personal connections with the teachings of Ibn 'Arabi in Ottoman Turkey, the culture of his birth and early education.

Chapter 2 details the emergence of the Beshara Trust in relation to Bulent Rauf. It shows how interest in the ideas and teachings of Ibn 'Arabi began to gain predominance over other forms of spiritual teaching initially pursued by the Trust. The chapter also demonstrates how this particular interest in Ibn 'Arabi came about, and connects this development with other scholars of Ibn 'Arabi and teachers of Islamic spirituality, such as Titus Burckhardt and J.G. Bennett.

Chapter 3 summarises the further historical development of the school, and goes on to describe the purpose and structure of its newly established courses.

Chapter 4 offers a summary of Ibn 'Arabi's key metaphysical concepts and teachings as they are actually studied on the Beshara courses and related study texts. In this chapter, his ideas are extracted primarily from *The Twenty-Nine Pages*[98] and the *Blue Fusûs*.[99] The chapter acknowledges early on the potential difficulties which could arise during the attempts at obtaining a true interpretation of what is meant by some of Ibn 'Arabi's concepts in translation and the risk of distortion in interpretation. The latter part of the chapter includes summaries of all the other texts used by the school.

Chapter 5, which begins the central phenomenological focus of the study, provides an analysis of the aims and objectives of the recent education and courses at the Beshara School. It examines the ways in which the meaning of 'Beshara' is understood by some participants, and the ways in which Ibn 'Arabi himself is understood by some of them as a 'spiritual meaning'.

Chapter 6 focuses on some students' experiences during and following their attendance on Beshara courses. It describes their motivations for being there and their memorable experiences during this time. This chapter also includes a representative selection of individual case studies illustrating the diverse ways in which the spiritual realisations attained

---

98. This teaching text is Bulent Rauf's condensed summary of the ideas of the *Fusûs al-Hikam* and the *al-Futûhât al-Makkiyya* from the English translations included in A.A. Affifi's *The Mystical Philosophy of Muhyid Dîn Ibnul Arabî* (Cambridge: Cambridge University Press, 1964).

99. The school's name for the English translation of Ibn 'Arabi's *The Wisdom of the Prophets* (trans. from Arabic to French by Titus Burckhardt and French to English by Angela Culme-Seymour; Gloucestershire: Beshara, 1975).

by some students on the courses are manifested in their daily lives, and how this manifestation goes on to affect those people with whom they come into regular contact.

Chapter 7 describes and analyses the school's annual pilgrimage to Turkey. During this trip, students and long-time adherents of the school visit a series of shrines dedicated to Muslim saints who have close connections with Ibn 'Arabi. The travellers also visit other historical sacred sites in this area such as of those from early Christianity (including the shrine of the Virgin Mary at Ephesus) and the Hellenistic era. This chapter is separate from the preceding one because, although the pilgrimage is part of the regular six-month courses, it is also open not only to other participants and friends of the Beshara School, but to anyone else with an interest in spirituality who can afford the journey. Usually the majority of these 'pilgrims' are not doing a formal course at the time. Therefore it must constitute a separate and distinct Beshara activity, especially important in maintaining contact among former course participants.

Chapter 8 explores the ways in which, from modest beginnings, the Beshara School has expanded its influence, first on a national level, then into Europe and the wider English-speaking world, and how it continues to generate interest now, thirty years after its initial emergence, even in parts of the Muslim world as far as Turkey and Indonesia. Here the theme that was initially explored in Chapter 6 (i.e. how the intended outcome of all Beshara courses and related activities is that participants should continue as active 'seeds' for effectively communicating and expressing Ibn 'Arabi's central spiritual understanding of the One Reality) is expanded into wider cultural spheres. This chapter shows how Beshara participants creatively relate its central ideas to a wide range of diverse disciplines, such as the physical sciences, cosmology, fine arts, literature, cuisine and economics, as demonstrated particularly in the school's periodical publications and website.

This study concludes, in Chapter 9, with a brief survey of the history and diverse influences of the Muhyiddin Ibn 'Arabi Society. It shows how the Society's activities began with networking throughout Europe and the West, where the majority of initial scholarly contributors to its journal and international symposia were originally English speakers, and included some long-time students of the Beshara School. It demonstrates how the Society's annual international symposia in Oxford and Berkeley have attracted scholars in disciplines ranging from philosophy, psychology, mysticism and Arabic Studies, to poetry, music and the visual arts, affording speakers, delegates and non-specialists the opportunities to increase their understanding of the relevance of the teachings of Ibn 'Arabi today. It also shows how the Society is active in the preservation of valuable copies of manuscripts of Ibn 'Arabi's works which are presently held in various locations in Turkey. The chapter concludes by illustrating how this expanding development, initially based in a network of Western academics and students of Ibn 'Arabi, has more recently begun to 'return' to its original and historical origins as the journal, symposia and related activities have attracted increasing Muslim scholarly interest and participation from North Africa to Indonesia.

Throughout this study, I have attempted to provide a representative and accurate presentation of my findings, in the hope that they will contribute to a deeper understanding of the many visible and less visible ways such forms of Islamic spirituality and philosophy, especially those associated with Ibn 'Arabi, are having an ever-increasing influence on many interested circles both in the West and throughout our increasingly compact global community.

NOTE ON TRANSLITERATION AND TRANSCRIPTION

Some key Islamic and Sufi terms used in the written sources for this study appear in very different spellings, depending on whether the particular sources I have quoted reflect Arabic, Persian or Turkish (Ottoman or modern) pronunciation and spelling conventions. When *quoting* published sources, I have retained the original spellings, despite the obvious variations involved. In describing common Beshara practices and terminology however, I have generally adopted the particular 'anglicised' spellings which the participants themselves normally employ in those contexts: e.g. *zikr*, rather than *dhikr*, *zekr*, etc. And when referring to Ibn 'Arabi directly I have again used the commonly 'anglicised' form of his name by dropping the definite article 'al', and refraining from use of the accent over the long vowel 'î'. Finally, in transliterating Arabic and Persian titles and in my own discussions of Ibn 'Arabi's Islamic terminology (when not quoting other translations), I have consistently attempted to adapt the standard (Library of Congress) scholarly transliteration system, showing long vowels (â, î, û), but not the diacritical marks under certain consonants, which in any case are readily recognised by those scholars familiar with those languages. A number of Islamic terms and proper names which have become familiar in Islamic and religious studies have been kept in their common, simplified and 'anglicised' forms, without italics or diacriticals (e.g. Sufi, tariqa, Shadhili, Sunni, Qunawi, etc.).

1

BULENT RAUF

The Beshara Trust was established in 1971 around the central figure of Bulent Rauf. Rauf was 'consultant' to the Trust and its school from this time until his death in 1987. He was also instrumental in the founding of the Muhyiddin Ibn 'Arabi Society in 1977.

Bulent Rauf was a highly educated scion of an aristocratic Ottoman family, who before becoming 'consultant' to the Beshara School had lived a life that moved between extremes of wealth and grinding poverty. These extremes of experience prepared him well for his later spiritual life, and allowed him to work effectively and closely with a broad spectrum of Beshara students.

EARLY LIFE

Mehmed Ali Bulent Rauf was born in Istanbul in 1911. His family, who were part of the Ottoman court, can be traced back to Mehmet Ali Pasha, who was born in 1769. Mehmet Ali Pasha's father, Ibrahim Aga, came from Konya and settled in Kavala. When he was thirty years old, Mehmet Ali went to Egypt where he gained favour with the Ottoman Sultan. The Sultan offered him the Vice-regency of Egypt and he accepted the position on the condition that it would be hereditary. Having agreed, the Sultan gave him the title of 'Khidiv'. The succession which followed was Ibrahim Pasha, then Ismail Pasha, Bulent's great grandfather, whose daughter Fatima was Bulent's grandmother. Bulent was her favourite grandson. He could remember her immense wealth and playing with her fabulous jewels and how, on a visit to Egypt, she either hired or bought her own passenger steamer, fitting it out for her own comfort and pleasure. Bulent grew up within the grandeur of the final days of the Ottoman Empire, and following its sudden termination after the First World War, he continued to live the life of a wealthy aristocrat.[1]

1. Bulent Rauf's work, *The Last Sultans*, in the foreword written by his second wife Angela Culme-Seymour (published posthumously by Meral Arim, 1995).

As a child Bulent studied French and English. As was typical during the later Ottoman period, Europe and particularly France was very attractive and fashionable to the Ottomans, and many upper-class households employed a live-in French woman, a 'mademoiselle', solely for the purpose of teaching the children fluent French. This was applicable to Bulent's home, which was a very substantial house in the Beylerbey district of Istanbul.[2]

As a teenager, Bulent attended Robert College, an American international high school in Istanbul, which educated children of the Ottoman elite for almost a century. At the age of seventeen, he went on to America and entered higher education, studying English at Cornell, and continuing graduate work in Hittite Archaeology at Yale. He had earlier developed a good knowledge of Ottoman Turkish and Arabic.

On completion of his university education, at the height of the Great Depression, he lived in Switzerland, indulging in an aristocratic lifestyle without any form of paid employment, pursuing this existence in smart hotels, attending evening bridge parties, operas and concerts.

In 1945 he married Princess Fayza, a distant cousin who was the younger sister of King Farouk of Egypt. She was also sister of Princess Sorayya, who was the first wife of the Shah of Persia, Riza Pahlevi. His marriage was arranged, which was customary within upper-class Egyptian and Turkish culture at that time. Following his marriage his 'high lifestyle' continued; there was no paid employment but rounds of elegant parties in the company of well-known European royalty and aristocracy. Following the Egyptian Revolution in 1952, Bulent and Fayza had to live in exile having lost all their wealth, which was confiscated by the new regime. Soon after this their marriage broke down. Fayza went to America and Bulent to England, where he made the first connections that were to lead to the establishment of Beshara.[3]

BULENT RAUF AND IBN 'ARABI

Since his first visit to Konya in 1205, Ibn 'Arabi had a lasting influence in Anatolia, particularly through the influential role of his step-son and foremost interpreter, Sadruddîn al-Qûnawî. The second Ottoman Sultan,

2. Information about Bulent's childhood and education were obtained through an interview with A. (a Turkish friend of Rauf), 11 February 2000.
3. Information about Bulent Rauf's life following university and up to the separation from with his first wife was obtained through interviews with S., 30 October 1999, and A., 11 February 2000. (S. was a very early and close acquaintance of Rauf following his initial arrival in England).

Orhan Ghazi, invited Da'ud al-Qaysarî (d. 1350 CE), a disciple of Kamâl al-Dîn al-Qûstânî, who had himself been a disciple of al-Qûnawî, to be director and teacher of the first Madrasa (school) founded by the Ottomans at Iznik. As a result of this line of influence, this master of Ibn 'Arabi's school of thought helped to set in motion the official religious teaching in the growing Ottoman Empire. This helped to establish Ibn 'Arabi's spiritual authority and intellectual influence throughout the later Ottoman Empire, continuing in Turkey to this day.[4]

At this point it is appropriate to introduce the *malâmî* ideals of sainthood and spiritual practice which were especially relevant to the teaching and philosophy of Ibn 'Arabi within the Ottoman Empire. These ideals ultimately helped to shape the educational outlook of Bulent Rauf and the Beshara School.

Ibn 'Arabi on Sainthood (*walâya*) and the 'Hidden Saint'

The Arabic word *walî*, usually translated as 'saint', derives from a root meaning 'to draw near'. This has two derived meanings. The first is 'to be a close friend', whilst the second has an active meaning 'to govern or take charge'. As the Arabic scholar and Beshara participant Stephen Hirtenstein explains 'the common understanding of saints refers to this second meaning, that of being a source of authority and assistance— people visit shrines or holy men in order to derive benefit and help'.[5] He further explains that this term is not closely related to the English understanding of the term 'saint' (*sanctus*, holy or pure), which is etymologically related to ideas often associated with a type of other-worldly purity.[6] This type of connotation is not quite consonant with the Quranic term *walî*, which some scholars translate instead as 'friend of God'.[7] Michel Chodkiewicz explains that ' the *walî* is simultaneously one who is close, the beloved, he who is protected, taken in charge, and the protector, the "patron" (in the Roman sense), the governor'.[8] And he quotes Ibn 'Arabi:

---

4. Mustafa Tahrali, 'A General Outline of the Influence of Ibn 'Arabi on the Ottoman Era', *JMIAS* XXVI (1999), pp. 43-54 (46). Ibn 'Arabi's line of influence in the Ottoman Empire will be explored in more depth in Chapter 7, below.

5. S. Hirtenstein, *The Unlimited Mercifier: The Spiritual Life and Thought of Ibn 'Arabi* (Oxford: Anqa, 1999), p. 70.

6. William James was one of the first to postulate the universal character of saints in *The Varieties of Religious Experience* (New York: Longmans, Green & Co., 1902; repr. Penguin Classics, 1985), p. 173.

7. Ibid., p. 70.

8. M. Chodkiewicz, *The Seal of the Saints: Prophethood and Sainthood in the Doctrine of Ibn 'Arabi* (Cambridge: Islamic Texts Society, 1993), p. 24.

> The *awliyâ* (plural of *walî*) are those of whom God has taken charge (*tawallâ*), by aiding them in their battles against the four enemies: the passions, the ego, the world and the devil.[9]

The highest category in Ibn 'Arabi's understanding of sainthood is the Sufi ideal of *Malâmiyya*. As he describes it:

> The *malâmiyya* are spiritual men (*al-rijâl*) who have received the highest degree of sainthood (*walâya*). There is nothing higher than them except the station of prophecy. [Their station] is the one referred to as the Station of Proximity (*maqâm al-qurba*)... No miracles (*kharq âdât*) are ascribed to them. They are not admired, because in the eyes of men they are not distinguished by behaviour which is ostensibly virtuous... They are the hidden ones, the pure ones, the ones in this world who are sure and sound and concealed among men...they are the solitary ones (*al-afrâd*).[10]

The French biographer of Ibn 'Arabi, Claude Addas, explains that the Sheikh al-Akbar ('The Greatest Teacher', one of the titles by which Ibn 'Arabi is traditionally known) also specifies that the 'solitary ones' fall into two categories: 'those who use their spiritual energy (*rukkâb al-himam*) as their "mount", and those who use their acts (*rukkâb al-a'mâl*)'. Those in the first category choose not to intervene in the affairs of the world, whereas those in the second category are compelled by divine command to assume a function of 'government' (*tadbîr*); the most eminent example is that of the 'Pole'. These people are called the 'Directors' (*mudabbirûn*). They are superior to the first category because they have returned, following the example of the prophets, to the created world, although they never actually leave God because they see His Face (*wajhu 'llâh*) at every instant in every single thing. Both categories, though, have full and total realisation of *ubûdiyya*, the total service of God.[11]

The special historical relevance of the spiritual ideal of *malâmiyya* in the Ottoman Empire is clarified in an article by Victoria Rowe Holbrook,[12] who explains:

---

9. *Futûhât*, vol. 2, p. 53; also cited in Hirtenstein, *The Unlimited Mercifier*, p. 70. For more detail regarding Muslim sainthood see Scott Alan Kugle, *Rebel Between Spirit and Law: Almad Zarruq, Sainthood and Authority in Islam* (Indiana: Indiana University Press, 2006) and Vincent Cornell, *The Realm of the Saint: Power and Authority in Moroccan Sufism* (Texas: University of Texas Press, 1998).

10. Quoted in Claude Addas, *The Quest for the Red Sulphur: The Life of Ibn 'Arabi* (Cambridge: Islamic Texts Society, 1993), p. 71. Discussed in Chodkiewicz, *The Seal of the Saints*, p. 181.

11. Addas, *The Quest for the Red Sulphur*, p. 72.

12. V.R. Holbrook, 'Ibn 'Arabi and Ottoman Dervish Traditions', Part I, *JMIAS* IX (1991), p. 18.

The *Melâmi*[13] are said to have emerged as a Turkish tarikat or sufi 'way' when Emir Sikkini walked into a blazing fire and came out having lost only his dervish robe and crown. This was in the Anatolian town of Goynuk, after the death of Sikkini's sheikh Haci Bayram Veli c. 1430. From the fifteenth century until now the Turkish *Melâmi* have worn the normal clothes of their day, and employed none of the other accoutrement by which dervish orders in Ottoman times identified themselves in public.[14]

Holbrook explains that Ibn 'Arabi has been associated with this particular Ottoman path both by the *Melâmi* themselves and in popular thought. She continues:

> The association is not one of initiatic chain (*silsile*); that is, no continuous connection between master and disciple leading back to Ibn 'Arabi was invoked. Rather, Ibn 'Arabi's many references to *malâmiyya* in his Meccan Revelations (*Futûhât al-Makkiyya*) were often cited by the *Melâmi* in definition of their 'way'. And they have been known as extremists in 'the oneness of being' (*vahdet-i vucud; a.wahdat al-wujûd*), a theory and practice which popular opinion attributed to Ibn 'Arabi.[15]

Holbrook then cites Spencer Trimingham, who explains the distinction between Sufis and *Malâmatîs* in the formation of their tariqas (orders) in the eleventh–thirteenth centuries:

> The distinction within Sufism between Sufis and *Malâmatîs* now becomes defined, the Sufis being those who submit to direction and conformity and the *Malâmatîs* are those who retain their freedom.
> ...The *sûfî* is concerned with *tawakkul* ('trust'; Quran, lxv.3) and that which involves *inkâr al-kasb* (severing the bonds of acquisition and personal action), with training, guidance, and even subjection to his shaikh, affirmed with oath and investment with a *khirka*, regulated exercises (*dhikr*) and *samâ*. All these the *malamatî* rejects, at least theoretically. At the foundation of the *malâmatî* tendency is the absolute nothingness of man before God. Contrary to the *sûfî*, the true *malâmatî* conceals his progress in the spiritual life. He aspires to free himself from the world and its passions whilst living in the world.[16]

It was within this ongoing tradition and through immersion in this type of spiritual thinking that Bulent Rauf was raised. As the chapter progresses, the relevance of these explanations of the *malâmatî* way will become progressively clearer. For Rauf's family had special traditional

13. Turkish spelling of the Arabic *Malâmî*.
14. Holbrook, 'Ibn 'Arabi and Ottoman Dervish Traditions', Part I, p. 18.
15. Ibid.
16. S. Trimingham, *The Sufi Orders of Islam* (Oxford: Clarendon, 1971), pp. 13, 265, quoted by Holbrook, 'Ibn 'Arabi and Ottoman Dervish Traditions', Part I, p. 19.

connections with the Sheikh al-Akbar, particularly through his mother and a cousin named Madame Hatice Munevver Ayashli (1906–1999).

Growing up in the midst of Ataturk's radically secularising revolution, Bulent was never formally involved with any established Sufi orders and had no official Sufi sheikh (master). He ostensibly maintained that 'all that he had learnt came through his mother'. This independent attitude later caused friction within some circles in Turkey because Islamic culture there was largely entrenched in the traditional local institutional forms of tariqas (Sufi order), sheikhs and disciples. However, the explanation above indicates that the *Malâmîs* of Turkey did not adhere to those historically recent forms, but rather followed a distinctive spiritual line self-consciously rooted in Ibn 'Arabi's approach. According to one of Rauf's students, his credentials were interior or purely spiritual, and he needed no external intermediary.[17]

Bulent's maternal grandfather is buried at the feet of Ibn 'Arabi in Damascus, and his mother was descended from the Sheikh Aziz Mahmud Hudayi Effendi, who in the seventeenth century founded the Jelveti Order in Turkey. This sheikh was a spiritual teacher of eight different Sultans. The significance of this particular Sufi order in relation to Bulent's approach to mysticism was that the distinctive aspiration of this order was that its members should not retreat from the world, but should live 'openly' (*Jelvet*) in it. This attitude contrasted with other orders such as the Helveti Order which propagated 'retreat' (*Helvet*) from the world.[18] The idea that those who are actively working upon a spiritual path should also fully engage with the world around them was central to Ibn 'Arabi's thought.

The last Jelveti sheikh in Istanbul, Sirrhu Baba, who was a post-master in Çengelköy, officially closed the Jelveti Order in the early 1950s. This sheikh wore a secular suit and a tie. One day he was walking down the street when Aziz Hudayi, the founder of this order who had been dead since the late 1600s, stood in front of him and grabbed him by his tie and

---

17. The common Arabic word for this type of inspired mystic is *uwaysi*, referring to someone whose link with his spiritual teacher (often a great spiritual figure, such as a prophet or earlier *walî*) is spiritual and not one of physical contact and outward initiation. Rauf's link was with Ibn 'Arabi, but he also always emphasised to those whom he counselled to look beyond him to where he pointed—and this was towards the Real or God (*al-Haqq*).

18. The word *Helvet* derives from the Arabic *khalwa* meaning 'retreat' and *Jelvet* derives from the Arabic *jalwa* or *jilwa* and means 'society', as well as the 'unveiling of a bride' so that her beauty as one 'dressed in the Divine qualities' may be displayed. This is addressed by Ibn 'Arabi in the *Futûhât*, Yahya ed., vol. 13, Chapters 78 and 79, pp. 352-71.

said: 'Enough of this form!'.[19] Sirrhu Baba partially interpreted this incident to mean that he should go beyond the 'form' of an official order, and he closed his tariqa; in this case the tariqa was not closed by the secular government as others had been under Ataturk, but by the sheikh himself.[20]

The significance of this event for Bulent and those who would come under his influence at Beshara was that it was taken to imply the end of the necessity for Sufi tariqas in their traditional form whilst indicating that it was time for a new form of spiritual training to appear without the institutional intermediaries of the sheikhs and the inherited system of tariqas. This idea of a more 'direct' and socially engaged spiritual training was central in Bulent's thinking and his conception of what Beshara was understood to be about, as will be shown below.

Another relative of Bulent Rauf who had an important influence upon his spiritual life, and who also had strong family connections with Ibn 'Arabi's tradition, was his cousin, Madame Ayashli. Her connections with Ibn 'Arabi were through her father, Caferi Tayyer, who was a colonel in the Turkish army. He had several spiritual encounters with Ibn 'Arabi in dreams,[21] and following the tragic death of his 3-year-old daughter of typhoid fever, he had her buried in the courtyard of Ibn 'Arabi's tomb in Damascus. Madame Ayashli had learned about Ibn 'Arabi from her father, who always had a copy of Ibn 'Arabi's *Fusûs al-Hikam* and the *Quran* at his bedside. As an adult she studied Ibn 'Arabi's works with Professor Louis Massignon at the Sorbonne. She was to become a prominent Turkish journalist and novelist, whose themes were historical, political and autobiographical. She once referred to Ibn 'Arabi as 'The man whoever lived' (who has always lived). On hearing this Bulent commented 'she is almost right' (almost, because Muhammad is the actual man).[22]

19. This account seems to be quite irrational, but it is not in Sufi circles nor is it unexpected for a researcher applying the methodology of the phenomenologist.

20. This well-known story was told to me during an interview with V., 11 February 2000. The interpretation of this incident may be understood on various levels, but the fundamental underlying meaning is one of 'simplicity'—for example 'placing before God no form as we understand it'. Thus the conception of the Sufi tariqa involving a formalised restrictive framework needs to end. Or, to take the symbolism of the tie, a tie represents formality. As Bulent Rauf noted to an early participant, referring to the loosening of formalities in the Western world in the 1960s, the dispensing of the wearing of ties symbolised this new liberation. From an interview with H., April 2002.

21. Another common occurrence between Sufi sheikhs and their disciples whether the sheikh is dead or alive. Ibn 'Arabi received a lot of his own instruction through meeting his sheikhs in dreams.

22. Interview with O., April 2002.

Although Bulent was undeniably touched by the Ottoman stream of Ibn 'Arabi's spiritual influence that was transmitted through his family, he did not live an outwardly ascetic existence as a young adult, particularly following his marriage to Princess Fayza. During this time a significant part of the couple's lifestyle consisted in attending lively parties with European royalty and aristocracy. When asked in later life if he regretted having lived this extreme lifestyle, Bulent said that he had no regrets and that God had allowed him to experience these things because eventually he wanted Bulent to come and do His work.[23]

THE BEGINNINGS OF BESHARA

After the revolution in Egypt in 1952, Rauf and his wife had all their property and money confiscated. Having survived in Spain and France for as long as they could, supporting themselves with money raised from selling her jewellery, Bulent and Fayza eventually separated and divorced. This was in 1962. By this time Bulent had reached a turning point in his life. On top of all his other troubles he had a car accident and, whilst in hospital in great pain, he contemplated suicide. His depression lifted only when a nurse told him that it was only his positive attitude to his injuries that was giving another accident victim the will to live. He thought then that humanity is in the world for a purpose, and he also realised how little humans actually know of their purpose in the world and of the nature of their very existence. From then on he was determined to live.[24]

In the late 1960s, Rauf settled in England and it was here, through a series of apparently chance meetings, that he came across those people who were to play such a significant part in the latter years of his life. His first contact was whilst he was working in an antiques shop in London. He found himself in conversation with a customer who organised workshops and study groups for people interested in spiritual matters. The customer's name was Reshad Feild.[25] Feild was deeply involved with the 'Sufi Order in the West', headed by Pir Vilayat Khan.[26] At around this

---

23. Similarly contrasting ways of life can be seen in the biographies of such great spiritual figures as St. Francis of Assisi, Augustine of Hippo and Gautama Buddha.

24. From a biographical article by Christopher Ryan, 'Conversion to the Essence', in *Papers of the International Symposium on Islamic Thought in the XIIIth and XIVth Centuries and Daud al-Qaysari* (ed. T. Koç; Ankara, 1998), pp. 335-43.

25. At this time Feild co-ordinated the activities of the 'Sufi Order in the West' in England.

26. See Introduction above.

same time, Bulent met an English lady, Angela Culme-Seymour, who was later to become his second wife.[27]

On a return journey to Turkey, after he had been in England for some time, he met a well-known dervish, who told him that he must return to England as this was where he was needed. This incident, having deep significance in Bulent's life, has become legendary within Beshara circles.[28] Because Bulent had outstanding knowledge of spiritual matters and Sufism, he soon became a regular speaker at the meetings, usually held in private homes in London, of the group held by Reshad Feild.

In 1971 the Beshara Trust was formed, a house in Archway opposite the famous Highgate cemetery in London was rented,[29] and Swyre Farm in Gloucestershire was purchased. These premises were both acquired by the Trust for the purpose of study for those people who were particularly interested in what Beshara was about. Bulent was always understood to be simply a consultant to the Trust and himself was never a Trustee.

In the early years following the inception of the Trust, there were no structured courses available. Interested people met in the London house or at Swyre Farm to study and discuss various areas of spiritual knowledge. The first central theme of the Trust and its school were those of the 'Unity of Existence', i.e., gaining an in-depth understanding and realisation of the intrinsic Oneness of Being, initially through a consideration of the basic unity behind all religious traditions. The second central theme was that of the 'Perfectibility of Man' (humanity), which involves the realisation, in accordance with the common teaching of all three Abrahamic religions, that the perfected human being manifests the image of God. The prime sources of study were the teachings of Ibn 'Arabi, whose writings expounded these central concepts in the most articulate way. It was for this reason that at this time (1971/72) Bulent formulated the *The Twenty-Nine Pages*, a summary based on the translations by A.A. Affifi of key passages from Ibn 'Arabi's famous works the *Futûhât al-Makiyyah* and the *Fusûs al-Hikam*. Rauf's summary quickly became the initial foundation of work and study at Beshara.[30]

Bulent's method of teaching was Socratic, in that the students were encouraged to draw knowledge of the subject from within themselves. His argument, in accordance with Ibn 'Arabi's central teaching, was that

---

27. See Chapter 3 below, for details of the period.
28. For details of this account see Chapter 3 below.
29. For a nominal sum of money, as it was derelict, study there having taken place by candlelight.
30. A.A. Affifi, *The Mystical Philosophy of Muhid Dîn Ibnul 'Arabî* (Cambridge: Cambridge University Press, 1969; originally published 1939).

we all innately know the truth about such things as God, existence and the nature of Being, but that we have failed to realise our immediate awareness of this knowledge because we are so involved in our activities in the world. What are needed are proper 'reminders' and the right environment in which to awaken these innate memories and knowledge.

At the time of the founding of the Beshara Trust, Bulent did give a few people individual spiritual teaching and exercises to practice on a weekly basis.[31] Some of these people were to become supervisors on the first residential courses.

Bulent was known as 'consultant' to Beshara, and this is an apt term to describe his activity within the school. He advised on the appointment of supervisors but was not one himself. He often sat in on the study sessions to see how both the students and supervisors were doing. He was adamant that he was not a teacher. He did not want to be understood as a Sufi sheikh, head of a tariqa or as any type of 'master'. This attitude is one striking illustration of the ongoing relevance of the above quoted story of Sirrhu Baba, the modern head of the Jelveti Order, and his remarkable encounter with its long-deceased founder Aziz Effendi and his instructions 'enough of this form!' Bulent's interpretation of the event was that there was now no longer an absolute need for the particular historical forms of the spiritual orders, or for there to be a human intermediary between God and the seeker in the person of a Sufi sheikh or 'guru'. This understanding was again quite in keeping with the deeper intentions of Ibn 'Arabi's overall approach.[32]

In the words of one student from that formative time, 'No-one was taught, the students had to learn from within themselves—otherwise Beshara would be a tariqa in disguise'. He added: 'It is important to note that it was always "source" material which was studied, therefore avoiding someone else's interpretation'.[33]

Bulent often described himself as a sort of 'signpost' pointing the way to those who recognised that he knew what they were looking for. He often emphasised this to his students: 'Don't look at me; look at what I

---

31. Interviewees were not prepared to divulge what this training involved; it was a purely private and individual matter between Bulent and each person. From an Interview with V., 11 February 2000.

32. For discussions of Ibn 'Arabi's major concepts as studied and practised by the school, see Chapter 4 below.

33. Interview with V., 11 February 2000. This statement about the use of source material only could be construed as controversial because of the risk of distortion or misinterpretation during translation. The statement was meant here to refer to translations from original sources and not commentaries through which another person's point of view might impart influence on the student.

see. Don't love me; love what I love'.[34] He also sought to teach by example and the students looked to what he embodied and strove to emulate his qualities, such as his humility, his constancy and his knowledge and understanding. His intention was to provide the environment and circumstances for esoteric knowledge to be imparted to the students who were then encouraged to use this knowledge in their everyday lives. He very much advocated living in the world and not retreating from it, and in this he followed the long-established method of the Jelveti Order and the *Malâmi* tradition, both of which were strongly aligned with Ibn 'Arabi's influence.[35]

In particular, Bulent Rauf manifested his own spirituality and realisation in the art of cooking. In addition to being an amateur archaeologist, well-versed historian, linguist, art connoisseur, poetry lover and raconteur of the final days of the Ottoman Empire, he was an expert chef. To him cooking was an art form and an important spiritual expression of divine manifestation. One of his earliest publications was a section in a cookery book on Ottoman cuisine.

An early student of Beshara wrote of Rauf:

> About mysticism, Bulent Rauf was never mystifying. It was for him the most simple and practical value based on the absolute unity of existence, and the love of that One in knowing itself as the Beautiful. And for human beings, as Bulent saw it, our real destiny lay in acquiring an awareness of that value in their lives. And cooking was for Bulent a very particular modus operandi in practising that awareness and reaching that value. Perhaps one could say that for Bulent cooking was a mystical art.
>
> In the kitchen at Chisholme House in the Scottish Borders where Bulent spent much of the remaining years of his life hangs his Notice to cooks. It begins: 'Now know this—that cooking is an art. It is also an integral part of esoteric training'. He then goes on to explain the cook's responsibility in serving both humanity and the food itself, and refers to the Mevlevi Dervishes for whom the training of novices was termed 'cooking' and achievement 'taste'. Bulent was steeped in the traditions of Turkish Sufism, and one only has to read the works of Turkish cooks like Nevin and Feyzi Halici, or Ayla Esen Algar to get some idea of the richnesses and depths of meanings which abound in the spiritual and culinary life of the Turkish civilisation.[36]

---

34. Hugh Tollemache, 'An Obituary of Bulent Rauf', *Beshara Magazine* 3 (Autumn 1987), p. 3.

35. Interviews with V. and A., 11 February 2000. Most former students and adherents who have been questioned also generally describe these qualities and attitudes typical of Bulent Rauf.

36. Christopher Ryan, 'Bulent Rauf: A Mystic in the Kitchen', paper presented at the *Fourth International Food Congress*, Istanbul, September 1992); published in *Beshara Newsletter* (Autumn 1996), pp. 3-4.

BULENT RAUF'S WRITINGS AND TRANSLATIONS

In addition to compiling and publishing the '*Twenty-Nine Pages*', Bulent went on to produce many other works for use on the Beshara courses. These included:

—*Kernel of the Kernel*: Ismail Hakki Bursevi's translation of the *Kernel*, by Muhyiddin Ibn 'Arabi, translated from Turkish by Bulent Rauf (Gloucestershire: Beshara, 1981).

—*Mystical Astrology According to Ibn 'Arabi*, by Titus Burckhardt, translated from French by Bulent Rauf (Gloucestershire: Beshara, 1987).

—*Fusûs al-Hikam*: Ismail Hakki Bursevi's translation and commentary on *Fusûs al-Hikam* by Muhyiddin Ibn 'Arabi, rendered into English with the help of R. Brass and H. Tollemache (4 vols.; Oxford: Muhyiddin Ibn Arabi Society, 1986–91).

In addition, in 1975 Bulent Rauf acted as historical advisor, contributor to the script and narrator of Diane Cilento's film *Turning*, about the Mevlevi Dervishes.[37] He also contributed to a publication on international cuisine.[38] Between 1979 and his death in 1987, he contributed several articles to Beshara Trust publications, such as its newsletter and magazine, and to the *Journal of the Muhyiddin Ibn 'Arabi Society*. In addition, a series of his talks presented to Beshara students were published in 1987 under the title *Addresses*. More recent publications include its continuation, *Addresses II*, a collection of translations and commentaries on the work of Ibn 'Arabi; essays on history and cookery; and a fragment of autobiography. Rauf also wrote a history of the declining years of the Turkish Sultanate entitled *The Last Sultans*, which was published posthumously in 1995.

BULENT RAUF AND THE 'HIDDEN SAINTS'

Bulent Rauf died in the summer of 1987. Obituaries paint a unique character who was immediately able to empathise and understand the deeper spiritual needs of anyone with whom he came into contact. He was conscious of the abilities of each person, always seeing an individual's good, never looking for negative qualities in someone. This quintessentially Sufi attitude led him to have a broad and tolerant view of life and people, and his rich experience of life had prepared him well for the

---

37. Produced and directed by Diane Cilento (1975).
38. Jennifer Feller, ed., *Great Dishes of the World in Colour* (London: Hamlyn, 1976).

development of his spiritual understanding. He had a strong sense of humour, his seriousness being balanced with a sense of fun.[39]

From descriptions compiled through the data contributed by participants of the Beshara School and Ibn 'Arabi Society, Bulent Rauf may be understood to have demonstrated the characteristics of a true spiritual teacher and even possibly of the 'hidden saint' (*walî*) as understood in Islamic terms, particularly in the understanding of Ibn 'Arabi.[40] In accordance with his profound modesty Rauf would have undoubtedly denied this, yet evidence indicates that he certainly had a charismatic personality, if we use Max Weber's definition of the term: 'a certain quality of an individual personality by virtue of which he is set apart from ordinary men and treated as endowed with supernatural, superhuman or at least specifically exceptional qualities'.[41] As for being a true spiritual teacher or even a saint, these characters are traditionally recognised for exhibiting certain specific qualities, one of the foremost being their *adab*—an Arabic word which may be defined as meaning to have the right manner and outer bearing, dignity and spiritually appropriate behaviour before God.[42] A Beshara participant further defined its meaning to stand for: 'this dignity being a mode appropriate for each state or station, the dignity of the reality of being a human being in the image of God and treating other people accordingly'.[43] Bulent was unflinching in this. The following anecdote, recalled by one of his students, illustrates this point. Bulent was staying in a house in the south of Turkey. In the afternoons after lunch he always had a siesta. A man whom he hardly knew suddenly arrived as he was finishing his lunch. Bulent asked the man to join him and, having accepted the invitation, the man began talking about his

---

39. Tollemache, 'An Obituary of Bulent Rauf'; and Richard Hornsby, 'Rememoration for Bulent Rauf', *Beshara Magazine* 4 (Winter 1987/88), pp. 10-11.

40. See the discussion of sainthood, *walâya*, *afrâd* and the *malâmiyya* above pp. 37-39, and in Chapters 4 and 5 below.

41. Max Weber, *On Charisma and Institution Building* (Chicago: University of Chicago Press, 1968), p. xviii.

42. '*Adab*': From the first century AH the term came to imply the sum of intellectual knowledge which makes a man courteous and 'urbane', based in the first place on poetry, the art of oratory, the festivals and tribal traditions of the ancient Arabs and on the corresponding sciences: rhetoric, grammar, lexicography etc., and the mystical meaning referring to the norms of conduct which governs relations between master and disciples and between the disciples themselves. *The Encyclopaedia of Islam: New Edition, Glossary and Index of Terms*, vol. 1–9 (ed. P.J. Bearman et al.; Leiden: Brill, 2000), p. 4.

43. Interview with V., 11 February 2000.

problems and his personal life. The student could see that Bulent was exhausted, but he sat there for a very long time, being there for his visitor. When the man eventually left, the student praised Bulent for his self-discipline. Bulent was astonished: for him, his behaviour was normal and the way any person should behave. This is an illustration of how evolved spiritual character should be displayed in the world, and was also the ideal of the Jelveti Order, reflecting the spiritual influence of Ibn 'Arabi.[44]

A further anecdote underlines Bulent's attitude to right behaviour and the impact that it had on those around him. This former student described the situation in which he and another early participant of Beshara lived in Rauf's house in London particularly to keep Bulent's wife company, as she did not like to be left alone when Bulent was away helping with the administration of the early Beshara courses. Whilst living in the house, the student was taught to cook by Bulent, and during these lessons he learnt from him the importance of being constantly aware of everything that he did and that others did. The student explained that he and the others were rather 'wild and hippy-like' at the time, not exhibiting much *adab*, even on trips to Turkey, and that Bulent would at times get very angry with them if their behaviour was inappropriate. His emphasis was always on the need for constant awareness of right and appropriate behaviour.[45]

Another student provided a further anecdote related to the subject of Rauf and *adab*. This concerned the fundamental importance of 'the right way of doing things', even if what is actually being done appears to be very mundane. One day Bulent got up from having a rest and the student accompanied him in order to assist in pulling on a tight pair of boots. The student took up the left boot and Bulent raised his eyebrows because this was 'wrong', the correct 'order' being for the right boot to be pulled on first. After this occurrence, the student recalled that he could never put on a left shoe or boot before the right. Two to three years later, he reminded Bulent of the incident. Bulent laughed at himself, saying 'you think you can teach—only God teaches'.[46] The concept of doing things in the right order is central to the teaching at Chisholme. A typical example of this is the way in which the dining-room table is set for meals; this is done in a particular order which is seen to reflect 'God's order of things'.

The above account also illustrates the central Sufi pedagogical process of *suhba*, or 'companionship'. The traditional quality of an effective

---

44. Interview with V., 11 February 2000.
45. Interview with M., Turkey trip, 2000.
46. Interview with V., 11 February 2000.

spiritual teacher is this *suhba*, an Arabic word for teaching by example.[47] The same former student explained that he understood that Bulent was always 'teaching but not teaching', by setting the right examples.[48] As that student went on to explain, for him Bulent had become a sort of image of God. Then through this 'chance' remark, his heart was opened, and he realised that in fact God is the only guide. Bulent wanted all things done as perfectly as possible because it was the aim of the students to strive for their own perfection and so become worthy servants of God which is the aim of all human existence, according to Ibn 'Arabi. This striving for perfection and true servanthood included all aspects of study and work. One student remembered how he had been instructed to repair a door handle at Chisholme and how he had failed to do this to the best of his ability. He recalls that Bulent was outwardly quite furious with him until he did the job again without fault.[49]

A third traditionally important quality of a spiritual teacher, one often demonstrated by Bulent, was *firâsa* or 'spiritual insight', meaning to be able to see who a person really is.[50] In the eyes of such an inspired teacher, the outward persona is stripped away, leaving behind the person's true qualities, motivations and intentions. One student recalled that he was attending a short course at Chisholme during which Rauf came to stay for a few days and attended one of the study sessions. All the students were 'struck dumb' by being in the presence of Bulent, but this student was determined that this was not going to happen to him and that he was going to speak about his own realisation of the unity of being including the Self (He explained that the most difficult thing to do is to speak about the latter.) Before he could speak, though, Bulent, leaning on his stick, gestured to him and called him over, then asked him his name and said: '…do you know that you are a very urgent case!'[51]

---

47. '*Suhba*': Meaning 'companionship' or 'company'. *Encyclopaedia of Islam*, vol. 1–9, p. 283.

48. Interviews with V. and A., 11 February 2000, but also this point is generally accepted by Beshara participants.

49. Discussion with T., Oxford, December 1999.

50. '*Firâsa*': Physiognomancy, a technique of inductive divination which permits the foretelling of moral conditions and psychological behaviour from external indications and physical states, such as colours, forms and limbs. *Encyclopaedia of Islam*, vol. 1–9, p. 110.

51. Interview with V., 11 February 2000.

A further characteristic closely associated with saints and spiritual guides in Islam is *karâma*.[52] This word can variously be defined as: acts of grace or the ability to affect people spiritually directly or through dreams; it can also extend to more unusual spiritual powers. This last definition, particularly, was *not* the 'way' of Bulent, Beshara and, of course, Ibn 'Arabi. His belief was that when such a *karâma* was granted to a true servant of God, he should refrain from using it (unless commanded to do so), because using it for random or worldly effect, would show a lack of *adab*. Regarding *karâmâ* and Bulent, a former student described usually feeling better and spiritually energised on seeing Bulent, but reflected that this feeling could probably have had more to do more with his love of Bulent and what Bulent loved (i.e., God) than any special act of grace.[53]

For some students, Bulent Rauf could fall into the category of Ibn 'Arabi's understanding of the 'hidden saints', the *afrâd*.[54] This is someone who is outwardly so humble and spiritually unpretentious that they are ordinarily unacknowledged and unrecognised as spiritually exceptional during their own time on earth. Ibn 'Arabi provides numerous examples of such people in his *The Rûh al-quds and al-Durrat al-fâkhirah*.[55]

Another anecdote provides an illustration of this. In his youth, Aziz Effendi, the founder of the Jelveti Order, was searching for a teacher. When he found a suitable one, the man told Effendi (who was of a prominent family) that the only way into the order was to get rid of all his property and sell cat food in the market. (Selling cat food was the lowliest occupation possible.) But Effendi did this, and was eventually initiated into the order. He used to look after the needs of his sheikh personally, and one of his jobs was to heat up water for the sheikh's ablutions. One day he overslept and had to take cold water to the sheikh, but when the sheikh lifted the bowl, the water inside it was boiling. His sheikh then told Effendi that there was no room for two sheikhs there since Effendi had now reached the level of spiritual awareness and enlightenment of the sheikh himself. This story illustrates how 'hidden saints' (*afrâd*) were often the most accomplished spiritual individuals but

---

52. '*Karâma*': A marvel wrought by a saint, mostly consisting of mystical happenings in the corporeal world, or else of predictions of the future, or else interpretations of the secret of hearts etc. *Encyclopaedia of Islam*, vol. 1–9, p. 181.
53. Interview with V., 11 February 2000.
54. For discussion on this topic, see Chodkiewicz, *The Seal of the Saints*.
55. Translated by R.W.J. Austin as *Sufis of Andalusia* (London: Alan & Unwin, 1971).

usually hidden in society, taking on the most humble of occupations. Indeed, it appears that Aziz Effendi was not even consciously applying his ability in this case.[56]

Those involved with Beshara today use the evidence of the unbroken continuation of the school since Bulent's death to argue further that it is not dependent on the earthly personality of a sheikh for its endurance. This evidence supports their arguments and Bulent's insistence that they look beyond Bulent the man, to what it was that he constantly pointed to, which is the divine impulse and Reality. Since Bulent's death, the Beshara School has had no one person to guide it or to be its focus, although there were several people, no longer involved with the school, who felt that they should take Bulent's place.[57] Again, for Beshara's participants, this supports their argument that there is a larger divine intention behind Beshara and its aims.

POSTERITY

Soon after Bulent Rauf's death a small memorial known as the 'Monument to Man' was constructed for him at Chisholme House in Scotland. It was designed according to his own wishes and erected over his place of burial. He had chosen the highest point of the Chisholme estate, which afforded splendid views of the place that he had grown to love. The memorial was cast from reconstituted white marble from the Isle of Skye, consisting of four slender columns eleven feet high supporting a circular entablature eleven feet in diameter. The columns stand on three concentric circular steps rising out of the hillside, with the grave at the level of the top step. The grave is grassed over and open to the sky— 'open above and open on all sides—in order that the rain, symbolising the Mercy of God, may pass freely through'.[58] The top step bears the famous Quranic inscription: 'They are from Him and to Him they return'.[59]

Since Bulent Rauf's death, no-one in Beshara circles has explicitly articulated the idea that he is a *walî* or saint.[60] But the actions and reactions of many of those whom he guided during his lifetime as well as many more who have experienced his spiritual influence since then,

---

56. Interview with V., 11 February 2000.
57. Particularly leaders of some other tariqas, as was common knowledge of those involved with Beshara at the time.
58. Anon., 'Memorial For Bulent Rauf', *Beshara Magazine* 7 (1988), p. 43.
59. Quran, Sura 2:156.
60. Interview with M., Turkey Trip, December 2000.

might lead to the conclusion that this is how he is in fact understood. For example, he is at times referred to as a 'friend of God' which is one of the meanings of the Sufi understanding of *walî*.[61] As with countless other saints throughout the Islamic world, people who knew him or know of him regularly visit his tomb and 'open up to him' in the hope of receiving guidance, answers to personal questions and spiritual knowledge.[62] Hundreds of visitors to the tomb feel that they are in contact with him and that he speaks to them through words or inspiration and in dreams. For example, a participant explained how shattered he was by Rauf's death and how, even after several years, he had not properly come to terms with it. He described how he had just concluded a visit to the tomb and was walking sadly away down the hill when he heard Bulent laughing. He stopped, turned and looked back, and Rauf said to him in a jocular fashion, 'You still think we can be separated!' The participant felt that this statement was true, and that he would have to work out its significance himself before returning to the tomb. When he did return, he sat down on a nearby bench and as the winter sun broke through the clouds casting his shadow over the grave, Bulent Rauf said to him, 'see, even your shadow can't be separated from me'. The participant then finally understood that 'there is no separation', even when somebody dies.

Another Beshara student explained that some people do have contact with Rauf through various ways such as dreams, visions or inspirations, and that, as is normal in such cases, these experiences and messages are intensely private. Occasionally, though, 'something is given' to be shared by everyone, and this often occurs when a course is running. What is 'given' in such a case is usually offered at the monument during prayer and could be guidance for everyone on the course. When this happens, the 'guidance' is often more general than it is when it is just meant for one person. She explained:

> The principle of it is that if something is 'given to the heart' but then sent out again, it can become diluted. Sometimes something is completely private—between God, Bulent and a particular person. At times this appears as words or sometimes as a feeling or sensations in the heart—it is very private, like the intimacy between lovers, it is an intimate secret exchange which takes place and it is tactless to spread it out.[63]

61. Interview with M., Turkey Trip, December 2000.
62. Interview with M., Turkey Trip, December 2000 and H., August 2001. A detailed discussion on visits and pilgrimages to the tombs and shrines of Muslim saints takes place in Chapter 7 above, which focuses on the Beshara School's annual pilgrimage to Turkey.
63. Interview with H., August 2001.

The student continued to explain that Rauf's monument is dedicated to Man, as in humanity, and that people sometimes approach it and 'feel that they are talking to Rauf and sometimes they feel that they are facing the Reality, their own reality and the Reality—the potential of the self, never specified as a man but as Man'.[64]

Another time at which Bulent's presence is sometimes strongly felt is at sessions of group meditation, or *Zikrs*.[65] He had said '…it is a nice thing to invite people to Zikr…invite them to share in this remembrance of God…'[66] It was explained by one interviewee that that Rauf's presence is strong at *Zikrs* is 'not laid down or it would become a religion'.[67]

CONCLUSION

As this chapter has shown, following the methodological approach of the phenomenologist, many aspects of the process of the establishment of the Beshara School parallel familiar universal processes found throughout spiritual movements in Islam and other religions, which are the central focus of Ibn 'Arabi's own writings and teachings. As is clear, those involved with the foundation of the organisation and particularly Bulent Rauf were in no doubt as to the reality of the long-established Sufi doctrines of an Ultimate Reality far removed but not beyond, under certain circumstances, the reach of our own. As this idea is central to Ibn 'Arabi's spiritual metaphysics, it will be a constantly recurring theme in the chapters to follow.

---

64. Interview with H., August 2001.
65. Interview with M., December 2000.
66. Interview with M., December 2000. It was also explained to me by another participant that 'they (the *walîs*) come when they want and it is a good thing to invite them, as their presence elevates the *zikr*'. Interview with E., April 2002.
67. Interview with E., April 2002.

2

THE BESHARA TRUST: EARLY YEARS

The present chapter traces the evolution and the activities of the Beshara Trust and its school from Bulent Rauf's arrival in England in 1967, to the Trust's inception at the time of the purchase of Swyre Farm in 1971. It describes how the foundational study text of the school was produced, and gives a summary account of the early participants. It also situates and relates the Trust to other scholars and teachers, such as Titus Burckhardt and J.G. Bennett, who were active in promoting Sufi ideas in the West in the early half of the twentieth century. This chapter, like the previous one, provides some prime examples of unusual spiritual circumstances in the emergence of the Trust. These I have set out through the usual approach of phenomenological students of religion who are familiar with these types of incidences and apparent co-incidences during the emergence of new spiritual movements in all historical settings and traditions.

BULENT RAUF AND THE ORIGINS OF BESHARA

Soon after settling in England in 1967, Bulent Rauf returned briefly to Turkey and it was there, in 1968, that an incident occurred which has become legendary in Beshara circles. This story is quoted frequently by students of Beshara to show that it was no mere chance that Bulent was in England when he was, but that it was a kind of divine intervention through the spiritual influence (*baraka*) of Ibn 'Arabi, providing the providential vehicle through which Ibn 'Arabi's teachings would be disseminated in the West.

There are several versions of this story, the consistent thread being that whilst in Turkey on this particular visit, Bulent met with a well-known dervish who told Bulent that he must go back to England because that was where he was needed. The most detailed account comes from an eyewitness,[1] who recalls that when the incident occurred she was living in the house of Madame Ayashli (the famous Turkish writer who was Rauf's cousin), assisting her as a typist. Madame Ayashli was working on a book at the time, and though the witness knew Bulent's mother and brother, Mahmud Rauf, she did not know Bulent as well. On this occasion Madame Ayashli was writing in bed as she did early each morning, when a respected Sufi dervish named Sheikh Dede came into the bedroom to talk to her. Some time later, Madame Ayashli's housekeeper, Fatima, came into the room announcing that 'Bulent Bey' had arrived. Madame Ayashli flew into a panic as she was not properly dressed, and told the witness to go and meet him whilst she rectified the situation.[2] Bulent then tried to enter the bedroom, but Sheikh Dede stood in the doorway and greeted Bulent and then said 'Where are you coming from?' Bulent replied that he had come from England. Holding his hand up and out as if refusing Bulent entry to the room, the sheikh then exclaimed, 'Go back, go back, don't you know that we've been thinking of England for forty years'. The witness was shocked, because in Turkish culture, to greet someone and then say 'Go back' was decidedly bad manners. She thought that Bulent too would be shocked, but he was smiling. The witness then recalls that at that moment she realised that this was a 'different language', and that the incident had for Bulent a deeply esoteric interpretation that was at variance with the way in which it would be interpreted conventionally.

Other accounts of the incident vary slightly, such as that of Hugh Tollemache in the obituary that he wrote following Bulent's death in 1987, in which the words used are 'Don't you know that you are required in England? We have been waiting for you for a long time, stop wasting your time and go'.[3] The gist is always the same, being that Rauf was required to return to England for some reason. A general interpretation of the incident by Beshara students is that Bulent and his brother Mahmud had already been devotees and students of Ibn 'Arabi for many years

---

1. Interview with A., 11 February, 2000. Although neither a dream nor a visionary experience, the story does have a similar flavour to that recounted in the previous chapter, which recalls the incident during which the current sheikh of the Jelveti order was approached by its long-dead founder and given instructions which he then interpreted in his own way.

2. The eyewitness did not explain why Madame Ayashli had not reacted in the same way about Sheikh Dede coming into the room when she was not properly dressed.

3. Hugh Tollemache, 'An Obituary of Bulent Rauf', *Beshara Magazine* 3 (Autumn 1987), p. 3.

when the dervish instructed Bulent to bring these teachings to the West. This was an urgent matter, as the Western world needed these teachings; and since English was becoming a global language, the project must start in England straight away.[4]

So Bulent returned to England in 1969, and found a job in an antique shop. He was also in the process of publishing a book on Ottoman cuisine for which he had been given an advance by the publishers.[5] It was whilst he was working in this shop that the person approached him who would become so significant to the initial establishment of the Beshara Trust.[6] This person was a man named Tim Feild (later to be given the name Reshad by Bulent), who was distributing leaflets advertising a lecture on meditation by the popular Sufi teacher, Idries Shah of the Naqshbandi Sufi Order.[7] Feild was at the time a 'seeker of truth' having experienced numerous spiritual and esoteric traditions, and some accounts reveal that at the time of this first meeting between the two men, Bulent was wearing a special symbol around his neck. This was the symbol of *Hû* which represents the divine Spirit or 'breath' of God underlying all creation, and it is one of God's most sacred Names in the Islamic tradition. Feild recognised the symbol because it had Sufi significance and therefore realised that he and Rauf had knowledge of Sufism in common. In his autobiographical book *The Last Barrier*, Feild narrates the story of his association with his spiritual teacher whom he names 'Hamid', but who is understood to be Bulent under a thin disguise. In the book he describes himself as a healer with the ability to treat people with illnesses that the orthodox medical professions had given up on.[8] He was also an antique dealer and a musician, who had sung in a band with the famous singer Dusty Springfield. Although he had knowledge and experience of a

---

4. Later, Bulent was heard to comment that England had been chosen because of its role in World War II—because 'England had fought a moral war'.

5. See Chapter 1 for details of his publications.

6. See Chapter 1 for a short account of this meeting between Rauf and Feild.

7. Interview with S., October 1999. Shah was very active in promoting Sufism in the West, particularly in the 1960s and '70s, publishing numerous books about Sufism. See the Introduction.

8. *The Last Barrier: The Universal Search for Self-discovery* (Shaftesbury: Element Books, 1976). To Bulent this book was apparently 'anathema', as it was to later participants of Beshara, partly because it presents an inaccurate portrayal of Bulent and his teaching, but also because Bulent was a very private person so that if he offered guidance to somebody this was an individual and private guidance between himself and that person, not to be projected into the public domain. Ref.: letter from T., February 2000 and general opinion in Beshara circles.

variety of spiritual paths, he was particularly interested in Sufism, and was at that time the personal assistant and representative in Britain of Pir Vilayat Khan, who was the sheikh (leader) of the 'Sufi Order in the West'. When Feild discovered that Bulent was Turkish and had a profound knowledge of Sufism, he soon became a disciple, and he followed Bulent to Turkey in January 1970 to become his student.[9]

During the periods in which Bulent was in England in the early 1970s, he began to speak to groups of Feild's associates about Sufism and Ibn 'Arabi. Many of these students were to become core students of Beshara as it developed. Feild, who was born in 1935, was from a privileged background and had been educated at Eton, a school which has a tradition of educating the sons of royalty, aristocracy and the wealthy. Several of the early trustees and patrons of the Beshara Trust were from a similar background, as indeed was Bulent who, when he first resided in England, was naturally drawn into such social circles.

The initial meetings between Bulent and his early students usually took place in the London flat belonging to Bulent and his future wife Angela. As the size of attendance expanded, the flat became too small.[10] Eventually, at a lunch meeting between Mrs. Culme-Seymour, Bulent, Feild and a lady from Baghdad, Feild broached the idea of a 'centre' in a house in the country. The lady from Baghdad made a significant contribution to the choice of the name of the 'centre' by suggesting that they should choose something that began with the letter 'B'. This was because of its Arabic connection with the word *Bayt*, which in addition to its basic meaning as a dwelling place, also means a spiritual home, temple or sacred centre (especially the Kaaba in Mecca).[11] This suggestion also connected with the idea of this 'centre' being a 'dwelling place' for truth about the knowledge of Reality.[12] Bulent agreed and then consulted the Quran and prayed, arriving eventually at the name 'Beshâra'.[13] This Arabic word means 'good news' or 'annunciation' and has a common Semitic root found in Old Testament Hebrew, in the Aramaic of the Christian Gospels and in the Arabic of the Quran. The word is reputed to have been used by the angel Gabriel to Mary mother of Jesus when he

---

9. See the related sections of *The Last Barrier*.
10. From a letter from S., January 2000.
11. The lady from Baghdad was one of the few Arabic speakers involved with Beshara at the time. From an interview with Sh., Chisholme, August 2000.
12. Interview with Sh., Chisholme, August 2000.
13. It is common Muslim practice to consult the Quran, after praying, to seek answers to important questions.

announced the coming of Christ, in that 'Beshara' was his first word: 'Good News, a son is to be given'.[14] Also at this same significant meeting, Feild was given the name 'Reshad' by Bulent.[15]

SWYRE FARM

Reshad Feild located Swyre Farm, and the recently founded Beshara Trust then acquired it in 1971. At the time of its acquisition it was in need of almost full refurbishment, which was largely accomplished by Feild and the other students.[16] Swyre Farm was situated near the village of Aldsworth in Gloucestershire. The property included a large farmhouse and numerous outbuildings which dated from the eighteenth century. These outbuildings were converted to provide accommodation for up to sixty people in a way that allowed for as many private rooms as possible. Within the farmhouse itself, there was further accommodation and two main study rooms and a library. A particularly large barn with a geodesic domed roof constructed inside (known as the '*mihrâb*') was specially designed for meditation and devotional activities.[17] A further barn was converted into a pottery, and a dairy and milking parlour were eventually built in an old stable block.[18] The land comprised nine acres, including pasture for the livestock, which included poultry, sheep and dairy cows. There were also landscaped gardens, herb and vegetable gardens and a well-stocked orchard. The livestock comprised mostly endangered species, for example 'Jacob's sheep'.[19] Bee-keeping was also developed at the farm.

Reshad Feild purchased Swyre Farm by putting up substantial finance himself and through the patronage of several parties sympathetic to the aims and ideals of the Trust. In its early days the farm was operated as an open study centre where students were free to come and go as they liked, staying for varying lengths of time. At this time there were no structured courses on offer, though there were some obligatory daily requirements

14. Interview with Sh., Chisholme, August 2000.
15. Although this sort of symbolic name-giving is common initiatic Sufi practice, it is also found in other religious traditions, for example, when Christian monks or nuns enter into monastic orders
16. Interview with S., January 2000.
17. *Mihrâb* is an Islamic word that refers to the arched niche in a mosque that indicates the direction of Mecca (*qibla*) for the ritual prayers.
18. Ref.: promotional leaflet advertising Beshara Swyre Farm, produced approximately 1977.
19. A rare breed of black and white or brown and white sheep with double pairs of horns.

for those in residence which involved meditation, study, work on the property and some form of devotional practice.

At the outset, although the approach was universalistic and inclusive of all traditions and the study of religions and spirituality was from a wide variation of traditions, there was a notable Sufi influence, particularly in the devotional exercises that included the Islamic *zikr* or 'remembrance' of God.[20] Also at the very beginning (1971–72), the teaching and study guidance was given predominantly by Reshad Feild. It was only in the winter of 1972/73 that Bulent decided to reside permanently in England, and thereafter became increasingly active in the studies at Swyre Farm.

Feild was personally involved with a variety of aspects of spirituality and 'new age' activities, including such themes as acupuncture, dowsing, detecting ley lines, 'seeing subtle bodies' and stimulating chakras and particularly various forms of medically non-conventional healing.[21] It was in relation to these more practical themes that he provided instruction and lectures, though there was an underlying structure of devotion by way of meditation, prayer and *wazifas*.[22] There were also more practical forms of sacred service in connection with cooking, housework and work on the land and care of the animals.

In addition to Feild's talks, there were other lectures and talks provided by guest speakers from various fields connected with the maturing ideals of the Beshara Trust. These speakers were representatives of various world religious traditions or from other areas of spiritual interest. For example, one speaker was a Zoroastrian named Kjosti Mistri. Warren Kenton, better known as Zev ben Shimon Halevi, was a regular speaker on the Kabala (Jewish mysticism); he was also an early patron of the Trust. The Hon. Rosemary Russell spoke about Radionics. Another regular speaker was Dom Sylvester Houedard, who was a well-known concrete poet and Benedictine monk. J.G. Bennett, a pupil of G.I. Gurdjieff and P.D. Ouspensky, also presented lectures to the students at Swyre.[23]

---

20. From Swyre Farm's promotional brochure (approximately 1977). The key Quranic term (*dhikr*) is normally pronounced '*zikr*' in English, and has been written in that form throughout this work.

21. From discussions with T., February/March 2000 and general knowledge amongst Beshara students.

22. An Arabic term for a common Sufi prayer form of *dhikr* or litany, but exclusively involved with the ninety-nine Most Beautiful Names of God from the Quran. A distinguishing feature is that it has a set number of repetitions depending on the Name used in each prayer.

23. Those in Beshara circles, then, were already well-acquainted with the work of those invited to speak at Swyre Farm. J.G. Bennett, his teachers and his early association with Beshara will be discussed in more detail below.

Although Swyre Farm at first had strong similarities to the proliferation of small intentional communities with religious and spiritual concerns which sprang up in Europe and America in the late 1960s and early 1970s, during what is now termed the 'hippy era', one significant difference between it and those other communities was its total prohibition on the premises of the use of any non-prescription drugs. Another difference cited by many participants is that it soon developed a real focus to its teaching by the mid-1970s, following Rauf's preparation of structured courses and the emphasis on the study of Ibn 'Arabi's concepts.

In the early days following the establishment of the Trust, Bulent and his future wife Angela Culme-Seymour resided mostly in Turkey. Feild would travel there regularly and receive teaching from Bulent, some of which he would pass on to Swyre residents on his return to England. As mentioned above, Feild was also deeply involved with Pir Vilayat Khan, head of the 'Sufi Order in the West' and several participants at Swyre Farm were also Pir Vilayat's disciples. Following Feild's increasing involvement with Bulent, the relationship between himself and Pir Vilayat became strained and eventually was severed. This caused some measure of divided loyalty amongst participants of Beshara and even some of the trustees, as some of them were under the impression that the Beshara Centre was for Pir Vilayat, though he was never in residence there. He is said to have felt 'betrayed' by Feild at the time, and he soon left England to continue teaching for the 'Sufi Order in the West' around the world, particularly in America.[24]

The Twenty-Nine Pages: Teaching Ibn 'Arabi at Swyre Farm

In the first two years following the formation of the Trust (1971–72), several small Beshara centres and study groups formed around the country, in Cambridge, Edinburgh, Blackburn, Brighton, Oxford and London. The London centre was particularly important because there were many interested people living in the city who had difficulty in travelling regularly to Swyre Farm. The London centre was on Raydon Street, Highgate, opposite the famous Highgate cemetery,[25] in a house that was empty and awaiting demolition when Beshara began to use it for study. Instead it was taken over, for a low rent, as a Beshara student housing project, but it still needed total renovation. The Trust moved in

---

24. From letters from T., February/March 2000.
25. The burial place of Karl Marx.

and used it for three or four years, running it concurrently with Swyre Farm.[26] The house had no electricity, and the students had to study by candlelight. It was here that Bulent Rauf first began to teach about Ibn 'Arabi. Grenville Collins has recalled in detail how Bulent produced *The Twenty-Nine Pages*, a summary of Ibn 'Arabi's central teachings derived from his major works the *Meccan Revelations* (*Futûhât al-Makkiyya*) and the *Bezels of Wisdom* (*Fusûs al-Hikam*), which was to become the foundation of study and spiritual work in Beshara in its early years.[27]

Collins recalls that whilst Bulent was still working in the antique shop in Chelsea in London in the late 1960s, they would have lunch together once a week. At these lunch meetings, Bulent would speak to him about Ibn 'Arabi and, for example, his concept of the Perfect Man.[28] Following the discussion, he would then give him certain spiritual exercises to do during the succeeding week. Because the subject of conversation was predominantly Ibn 'Arabi, Collins went in search of a book about Ibn 'Arabi.[29] He gave it to Bulent to have a look at. At lunch the following week, Bulent reported that he found the book interesting and inquired whether Collins minded if he crossed some things out which were not correct. At the next lunch meeting, Bulent explained to Collins that rather than cross out errors, he had underlined those things in the book which were 'true'. This editorial activity continued for three weeks, after which Bulent asked Collins to find him a typist to type up the underlined bits so that other people could read them. Collins undertook this task and with great difficulty found a typist who was a guardian, with her husband, of a house belonging to a member of the famous rock music group, the Rolling Stones. Collins took the typist two pages to work on at a time, and the whole task took around three months to complete. So many people wanted to read the resulting work that it had to be photocopied. At this point Collins recalled some unusual circumstances, which were interpreted by himself and other early students of Beshara as having certain significance beyond the normal, implying the direction of a strong positive spiritual influence. Having made the decision to photocopy the

---

26. Interview with K., March 2000.

27. Mr. Grenville Collins, who with his wife was one of the initial trustees of the Beshara Trust and a friend of Reshad Feild's, had known Bulent since soon after his arrival in England. Interview with Mr. Collins, Oxford, November 1999.

28. The 'completed human being' or a human being in perfection as the image of God.

29. Interview with Grenville Collins, Oxford, November 1999. The book he found was A. A. Affifi, *The Mystical Philosophy of Muhyid Dîn Ibnul Arabî* (Cambridge: Cambridge University Press, 1964).

papers, Collins had difficulty in finding a location where this could be done, since photocopying machines were then still quite rare. There was, though, in Sackville Street, the only central London photocopying shop, owning seven machines 'on the leading edge of technology'.[30] Collins handed over *The Twenty-Nine Pages* and was assured that twenty copies would be ready the next evening. On his return to collect the copies the next evening, he found that all seven machines had broken down one after the other. Engineers did manage to fix them, and three days later the copies were made. Regarding this, Bulent Rauf commented that sometimes when something especially positive occurs, such as in this case the compilation of the *The Twenty-Nine Pages*, there can be a peculiar counter-reaction. Collins remarked that a similar incident took place when the Oxford University Press was printing Bulent's translation of *The White Fusus*.[31]

One participant recalls the initial introduction of *The Twenty-Nine Pages* to Swyre Farm. She explained that in 1972, Mr. Collins arrived from a stay in Turkey with Bulent, bringing with him a transcript of *The Twenty-Nine Pages*. Reshad Feild informed the students, under instruction from Bulent, that this was to be 'the foundation of our study and work at Beshara'. That evening every single person staying at Swyre Farm was given a personal interview and undertook intensive reading of the work for two hours each—this carried on through the night. Couples were interviewed together by Mr. Collins. The report states that exact numbers of students cannot be recalled but that the process of interviews and reading seemed to go on for at least 24 hours. The students found the subject matter very difficult to grasp.[32] An interesting point is that a number of Beshara participants interviewed recently have pointed out that as time has passed, new students coming to the text for the first time have found it increasingly easy to understand. This was apparently as Bulent had predicted, since he had said that people born of the post World War II generation had a spiritual potential that predisposed them to this understanding.[33] The belief of Beshara participants is that by its nature, Beshara is connected with an underlying wider global evolution of consciousness.[34]

30. Interview with Grenville Collins, Oxford, November 1999.
31. Details of this publication are given in Chapter 4 below.
32. This was because of the high level of abstraction of Ibn 'Arabi's ideas. Discussion with T., March 2000.
33. Discussion with T., March 2000 and general opinion.
34. See Chapter 5 below on the meaning of Beshara.

EARLY STUDENTS OF BESHARA AND SWYRE FARM

It was after the introduction of *The Twenty-Nine Pages*, in late 1972, that the group at Swyre Farm began to focus on the teachings of Ibn 'Arabi. After this, only those who were truly interested in Ibn 'Arabi's teaching remained with Beshara, whilst the others gradually dropped away.

Among the initial participants in Beshara, a majority of a particular type of person stand out, including those people who are still active within the Trust today. This group included a number of aristocratic people, among those whom Bulent first associated with after his arrival in England.[35] In addition to this group were a majority of very well-educated young middle-class people of both genders, several being Oxbridge graduates or graduates of other top British universities.[36] Other early participants included some with perhaps less prestigious educational backgrounds, but with obviously enterprising, enquiring, inquisitive intellectual attitudes. These were people who were not prepared to accept the 'traditional' lifestyle of their parents. Many of them had travelled widely and many had a strongly developed artistic ability. The first students were also predominantly from English speaking nations, for example, Britain, America, Australia and New Zealand. There were, though, some early participants from the Middle East such as a man from Saudi Arabia who taught Arabic for the school, a lady from Iraq, a Turkish friend of Bulent's and a man from Israel. The majority of students were relatively young, in their early to mid-twenties, although some were middle aged.[37]

Although when interviewed some early participants reported having naturally positive attitudes to life throughout all or most of their lives, being 'happy' people by nature, a majority described themselves as being in a fairly low or depressed state of mind at the time of their first contacts with Beshara. This state seemed to be a continuation of an adolescent type of 'existential angst', a feeling of the meaninglessness of life

---

35. See Rauf's biographical Chapter 1 above.
36. The high intellectual level of the first adherents of Beshara would support the hypothesis that a student would need a well-developed academic ability to understand the concepts of Ibn 'Arabi. However, as will be shown in a later chapter, this is not necessarily the case. As Bulent Rauf advocated, in accordance with Ibn 'Arabi, a developed spiritual intuition was quite as important (if not more important) than intellectual ability in enabling an understanding of Ibn 'Arabi's complex mystical philosophy.
37. Ref.: this is general knowledge in Beshara circles.

continuing through the teens into the twenties. Some mentioned a search for the meaning of life and a frustration with the answers provided by established religious institutions, whilst others had no formal religious upbringing. For example, an early participant, who was an Oxford graduate, described being prone to depression and anxiety in her teens and constantly questioning the purpose of existence. She experimented with non-prescription drugs and was on anti-depressants until discovering 'Transcendental Meditation', and through this she 'realised' the existence of a 'higher being'. Through her contacts with the T.M. movement, she found out about Swyre Farm. Once she had visited the place, she 'knew' that it was right for her.[38]

Another common group were those who had been through disastrous relationships or a traumatic youth, experiencing death and illness or other traumas (such as stressful divorces), and who then found spiritual solace in Beshara and the study of Ibn 'Arabi.

Clearly it is not possible to generalise widely about the psychological type of person originally drawn to Beshara. Although those who were 'anxious' and searching for one reason or another were in the majority, there were some examples of people who had always had a positive, cheerful approach to life. For example, a participant who had been a Beshara student from very early on (having become involved with Beshara in her twenties), described not seeking anything in particular but being filled with 'joy, energy and love', writing poems for pleasure which were 'intuitive, inspired, tumbling out unintentionally'. She found that reading *The Twenty-Nine Pages* brought how she felt into a 'type of focus'.[39] Interestingly, there was a significant group of people who all attended Cambridge University at the same time (1969–72), who were involved with Beshara from early on and are still participating.

Whatever their background, and whatever way these early participants arrived at the Beshara Centre, the common thread which runs through all accounts appears to be the search for 'something' indefinable which involved a deeper meaning to life and existence, so that their searches began to come to fruition and their yearnings were satisfied on discovering the teachings of Ibn 'Arabi.[40]

---

38. Interview with G., June 1998. This participant describes knowing that Swyre Farm was 'right for her' as soon as she visited it; this kind of comment is fairly typical of many interviewees.

39. Interview with R., December 1999.

40. In some ways, this is a recurrent story, shared by most adherents of Sufism at any time.

BULENT RAUF IN RESIDENCE AT SWYRE FARM

By the winter of 1972/73, Bulent Rauf had settled in the United Kingdom and divided his time between a flat in Eccleston Square in London and Swyre Farm. He never wanted to be thought of as a teacher, but as a 'co-student'; he was later known as a 'consultant' to the Beshara School.[41] Bulent was adamant that the time had come for a new universal understanding and that there was no longer a need for the mediation of 'gurus', as humanity had the potential to know God directly.[42] The scriptural passage transcribed below has been used at various times by participants of Beshara as an appropriate illustration of this approach.[43] This passage could also be understood to be prophesying the emergence of what they understood Beshara's meaning to be, although in this context it would be understood not only to refer to the House of Israel but to humanity as a whole. It is from Jeremiah 31:31:

> Behold, the days come saith the Lord, that I will make a new covenant with the House of Israel... Not according to the covenant that I made with their fathers... But this shall be the covenant that I will make... After these days, saith the Lord I will put my law in their inward parts, and write it in their hearts; and will be their God and they shall be my people. And they shall teach no more every man his neighbour and every man his brother saying, know the Lord, for they shall all know me, from the least of them unto the greatest of them, saith the Lord...

The students of the Beshara School believed, then, that they had important work to do in bringing to humanity the knowledge of the Unity of Existence as expounded by Ibn 'Arabi, offering all students the opportunity of 'knowing themselves' and having a direct connection with God without having to go through intermediaries, dogmas or any particular limited form of belief.[44]

Following Bulent's decision to live in England and reside frequently at Swyre Farm, and his growing emphasis on expounding the ideas of Ibn 'Arabi, the students' identification gradually shifted to his approach.

---

41. From a letter from T., January 2000 and several Beshara participants from 1998–2000.
42. From a letter from T., January 2000, and see Chapter 1.
43. Mansura Thomas, 'A Unique Message for Our Time: An Introduction to Beshara', *Beshara Newsletter* (Spring 1979), pp. 1-2; and Peter Young, 'The New Covenant', *Beshara Newsletter* (Spring 1998), pp. 1-2.
44. The school's Principal recently remarked that whilst this is doubtless true, he also hoped that some humility has been learned as well! From a discussion in April 2002.

Reshad Feild left Swyre Farm and the United Kingdom soon after Bulent took up residence. This was in 1973, and some controversy surrounded his departure, with the general consensus being that he left 'under something of a cloud'.[45] There had been some serious conflict and disagreement between him and those students who had begun to follow Bulent Rauf's interpretation of Ibn 'Arabi. Feild himself admits, in his biographical account of his spiritual development,[46] that many people thought that he had been 'thrown out of the circle'. He counters this assumption, though, by explaining that he had left England for Canada with his teacher's blessing, and he fully quotes a letter written by his teacher at this time. This teacher whom he refers to by the name of 'Hamid', is apparently Bulent Rauf only thinly disguised. Before he journeyed to North America, Feild gave his allegiance to Sheikh Dede of the Mevlevi Order of Dervishes in Konya, claiming later to have been made a Sufi sheikh in his own right by Sheikh Dede.[47]

Feild's departure coincided with a new era for Beshara when the school's teaching became fully focused on the works of Ibn 'Arabi under Bulent Rauf's guidance. Rauf, as 'consultant' to the school, never became a trustee and was never personally involved with the school's administration. Therefore, when Feild left, the vacancy occurred for someone to become 'head' of the Beshara School, and this position was filled by various people at different times.

THE *BLUE FUSÛS* AND TITUS BURCKHARDT

Immediately following the decision of Bulent Rauf to reside in England and spend his time between London and the Beshara Centre at Swyre Farm, the only work of Ibn 'Arabi that was studied at Swyre Farm was *The Twenty-Nine Pages*. Then in 1973, Bulent asked Angela Culme-Seymour to translate Titus Burckhardt's French translation of part of Ibn 'Arabi's famous late work the *Fusûs al-Hikam* (*Wisdom of the Prophets*).[48] This work of Burckhardt included only twelve of the twenty-seven chapters of Ibn 'Arabi's original work. These were the chapters that Burckhardt thought were the most important in terms of their

---

45. Discussion with R., December 1999 and general opinion amongst Beshara participants.
46. Reshad Feild, *Going Home* (Shaftesbury: Element Books, 1996), p. 4.
47. Interview with A., February 2000 and other Beshara participants.
48. This work will be discussed in detail in Chapter 4 below. Ibn 'Arabi, *The Wisdom of the Prophets* (trans. from Arabic to French by Titus Burckhardt and French to English by Angela Culme-Seymour; Gloucestershire: Beshara, 1975).

doctrinal content. When Angela had completed the English translation, the book quickly became known in Beshara circles as the *Blue Fusûs* (because of its blue cover). From early on it was central reading for Beshara students, along with *The Twenty-Nine Pages*.

Titus Burckhardt (1908–1984) had belonged to another influential Sufi 'school' inspired by Ibn 'Arabi, with a somewhat different approach to Ibn 'Arabi's works. He came from an important Swiss family from Basel, which included a long line of artists, historians and explorers. Beyond acquiring world renown with his monographs on the sacred art of different civilisations, he was considered one of the greatest authorities on Sufism. He was also one of Europe's foremost metaphysicians, producing important studies on alchemy and traditional cosmology.[49] Also in connection with the school of Ibn 'Arabi, he produced a translation of Jîlî's *al-insân al-kâmil* (*De l'Homme Universal*), which Angela Culme-Seymour later translated into English, in 1983, as *The Universal Man*. This treatise of 'Abd Al-Karîm Al-Jîlî is an extended commentary on Ibn 'Arabi's concept of the 'Perfect Man', or fully realised human being. This book was also to become a central study text for the Beshara School in later years.

Burckhardt's thought has often been classified as belonging to the French 'Traditionalist' school founded by Rene Guénon.[50] Guénon's objective in his writing was an urgent call to what he saw as a perennial spiritual 'Tradition'. He attacked the individualism of the early twentieth century and recalled Europeans to their own genuine Christian tradition, Muslims to primordial Islam and Indians to true Hinduism. In an article that refers to his work, Bernard Kelly suggests that to Guénon, 'it is tradition as such which possesses authority in passing on the knowledge of Divine truth…'[51] Guénon believed that strict practical faithfulness to one's own particular tradition was the prerequisite for any meaningful discourse between the traditions themselves. As Kelly points out, his perspective was focused in the 'transcendent' unity of traditional doctrines, not in a theory of their unity but in that unity itself.[52] Other

---

49. *Introduction aux Doctrines Esotériques de l'Islam* (Paris: Dervy-Livres, 1969); *Principes et Methodes de L'art Sacré* (Lyons: Derain, 1958); *Alchemie: Sinn und Weltbild* (trans. from English edn by Madame J.P. Gervy; Basle: Foundation Keimer, 1974; Milan: Archè, 1979).

50. See the Introduction.

51. Bernard Kelly, 'The Light of the Eastern Religions', in *Religion of the Heart: Essays Presented to Frithjof Schuon on His Eightieth Birthday* (ed. Seyyed Hossein Nasr and William Stoddart; Indiana: Foundation for Traditional Studies, 1991), p. 159.

52. Ibid., p. 160.

prominent authors connected with or influenced by this school of thought included Ananda K. Coomaraswamy, a Hindu scholar and art historian who contributed to the call to tradition through his exegetic work on Hindu art and the Vedic texts; Frithjof Schuon, a highly influential Sufi writer who developed the school of perennial wisdom and advocated the idea of the transcendent unity of religions; and Martin Lings, who devoted an essential part of his work to making Islamic esotericism better known in the West.[53]

J.G. BENNETT AND THE BESHARA SCHOOL

As mentioned above, a wide range of experts and scholars who represented various aspects of spirituality and religion were frequently invited to Swyre Farm to lecture to the students there. One speaker whose regular presence had a particular significance in the development of the Beshara School was John G. Bennett. He had a special relevance for Beshara in two respects. First, his early lectures to the school were collected and published by the Beshara Press;[54] and secondly the stately home at Sherborne in which he ran his own school of spiritual study was acquired by the Beshara Trust sometime after his death in 1974.

J.G. Bennett or 'J.G.B'. as he was most commonly known, had become at an early age a student of G.I. Gurdjieff, and eventually became one of his closest and most highly regarded followers.[55] Gurdjieff was one of the first people to introduce Sufi ideas and practice into Europe and America in the early part of the twentieth century. He was also later a student of Peter Ouspensky, himself a former leading student of Gurdjieff. Another 'spiritual teacher' who among others had a profound influence on Bennett's thinking was a Javanese Muslim named Mohammad Subuh.[56] Beyond having his ideas shaped by particular teachers, Bennett

53. See the Introduction.
54. John G. Bennett, *Intimations: Talks with J.G. Bennett at Beshara* (Gloucestershire: Beshara, 1975).
55. For details on Georgei Ivanovitch Gurdjieff and Peter Ouspensky, see the Introduction.
56. Subuh had introduced a way of spiritual realisation which was known as 'Subud'. The teaching centred around a system of meditation known as the 'latihan', which is based on traditional Sufi practices of South East Asia. It involves a formal opening or initiation that gives contact with the Life Force, during which a conscious declaration of faith and submission to God's Will takes place. See J.G. Bennett, *Witness: The Story of a Search* (New Mexico: Bennett Books, 1997), pp. 260-71; and *Christian Mysticism and Subud* (London: Institute for the Comparative Study of History, Philosophy and the Sciences, 1961).

experienced Eastern spirituality first hand whilst spending many years in the Near and Middle East, particularly in Turkey, where he gained knowledge and experience of Sufism in its various forms.

In the Introduction to Bennett's book *Intimations*, the collection of talks which he gave to Beshara at Swyre Farm between 1972 and 1974, Rashid Hornsby describes Bennett as someone who had totally immersed himself in the struggle for self perfection; who had, to the perceptive seeker, recognisably extraordinary qualities which were signs of his own inner achievement; and someone who was in touch with the actual 'living Source' from which he derived his teaching.[57] Bennett was convinced that real spiritual change was needed in his age and that only a fundamentally different set of values and different motivations could save humanity from disaster. This attitude coincided to an extent with Bulent's ideas for the present age in that he also felt that the future lay with young people of the post World War II generation. He believed, as did Bulent, that these people were able to assimilate some types of spiritual realities at an accelerated rate. John Bennett spent his final years as Principal of the 'International Academy for Continuous Education' at Sherborne House.

Bennett had been helpful and encouraging with the development of Beshara, believing that it was no mere accident that Swyre Farm, the first major Beshara Centre, was only a few miles from Sherborne House.[58] He felt that his mission was the same as that of Beshara. He also believed, as did the Beshara participants, that small self-sufficient centres should be established nationally and internationally, where people could pursue their personal development and become aware of what the responsibility of being human entails. These centres, he thought, should not be cults or sects with particular gurus or teachers; instead he believed, as did the Beshara students, that those who seek for gurus are seeking only for a glorified reflection of their own personality.[59] His thinking demonstrates strong, though not always openly acknowledged, influences by Ibn 'Arabi, as will be shown below.

His connection with Beshara, and the idea that it was a continuation of an impulse in which he was already instrumental, is highlighted in the following anecdote offered by one of the first students of Beshara, who is still actively involved today.[60] One day Bulent Rauf was away and John Bennett was lecturing a group of Beshara students. Rauf returned towards the end of the lecture. Bennett turned to the students and told them that

---

57. Rashid Hornsby, 'Introduction', in Bennett, *Intimations*, pp. vii-xi (vii).
58. Ibid., p. 10.
59. Ibid.
60. Interview with K., August 1999.

he was no longer needed.[61] The student then recalled the strong inner impact of being in the presence of the two powerfully spiritual but extremely 'courtly' gentlemen, talking together in mutual respect and acknowledgment. Bennett died shortly after this incident.

Bennett's *Intimations*

J.G. Bennett's compact work, *Intimations,* is of particular interest within the context of the emergence of the Beshara School, because of the way in which Bennett ran his own facility, the International Academy for Continuous Education, and the structure and materials used in his courses. Early participants of Beshara have admitted that Bennett did have some influence upon the way in which their own courses were constructed.[62] These same participants have pointed out, though, that stark contrasts also existed between the two types of teaching. For example, Bennett's courses followed a line of procedure whereby the progress of the student took place stage by stage. In contrast, the Beshara teachings were presented in a way that essentially reversed or inverted Bennett's procedure. For example, the Beshara School uses the imagery of viewing a pyramid from its apex, an image which, in summary form, describes Ibn 'Arabi's philosophical metaphysics of the diversity within Unity.[63] Their method is to confront Ultimate Reality as a whole, and to realise it as One without focusing on intermediaries or stages. Students of Beshara point out that Bennett's approach is one common to most spiritual paths; i.e., the student starts at the bottom and rises up to greater spiritual knowledge and experience through gradual stages and initiations.

Before his death in 1974, Bennett was a regular visitor to Swyre Farm, where he would lecture the students using an approach particularly suited for Beshara in contrast to his methods at his own school. The resulting book of lectures, *Intimations*, explores subjects of spiritual relevance, ranging from the need to act in support of improving the constantly deteriorating world situation,[64] in Chapter 1, to the meaning and nature of

---

61. To some students of Beshara, this statement had a double meaning. First, it could be taken in the literal sense (i.e., now that Bulent had arrived he could take over the lecture); and second, it could mean that Bennett was no longer needed to continue his own mission in the West now that Bulent was there to carry on where he had left off.

62. Interviews with Sh., and Ss., Chisholme, August 2000. This is a general view in Beshara circles. Due to the fact that Bennett had been a student of Gurdjieff, his courses were run partly on the lines of Gurdjieff's teachings.

63. See the opening chapter of *The Twenty-Nine Pages*.

64. This was a strong social and political issue when the book was written in the 1970s, as it is, under different conditions, today.

the Divine Name *Hû*, in the final chapter. Throughout the book, glimpses may be gleaned of these points where the objectives and ideals of both schools of thought coincide, as well as their contrasting aspects. In the Introduction, a founding member of the Beshara School, Rashid Hornsby, suggests some complementary approaches, such as the agreement that small centres should be established globally where people could come to listen and learn, without having to adhere to a particular sect or teacher. Bennett's approach advocated, as does the Beshara School, the avoidance of adhering to a single 'exclusive' religious or spiritual form or belief, whilst striving to recognise the truth in all. However, Beshara's approach goes even further back, beginning at a point beyond religious form and proceeding into manifestation from there. In common with Beshara, Bennett had the idea that humanity is entering into a new cycle which could possibly involve a new dimension of human nature. He felt that it was time for humans to prepare to change and to accept a higher aim related to a 'higher power' (God).[65] What is needed is trust in or, as the Beshara School would put it, submission to this 'higher power'.

Chapter 2 concerns the transformation of energies with a section on transformation and food. Food and its preparation are very important to Beshara, as already mentioned above in connection with Bulent Rauf. In the Beshara School, cooking is understood to be a form of sacred service, not only to other people through their eating of the food, but also to the ingredients of the food, in that it is transformed from one state to another, and when it is actually consumed it is again transformed into an even higher state of energy.[66]

In Chapter 3, there is an interesting section concerning the 'ego' that would be readily recognisable to Beshara students. Here it is suggested that there is a need to learn from one another and to avoid trying to be different or individual and therefore feeling 'special', because by feeling artificially unique a person is likely to acquire an inflated idea of him/herself resulting in the problem of a dominant ego. The spiritual aim in both schools of thought is to humble the ego. However, the Beshara School contributes a more sophisticated understanding of uniqueness and the human being from Ibn 'Arabi's understanding, i.e., that 'each person is unique because He (God) is unique—a new configuration in each one of His manifestations. The aim is not to be unique oneself, but to see *His* uniqueness in everything'.[67]

---

65. Bennett, *Intimations*, p. 10.
66. Ibid., p. 20.
67. Discussion with the current Principal of the Beshara School, April 2002.

This chapter also deals with the idea of service, service to God and service to God's creation in all its forms, because God is within all His creation and therefore any service is ultimately to Him. This is a central theme for Beshara and especially for Ibn 'Arabi, as it is to many other spiritual paths.

The rest of the book touches on subjects which have relevance to Beshara and which are also common Sufi concerns, most of which are naturally to be found in the teachings of Ibn 'Arabi. These concepts include discussions about *Zikr* and Sufism, the spiritual nature of suffering, the creative imagination, *Baraka* or spiritual influence and a very enlightening chapter on the nature and person of Khidr, a key initiatic figure in Islamic esotericism.

The final chapter, which focuses on the Arabic divine Name *Hû*, is the most directly relevant to Beshara and provides a prime example of where the two schools also diverge in their thinking. In the glossary of the book, Bennett describes the word *Hû* as being 'the First Sound or annunciation of Ipseity'.[68] It is the most sacred sound, and in this chapter he even scolds the Beshara School for their apparent lack of respect for it and its use. He was referring to the first Glastonbury Festival (in 1973 or 1974), at which a group of Beshara participants who were in attendance performed a public *Zikr* and repeatedly chanted the words *Hû* or *Yâ Hû* or *Allâh Hû*. To Bennett, this was an act of profound disrespect. He mentions that, for many years, he could not even pronounce out loud the words 'God' or 'Love' because he felt 'so far away from them'.[69] Eventually, he explains, he was able to use the words, but only with the greatest respect. He stresses that the word that needs the most respect is '*Hû*', because it stands for everything (the Source of everything) because It is beyond all existence and all being. Not treating such a word with respect amounts to sacrilege.

In contrast, this public performance of *Zikr* by the Beshara group at Glastonbury at that time was what the festival was all about. It then had more to do with a gathering of spiritually like-minded people than the music festival that it has become today. That *Zikr* symbolised the meaning of Glastonbury, a gathering of people coming together through the call of 'the heart'.[70] To Beshara people, spiritual awakening and experience should be available immediately to all, but to Bennett, continuing in the line of Gurdjieff's teaching, things needed to be done properly and

---

68. Bennett, *Intimations*, p. 99.
69. Ibid., p. 97.
70. Interview with Ss., August 2000.

privately and only a bit at a time.[71] Both schools were in agreement, though, that to activate any deep spiritual awareness or realisation, preparation was needed of the Self through hard dedicated work, both mental and physical.

As is demonstrated above, the Beshara School had at the outset of its development several distinct strands of spiritual influence woven into its emerging ethos. However, even at an early stage, a focus upon Islamic mystical thought, particularly through the works of Ibn 'Arabi, was clearly becoming apparent. It was during this process that the organisation began to steer away from other initially similar types of spiritual/religious communities that had emerged in the 1960s and 1970s, and gradually became the focused and serious school of esoteric education that it is today.

---

71. Interview with Ss., August 2000.

3

CHISHOLME AND SHERBORNE: THE INTRODUCTION OF STRUCTURED, RESIDENTIAL COURSES

Once Bulent Rauf was constantly in residence at the Beshara Centre at Swyre Farm as its consultant (from the winter of 1972/73), it began to become apparent to him that the esoteric education offered at the centre required a more formal structure. Up until that time, when the teachings of Ibn 'Arabi began to become central study material at the school through his introduction of *The Twenty-Nine Pages* and the *Wisdom of the Prophets*,[1] a wide range of spiritual and religious themes had previously been offered for study there. But once he had established the focus of study on Ibn 'Arabi, many less interested students dropped away. This was when Bulent Rauf devised the first long residential course, which still follows a similar structure today to that which he inaugurated in 1975. That core intensive course was built around the four spiritual disciplines that were already central to the work of residents at Swyre Farm—work, study, mediation and devotional practice. This chapter discusses the structure and detail of the new intensive courses, beginning with the acquisition of two new sites for the courses.

THE ACQUISITION OF CHISHOLME AND SHERBORNE

Once the Beshara Trust had decided to structure an intensive six-month residential course, they faced the necessity of finding a suitable location and environment for such a course.[2] The ideal type of property needed to be large enough to accommodate a significant number of people including up to around sixty students and twenty staff; it also needed land suitable

---

1. The publication of this latter translation coincided with the 1975 course, though there was a typescript copy of it available before then.
2. The first structured courses of any kind to be run by the Beshara Trust were a series of nine-day introductory courses at a privately owned property known as 'The Warren' in Radnorshire, in Wales, in 1974.

for cultivation and pasture for stock grazing.[3] Ideally, the location also required some degree of seclusion from the outside world.

In 1974 Chisholme House, a Georgian house in the Scottish Borders region, was discovered purely by 'apparent' chance.[4] A lady who was a participant in the Beshara Trust was out hunting on horseback on the moorland that surrounds Chisholme, when she spotted the house. It was in a state of almost total dilapidation. But she told the Beshara trustees about it and they agreed that after restoration it would be ideal for the Trust's purposes.[5]

In its prime, Chisholme had been the home of the clan head of the southern Chisholmes. It had been surrounded by its own substantial estate, including four cottages and an extensive steading which could accommodate a large number of farm animals. But the house had been abandoned and left to fall into ruin and the surrounding estate land sold off, so that when the Beshara Trust eventually purchased it, all that remained of the property was the crumbling house and the immediately surrounding buildings. In the years succeeding its initial purchase, though, the Trust gradually bought back much of the land which originally belonged to the estate. Today the property comprises nearly two hundred acres, including a walled garden, a lake, pastures and woodlands.

Having decided that Chisholme would be a perfect venue for the purposes of the Beshara School, the Trustees sent several supporters to the house in order to 'squat' in it. (They did this because there were some complications over the actual purchase of the property to begin with.) Those initial occupants began the renovations, which ultimately turned out to be far more extensive than they had first estimated.

The first six-month intensive residential course was planned for October 1975, and during the preceding summer a large number of potential students and Beshara sympathisers worked together on a voluntary basis with the intention of restoring the house enough for it to be usable for the course. These people all learned how to build and restore and for many of them this was in itself a new experience. But by October and the start of the course, the house was still not usable for

---

3. Poultry were raised for meat and eggs, and sheep for meat, wool and as a contribution to the preservation of some rare breeds of sheep. The care of the animals, pastures and fencing as well as the cultivation of the land for the production of vegetables for the table also provided a necessary source of practical spiritual work for the students on the courses.

4. According to Ibn 'Arabi and many Beshara students, nothing spiritually significant happens by chance or by pure coincidence; such occurrences are part of 'the order of things' and happen according to the will of God.

5. Interview with W., December 1999.

accommodation, although the first floor was renovated enough to use for study, lectures, *zikr* and dining, so it was decided by the Trustees to use the steading for accommodation instead. When the first group of students did arrive, although the steading had been fully converted to accommodate them, there was still no heating or hot water available for washing. Then again another 'chance' incident occurred. One of the students happened to give a lift to a hitchhiker, a young German, and she brought him to Chisholme. It turned out that he was a plumber, but involved in a legal problem. Given his situation, he was quite happy to go 'underground' at Chisholme; in return for board and lodging, he installed a wood burning boiler which provided heat and hot water for the steading, and as a result the first course was able to go ahead.[6]

When it became apparent that the restoration of Chisholme House was going to take significantly longer to accomplish than had been originally anticipated, and that the semi-renovated buildings were not yet altogether conducive to running an effective residential course, the Trust then acquired Sherborne House near Cheltenham, in order to provide an immediate location for further intensive residential courses.

Sherborne House was an enormous late eighteenth-century stately home, which even included its own adjoining church. It had forty bedrooms, a large stable block, but an estate of only around four or five acres, the rest of its land having been sold off separately at an earlier date. It had been the country seat of Lord Sherborne, who had also owned the surrounding picturesque village. Originally it had been a monastic building, with eighteenth-century aspects being added later.

The first course to be run at Sherborne was in 1976; it was six months long, and about fifty students participated. The participants who attended that particular course are all consistent in their recollection of the intense cold and draughtiness of the great old house during their stay. The house did not have central heating, and a pivotal part of the daily work consisted of chopping wood and lighting fires. A great effort was needed to keep the fires going, and sixteen fires had to be lit first thing in the morning, before the six o'clock meditation session. Memorable also from that course was that, apart from the other routine work in the house and grounds, another central duty was child-care. Many of the students had young children whom they had brought with them. These children were accommodated in a nursery, and all the students had to take turns in looking after them, which included all aspects of their care.

Sherborne House was sold in 1981, but study activities continued to take place in the converted stable block of the house, which had been

6. Interview with R., November 1999 and L., August 2000.

leased back by the Trust. In 1988, the lease on the property expired and the Trust purchased another property, Frilford Grange near Oxford. Frilford was used primarily for conferences, seminars and study groups but not for the extended residential courses and was finally sold in 1990, after which the sole property owned by the Trust in England at which the residential courses were run was Chisholme.[7]

THE INTRODUCTION AND PURPOSE OF A STRUCTURED RESIDENTIAL COURSE

When Bulent Rauf established the first intensive introductory residential six-month course in esoteric education, it was planned to be the only course of its kind offered by the Beshara Trust. Nearly thirty years later, the Trust is still running the same course.[8] In the meantime it has also developed an advanced six-month residential course,[9] and a nine-day residential course based on the structure of the long courses, as well as an introductory residential weekend course.

Following the completion of the first two courses at Chisholme and Sherborne, the course period was extended to eight months in order to accommodate an increased volume of study material through more works of Ibn 'Arabi becoming available in translation. The course was only run for eight months over a two-year period, after which it was again reduced to six months, as the students were able to assimilate the increased amount of reading in that time. Initially the first course took place during

---

7. In addition to Sherborne House and Chisholme, the Trust also owned a property in London, in Charlwood Street, Pimlico which was used for study until the early 1980s. In the early 1980s, a property in New South Wales, Australia was purchased by 'Beshara Australia Incorporated', which was an autonomous Australian charity founded by Australian students of Chisholme and Sherborne with the same aims as the Beshara Trust. The intention was to run long residential courses at this property but this never happened although short courses did take place there. This property was sold in 2001. For details, see Chapter 8 below.

8. The daily focal points are still study, meditation, devotional practice and work on the estate and in the house. The only variation is that due to the steady increase in translations of Ibn 'Arabi's writings and related works (many by associates of the Muhyiddin Ibn 'Arabi Society), there are more of his texts available for study periods.

9. The Beshara School offers an advanced six-month course, first run in 1978, for students who have completed the first six-month intensive residential course. This course differs from the first in that conversation replaces study of texts, and the system of two days work followed by two days of study does not operate. Otherwise the structure is similar in that the other daily requirements are the same.

the summer and the second, in the winter, but eventually it became standard practice to offer the six-month courses from October to March.

Bulent's objective in inaugurating the long residential course was to encourage the development of each student as a Complete Human Being.[10] The course provided an appropriate environment and circumstances where students could begin to undertake a genuinely comprehensive spiritual education in accordance with Ibn 'Arabi's concept of the 'Perfect Man'.[11] The students initially drawn to the course were intelligent and for the most part highly educated, but felt the need for a more comprehensive and profound education.

Rauf understood this spiritual pedagogy to follow two key principles. The first principle was that Existence is One, Unique and Indivisible and Absolute and that there is nothing apart from It which is fully real. The second principle, a human 'reflection' of the first, is the Perfectibility of Man (humanity) through knowing ourselves: i.e., who we are, where we are from, and that we are in reality nothing but potentially a self-conscious 'reflection' of the One in this relative world, rather like the perfect mirror image of 'an object reflected'.[12] Therefore the purpose of the course was to present a body of knowledge which potentially allowed people to align themselves with that which they really are and thereby to know what their relationship to Reality really is. This includes other people, society, work and the universe as a whole with all its responsibilities, including most fundamentally our appreciation of existence and being itself.[13]

Because Ibn 'Arabi's perspective was understood by Bulent Rauf and the early participants of Beshara to be a universal one, his ideas were from the beginning used to expound these basic course objectives. The present Principal of the school states that Ibn 'Arabi's viewpoint is spiritual rather than 'religious' in the modern limited political and sectarian sense; and although Ibn 'Arabi came from a Muslim culture and background, his viewpoint was explicitly founded on this universal

10. A rough English equivalent to Ibn 'Arabi's central metaphysical concept of *al-insân al-kâmil*, often somewhat inaccurately translated as 'The Perfect Man'. *Insân* is the logos or theomorphic reality, fully exemplified historically in the prophets and saints; *kâmil* refers to the complete human actualisation of all the divine 'Names' or attributes and modalities.

11. Interviews with C. and K., August 1999.

12. Peter Young (present Principal of The Beshara School at Chisholme), from an article paraphrasing the key opening chapter on '"Adam" in Ibn 'Arabi's *Fusûs al-Hikam*', *Beshara Newsletter* (Spring 1994), p. 1.

13. Summarised from an unpublished interview for the *Beshara Magazine* with Peter Young, by Cecilia Twinch, from the mid-1980s.

Reality. Reality may be expressed by each revealed religion, but it is also beyond particular religions.[14] He suggests that all that Ibn 'Arabi wrote is qualified by such an explicitly universal understanding. Therefore, by establishing in the students the awakened awareness that Reality is one and universal, then that Truth may be recognised however it appears. Thus the students will have a touchstone of understanding which will place their subsequent spiritual learning and activities in a wider universal context.

From the beginning of the first structured course, Bulent Rauf and the Beshara trustees emphasised that the Beshara School was not an 'Ibn 'Arabi school', but rather that because the school was interested in promoting knowledge of the 'Unity of Existence', Ibn 'Arabi's works were to be used in the main. This was because he articulated the central ideas of this course more comprehensively and fully than other well-known mystics, many of whose writings from various traditions are used as supplements to Ibn 'Arabi on the course.[15]

COURSE SCHEDULE

The intensive introductory residential course runs over a six-month period, through the winter from October to March.[16] During that time the students are discouraged from leaving the premises except for reasons of emergency, and there is normally no time off apart from Christmas afternoon.[17] The daily timetable is still more or less as it was when the course was first begun, and runs as follows:

6.30 am:	Rise. Full Ablution
7.00 am:	Meditation
7.30 am:	Breakfast
9.00 am:	Study/Work
10.15 am:	Coffee
10.45 am:	Study/Work
12.00 pm:	Ablution (Partial)

14. The key Arabic expression 'Reality' (*al-Haqq*) also includes the ideas of divine 'Truth' and 'Justice'.
15. These works will be discussed in Chapter 4 below. See interviews with Peter Young and Angela Holroyd (at the time a potential student) mid-1980s, *Beshara Magazine* 8 (c. 1988/89), pp. 26-31. Also interview with E., August 1999.
16. The intensive six-month course and its structure is summarised here. It will be analysed in detail in Chapters 5 and 6 below.
17. The intensity of the daily routine relaxes somewhat during the annual trip to Turkey, but this visit is still not to be understood as a 'holiday' by the students. See the discussion about this annual pilgrimage in Chapter 7 below.

12.15 pm:	Meditation
12.45 pm:	Set table for lunch
1.00 pm:	Lunch
2.15 pm:	Work
4.00 pm:	Tea
4.30 pm:	Work/Study
5.45 pm:	Ablution (Partial)
6.00 pm:	Meditation
6.30 pm:	Work
7.45 pm:	Set table for supper
8.00 pm:	Supper
9.00 pm:	Full Ablution
9.30 pm:	*Zikr*

Purification and Meditation

Full ablution is required twice daily, as is partial ablution as indicated in the schedule above.[18] Ablution in the context of the course, reflecting an Islamic influence, is practised before approaching God in devotion such as prayer, meditation or *zikr*. It is based on the principle that the body and mind must be pure. Therefore the body is cleansed by washing and the mind should be cleansed of impure thoughts. The external aspect of full ablution involves washing the whole body by way of a shower,[19] whilst partial ablution comprises washing one's hands, face, head and feet. During the six-month course, full ablution was obligatory upon rising in the mornings and before evening *zikr*, whilst a partial ablution was required before the noon and early evening meditation sessions.

The type of meditation practised by the students is a 'passive' type (similar to Zen 'sitting'), in that rather than using a theme upon which to

---

18. '*ghusl*' : this is the term for the general ritual ablution in ritually pure water, of the whole body. This ablution is required for a person who finds himself in a state of major ritual impurity (*a janâba*) caused by marital intercourse, to which the religious law assimilates any *effusio seminis*. Second, ablution refers to *wudû*, the term for minor ritual ablution, consisting of, in this sequence, washing the face, the hands and the forearms, rubbing the head with the wet hand and washing the feet. The intention of the *wudû* must be duly formulated. The simple ablution is to be performed after incurring a minor ritual impurity which is caused by contact with an unclean substance or by certain facts explained in Muslim law. E. Van Donzel, ed., *The Islamic Desk Reference: Compiled from the Encyclopaedia of Islam* (Leiden: Brill, 1994), p. 12. '*ghusl*': is necessary having washed a corpse, and is obligatory before performing the ritual daily prayers. *The Encyclopaedia of Islam: New Edition, Glossary and Index of Terms*, vol. 1–9 (ed. P.J. Bearman et al.; Leiden: Brill, 2000), pp. 118-19.

19. The water has to be running and if a bath is taken, it must be followed by a shower.

meditate or a mantra or visualisation, the mind is to be kept passive and receptive 'before the face of God'.[20] No particular technique is used, and very little explicit guidance is given. It is only at the commencement and completion of the half-hour sessions that obligatory words and actions are required. The words used at the beginning of a session are the Arabic formula '*Bismillâh ar Rahmân ar Rahîm*', meaning 'In the Name of God, the Compassionate and Merciful'. At this point the students are surrendering themselves completely to the loving mercy and will of God, the Real. Sometimes they will receive a vision or realisation connected in some way with the study on the course; at other times they may receive no kind of inspiration at all. At the conclusion of such a session, the Arabic word *Hû* is intoned (the Quranic pronoun usually referring to the divine Essence), and all the students prostrate themselves in the way that Muslims do during prayer.

The meditation venue needs to be quiet and warm in order to avoid distractions, and the students normally meditate whilst sitting on especially constructed stools. If for some reason the stools are not practical to use, then the students may sit in whatever way is most comfortable and conducive to concentration, usually cross-legged on folded blankets or on chairs with their backs straight and eyes closed. Each session is opened and closed by an attending supervisor.

The purpose of the sessions is to open the mind and soul to God, to be in submission to God's will; therefore the mind should be clear and receptive. This is easier said than done, as unwanted thoughts habitually intrude. The students are sometimes advised to allow these unwanted thoughts to rise in the mind, acknowledge them but not to follow them. As indicated in the schedule above, the meditation sessions take place for half an hour, three times a day, preceded each time by a ritual of inner and outer purification.

Study

The study periods extend to around four hours per day on study days, and the course format is normally arranged so that two consecutive study days are followed by two work days. The study periods take place within seminar-type discussion groups, with from three to ten students taking part at a time. The sessions are presided over by a course supervisor who facilitates the discussion through the choosing of appropriate texts, but does not actually lead the session or impose his or her own ideas; they do, though, help ensure that a focus is kept.

---

20. As explained during participation in the nine-day course in November 1998.

The text is approached in a manner similar to that of a seminar in scriptural exegesis or literary criticism, in that a student or the session supervisor first reads out loud a passage from the text, then all the students re-read it (silently) and contemplate it. The passage is then discussed and reflected upon by the whole group. Quite frequently the text is actually approached sentence by sentence, depending on how easily the students are able to absorb the content. This approach has the effect of initially acting on the intellectual level of the student's psyche, so that the content is first approached intellectually through a mental understanding of the words. But according to the school's supervisors, this intellectual level only offers one aspect, a surface or superficial understanding of the meaning of the text; it is only through contemplating its meaning that the deeper spiritual intuition begins to act, so that realisations which cannot be intellectualised begin to rise in the consciousness of the student.[21] The students frequently find relevance for themselves in the passage that they are studying and as a former student has pointed out, without that central element of personal relevance the study necessarily becomes abstract, the focus metaphysical and ultimately pointless.[22] This type of approach to the text can produce interesting results, such as the revelation of sub-conscious contents, buried ideas, memories, associations and a heightening of intuitive ability.

Work

The work periods consist of working outside on the estate, for example, looking after animals, tending the pleasure or productive gardens, maintenance of outbuildings, attention to pasture, forestry and fencing; or the work may be in the house and involve cooking, cleaning, laundry or house maintenance.

These work periods provide a counter-balance to the intense study of the texts, and at the same time contribute vital support to the running of the establishment. But the primary purpose of these work periods is to put what has been studied into practice and to begin to assimilate it more concretely. Such work is integral to Ibn 'Arabi's central guiding idea of 'service'.[23] Within the context of the school, this means that all work

---

21. See the description and analysis of the effect that the study of the texts has on some students in Chapter 6 below.
22. Interview with V., 11 February 2000.
23. For Ibn 'Arabi's concept of divine 'service' (*ibâda*) as the embodiment of the *insân al-kâmil*, the 'Perfect Servant', see the synopsis of *The Twenty-Nine Pages* in Chapter 4 below.

undertaken has to be done as perfectly as possible. This idea of *ihsân*,[24] true divine service ('perfected realisation of good and beauty'), is central to the Sufi conception of our human purpose and perfection. 'Abd al-Karîm al-Jîlî[25] describes the situation as follows:

> For if the servant (*al-'abd*) is elevated by cosmic degrees towards the degree of the Eternal Reality and he discovers himself, he recognises the Divine Essence as his own essence, so that he really attains the Essence and knows It, as the Prophet expresses it thus: 'He who knows himself, knows his Lord'.[26]

Zikr ('Remembrance' of God)

The waking day ends with *zikr*, which is a traditional Islamic devotional practice of prayer in which a selection of the ninety-nine 'Most Beautiful Names' of God are repeatedly intoned. The key Quranic word *dhikr* (pronounced '*zikr*') means 'Recollection' or 'Remembrance' of God, and during this practice the participants undergo an intense recollection of the divine Source.[27] The participants sit, stand, circle or sway throughout the session. The regular nightly *zikrs* are led by a supervisor and last for around half an hour. Following these sessions, the students say *wazîfas*, which again involve repetition aloud of the 'Most Beautiful divine Names' (*al-asmâs al-husnâ*) on a string of prayer beads, a practice outwardly resembling the Catholic rosary or *mantras* in Hindu and Buddhist tradition. Each Thursday night, a longer *zikr* takes place at which, in addition to the current students, all other residents and guests of the school are invited to take part.[28] At certain times special *zikrs* take place, such as on the Prophet's birthday (*mawlid*) or the 'Night of Power', a particular night during Ramadan on which it is said the Prophet Mohammed received the whole of God's revelation at one time.

---

24. Aisha Bewly, '*ihsân*': absolute sincerity to Allah in Oneself: it is to worship Allah as though you were seeing Him because He sees you, *Glossary of Islamic Terms* (Norwich: Ta-Ha, 1998), p. 214.

25. The fourteenth-century Sufi, who continued the metaphysical teaching of Ibn 'Arabi.

26. *Universal Man*, extracts from his work *al-insân al-kamîl* (trans. from Arabic to French by Titus Burckhardt and French to English by Angela Culme-Seymour; Gloucestershire: Beshara, 1983), p. 13.

27. '*dhikr*' remembering God, reciting the Names of God: the tireless repetition of an ejaculatory litany; a religious service common to all the mystical fraternities performed either solitarily or collectively, *Encyclopaedia of Islam*, vol. 1–9, p. 78.

28. Thursday night is special because it is the evening before the Islamic sacred day of the week which is Friday. During the day, particular attention is given to cleansing or abluting the whole house in general and the room in which the *zikr* is taking place in particular.

Meals

Food preparation and meals are also a required, integral part of the course. The preparation of the food is understood to be a transformative operation, akin to the transformation that should be taking place within the students as they work towards perfecting themselves to be as a mirror of God's own perfection.[29] Even the way in which the dining tables are set and the seating plan is arranged is understood as part of the education taking place and is intended to reflect God's perfection and the order in creation. The deeper intentions here are expressed in a recently published article about Bulent Rauf and his culinary skills:[30]

> He referred often and in many ways to the idea that cooking was never just simply a mixture of ingredients, but rather a harmonious composition, capable of expressing the inherent potential of both the individual ingredients and the total composition. And the most necessary ingredients in the cook's own personal composition for this to occur, he would say, was an attitude of deep respect, and consideration and full awareness of the bounty and clemency of existence itself. And this word clemency would have all the connotations of the word '*rahmet*' in Turkish or '*rahma*' in Arabic, the Divine Mercy which bestows existence on all creation.[31]

So as we may understand from these above remarks, meals and their preparation at Chisholme or Sherborne demand constant awareness and right spiritual intention throughout the whole process including the key spiritual virtues of thankfulness and praise. This heightened awareness involves the endeavour for perfection in the realisation that the Essence of the Real is the *true* essence of the completely realised human being. And it is only through the polishing of the mirror of the self that a human truly begins to reflect that divine Essence.[32]

Languages and Other studies

A language is often taught during the long residential course, although it is not integral to the course and depends on the availability of an appropriate teacher. If a teacher is available, the language taught is usually Arabic, Hebrew or Turkish, although ancient Greek has at times been

---

29. Concerning the attitude to meals and cooking at the Beshara School, see the above biographical Chapter 1, on Bulent Rauf, particularly the quote from the article by Christopher Ryan, 'Bulent Rauf: A Mystic in the Kitchen', *Beshara Newsletter* (Autumn 1996), pp. 3-4. Also see, in the same chapter, a description about Rauf's spiritual methods of teaching culinary skills described by an original student.
30. Ibid.
31. Ibid., p. 3.
32. See the famous opening chapter on Adam in Ibn 'Arabi's *Fusûs al-Hikâm*.

taught and even Chinese was offered on one particular course. All the students are provided with a short lesson on Arabic at the beginning of the course, in order to have a better understanding of the divine Names. They are also taught a small amount of Turkish before embarking on the pilgrimage to Turkey. A further reason for being taught an unfamiliar language, particularly one that the student is unlikely to use in the future, such as Chinese, is in order 'to use the mind in a different way, loosen the mind, think in a different way'.[33]

In addition to the texts studied, other lectures are presented, normally towards the end of the courses, by staff members or visiting speakers who talk on spiritual matters or related subjects, such as literature, expressive art, poetry, architecture, economics or archaeology. Or there may be a visit, for example, to the Tibetan Buddhist temple and retreat centre of Samye Ling, only twenty miles away from Chisholme. These additional lectures, particularly those presented by adherents of various religious traditions, give the students an added perspective to their own studies.

Silent Days
Included in the structure of the six-month courses are certain days upon which total silence is to be maintained. This requirement involves all aspects of the day, including meals and work in the house or on the estate. In addition to imposing a firm discipline upon the ego, it also allows the students to increase and deepen their constant awareness of Reality and their place within it, without the distraction of conversation.

The Pilgrimage to Turkey
In December each year, the school arranges a trip to Turkey which is required for the course students, but is also open to non-students. The trip offers a chance to encounter more directly significant monuments and practices of several traditions, as well as to visit the shrines of several Sufi saints and other spiritual figures such as the Virgin Mary. Typically, the journey begins at Istanbul and proceeds through Bursa, Pergamon, Ephesus, Priene, Didyme and Pamukkale, culminating in Konya with participation in the 'Nuptial Night' celebration (the anniversary of the death) of Mevlana Jalâluddîn Rûmî, on the 17 December. The 'Sema', the complex ceremony in which the Mevlevi Dervishes 'throw off the cloak of physical existence' and participate freely in the Divine Existence, celebrates this reunion each year. The journey then continues to Ankara and then back to Istanbul.[34]

33. Discussion with O., April 2002.
34. Chapter 7 below is entirely dedicated to the annual Turkey trip.

BASIC RULES OF BEHAVIOUR

There are two sets of important rules that students of the Beshara School are required to adhere to during their time of residence. The first are the 'Rules of the Kitchen' as laid down by Bulent Rauf. These have already been mentioned with reference to his particular skill as a chef and his expectations of students. The second set of rules involves a more general overall demand for 'appropriate behaviour' (*adab*). This key spiritual term refers not just to apparent, external right behaviour, but above all to interior control and awareness of negative thoughts and emotions. These brief rules are quoted in full because of their significance:

> Students taking part in esoteric study will comply without hesitation with the rules and regulations set out by the Beshara School of Intensive Esoteric Education.
>
> Therefore also, students are asked to keep check and at bay all natural impulses of primitive expression. Such as: Anger, garrulousness, avarice, meanness and miserliness in heart and mind, constrictedness of consideration and compassion, lust, luxuriousness, ableness, sloth, unawareness, mental and moral and physical uncleanliness, lack of respect and lack of balance between duty and privilege, obligation and right, self-righteousness and pride, and above all indulging in passing judgement.
>
> A student is a willing scholar and as such is obedient to these rules of study and is expected to act in complete accordance with them.[35]

COURSE SUPERVISION

All the courses are now supervised by a range of people who have themselves completed both of the six-month courses. The policy of the school is that there may be a staff reshuffle after the first three months, halfway through each course. For one thing, this allows for alternative approaches to the study and the texts. It is also in keeping with the ethos of the school, which maintains that in contrast to the monastic approach to spirituality, former students and adherents of Beshara should manifest what they have experienced and 'realised' in the outside world, so neither staff nor students are encouraged to stay at the school for too long at any one time. The school also has a tutorial system for the students in place, whereby once a week they have the chance to speak to a supervisor on a one to one basis on a range of issues arising out of the course experience.

---

35. This list of rules is close to the door of the meditation room at Chisholme in Scotland.

Other staff in attendance at the school over the duration of the six-month courses include a house-keeper and an estate manager, both usually former students under whom the current students work, and the school's administrators. For the reasons explained above, although these positions are relatively permanent, the people who actually occupy them change. All these positions are undertaken on a voluntary basis and the only permanent position is that of the Principal.[36]

Although the above description refers to the structure of the intensive six-month residential course which was first introduced into the Beshara School in 1975, that structure itself has not changed significantly since then. When this course had been established for two years, the advanced six-month residential course was introduced which is run on a similar structure to the first course, except that during the study periods and work days, conversation takes place rather than study of texts.[37]

In addition to the nine-day and weekend introductory courses, the school also offers talks and seminars by visiting authorities from related fields as well as the possibility of individualised retreats of varying lengths. In recent years, introductory nine-day courses have also been held in private houses or public buildings in Indonesia, the USA and Australia.

ORGANISATION AND FUNDING

In 1979, the Chisholme Institute was set up as a charitable company under Scottish law to administer the teaching activities of the Beshara School at Chisholme, now known as the 'Beshara School of Intensive Esoteric Education'. The directors of the Institute were drawn from the founders and early participants of the Beshara Trust. The Trust and the Institute were at that time separately constituted legal bodies, each with its own charter. Today (2002), the Trust is dormant and the Chisholme Institute is now the active body administering all the activities which were previously within the domain of the Beshara Trust, such as the courses held at Chisholme, the Beshara Foundation in the USA and Beshara Australia Incorporated.[38]

---

36. The position of Principal is permanent but the person who occupies that position is clearly selected by mutual agreement and consensus, even though it has now been occupied by the same person for many years. Written information from HP., May 2002.
37. The conversation, form and content of the advanced six-month course will be discussed more thoroughly in Chapters 5 and 6 below.
38. Details of these organisations are discussed in Chapter 8 below.

In its early days the Trust was supported by charitable contributions and the courses were largely self-supporting, but it still needed funds for such things as equipment, restoration and the upkeep of properties, and for scholarship and loan facilities for less well off students. This money was initially raised through participants' covenants and charitable donations (which continue to support the Trust's activities today) as well as through the Trust's own money-making enterprises.

Conclusion

The account above has demonstrated how from modest beginnings the activities of the Beshara School expanded rapidly in a short space of time. It also reveals, in the breakdown of the course structure, the considerable extent of Islamic and traditional Sufi influence within the course content. This in turn goes to illustrate the understanding of the participants of the school, regarding the root meaning of *islâm* as 'submission to God'. In addition this highlights their typical (and highly 'akbarian') interpretation of Ibn 'Arabi's metaphysical concepts as having universalistic meaning. The approach of the Beshara School to historical and culturally specific forms of Sufi practice forms one part of the much wider spectrum of Westernised Sufi movements, briefly introduced in the Introduction above.

4

AN INTRODUCTION TO THE TEXTS AND TEACHINGS OF IBN 'ARABI USED FOR STUDY BY THE BESHARA SCHOOL

This chapter provides summaries of the principal texts and teachings of the works of Ibn 'Arabi used for study by the Beshara School. The first part of the chapter discusses themes drawn from *The Twenty-Nine Pages* and the *Wisdom of the Prophets*, both of which illustrate Ibn 'Arabi's key mystical and metaphysical ideas extracted from his most important and influential works: the *Bezels of Wisdom* (*Fusûs al-Hikam*) and the *Meccan Revelations* (*al-Futûhât al-Makkiyyah*). Also included in this section are some comments and discussions related to these principle themes extracted from William Chittick's recent book *Ibn 'Arabi: Heir to the Prophets*.[1] Although Chittick's works are not central to the study of Ibn 'Arabi by the Beshara School, the extracts were chosen because they offer a concise and comprehensive rendering of Ibn 'Arabi's central teachings, and were added since the completion of the original doctoral thesis in 2003. The intention in doing this is to provide the general reader with additional clarification of some of the complicated themes encountered. The latter part of this chapter discusses other key texts, primarily those produced by Ibn 'Arabi's original followers, as well as other Sufi 'classics' used for study at the school.

Because the two partial versions of the *Fusûs al-Hikam* (with extracts from the *Meccan Revelations* (*al-Futûhât al-Makkiyyah*), provide the central metaphysical ideas that form the foundation for all other writings studied throughout the Beshara courses, as well as the dimensions of practical and devotional work, the key themes will be examined in some detail below. Before summarising them it is necessary to point out that I am aware that the school uses Ibn 'Arabi's works from translations which could themselves be liable to misinterpretation. (Although *The Twenty-Nine Pages* is derived more or less directly from Affifi who

---

1. W.C. Chittick, *Ibn 'Arabi Heir to the Prophets* (Oxford: Oneworld, 2005).

translated it from the Arabic, other versions of the *Fusûs* that are studied are translations from Arabic to French, or Arabic to Turkish and then to English, and the problem would be more likely to occur with these.) The possibility of misinterpretation is undoubtedly there, but it is also true to say that ever since his lifetime, Ibn 'Arabi's works have been particularly open to creative interpretation and hostile misinterpretation. This was partly due to the enigmatic nature of the essential meaning of his complex metaphysics, and also to his tendency towards an apparently unstructured style of writing, particularly in his magnum opus the *Meccan Revelations* (*al-Futûhât al-Makkiyyah*), which many early and even contemporary scholars and commentators of his works have found confusing.[2] Indeed the historical evidence would indicate that Ibn 'Arabi was quite as likely to be misrepresented in the centuries following his death as by the participants of the Beshara School. On the other hand, his key metaphysical themes taught in the Beshara School have not shifted since his lifetime, and these are the themes that will be explored below.

THE TWENTY-NINE PAGES: AN INTRODUCTION TO MUHYIDDIN IBN 'ARABI'S METAPHYSICS OF UNITY

The Twenty-Nine Pages was the first study text used by Bulent Rauf for those students of Beshara at Swyre Farm who had a particular interest in Ibn 'Arabi.[3] This text, whose official 'title' refers to its original photo-copied format, was based on translated passages from Ibn 'Arabi's *Bezels of Wisdom* (*Fusûs al Hikam*) and the *Meccan Revelations* (*al-Futûhât al-Makkiyyah*) included in *The Mystical Philosophy of Muhyid Dîn Ibnul Arabî*.[4] Affifi was a student of the renowned Cambridge scholar of Islamic mysticism, Professor A.R. Nicholson. Rauf, who was intimately familiar with Ibn 'Arabi's writings as they had been interpreted through a long tradition of later commentators, self-consciously condensed and adapted Affifi's English translations of Ibn 'Arabi's *Fusûs* and *Futûhât* for his own teaching purposes.

The Twenty-Nine Pages summarises, in a extremely condensed introductory manner, all the main themes contained in Ibn 'Arabi's spiritual

---

2. Alexander Knysh (among other scholars of Ibn 'Arabi) addresses this issue in the Introduction of his book *Ibn 'Arabi in the Later Islamic Tradition: The Making of a Polemical Image in Medieval Islam* (Albany: SUNY Press, 1999), pp. 1-16.

3. *The Twenty-Nine Pages: An Introduction to Ibn 'Arabi's Metaphysics of Unity*, was finally published in book form by Beshara Publications in 1998.

4. A.A. Affifi, *The Mystical Philosophy of Muhid Dîn Ibnul 'Arabî* (Cambridge: Cambridge University Press, 1969; originally published 1939).

teaching especially as articulated in later philosophic commentary traditions. That role of Ibn 'Arabi's ideas had been particularly marked throughout the Ottoman world and its high culture, which had been central in Bulent Rauf's own early education and family milieu. In Turkey and throughout the Ottoman Empire, Ibn 'Arabi's ideas had come to play a central role in many areas of religious and cultural life since he first expounded them there in the early thirteenth century.

The contents of *The Twenty-Nine Pages* relate to themes of Ibn 'Arabi which have continued to be of central importance to the participants of Beshara, especially the Unity of Existence and the spiritual perfectibility of the fully human being (*al-insân al-kâmil*). Rauf's summary is most notable for its purely metaphysical, abstract language (based on centuries of commentaries on Ibn 'Arabi's *Futûhât* and *Fusûs*), carefully avoiding direct reference to the multitude of complex Quranic verses and *hadith* through which Ibn 'Arabi himself typically expresses his ideas in most of his writings.

The *Blue Fusûs*

The dense summary of Ibn 'Arabi's teachings in *The Twenty-Nine Pages* was soon supplemented in Beshara courses by the actual translation of the key chapters from his *Fusûs al-Hikam* contained in what some participants usually call the *Blue Fusûs*.[5] The full original title of that work is *The Wisdom of the Prophets*. This was the title given to Titus Burckhardt's French translation from the Arabic of selected chapters from Ibn 'Arabi's work, and was retained in Beshara's later English version. The Arabic title is *Fusûs al-Hikam*, which translated literally means the 'ring-settings' or 'bezels' of wisdom. The Arabic word *al-fass*, the singular of *fusûs*, refers to the setting that holds a precious stone or jewel in a ring. In the context of Ibn 'Arabi's work, *al-hikam* means 'wisdoms', referring here to the different prophetic aspects of the universal divine Wisdom. So in Ibn 'Arabi's title, the settings or bezels holding the jewels that manifest the eternal divine Wisdom are the forms of the different prophets. These human receptacles provide form for manifesting a 'jewel' of Truth (Reality or Logos), which represents a particular aspect of Divine Wisdom. For example, in the first chapter entitled 'The Setting of the Wisdom in the Word of Adam', the Divine Truth is manifested in the form of the 'Word' of Adam, and the same principle applies to each of the twenty-six other prophets who have chapters named after them in the book.

---

5. Ibn 'Arabi, *The Wisdom of the Prophets* (trans. from Arabic to French by Titus Burckhardt and French to English by Angela Culme-Seymour; Gloucestershire: Beshara, 1975) (hereafter *WP*).

Burckhardt's original translation and commentary contained only twelve out of the twenty-seven chapters of the *Fusûs*. He explains that he chose these because he felt that their doctrinal content was the most important, and also because he considered some other chapters to contain exegesis too difficult to render into a European language. He suggests that the first two chapters in themselves, on Adam and Seth, actually summarise Ibn 'Arabi's metaphysical doctrine. This work refers to all the main focuses of Ibn 'Arabi's teaching including the concepts of Unity and Multiplicity, the nature of God and humanity, and the metaphysical ideas which are associated with these central schemes of thought. Ibn 'Arabi's main scriptural sources for his work are the symbols and teachings in the Quran and related reported sayings (*hadith*) of Muhammad. His most important concepts tend to recur from chapter to chapter. Burkhardt's twelve chosen chapters also provide material that is central to the Beshara courses.

The key metaphysical themes extracted from these works[6] and studied at the Beshara School are organised broadly within the same categories in which Affifi presented his in his ground-breaking work *The Mystical Philosophy of Muhyid Dîin Ibnul 'Arabi*, and may be summarised as follows:

ONTOLOGY AND COSMOLOGY

Being

To Ibn 'Arabi the primary focus of his metaphysics is the truly Real, i.e., God. He then turns his attention to the cosmos which is, to him, everything other than God. He typically calls God *wujûd*, which translates most frequently as 'being' or 'existence'.

The opening chapter of the *The Twenty-Nine Pages* introduces Ibn 'Arabi's approach to the metaphysics of existence. It describes his perspective as compared to a bird's-eye view, looking down on a pyramid from above its apex, in contrast to viewing it from its base, looking up towards the apex. Therefore, it becomes apparent that in Ibn 'Arabi's thought, the apex corresponds to that metaphysical 'Point' which is Absolute Being.

The focus of the chapter is how, in Ibn 'Arabi's understanding, Reality (*al-Haqq*)[7] termed as 'Absolute Being' (*wujûd al-mutlaq*) or 'Entire

---

6. With additional comments extracted from W. Chittick's *Ibn 'Arabi Heir to the Prophets*, as mentioned in the introductory paragraph of this chapter.
7. The most inclusive Quranic divine Name, *al-Haqq* refers at once to the highest Reality, Truth, Right, Justice; it is thus understood to encompass all the other divine Names and Attributes.

Being' (*wujûd al-kulli*), is ultimately One and the Source of everything in existence. To reinforce this idea, Ibn 'Arabi is quoted as saying 'Were it not for the permeation of God, by means of His form, in all existents, this world would have no existence just as it were if not for the intelligible universal realities, no predications (*ahkâm*) of external objects would be possible'. Therefore, 'the real source of all beings is Absolute Being: a Reality or Being whose existence is identical with its Essence—a Being whose existence is necessary (*wâjib al-wujûdi bidhâtihi*). This Essence is at once all the realised and the realisable quiddities (*mâhiyyât*) in the external world with all their properties and accidents...'[8]

William Chittick, who is a foremost expert on the metaphysics of Ibn 'Arabi, makes some very comprehensive points about what the word *wujûd* means to Ibn 'Arabi. I have incorporated a substantial quote here from Chittick because I feel that it contributes to the clarification of Ibn 'Arabi's metaphysical perspective on God and Reality and it also highlights the way in which the students of the Beshara School approach an understanding to what is the keystone of all Ibn 'Arabi's teachings.

> For Ibn 'Arabi, the word *wujûd* carries both the Sufi and the philosophical meanings. No matter how 'ontological' his discussions may appear to modern readers, he never loses sight of the fact that *wujûd* designates not only the incomparable and ineffable Reality of the Real, but also the immanent presence of God in the knower's awareness. The Gnostics look with both eyes, and they perceive *wujûd* as both absent, because it is none other than the Divine Essence, and present, because it is none other than God's self-disclosure as the selfhood of the knower.
>
> In Ibn 'Arabi's terminology, then *wujûd* means not only being and existence (the 'objective' side of reality), but also finding and awareness (the 'subjective' side of reality). He highlights the latter sense in expressions like *ahl al-kashf wa'l-wujûd*, 'the folk of unveiling and finding,' or *ahl ash-shuhud wa'l-wujûd*, 'the folk of witnessing and finding.' These are precisely the Gnostics those who see with both eyes.
>
> It hardly needs to be pointed out that in English neither 'being' nor 'existence' has the connotation of awareness and consciousness. Even when we talk about God as 'Being,' we know that God has knowledge and awareness because we say so, not because the word itself demands it.
>
> The results of disassociating being and consciousness become obvious when we glance at history of Western thought, especially in recent times, Scientists, philosophers, and even some theologians look upon life and consciousness as epiphenomena of existence, latecomers on the cosmic scene. We moderns are happy to think that 'existence' came before consciousness, or that living things gradually evolved from dead and inanimate matter. For Ibn 'Arabi and much of Islamic thinking (not to

---

8. *The Twenty-Nine Pages*, p. 1.

mention kindred visions in other traditions), no universe is thinkable without the primacy of life and awareness, the presence of consciousness in the underlying stuff of reality.[9]

Unity and Multiplicity

Ibn 'Arabi's idea is that although Reality is One, it can be viewed from various perspectives: thus it may be named 'the Real' (*haqq*) when viewed as the Essence of all phenomena, or 'creation' (*khalq*) when viewed from the angle of the manifestation of the phenomena of that Essence. *Haqq* and *khalq* could then be termed, for example, 'Reality' and 'appearance', or 'the One' and 'the many', with these two names being used in either case to describe two aspects of that one Reality. According to Ibn 'Arabi: 'If you regard Him through Him (i.e. if you regard the Essence from the point of view of the Essence), then He regards Himself through Himself which is the state of Unity; but if you regard Him through yourself (i.e. from your point of view as a form) then the unity vanishes'.[10] Usually it is difficult for people to regard that whole as a whole, since we typically regard the manifested world as a plurality of beings. Ibn 'Arabi asserts that it is only a true 'knower' who has the ability to transcend the 'dispersed' vision of the world of forms and simultaneously see their underlying Reality.

The themes concerning Unity and multiplicity and the Oneness of Being run through all the chapters of the *Fusûs*. This is not surprising, as these ideas lie at the heart of Ibn 'Arabi's philosophy. The other central themes also tend to recur in various chapters, but there are some chapters in which certain themes command more centrality than in others. This is so in the case of the themes of Unity and multiplicity, dealt with in particular detail in the chapter 'Of the Wisdom of Being Lost in Love in the Word of Abraham'. The Quranic epithet for Abraham (*al-khalîl*) means 'the intimate friend of God'.[11] The root of *al-khalîl* is *khalla*, which means 'permeation' or inter-penetration. Ibn 'Arabi uses this image to explain the way in which the reality of God permeates or inter-penetrates everything in existence in all its complexity and multiplicity. This extends even to qualities of imperfection and blame. He shows here that God and the cosmos are interdependent and that neither God nor the ephemeral beings may be known except in relation to each other. He uses as an example of the permeation of God in creation the way that 'water spreads itself in wool and makes it heavier or more voluminous'.[12] He

9. Chittick, *Ibn 'Arabi Heir*, p. 37.
10. *The Twenty-Nine Pages*, p. 2.
11. *Blue Fusûs* (*WP*, p. 40).
12. *WP*, pp. 41.

explains that if it is Divinity which appears as manifest and the creature is hidden within divinity, the creature will be assimilated with all the divine Names, e.g., His hearing, His seeing, all His attributes and His knowledge. But if it is the human creature which is apparent and the Divine manifest in him, God then becomes the hearing of that person, his sight, hand, foot and all his faculties.[13]

In this chapter Ibn 'Arabi writes statements and poems which were intended to be paradoxical to his contemporaries, such as:

> He praises me and I praise Him;
> He serves me, and I serve Him;
> By my existence I affirm Him;
> And by my determination I deny Him...
> Where then is His independence, when
> I glorify Him and help Him?
> In the same way, as soon as God manifests me,
> I lend Him science and manifest Him...[14]

Another chapter that includes a strong flavour of the theme of the Oneness of Being is the chapter entitled 'From the Wisdom of the Prophecy in the Word of Jesus'. As Austin explains in his introduction to this chapter in his translation of Ibn 'Arabi's work,[15] throughout the chapter Ibn 'Arabi tries to tackle the problem of 'He' and 'other than He', using the nature of Jesus to illustrate this paradox, i.e. to show to what extent Jesus (or for that matter any created thing) is 'himself rather than Himself'. Ibn 'Arabi says of the Divine 'Breath' through which God manifested creation:

> He who wants to know the Divine Breath (*nafas*) let him consider the world, for (according to the word of the Prophet) he who knows his self (*nafsahu*) knows his Lord who manifests Himself in him; I mean that the world is manifested in the Breath of the Clement, by which God 'dilated' (*naffasa*) the possibilities implied in the Divine Names, relieving them (*naffasa*) so to speak from the restraint of the state of non-manifestation; and doing this, He was generous towards Himself (*nafsahu*) because He manifests in Himself...[16]

---

13. Ibid. This refers to the words of the famous *hadith qudsi* (a *hadith* or saying which denotes a direct revelation, where God speaks in the first person, transmitted by the Prophet): '...My servant continues to come nearer Me through the acts of piety, until I love him. And when I love him, I am his hearing with which he hears, his sight with which he sees, his tongue with which he speaks, his hand with which he grasps, and his foot on which he walks'.

14. Ibid., p. 44.

15. *The Bezels of Wisdom* (New York: Paulist, 1980), p. 174.

16. *WP*, p. 76.

A further chapter that has a particular emphasis on the Oneness of Being is known as 'From the Sublime Wisdom in the Word of Moses'. From the perspective of analogy, this chapter concerns the relationships between Moses and Pharaoh and Moses and al-Khâdir ('*Khidr*').[17] The chapter also discusses an idea that is central to Ibn 'Arabi's philosophy, which is of the Divine 'love' to create all creation, in order to be known. He explains that the impulse of movement is always love. Thus the passage of the world from a state of non-manifestation (a state in which it is pure possibility) to one of manifestation is the essential Divine movement of love. He illustrates this by quoting the *hadith qudsi* (divine saying): 'I was a hidden treasure and I loved to be known; so I created the world and human beings in order that I might be known'. Without this divine Love the world would not have been created. So therefore the divine creative movement of non-manifestation into manifestation is of God's love manifesting itself in creation and humanity as its/His mirror.[18]

William Chittick further remarks on this subject explaining that God 'gives to his creatures the best he has, and that is *wujûd*, his own reality. The creature is by definition a lover, for the entity loves the Beautiful who discloses himself to it through the effusion of light. God's mercy, then, is directed at his lovers, who are all the creatures of the universe'.[19] In Ibn 'Arabi's words:

> He has mercy only on the ardour of the lover, which is a delicate yearning for the encounter with the Beloved. No one encounters the Beloved save with His attribute, and His attribute is *wujûd*. Hence He bestows *wujûd* upon the lover. Had there been anything more perfect than that with Him, He would not have been stingy with it..., for God reported that He is 'the Forgiving, the Loving,' which is to say that in His unseen reality He is fixed in love, for He sees us, so He sees His beloved. Hence He delights in His Beloved.[20]

Transcendence and Immanence

According to Ibn 'Arabi, the proposition that God is immanent in all creation does not mean that He possesses hands or hearing or sight, but that He is immanent in all that has hands, hears and sees. His Essence is not limited to one being or a particular group of beings but to *all* manifested beings. God is therefore regarded as transcendent in this sense,

---

17. Al-Khâdir is the traditional Arabic name for the mysterious divinely inspired sage who is alluded to in relation to Moses in the Sura of the Cave (where he is not named).
18. *WP*, pp. 104–5.
19. Chittick, *Ibn 'Arabi*, p. 45.
20. *Futûhât* IV, 260.6 in Chittick, *Ibn 'Arabi*, p. 45.

because He is above all individualisation and limitation; He is the Essence of all that is. Therefore from this perspective, transcendence and immanence are two aspects of the one Reality: 'the "*Haqq*" of whom transcendence is asserted is ultimately the same as the "*khalq*" of whom immanence is asserted, although the Creator is distinguished from the created'.[21]

This theme is stressed in the chapter on Noah in the 'Wisdom of the Prophets', of which only the first part has been translated from the Arabic. Ibn 'Arabi explains:

> If thou dost affirm the Divine transcendence, thou dost condition (the conception of God) and if thou dost affirm His immanence, thou dost limit Him: but if thou dost affirm simultaneously the one and the other point of view thou wilt be exempt from error and be a model of knowledge.[22]

The Divine Names

According to Ibn 'Arabi, the 'Names' of God are the cause of the manifest universe, which he regards as 'lines of force'.[23] Being Names of the Godhead, they necessarily demand their 'logical correlatives' which must be expressed by outward manifestation in the external world.[24] Through their manifestation the (divine) knower becomes known; thus Ibn 'Arabi describes them as instrumental causes or tools by which God performs His creative actions in the cosmos. Although the Names possess a hierarchical order, everything created ultimately owes its existence to the divine Names which act as prototypes for its being. This therefore repeats what Ibn 'Arabi says about the external world being the manifestation of those attributes with which God is scripturally described. 'God was whilst the world was not and He was named by all the divine Names'.[25]

Chittick adds that Ibn 'Arabi insists that names make remembrance possible and that this holds true for God as well as humanity. God knows things through their names, which are nothing but their traces in his own omniscience, traces known as 'entities': 'Were it not for the names, God would remember nothing, and nothing would remember God. So, God remembers only through the names, He is remembered and praised only through the names'.[26]

21. *The Twenty-Nine Pages*, pp. 4-5.
22. *WP*, p. 34.
23. *The Twenty-Nine Pages*, p. 8.
24. Ibid.
25. Ibid.
26. *Futûhât* II, 489.26 in Chittick, *Ibn 'Arabi*, p. 62.

The A'yân Thâbita

Affifi proposes that Ibn 'Arabi was the first to use the technical physical term *a'yân thâbita*, which can be interpreted as 'fixed entities', or 'fixed prototypes', 'latent realities of things' or 'established potentialities'. This concept was a prominent and notoriously problematic position in Ibn 'Arabi's metaphysical scheme.[27] According to Ibn 'Arabi, before becoming manifest, all things in the phenomenal world are in a state of ontological potentiality in the Divine Essence of God, as ideas related to His future 'becoming'. These *a'yân* are the content of His eternal Knowledge, which is identical with His Knowledge of Himself. Therefore God reveals Himself to Himself in a primordial state of Self-consciousness (not in a point of passing time), in what Ibn 'Arabi calls God's 'first epiphany' or 'first particularisation', in which God sees in Himself the infinity of these *a'yân* which are the primordial particularised forms of His own Essence.[28] These *a'yân thâbita* could therefore be described as the 'latent particulars' in the Mind and the Essence of God.

Chittick offers further comprehensive interpretation:

> The entities are 'fixed' because, despite their non-existence in themselves, they are eternally known to God. They are 'things' even before God brings them into existence. On the basis of his knowledge of them, he creates them and they become manifest as 'existent entities' (*a'yan mawjuda*). However, their existence is not their own, because *wujûd* belongs to God. There is only one *wujûd*, and that is the *wujûd* of God... the *wujûd* that is identical with God. As Ibn 'Arabi remarks 'The fixed entities have never smelt a wiff of *wujûd*', and they will never smell it, because they are non-existent by definition.[29]

Chittick explains that in our empirical world, the things that we experience and perceive are called 'existent entities'. He warns that the name is deceptive because the sustenance that is implied by it does not belong to these entities and that in themselves they are identical to non-existent fixed entities. He concludes 'Whether we call them "fixed" or "existent", it is not they that smell the wiff of *wujûd*. Rather, Real *wujûd* itself is the hearing through which they hear and the eyesight through which they see'.[30]

---

27. *The Twenty-Nine Pages*, p. 11.
28. Ibid.
29. Chittick, *Ibn 'Arabi*, pp. 40-41, and *Futûhât* 76 in Chittick, *Ibn 'Arabi*, p. 41.
30. Chittick, *Ibn 'Arabi*, p. 41.

Self-Revelation of the One (*tajalliyât*)
Here Rauf has highlighted Ibn 'Arabi's central dynamic concept of God's self-revelation using Affifi's quotes from Ibn 'Arabi's work such as: 'Glory be to God who created things, being Himself their Essences'.[31] 'He alone is proof of His own existence which is manifested in the *a'yân* (particulars) of contingent beings'.[32] 'There is nothing but God, nothing in existence other than He. There is not even a "there" where the essence of all things is one'.[33] 'From whom does thou flee and there is nought in existence but He'.[34] 'My eye sees nought but His face (Essence) and my ear hears no other than His speech'.[35] Thus Ibn 'Arabi denies that mystics somehow 'become one' with God, interpreting such experiences as the individual realisation of the fundamental reality that all existents are *already* one with God (*al-Haqq*).

DOCTRINE OF THE LOGOS

The Reality of Realities
Ibn 'Arabi's approach to the Islamic equivalent of the doctrine of the Stoic 'Logos' or Christian divine 'Word', may be understood from several different perspectives. For example, from a metaphysical stance it is called the 'First Intellect', whilst in relation to the cosmos may be understood to be the 'Reality of Realities'. From the practical spiritual angle it is called 'The Perfect Man' (*al-insân al-kâmil*),[36] and is regarded as the active principle in all divine and esoteric knowledge. In Ibn 'Arabi's doctrine, it could be described as the consciousness of God, since it includes the substance and content of divine Knowledge.[37] 'In it the knower, the known and the knowledge are one, and through it the universe is brought into manifestation'.[38]

---

31. *The Twenty-Nine Pages*, p. 14.
32. Ibid., p. 15.
33. Ibid.
34. Ibid.
35. Ibid.
36. Or 'fully human being': the term *insân*, following Quranic usage, refers to the theomorphic spiritual reality (logos) fully realised by the prophets and saints, always as contrasted with *bashar*, the mortal, terrestrial human animal and its qualities. In the *Fusûs* (and throughout Ibn 'Arabi's work) *insân* is also identified with the primordial 'Reality of Muhammad'.
37. Ibn 'Arabi also refers to the Logos as the Supreme Isthmus, Non-delimited Imagination, the Reality of the Perfect Man and the Breath of the All-merciful.
38. *The Twenty-Nine Pages*, p. 16.

The Perfect Man (*al-insân al-kâmil*)

Ibn 'Arabi's teaching concerning the 'Perfect Man' is, along with his philosophy of the Unity of Existence, of central *practical* importance to the intention of the Beshara School. In *The Twenty-Nine Pages* Ibn 'Arabi's treatment of the First Intellect (logos) is usefully summarised as follows:
1. As the Reality of Realities: the metaphysical aspect.
2. As the 'Reality of Muhammad': the mystical aspect.
3. As the Perfect Man.

Although this Universal Reason is immanent in everything and could be understood to constitute the divine consciousness, and although it is identified with the Reality of Realities and the Reality of Muhammad, it is not equally present in all things. However, all things, even inanimate objects, do manifest this hidden logos to a degree, but it is manifested in humanity to such an extent that human beings are potentially the 'vice-regent' of God (*khalîfa*), the image of God (*sûra*), the microcosm (*al-kawn al-jâmi'*) or the 'mirror' which reflects the attributes of God and God Himself.

According to Ibn 'Arabi, 'No-one knows the dignity of Man (*insân*) and his place in the universe except those who know how to contemplate God perfectly'.[39] The fully 'human' (*insân*) is the only creature who has the potential to know God fully, and it is through the 'human' (*insân*) that God knows Himself, because the 'human' is the manifest consciousness of God. Even archangels only know God partially—i.e. as a transcendent Reality which is not related to the phenomenal world—but human beings know God as both *Haqq* (the Real) and *khalq* (the phenomenal). It is the heart of the Perfect Human that is the focus of manifestation of the universal Intelligence, and it is here that that principle is fully expressed. Although every human is a microcosm, they are only potentially so. The Perfect Human manifests *all* God's attributes and perfections (i.e., God's divine Names), since without full realisation of one's unity with God, those manifestations are incomplete. Therefore, according to Ibn 'Arabi it is only the prophets and saints who become perfectly human, since it is only in their awareness that this realisation is fully attained.

Ibn 'Arabi refers to the Perfect Human as an intermediary (*barzakh*) in that such a person unites and manifests both the attributes of God and the universe, the divine and the creature perfectly. He says: 'He is to God

---

39. Ibid., p. 18.

what the eye-pupil is to the (physical) eye...and through him God beholds His creatures and has mercy upon them, i.e. creates them'.[40]

The chapter of the *Fusûs* which deals most rigorously with this concept is the opening chapter on Adam entitled 'The Wisdom of Divinity in the Word of Adam'.[41] As the title suggests, the central focus here is the relationship between God and human beings symbolised by Adam, who represents the archetype of the divinely inspired, fully human being (*insân*).[42] Ibn 'Arabi begins by explaining that God or Reality (*al-Haqq*), in his Essence as the Absolute Being, wanted to see the essences (*a'yân*) of His most Beautiful or Perfect Names, or rather that God wanted to see His own Essence in one particular inclusive object, i.e. something which by its existence encompassed the Divine Order, so that He could manifest to Himself His own mystery.[43] Because seeing a thing itself by itself, is not equal to seeing itself in another, which acts as a mirror to it.

Austin explains, in his commentary to the opening chapter of the *Fusûs*, that in the mirror are two elements, these being the mirror itself and the observing subject who sees the image of himself as an object.[44] Adam is the factor which links the mirror and the observing subject, representing both the mirror and the observer. The observing *subject* is God and the 'mirror', the Perfect Man, is the symbol of the reflective receptivity of the cosmos.[45] Ibn 'Arabi describes Adam as becoming the 'light itself of the mirror and the spirit of this form'. The mirror of the heart does, though, need to remain highly polished, or the reflection will become distorted and imperfect. Austin suggests that in the mirror we have an apt symbol of the Divine/cosmic polarity.[46] Adam as the archetype of humanity becomes the medium through which God observes His own image in all creation. As such, Adam/Man is a microcosm, containing within him all that manifests in the macrocosm, yet to perfectly reflect God he has to polish the mirror of himself by working toward perfection.

40. Ibid.
41. And the closing chapter on Muhammad.
42. For readers unfamiliar with the Quranic (and wider Islamic) image of Adam, he is portrayed there as a divinely inspired, fully theomorphic human being, and considered, therefore, the first divine prophet. Adam's image there contains none of the particular theological implications of human fallibility, 'original sin' etc. typically associated with the figure of Adam in Christian theological and cultural settings.
43. *WP*, p. 8.
44. *Bezels of Wisdom*, p. 48.
45. Ibid.
46. Ibid.

Epistemology

Sainthood

According to Ibn 'Arabi (and the larger Islamic spiritual tradition), the Quranic expression often translated as 'sainthood' (*walâya*) does not mean simply holiness or piety, although these attributes could constitute some of the characteristics of a saint (*walî*).[47] The main attribute of a saint is spiritual gnosis (*ma'rifa*); or in other words, a saint is a Perfect Human, one truly 'close to God' (the root meaning of *walî Allah*). That term is applicable to a wide spectrum of human spiritual exemplars, particularly divine messengers, prophets and the larger body of the 'hidden saints'. The common element which unites all the 'saints' (*awliyâ'*), is thus their realisation of the logos as the 'Muhammadan Spirit'.[48] This Reality is the real, eternal 'vice-regent' of God and is forever manifesting itself in the forms of prophets and saints, each of whom may therefore be considered a kind of *khalîfa*.

In the *Fusûs* Ibn 'Arabi's approach to sainthood is explored in the chapter on Seth, 'The Wisdom of Expiration in the Word of Seth'. Here he discusses the idea of gnosis or knowledge of the self and of Divine Reality in relation to the saint (*walî*), prophetic messenger (*rasûl*) and apostle (*nabî*). Although this gnosis is fully realised in the above categories, it is potential in all humanity. This chapter also introduces the idea of the 'Seal of Saints' (Jesus) and the 'Seal of Muhammadan Sainthood' (who Ibn 'Arabi implies is himself), meaning that the Seal of Muhammadan Sainthood completes the line of 'Muhammadan' influence and prophecy, which is to be understood as the spirit or light of Muhammad, which is equivalent to the whole principle of prophecy.

Knowledge

This chapter of *The Twenty-Nine Pages* concerns Ibn 'Arabi's approach to spiritual knowing and its attainment in various forms. Ibn 'Arabi proposes that knowledge is usually obtained through six faculties, which are the five senses and the intellect; he describes these as being numerically different but essentially one. He also describes another faculty through which to attain spiritual knowledge, which he calls 'intuition'.

---

47. See Chapter 1 for detailed discussion on various interpretations of the word *walî*.

48. *The Twenty-Nine Pages*, in keeping with its concise philosophic expression and concomitant avoidance of Ibn 'Arabi's elaborate religious language and expression, does not discuss the logos in its aspect as the Muhammadan Reality in any detail.

To him, this is the most important faculty of all. It is through this intuitive knowledge that humanity acquires immediate perception of the Truth itself and the realities as they are, in contrast to the very partial, probable or conjectural knowledge acquired by the normal intellect.

As Ibn 'Arabi explains to Fakhr ad-Din Razi, the famous theologian and commentator of the Quran, an intelligent and wise person seeks only knowledge that will assist him in perfecting his soul and in the 'homesteads of the underworld' i.e., the stages of becoming after death where this knowledge will accompany him. He says:

> Hence the intelligent person should not partake of any knowledge save that which is touched by imperative need. He should struggle to acquire what is transferred along with him when he is transferred. This is none other than two knowledges specifically—knowledge of God, and knowledge of the homesteads of the afterworld and what is required by its stations, so that he walk may there as he walks in his own home and not deny anything whatsoever.[49]

As Chittick points out, according to Ibn 'Arabi true knowledge attaches itself to its 'essence' (*dhat*) which is its fixed entity, or its reality as known to God. Knowledge has a divine root and God knows everything. 'To say that God has knowledge means that real *Wujûd* has permanent consciousness of its own reality; it is aware of itself and everything demanded by its absoluteness and infinity'.[50]

The Heart
In accordance with other Sufis, Ibn 'Arabi metaphorically describes the 'heart' (*qalb*, another key Quranic expression) as the focus for transmission or revelation of esoteric knowledge. This is not the physical heart. The 'heart', though, is used as a symbol for the logos aspect of the human, or the Spirit. He compares it to an inward eye, its object of perception being Reality itself. The distractions of the lower animal (*basharic*) soul and the temptations of the material world normally blind this inward 'eye'. But once it has been freed from those veils, the heart may fully perceive and communicate with the Real. Reality, which is continually manifesting itself in an infinity of forms, is most fully reflected in the heart of the true gnostic. By this Ibn 'Arabi explains what is meant by the saying of al-Bastâmî, that 'God is contained in the heart of the gnostic'.[51]

---

49. Chittick, *Ibn 'Arabi*, p. 73.
50. Chittick, *Ibn 'Arabi*, p. 70.
51. *The Twenty-Nine Pages*, p. 27.

In discussing the Sufi practices of retreat (*khalwa*), which involves seclusion from the world in order devote oneself to meditation, prayer and remembrance (*zikr*), i.e., continuous repetition of the divine Names, Ibn 'Arabi advises:

> When the aspiring traveller clings to retreat and the remembrance of God's name. when he empties his heart of reflective thoughts, and when he sits in poverty at the door of his Lord with nothing, then God will bestow upon him and give him something of knowledge of Him, the divine mysteries, and the lordly sciences.[52]

This passage illustrates that it is the heart that must be emptied of reflective thoughts, because in the Quran and other Islamic sources, it is the heart, not the head, that is the centre of consciousness, intelligence and awareness. This contrasts other cultures whereby the heart is symbolically the centre of the emotions and the head the consciousness and intelligence.

MYSTICAL AND METAPHYSICAL PSYCHOLOGY

The Soul

Chittick explains that translators of Greek texts into Arabic rendered *psyche* as *nafs*, which is usually the equivalent of 'self' or 'soul' in English. *Nafs* functions as the reflexive pronoun in Arabic, unlike *psyche* in Greek but like *self* in English. Therefore, it can be applied to absolutely anything—God himself. In the Quran, however, it is used frequently with the definite article but with no reference to a noun. On these occasions, it is utilized to designate the human self as a generic term, and translators typically render it as 'the soul'.[53]

According to Ibn 'Arabi, human beings are made up of three different elements; the body, the soul and the spirit. The body is material in form and extended in time and space; it is mutable and perishable. The soul (*nafs*) he defines as the vital principle, the mortal animal life in the human organism. The spirit (*rûh*) is the rational principle; its purpose is to seek true knowledge, and it is a mode of the universal intellect.[54] Ibn 'Arabi defines three distinct aspects of the soul, which are the vegetative, the animal and the rational; he relates the vegetative and animal specifically with the body. The rational is not identified with the intellect or the body, although the intellect is one of its subordinate powers. At death

---

52. *Futûhât* 131.4 in Chittick, *Ibn 'Arabi*, p. 15.
53. Chittick, *Ibn 'Arabi*, p. 101.
54. *The Twenty-Nine Pages*, p. 27.

there is no destruction of the human spirit, but only dissolution of the physical form. Ibn 'Arabi asserts that all forms are but 'passing shadows', with a Reality behind them that constitutes their very being. The same is so of the human being whose reality ultimately returns to God.[55]

William Chittick makes the interesting observation that from a certain perspective, the soul is Ibn 'Arabi's only topic:

> He frequently tells us that we can only know what we are. All human knowledge is simply the articulation of human awareness and consciousness. Everything we know is our self, because awareness and knowledge are situated inside the self, not outside it. What we know is the image of what lies outside, not the thing itself. All outside things are themselves images cast into the mirror of nothingness. Things have no permanence or substantiality, despite the power of the divine imagination to display them as integral parts of an entrancing dream.[56]

Khayâl (Divine 'Imagination')

Ibn 'Arabi uses this term to refer to an intermediary between two ontological stages: for example, as the intermediary stage between Absolute divine Essence and the phenomenal, creative world. Other examples of *khayâl* are symbols, because they are the intermediate between the spiritual and the visible world. Dreams are another example of being a state between the Real and the phenomenal world; and mirror images, for similar reasons, could also be classified as *khayâl*.

It is necessary to divide Ibn 'Arabi's interpretation of the word into two categories, the first being psychological, referring to mental images which have no existence away from the mind. This category includes dreams, illusions and images from ordinary waking life. Ibn 'Arabi's second category is the metaphysical or ontological *khayâl*: for not all images are wholly psychological or mind-dependent, having no being in themselves. Many images, he believes, come from the 'Essential Presence' (*al-hadara al-dhâtiyya*) and are ready to receive 'meanings' (*ma'ânî*) and 'spirits' (*arwâh*).[57] In this way higher spiritual Reality can be communicated to the human spirit.

Ibn 'Arabi regards these images as more elevated than forms in the phenomenal world. Such images often appear in dreams, where they usually occur as symbolic forms, the imagination supplying the symbols. For example, when Mohammed saw milk in a dream he saw a symbol, this symbol being the vehicle for divine Knowledge. According to Ibn

---

55. Ibid., p. 28.
56. Chittick, *Ibn 'Arabi*, p. 108.
57. *The Twenty-Nine Pages*, p. 30.

'Arabi there are also purely spiritual dreams that need no interpretation; they are revelations of the Real and are reflected directly in the heart without the imagination needing to supply symbols.[58]

In the *Fusûs*, these ideas are discussed in the chapter entitled 'The Wisdom of Light in the Word of Joseph'. Here Ibn 'Arabi approaches imagination and humanity in a twofold way in that humanity, as the microcosmic image of the macrocosm, experiences the divine imagination in part as its own imaginative faculty and also as part of God's imaginative process. He proposes that the whole creative process can be understood as God's imagination in a type of divine 'dreaming':

> Now as Reality is such as we have affirmed, know that thou art imagination and that all thou perceivest and that thou dost designate as 'other than me', is imagination; for all existence is imagination in imagination; whereas the veritable Being is God alone...[59]

In the chapter on Moses, Ibn 'Arabi reaffirms that the form of Adam is:

> ...none other than the Divine Presence itself, so that God manifests in this noble 'resumé' which is the Perfect Man [or Universal Man; *al-insân al-kâmil*] all the Divine Names and the Essential Realities of everything that exists outside of Him, in the Macrocosm, in a detailed manner.[60]

The chapter which discusses *khayâl* in *The Twenty-Nine Pages* concludes with a rendering of Ibn 'Arabi's concept of *'himma'*, the creative power of the intention of the saints/mystical 'knowers' whereby they are able to affect the material and psychic worlds. According to Ibn 'Arabi, the true spiritual 'knower' does not make personal use of this power, both because he realises that he is a servant of God and therefore leaves creation to Him; and also because he understands the Unity of Being, in that the Creator and what is created is already one.

MYSTICISM

Fanâ' and *Baqâ'*

The English translation of the Arabic word *Fanâ'* is 'annihilation' or passing away (in God); the contrasting Quranic term *Baqâ'* means 'subsistence' or remaining (in God).

---

58. Indeed, Ibn 'Arabi's main focus in most of his writings on *khayâl* (including the famous chapter on Joseph in the *Fusûs*) is that all of creation/manifestation being ultimately *khayâl*. From this perception, everything that exists is 'revelation' (or the divine 'book', in the language of the Quran).

59. Ibid., p. 65.

60. *WP*, p. 99.

According to Ibn 'Arabi, a mystic does not, in his moments of ecstasy, experience some special 'unity' with God, because all creatures are already one with God. Instead he typically understands *fanâ'* and *baqâ'* in one of two different ways. First, *fanâ'*, in the mystical sense, means the 'passing away' of ignorance, whilst *baqâ'* is the subsistence (remaining) of the inspired spiritual knowledge intuitively gained. His second, metaphysical interpretation of *fanâ'* is in reference to the 'passing away' of the soul's awareness of material forms, whilst *baqâ'* is the eternal continuation of the one universal Essence.

Fanâ' is a progressive process, according to Ibn 'Arabi, during which the mystic passes through various stages realising through intuition (*dhawq*) his real place in relation to God. He does not necessarily have to go through them all. Some of the stages are listed in *The Twenty-Nine Pages* as follows:

- The passing away from all actions whatever. In this stage the mystic realises that God alone is the absolute and only agent in the universe. The real agent is God Himself.
- Passing away from one's own personality (*dhat*), by which he means that the mystic realises in such a state the non-existence of his phenomenal 'self' and the subsistence (*baqâ*) of the unchangeable, imperishable substance which is Essence.
- Passing away from the whole world, i.e., the cessation of contemplating the phenomenal aspect of the world, and the realisation of the real aspect which underlies the phenomena.
- Passing away from all that is 'other than God', even from the very act of passing away. One of the conditions of this stage is that the mystic must cease to be conscious of himself as a contemplator. It is God Himself that contemplates and is contemplated. He is seen in every one of His infinite 'states' (*shu'un*) i.e., manifestations.
- The passing away from all the attributes of God and their 'relations', i.e., the contemplation of God as the Essence of the universe rather than the 'cause' of it, as the philosophers say. The mystic then does not regard the universe as an effect of a cause, but as 'Reality in Appearance' (*haqq fi zuhûr*). He realises the meaninglessness of causality and such divine Names as the Creator, the Designer, the Giver and so on. This stage is the ultimate goal and is what Ibn 'Arabi calls the absolute transcendence of the unity.[61]

---

61. *The Twenty-Nine Pages*, pp. 34-35.

Religion, Ethics and Aesthetics

Beliefs and Real 'Knowing'

According to Ibn 'Arabi, all 'paths' lead to one 'Straight Path' (the Quranic expression), which leads to God. This is universal and is the path of the essential Unity. For example, he does not reject outward polytheism, provided that the worshippers of images and idols realise that there is one Reality behind these forms.

There are three ways in which people relate to God:
1. The way of the common followers of the prophets.
2. The way of the rationalist philosophers and theologians.
3. The way of the spiritual 'knower' (*ârif*).[62]

The believer 'simply' believes and follows the received external forms of the teachings of his prophet. The followers of 'rationality' (theologians and philosophers) form their beliefs based on their limited personal reason. But the spiritual knower knows through direct perception or intuitional 'tasting' of the Truth of Reality.

Each type develops its own characteristic, unavoidable perception of God and 'each will, when the Truth is revealed in the next world, recognise the object of his beliefs (i.e. his God) in the infinite Being who will then appear in all the forms of belief'.[63] Thus only the 'knowers' are aware of and fully comprehend the one Reality underlying the endless possibilities of individual beliefs.

According to Ibn 'Arabi, an awareness of immanence alone leads to polytheism, which he strongly denounces. But he also denounces the purely 'rational' belief in transcendence alone, as this leads to a dualism of spirit and matter, or creator and creation. What concerns Ibn 'Arabi is that one universal Religion (*al-Dîn*) includes all human beliefs. The enlightened 'knower's' immediate awareness of *Dîn*, in this view, necessarily includes *all* religions and beliefs. He sums up his all-encompassing religious philosophy in the words: 'People have formed different beliefs about God, and I behold all that they believe'.

To Ibn 'Arabi, divine Love is the basis of all worship, and the only true worship is love of God. It is love, which is the creative principle pervading all divine manifestation. Although the divine appears in the multiplicity of forms, it is One universal Reality. Indeed it is the knowable aspect of the divine Essence itself. Love therefore is the highest

---

62. Ibid. p. 35.
63. Ibid.

form in which God is worshipped, and he says: 'I swear by the Reality of Love that Love is the cause of all Love; were it not for Love (residing) in the heart, Love (God) would not be worshipped'.[64]

Good and Evil
Ibn 'Arabi understands evil as not an intrinsically existent quality. 'Pure evil is the equivalent to non-being and to pure darkness whereas pure good, is pure being and pure light'.[65] To his mind, following the Quranic indications, the difference between Light and darkness is one of existence and non-existence. He believes that nothing real is evil, because God does not create evil. According to his doctrine, 'evil', be it ethical or otherwise, is relative, and things or actions can thus be labelled as evil under the following conditions:
1. Because one religion or other regards them as such;
2. Relative to a certain ethical principle or customary standard approved by the community;
3. Because they are incongruous with some individual temperament;
4. Because they fail to satisfy some natural, moral or intellectual desires of an individual; and so on.[66]

It is explained in *The Twenty-Nine Pages* that Ibn 'Arabi teaches that beyond those conditions described above and other similar standards by which good or evil may be measured, there is nothing but the pure essence of things (*a'yan al-muwjûddât*) which is not possible to describe in terms of good or evil.

Added to Ibn 'Arabi's categories of evil include such states as sin, infidelity, disharmony, disorder, falsehood, ignorance and uneven temper. All these conditions involve a lack of something, a positive quality, that if added to the apparent actions or things that we call evil would convert them to good. To Ibn 'Arabi, nothing is evil, all is good.[67]

Love and Beauty
The final chapter of *The Twenty-Nine Pages* concerns love and beauty, particularly three aspects of love, as Ibn 'Arabi understands them. These aspects are natural love, spiritual love and divine Love, the first two being species or subsets of the third. Divine Love is essential love of the One.

64. Ibid., p. 36.
65. Ibid.
66. Ibid., p. 37.
67. Ibid.

Before any form of modalisation, the One, in His supreme isolation and simplicity, loved Himself for and in Himself, and loved to be known and to be manifested. This was the cause of creation. In loving Himself, the One loved all the *a'yân* of things latent in His Essence, and hence they are impregnated with love they now manifest in different ways. 'The love of the *a'yân* began', Ibn 'Arabi says, 'when they were still in the Blindness (*amâ*), when they first heard God's creative word (Be)'.[68]

Spiritual love is mystical love, its aim being the realisation of the essential oneness (unity) of the lover and beloved.

> Ibn 'Arabi says that the ultimate goal of love is to know the reality of love and that the reality of love is identical to God's Essence. Love is not an abstract quality superadded to the Essence. It is not a relation between a lover and an object loved. This is the true love of the Gnostics, who know no particular object of love. It is the profane that loves forms. Nothing is loved except God, just as nothing is worshipped except Him.[69]

Natural love is physical, elemental love. Ibn 'Arabi classes within this category physical, psychological and mechanical attractions, the objective here being self-satisfaction, regardless of the object loved. However, he understands this form of love to be a manifestation of the divine Love in its crudest and lowest form. Ibn 'Arabi says of divine Love:

> Love is the working principle in all manifestations of the One, from the highest to the lowest. It reaches its zenith in Man, the Perfect Man, who above all creation experiences all the three kinds of Love. Through Love, the Whole is bound together and through it the object of creation is realised. Thus the whole system is perfectly complete.[70]

Servantship and Lordship

Ibn 'Arabi's concepts concerning servantship and service of God (*'ibâda*) contribute a further vital thread to the teaching on offer at the Beshara School. Participants on the courses, particularly the six-month courses, are encouraged to approach all their actions as acts of service. The intention of the service is directly to God and God's Order in the cosmos, but also indirectly to God through acts of service to other people and in ordinary work. As understood by Ibn 'Arabi and the adherents of Beshara, any act of service is in reality offered to God or to God as the Reality both above (transcendent) and within (immanent) everything in existence. Although *The Twenty-Nine Pages* does not engage directly with this theme, the chapter in the *Fusûs* which focuses particularly on

---

68. Ibid., p. 39.
69. Ibid., pp. 39-40.
70. Ibid., p. 40.

the idea of servantship and Lordship is the chapter entitled 'The Wisdom of Sublimity in the Word of Ismaël'. Here Ibn 'Arabi's discussion concerns the relationship between Lord and servant, or the individual created thing and its Lord. Its 'Lord' (*rabb*) is a particular aspect of God that creates a thing according to its essential reality in God and therefore also determines its destiny. Ibn 'Arabi explains:

> Know that He who is called Allah is One in the Essence and all by His names and that all conditioned being is only attached (as such) to God by his own Lord (*rabb*) exclusively; for it is impossible that the totality (of the Names or the Divine Aspects) correspond to a particular being.[71]

The idea of 'lordship' (*rubûbiyya*) derives from the divine Names in that each divine Name could be understood to be a 'lord' (*rabb*). This relationship of lordship is assigned from God in respect to His Names, not His Unity. Ibn 'Arabi explains that because of this, humanity cannot receive the revelation of God in His Unity, because if a person contemplates Him (God) through Himself, it is He who contemplates Himself; but if a person contemplates Him (God) through himself (a human), 'unity ceases to be unity'.[72] Because of this a polarity is implied, but it is important to note that this polarity is a *relationship* between a Name of God and its manifest servant and does not assume a duality in the divine Essence, which is One in Itself.

Ismaël was distinguished from other ordinary individuals because it was said of him that he was 'pleasing to his Lord'. It is necessary to become pleasing to One's Lord in order to return to Him.[73] By becoming a good and faithful servant, a human begins the process of 'returning to his Lord'.

THE FIGURE OF JESUS AND THE 'SEAL OF SAINTHOOD'[74]

The figure of Jesus holds a central position in eschatology in Sunni Islamic belief, and in a more specific way, in the metaphysics of Ibn 'Arabi.[75] The figure of Jesus is also of prime importance to

71. *WP*, p. 57.
72. Ibid.
73. Ibid., p. 58.
74. I have focused particularly on the figure of Jesus here and not placed so much emphasis on investigation of the other prophets mentioned in the *Fusûs* because of the particular importance Jesus had in Ibn 'Arabi's own mystical development and also to the students of the Beshara School.
75. See M. Chodkiewicz, *The Seal of the Saints: Prophethood and Sainthood in the Doctrine of Ibn 'Arabi* (Cambridge: Islamic Texts Society, 1993), Chapter 5, pp. 75-83, and Chapters 8 and 9, pp. 116-41.

Beshara.⁷⁶ The Arabic word *beshâra* and its cognates in other Semitic languages means 'Good News' or the 'annunciation of good news'. For some adherents of the Beshara School it is also concerned with the preparation of the ground and the heralding of the eschatological 'Second Coming'.⁷⁷ This idea ties in with the theme of millenarianism and the expectation of a new universal spirituality.⁷⁸

In the 1970s, a useful paper was produced for the Beshara School by one of its early participants which explains the meaning of the 'return' of Jesus in Islamic understanding, and in relation to Ibn 'Arabi as the 'Seal of Muhammadan Sainthood'.⁷⁹ In brief, Ibn 'Arabi's understanding of himself as the Seal of Muhammadan Sainthood meant that he was the saint most fully manifesting that divine Essence which is the 'Muhammadan Spirit'. In the present, humanity is between this Seal and the Seal of Universal Sainthood, who will become manifest in the person of Jesus in his second coming.

According to some current senior co-ordinators of the Beshara School,⁸⁰ they believe Christ will come as a person and not as an abstract idea, energy, realisation or impulse, such as a new form of spirituality or religion. Humanity is, according to this point of view, situated between the two Seals and building on what was brought by the Seal of Muhammadan Sainthood (Ibn 'Arabi), and expanding out the awareness of Reality so that it is recognised at a universal level and not limited to

---

76. As above in the section on 'Servantship and Lordship', the figure of Jesus is not engaged with in *The Twenty-Nine Pages* but is in the *Fusûs* and other literature.

77. The advent of a saviour or Messiah is common to most of the major world religions. In Islam itself there are no explicit prophecies in the Quran about his advent but there are numerous statements about the advent of the Mahdi and the return of Jesus in the *Hadith* of the Prophet Muhammad. In the Islamic Shi'i tradition the Mahdi is the twelfth Shi'i Imam, who went into hiding in 874 CE and whose life has been miraculously prolonged by God until the time when he will reappear. A common thread running through these various expectations is that the saviour will make his or her appearance when affairs of the world have reached their lowest point and the saviour's arrival will be preceded by miraculous signs and portents. Their manifestation will bring with it a golden age of justice, peace, rehabilitation of the world, revival of religion and an establishment, from the perspective of the theistic religions, of God's rule on earth.

78. Thus the theme of the Ibn 'Arabi Symposium held at Chisholme in August 2000 was entitled *The Spirit of the Millennium*, and several of the papers presented there touched on ideas connected with Christ and eschatology.

79. The paper, entitled 'Christ', was written by R. Hornsby for Beshara in the 1970s. For a fuller account of Ibn 'Arabi's own ideas, see Chodkiewicz, *Seal of the Saints*.

80. Interviews with E., August 1999, and R., December 1999.

some particular individuals. Whatever the second coming is, it will have a global impact. That person will not be another 'legislating' messenger, but will be a universal saint, universally recognised as such.

Indeed at least one key figure in Beshara today has openly stated that this is a major concern of the school: 'it is a platform of knowledge for the preparation of the Second Coming of Christ'.[81] In a paper presented at the Ibn 'Arabi Symposium at Chisholme in August 2000, the Principal of the school further explained this concept in relation to Adam as the universal archetype of humanity.

> This event, known as the Second Coming of Christ, is the completion of the potential for Mankind which was embodied in Adam as the tree is contained in the seed, and is the appearance here as the Seal of Universal Sainthood. It is we then, the present human population, who were and still are contained in the Adamic soul, who now contain the tree that is yet to emerge, containing as we do the completion of Man as an unborn child in the womb. It is we who are the container of the Uncontainable, the unlimited spirit of Man.[82]

It is worth noting that the spiritual figure of Jesus played a significant role in Ibn 'Arabi's early spiritual development. Ibn 'Arabi met Jesus in many visions, along with many other personal teachers, among the most important being Muhammad and Moses. Jesus was Ibn 'Arabi's first teacher, and Ibn 'Arabi says of him:

> I have had many meetings with him in visions and at his hands I turned (to God). He prayed for me that I might be established in the religious life (*dîn*), both in this world and in the hereafter, and he called me beloved (*habîb*). He ordered me to practice renunciation (*zuhd*) and detachment (*tajrîd*).[83]

It was whilst experiencing a vision in 1199 CE, in which he participated in an encounter with all the prophets, that Ibn 'Arabi received details of the role of Jesus as Seal of Muhammadan Sainthood. He says in the *Futûhât*:[84]

> One of the (men of God) is the Seal, and there is only one, not (simply) in each age but in the sense of there only being one in the whole world. By him God seals the Muhammadan Sainthood and there is none greater than

---

81. E., August 1999.

82. Peter Young, 'United by Oneness: Global Considerations for the Present', paper presented at the Ibn 'Arabi Symposium, Chisholme, August 2000.

83. *Futûhât* XI, p. 49 and vol. 12, p. 123, quoted in S. Hirtenstein, *The Unlimited Mercifier: The Spiritual Life and Thought of Ibn 'Arabi* (Oxford: Anqa, 1999), p. 53.

84. *Futûhât* XI, pp. 9, 290, quoted in Hirtenstein, *The Unlimited Mercifier*, p. 131.

he among the Muhammadan saints. Then there is another seal by whom God will seal the universal sainthood, which runs from Adam to the last saint, and that is Jesus the Seal of the Saints, sealing the cycle of the Kingdom.

In the chapter in the *Fusûs* entitled *From the Wisdom of the Prophecy in the Word of Jesus*, reference is made to the Second Coming in the opening lines:

> The Spirit (*ar-rûh*: that is to say Christ) was manifested by the water of Mary and the Breath of Gabriel, in the form of a man made of clay. In the purified body of (corruptible) nature that he calls 'prison'—(*sijjîn*) so that he is staying there more than 1000 years.[85]

Titus Burckhardt's footnote on this passage in the *Wisdom of the Prophets* explains:

> That is to say the time passed since the ascension of Christ until the moment when this book was written; he will remain there until his 'Second Coming' at the end of the cycle.[86]

IBN 'ARABI AND THE FEMININE DIMENSION IN THE DIVINE

The concept of the feminine in divinity holds particular significance for the Beshara School because of Ibn 'Arabi's attitude in this regard which has been noted by many interpreters in the past.[87] Ralph Austin has explored this aspect of Ibn 'Arabi's approach in depth. In an article in the *Journal of the Muhyiddin Ibn 'Arabi Society* he presents some useful arguments.[88] He approaches his proposition from three angles, first suggesting that to understand the real character of Ibn 'Arabi's mystical vision as being a whole and universal one, the feminine dimension in his thought cannot be ignored. Second he proposes that Ibn 'Arabi's own spiritual experience was much enriched by his perception of the feminine dimension. Third he addresses Ibn 'Arabi's approach in relation to the significance and function of the feminine in all spheres of the contemporary world.

---

85. *WP*, p. 68.
86. Ibid.
87. As in the previous two sections involving Servantship and Jesus, Ibn 'Arabi's concepts of the feminine in the divine are not discussed in *The Twenty-Nine Pages*, but in the *Fusûs* and other literature used by the Beshara School.
88. R.W.J. Austin, 'The Feminine Dimensions in Ibn 'Arabi's Thought', *JMIAS* II (1984), pp. 5-14.

Regarding the first angle, Austin suggests that the key to Ibn 'Arabi's view of the feminine dimension in Reality is to be found in the chapter in the *Fusûs* entitled 'From the Wisdom of the Singularity in the Word of Mohammad'. He points out that in the middle of the chapter Ibn 'Arabi sets forth an interesting proposition concerning the famous saying of the Prophet: 'Three things of this world have been made beloved to me, women, perfume and prayer'. Ibn 'Arabi shows that the Prophet, by using the form *thalath*, gave precedence to the feminine gender. He also pointed out that 'perfume', which is a masculine term, comes between two feminine terms, i.e., 'women and prayer' in the same way that a man is between the divine Essence (feminine) from which he came and the human woman who comes from him. Austin suggests:

> that this microcosmic triad is indeed a reflection of a greater, namely one in which Allah, the creating God, the first and supreme Name, is between His own secret Essence which, from its eternal treasury of latency, provides Him with contents of His knowledge of Himself as creation and the created Cosmos, and the world which comes from Him; or between His own latent wisdom, Sophia, and the Universal Nature which is the theatre of His infinite self-manifestation and elaboration. Thus both micro-cosmically and *in divinis*, man in the first and the worshipped God in the second, look upon two objects both regarded as symbolically feminine, the one inner and essential, a hidden secret mystery, the treasure of being, the other outward, apparently other and multiple...[89]

Austin suggests that even more astonishing is the implication by Ibn 'Arabi that the great creative force of the Breath of the Merciful could be conceived as feminine. Ibn 'Arabi says of this:

> The prophet mentioned women in the first place, because they represent the passive principle and Universal Nature (which is the universal plastic principle) precedes whatever manifests itself, from it by (action of) the 'form'. But, Universal Nature is none other, in Reality, than the Breath of Mercy (*an-nafas ar-rahmani*) in which are employed the forms of the world, from the highest to the lowest by infusion of the Divine Breath in the 'materia prima' (*al-jawhar al-hayulani*)...[90]

Austin's second angle of exploration of the feminine in Ibn 'Arabi's thought involves particularly Ibn 'Arabi's collection of poems *Tarjuman al Ashwaq* (The Interpreter of Desires) in which he builds especially on Henri Corbin's insights.[91] In these poems, Ibn 'Arabi writes in praise of

---

89. Ibid., p. 7.
90. *WP*, p. 122.
91. Henri Corbin, 'Sophiology and Devotio Sympathetica', in *Creative Imagination in the Sufism of Ibn 'Arabi* (Princeton: Princeton University Press, 1969), Chapter 2; now reprinted as *Alone with the Alone* (1998).

the beauty and grace of a young woman, Nizam, the daughter of a friend of his. It is through her loveliness that he seems to witness God's perfection. Austin says of this:

> Here all his threads of the feminine dimension of Reality come together in a wonderfully synthetic image in which a powerful sensuousness mingles with a rare wisdom, and in which all the combined attraction of the earthly and essential feminine fuses... In a deliberate conjoining of classical Arab love themes and metaphysical insights...the master brings us as close as possible...to an appreciation of the living experience of the aspiring Gnostic in all his anguish and bewilderment in the face of the infinite mystery of Reality as the object of perception and awareness.[92]

In his third approach to Ibn 'Arabi and the feminine dimension in the divine, Austin proposes that Ibn 'Arabi would probably not have been very interested in the contemporary phenomena of feminine resurgence and reassertion because he is not concerned with the 'personal and individual female, but with a trans-personal archetype albeit reflected in the instance of his meeting with Nizam, in a particular human woman, that is to say, he is interested and effected by her only in so far as her person is a medium of supra-human realities'.[93]

This summary of Ibn 'Arabi's key metaphysical concepts illustrate the fundamental themes that have been emphasised beginning with the earliest courses of the Beshara School. It is also intended to provide a helpful reference point for discussing related themes, subjects and emphases of different students of Ibn 'Arabi throughout the later chapters.

OTHER TEXTS USED ON BESHARA COURSES

Other central texts that have come to be used for study on the Beshara courses include the following, almost all of which were either written by Ibn 'Arabi or by Sufi authors who were later aligned with his spiritual influence. They expand, elaborate or offer a supplemental perspective to themes already expounded in his best-known work, the *Fusûs al-Hikam*.

The *White Fusûs*
This is the name—referring to the white binding of the four volume English translation—by which Beshara students usually refer to Bulent Rauf's English version of the influential Turkish translation and

---

92. At the time that he wrote these poems, Ibn 'Arabi was fiercely criticised for producing what his critics took to be erotic poetry. Austin, 'The Feminine Dimensions', p. 13.

93. Ibid.

commentary on Ibn 'Arabi's *Fusûs al-Hikam* traditionally attributed to Ismail Hakki Bursevi.[94] Following Bulent Rauf's translation of this version of the *Fusûs* (which he started translating in 1980 and which was first printed in 1987), it became of primary importance to the Beshara School. R. Brass, who assisted Rauf with the translation, explained some of the reasons for its special role:[95]

> Although there have been many commentaries of the *Fusûs al-Hikam*, this one of Ismail Hakki Bursevi is of special importance and significance. First, he is a great saint, and in order for a commentary on the *Fusûs* to properly draw out and magnify the meanings intended by the Shaykh, in order for it to truthfully explain the knowledges and mysteries and realities and indications and allusions, sainthood and perfect servanthood is without a doubt the necessary pre-requisite. But the point to be made here particularly is the following: Bursevi was a Jelveti Shaykh who lived from 1652–1728, and the Jelvetis emerged in the 16th century from the Helveti Order through the great Shaykh Mahmud Muhyiddin Uftade instructing his principle disciple, Aziz Mahmud Hudayi Effendi, in the manner which was to become that of the Jelveti Order, and Hudayi became the first Shaykh of that order. Ibn 'Arabi did not found a tariqa as such, but the Jelveti manner reflected most closely his teaching. The Helvetis are disposed towards retreat (*khalwah*) and seclusion with the Beloved through retirement from this world, but the taste of the Jelveti is at the same time for the return to this world after Union, the coming out of that seclusion adorned with the Divine characteristics which is regarded as progress, as an added gift (the bridal present—(*jilwah*)), the superlative perfection of expression, and this manner very clearly signifies that which is central to 'Arabi's teaching and the Mohammedian Way. It is therefore most appropriate and not at all surprising that a Jelveti Shaykh should have written the definitive commentary.

In the *Journal of the Muhyiddin Ibn 'Arabi Society*, vol. VII, a review of the second volume of this version of the *Fusûs* goes to explain further its importance and significance to those involved with Beshara. The reviewer, a long-time Beshara participant, focuses on Ibn 'Arabi as a

---

94. Ibn 'Arabi, *Fusûs al-Hikam* (rendered into English by Bulent Rauf with the help of R. Brass and H. Tollemache, from the 1832 Boulaq Edition of a manuscript written in Turkish and Arabic c. 1700; 4 vols.; Oxford: Muhyiddin Ibn 'Arabi Society, 1986–91).

95. From a paper given by Rabbiya Brass on the new translation of the *Fusûs al-Hikam* presented at an Annual General Meeting of the Muhyiddin Ibn 'Arabi Society, 1985. For discussion on the Helveti and Jelveti Orders, see Chapter 1 on Bulent Rauf.

'Meaning' in relation to Bursevi and Bulent Rauf. He begins by quoting a passage from the foreword of the first volume written by Rauf.[96]
He then explains:

> The emphasis on and subservience to Meaning is the dominant strand which links the original through Bursevi's commentary, to Bulent Rauf's translation into English. Both Bulent Rauf and Bursevi remain true to this principle, that in as much as there is any interpretation it is according to the Meaning of Ibn 'Arabi...[97]

The reviewer further explains that rather than use 'standard English', Bulent Rauf 'uses the elasticity of the language with a thesaurus of subtle meanings, to communicate to the full, the "That" which is not ordinarily accessible in English'. He continues by suggesting that depending on the attunement of the reader, the book can have an 'exhilarating or a disturbing effect', acting as a mirror to the soul. He concludes by suggesting that when the meaning becomes 'transparent', the reader may begin to understand why the book is so important and why its translation into English is so important to our era.[98]

Kernel of the Kernel

This book, including the commentary by Ismail Hakki Bursevi, is one of the shortest and most essential works of Ibn 'Arabi.[99] It describes 'what a human needs to know to realise their completion'. It is presented as a dialogue with a person who is ready to examine the depths of their own being, i.e. 'the kernel of the kernel', which is one's own essence. As Rauf describes it, 'he is likened to a fruit which must search its own kernel for the cause and possibility of its ripening'.[100] In this work the stages of this progress are clarified. However, it is explicitly intended as not just a

---

96. The reviewer was Peter Yiangou, an original participant of Beshara: '...For Muhyiddin Ibn 'Arabi is not only a man of Wisdom, the greatest Shaykh, Doctor Maximus, but a Meaning...' A definition of the word 'Meaning' in this context could refer to a 'spiritual reality'. For an extended quote and a discussion of the Beshara School's understanding of Ibn 'Arabi as a 'Meaning', see Chapter 5 below.

97. P. Yiangou, review of *Fusûs al-Hikam*, *JMIAS* VII (1988), pp. 85-86.

98. Ibid.

99. Ibn 'Arabi, *Kernel of the Kernel* (trans. into Turkish with a commentary by Ismail Hakki Bursevi and into English by Bulent Rauf; Gloucestershire: Beshara, 1979).

100. From an article by Bulent Rauf, 'Concerning the *Kernel of the Kernel*', *Beshara Newsletter* (Summer 1981), p. 1. An *'ârif* is one who in Sufi tradition has reached, through a series of steps, *ma'arifa* (divine Knowledge), whence he is known as the *'ârif* (the 'knower').

work for anyone, but for the 'knower' (*'ârif*) who is searching for the structure of his own kernel. The beginning of the first chapter illustrates perfectly the essential premise of Ibn 'Arabi's metaphysics of the Unity of Existence, where it is explained:

> One of the special matters that Ibn 'Arabi wants to explain in his *Futûhât al-Makkiyah* is this: 'If a gnostic (*'ârif*) is really a gnostic he cannot stay tied to one form of belief.'
> That is to say that a possessor of knowledge is cognisant of the being in his own ipseity,[101] in all its meanings, he will not remain trapped in one belief. He is like materia prima (*hayûla*) and will accept whatever form he is presented with. These forms being external, there is no change to the kernel in his interior universe.
> The knower of God (*'ârif bi'llâh*), whatever his origin is, remains like that. He accepts all kinds of beliefs, but does not remain tied to any figurative belief. Whatever his place is in the Divine Knowledge, which is essential knowledge, he remains in that place; knowing the kernel of all belief he sees the interior and not the exterior. He recognises the thing, whose kernel he knows, whatever apparel it puts on, and in this matter his circle is large. Without looking at whatever clothing they appear in under the exterior he reaches into the origin of those beliefs and witnesses them from every possible place.[102]

Sufis of Andalusia

This important translation of Ibn 'Arabi's *Rûh al-quds and al-Durrat al-fâkhirah* by R.W.J. Austin[103] is primarily a collection of biographical sketches of some of the spiritual masters and hidden saints from all walks of life who Ibn 'Arabi had personally known in his early years. These sketches come from two works of Ibn 'Arabi, the first and most important being the *Spirit of Holiness in the Counselling of the Soul*,[104] composed after Ibn 'Arabi's migration to the Eastern Islamic world. Like the *Futûhât*, it is addressed in the form of an epistle to Ibn 'Arabi's friend Abû Muhammad 'Abd al-'Azîz b. Abû Bakr al-Qurayshî al-Mahdawî who lived in Tunis. The work is in three sections, the first beginning with the author's complaints about the degeneration of Sufism at the time.[105] The second section concerns the lives of fifty-five

---

101. The essence of Being.
102. *Kernel of the Kernel*, p. 1.
103. This edition published by Allen & Unwin, 1971. A later edition has also been made available by Beshara Publications, 1988.
104. *Rûh al-quds fî munâsahat al-nafs*.
105. Not translated by Austin, but now available in translation by Roger Boase and Farid Sahnoun as 'Excerpts from the Epistle on the Spirit of Holiness (*Risâlah*

spiritually influential individuals whom Ibn 'Arabi had met and been taught by during his early years in Spain and North Africa. This second section compensates for the first, showing that in spite of the deficiencies in the contemporary state of Sufism, there were still some who have reached a high level of spiritual attainment. The third section deals with difficulties encountered on the Sufi path, and here in places Ibn 'Arabi uses some of his own experiences as illustrations.

The second work of Ibn 'Arabi included in this book is *The Precious Pearl concerned with the Mention of those from whom I have derived Benefit in the Way of the Hereafter*.[106] This is a synopsis of a work that Ibn 'Arabi left in Spain or North Africa when he travelled East. Much of the material in it is similar or identical to that which is in the *Spirit of Holiness*, and the translator explains that this is why he only translated portions of it which do not already appear in the *Spirit of Holiness*.[107]

The whole book is relevant to Beshara students because it provides a useful biography of Ibn 'Arabi at the beginning (the longest English biography available until recently), and particularly because it illustrates the qualities of true Sufis and saints according to the 'greatest sheikh' (*al-Shaykh al-Akbar*). In Austin's biographical overview, there is a quote from Ibn 'Arabi's greatest work the *Meccan Revelations*, concerning his wife Maryam who shared his aspirations to follow the Sufi Way. In this quote, 'five things' are mentioned,—these 'five things' are of such central importance to Beshara students on the six-month intensive course that they are told about them at the very beginning of their work:

> My saintly wife, Maryam bint Muhammad b. 'Abdun, said, 'I have seen in my sleep someone whom I have never seen in the flesh, but who appears to me in my moments of ecstasy. He asked me whether I was aspiring to the Way, to which I replied that I was, but that I did not know by what means to arrive at it. He then told me that I would come to it through five things, trust, certainty, patience, resolution and veracity'. Thus she offered her vision to me (for my consideration) and I told her that that was indeed the method of the folk.[108]

Rûh al-Quds)', in *Muhyiddin Ibn 'Arabi: A Commemorative Volume* (ed. S. Hirtenstein and M. Tiernan; Shaftesbury: Element Books, 1993), pp. 44-72.
    106.   *al-Durrat al-fâkhirah fî dhikr man intafa'tu bihi fî tarîq al-âkhirah.*
    107.   *Sufis of Andalusia*, pp. 17-19.
    108.   In ibid, pp. 22-23. The word 'folk' refers specifically to those on the Sufi Path.

Whoso Knoweth Himself[109]

Although this book was the earliest translated work (in 1901) attributed to Ibn 'Arabi in both English and French, it is actually the work of a later thirteenth-century Persian Sufi teacher, al-Balyânî.[110] One of the chief emphases of the Beshara School highlighted in this work is that through coming to know oneself, an individual gets to know God, because in all reality there is nothing in existence other than God. Balyânî's book illustrates this teaching comprehensively and was studied early on in some courses.[111]

The book begins by emphasising the Oneness of God, then underlines the theme with such phrases as:

> There does not see Him, save Himself; nor perceive Him, save Himself. By Himself He sees Himself, and by Himself He knows Himself... His Prophet is He, and His ending is He, and His word is He. There is no difference between the sender and the thing sent, and the person sent and the person to whom he is sent...There is no other, and there is no existence to other, than He... And for this the Prophet (upon whom be peace) said: 'Whoso Knoweth himself Knoweth his Lord'. And he said (upon him be peace): 'I know my Lord by my Lord'. The Prophet (upon whom be peace) points out that, that thou art not thou: thou art He, without thou, not He entering into thee, not thou entering into Him, nor He proceeding forth from thee, nor thou proceeding forth from Him.[112]

Although it does not take too much effort for spiritually or religiously inclined people to intellectualise or verbalise the idea that we all as humanity and as a part of creation contain a 'divine spark', 'God within' or such like, it is radically different to actually realise and internalise the concepts cited above. The process of gradually developing this deeper

---

109. *Whoso Knoweth Himself* (trans. T.H. Weir; repr. Gloucestershire: Beshara, 1976).

110. See Michel Chodkiewicz's French translation and important study *Awhad al-dîn Balyânî, Épître sur L'unicité Absolue* (Paris: Les Deux Océans, 1982); J. Morris, 'Ibn 'Arabi and his Interpreters. Part II. 'Influences and Interpretations', *Journal of the American Oriental Society* 106, no. 4 (1986), pp. 736-41; and Morris, ''Theophany or "Pantheism?": The Importance of Balyânî's Risâlat al-Ahadîya; and Jâmî's Description of Abû 'Abdallâh Balyânî', in 'La Walâya,étude sur le soufisme de l'école d'ibn 'Arabî', *Horizons Maghrébins* 30 (1995), pp. 43-54.

111. During the nine-day course in which I participated in 1998, this book was studied on the first day.

112. *Whoso Knoweth Himself*, pp. 3-5. The work has now been newly translated from the Arabic into more accessible modern English especially for the courses. See online: http://www.beshara.org/essentials/text_whoso.html.

'realisation' can sometimes involve unsettling emotional and psychological reactions in students as they begin to assimilate Ibn 'Arabi's ideas.[113]

The Universal Man[114]

'Abd al-Karîm Ibn Ibrâhîm al-Jîlî, who was born in 1366/767 at Jîl near Baghdad, is one of those who continued the line of the metaphysical teaching of Ibn 'Arabi. In Burckhardt's Introduction to this book, the translator mentions that Jîlî's approach is more systematic than Ibn Arabi's, that Jîlî provides a more 'dialectical architecture' which is advantageous to students unfamiliar with Sufism.[115] This is particularly apparent in the way in which he presents the degrees of manifestation of Being and Its Self-revelation. As pointed out by an early adherent of Beshara, these metaphysical principles go far beyond the merely theoretical, in that when he describes the realisation of these same degrees in humans, Jîlî says:

> I will mention of all that only that which happened to me on my own journey to God; moreover, I recount nothing in this book, neither of myself nor of another, without my having tested it at the time when I travelled in God by the path of intuition and direct vision.

Burckhardt's Introduction also provides a useful definition as to the meaning of the 'Universal Man' (*al-insân al-kâmil*, literally, the 'Completed Human Being') to Sufism in general and Jîlî in particular. It explains that Universal Man is not really distinct from God; it is like the 'Face of God' in all creation, it is the inherent Unity of all creatures. As one of Burckhardt's footnotes suggests, this concept can be compared to the Christian (and Quranic) concept of the divine 'Word' (logos). When the spirit within a human unites with the Universal Man, it unites with God. Thus a spiritually realised human or 'Perfect Man' manifests to the full all the divine Names and qualities, becoming a 'synthesis of all the essential realities (*haqâ'iq*) of existence', and the microcosmic or earthly human form of the Universal Man. For Muslims this eternal Reality is usually identified with the Prophet Muhammad, and as Jîlî says:

---

113. See Chapter 6 below.
114. 'Abd al-Karim al-Jîlî, extracts translated with commentary by Titus Burckhardt, English translation by Angela Culme-Seymour (Bulent Rauf's wife and translator of Burckhardt's version of the *Fusûs al-Hikam*), being the first version available in English.
115. Burckhardt, 'Introduction', in *Universal Man* (Eng. trans. Angela Culme-Seymore; Gloucestershire: Beshara, 1985), p. 1.

Universal Man is the pole around which revolve the spheres of existence, from the first to the last; he is unique as long as existence lasts... However, he puts on different forms and is revealed by different cults, so that he receives multiple names.[116]

Mystical Astrology According to Ibn 'Arabi[117]

This book is not so central to the study on the Beshara courses, but it is studied to some extent on the first six-month course. In the foreword to the English version, Keith Critchlow[118] explains that in this translation Titus Burckhardt has distilled the essential symbolism underlying spiritual astrology—in contradistinction to divinatory astrology. He quotes Burckhardt as saying '...for the individual curiosity, all "oracle" remains equivocal and may even reinforce error...' as '...man cannot remove the veil of his ignorance except by or through something which transcends his individual will'. Critchlow suggests that in order to understand astrology in the traditional sense by which Ibn 'Arabi presents it here, we in the West need to make an effort of reorientation away from the Aristotelianism, under the influence of which we have been since the middle ages (through such theologians as Thomas Aquinas), and embrace the concept of the tradition of Plato known as *perichorêsis*, the permeation of the divine presence in the material world.[119] Critchlow explains that Ibn 'Arabi was later termed 'Son of Plato' (Ibn Aflâtûn), because of the viewpoint within Islamic revelation that 'asserts the dependence of the sensible world on the intelligible world, and the intelligible world in return on the ontological principle of Unity'. The result therefore of studying this book could lead to a deeper appreciation of the significance of astrology in the traditional sense and to an understanding of what it means for a human to 'seize their favourable moment'.[120]

---

116. Burckhardt's footnote (p. xx) explains that this Reality is therefore Muhammad for the Muslims, Christ for the Christians, every Avatara for the Hindus, Buddha for the Buddhists. 'In this last case, the idea of Universal Man absorbs all qualities positively ascribable to God, the Essence as such being expressed only by negations'.

117. Titus Burckhardt, *Mystical Astrology According to Ibn 'Arabi* (trans. Bulent Rauf; Gloucestershire: Beshara, 1977).

118. Critchlow is an expert in sacred architecture and founder of the school of 'Visual Islamic and Traditional Arts' (VITA), who has been associated with the Beshara School since its emergence.

119. Ibid., pp. 6-7.

120. As Critchlow suggests (p. 5), this favourable moment relates to the idea of a 'timeless present' and can be likened to a 'glance outside time'. The concept of timelessness is a frequent subject for discussion on the Beshara courses, but is too complex a subject to discuss here.

Rûmî—Mathnâwî

Jâlluddîn Rûmî was born in Balkh (in present Uzbekistan) in 1207. His most famous work is his immense didactic collection of spiritual epic poetry known as the *Mathnâwî*.[121] Rûmî's connection to Ibn 'Arabi was through Ibn 'Arabi's stepson and spiritual heir, Sadruddîn al-Qûnawî, some of whose lectures Rûmî attended prior to his decisive spiritual encounter with Shams-i Tabrîz.[122] Although the outward form of literary expression differs characteristically between Ibn 'Arabi and Rûmî, there is also a strong spiritual connection between the two. Henry Corbin points out that:

> The same theophanic sentiment, the same nostalgia for beauty and the same revelation of love inspire both. Both tend toward the same absorption of the visible and the invisible, the physical and the spiritual.[123]

Rumî has often been known throughout the Ottoman realm as the 'Pole of Love' and Ibn 'Arabi as the 'Pole of Knowledge', but ultimately there cannot be true spiritual love without knowledge, or knowledge without love, in the place of absolute unity in the essence of the Real.

Addresses by Bulent Rauf[124]

Following Bulent Rauf's death in 1987, the Beshara Trust published extracts of his work *Addresses* in the *Beshara Magazine*.[125] This work includes eleven addresses originally written for students of the Beshara School, together with the paper 'Union and Ibn 'Arabi'. The following quote, opening the first selection, illustrates the emphasis of his guiding purpose, which was to assist the students to arrive at a realisation of their essential Unity with the one Absolute Existence. One of the first steps towards this aim is to bring their egos into a state of humility, i.e., the 'effacing of the ego', a central teaching of Ibn 'Arabi:

> The purpose of all your study is to bring you to a realisation of your 'essential' oneness with the One and Only Absolute Existence. Here remember that the word 'essential' mainly means 'in your essence' as

---

121. The version used by the Beshara School is: Extracts from *The Mathnawî of Jâlâl 'uddin Rûmî, Books I–VI* (London: E.J.W. Gibb Memorial Trust, 1926, 1930, 1934; latest repr. 1982).

122. See Chapter 7 for more references to Rûmî, his relationship to Shams-i Tabrîz, his sainthood, the Mevlevi Dervishes and the Sema.

123. Henry Corbin, *Creative Imagination in the Sufism of Ibn 'Arabi* (London: Routledge & Kegan Paul 1969), pp. 70-71.

124. Bulent Rauf, *Addresses* (Gloucestershire: Beshara, 1987). A sequel to this book has now been published as *Addresses II* (Gloucestershire: Beshara, 2001).

125. *Beshara Magazine* 4 (Winter 1987/88), pp. 20-21.

well as your origin and your reality. The realisation of 'your essential oneness' can only be consequent to the complete humility of your ego to accept this knowledge and make it its own belief; because this knowledge is not the mere acceptance of a 'concept' or 'theory' etc. which may be received by an instrument of the ego to tolerate, or even to consider this theory or concept or what you will, and still continue unaffected in its (the ego's) separate illusory self-existence as something apart from the basic reality of your 'essential oneness'.

As we can see when you make this reality your realisation, you implicitly admit the non-existence of a relationship of the ego to the One, or through the One, or with the One, or in the One, or together with the One, etc. except that this ego is no longer the ego you have known up until now, but the extension of the ego of the One in a single determination, which is differentiation and which is His individuation as you.[126]

Other concepts focused on in this collection include, for example, discussions ranging from the nature of '*fanâ and baqâ*'—'passing away and remaining'—to what is meant by perfect servanthood and the necessity of total dependence on God.[127]

In 2001, Beshara Publications produced the sequel to the above work, *Addresses II*. This book includes, in addition to spiritual and metaphysical discussions particularly related to Ibn 'Arabi's mystical conceptions, a chapter on Turkish cuisine and a biographical account by Rauf on the highlights of his childhood, as well as an account of a sixteenth-century 'Sufi' Indian emperor, 'Abdul Fattâh Jalâludîn Muhammed Akbar. This is a useful book for students of Beshara who wish to obtain a deeper insight into Rauf's way of thinking, his approach to the principle of the Unity of Existence and the type of person that he was.

Writings of Other Spiritual Traditions

As explained in an earlier Beshara promotional pamphlet,[128] the courses of study begin with the works of Ibn 'Arabi because of the way in which he explains with 'exceptional clarity, the principles of Being and the place of Man, taking as his starting point not the present condition of ordinary man, but the conclusion of Union or Realisation expounding everything from that point of view...' When the students have understood the view from the top downwards,[129] they go on to study a selection of

---

126. Ibid.
127. For details, see the section on *The Twenty-Nine Pages* above.
128. Promotional pamphlet from the late 1980s or early 1990s, author anonymous.
129. See the analogy of the pyramid in this chapter above, section on *The Twenty-Nine Pages*.

works of other traditions, such as the *Tao Te Ching*,[130] the *Baghavad Gita*[131] and Christian writings, such as certain apocryphal gospels or the works of Meister Eckhardt. Which aspects and writings from other traditions they actually study vary slightly from course to course, and this usually takes place through texts and lectures presented by staff members or visiting speakers. For instance, a highly esteemed regular speaker and friend of the Beshara School was the Benedictine monk Dom Sylvester Houedard OSB.[132] In the words of the Principal of the school:

> It seemed sometimes as if his knowledge of the field of Tibetan Buddhism was equal to his familiarity with Meister Eckhart and the whole Christian contemplative tradition and he was equally at home with the works of Ibn 'Arabi...[133]

His series of lectures were published as *Commentaries on Meister Eckhart's Sermons*, which was published by Beshara Publications and often used as study text on the courses.

If no aspects of Buddhism are formally studied at the school, this is because only twenty miles away from Chisholme is the Tibetan Buddhist temple and monastery/retreat centre of Samye Ling, to which Beshara students are at times taken to learn something of the mystical aspects of that tradition.

CONCLUSION

This chapter has discussed the principal texts used by the Beshara School and has summarised Ibn 'Arabi's key metaphysical concepts as articulated within these texts. As mentioned in the introductory pages, the possibility of distortions or inaccuracies to the meanings of Ibn 'Arabi's teachings found in certain texts in which double translations have taken

---

130. Gia-fu Feng, *Tao Te Ching* (trans. Jane English; Hampshire: Wildwood House, 1973).

131. *Baghavad Gita* (trans. Juan Mascaro; Harmondsworth: Penguin, 1962).

132. Born in 1925 in Guernsey and having graduated from Oxford University, he became a monk of the Benedictine Order in 1951. He was ordained in 1960. He lived for most of his life at Prinknash Abbey in Gloucestershire, where he died and was buried in 1992. In addition to being a poet, he was a member of the Committee for Dialogue with other Monastic Traditions. He was appointed to welcome the Tibetan Buddhist teachers, Trungpa and Akong Rinpoche, when they first arrived in England from India.

133. Extract from an article by Peter Young, 'Dom Sylvester Houédard O.S.B., Drawninward', *Beshara website*, www.beshara.org (magazine section, accessed 2002, no longer accessible).

place could arguably be problematical. However, as may be perceived in the chapter, the meaning of Ibn 'Arabi's teachings as presented by the school appears to be as clear (or as enigmatic) as any metaphysical concepts from any spiritual tradition are likely to be and it is ultimately down to the intellectual and intuitional capacity of the individual students to realise the meaning of the esoteric content of the texts for themselves. This was so in Ibn 'Arabi's lifetime as it is today.

5

RECENT BESHARA EDUCATION: THE COURSES AND THEIR AIMS

THE MEANINGS OF 'BESHARA' AS UNDERSTOOD BY SOME PARTICIPANTS

This chapter reflects on what Beshara means to those involved with the school and in the light of this discussion then focuses on the courses and their aims. It includes a range of written, interview and participant observer sources whose collection was described and contextualised in the Introduction above.

> The word Beshara means 'Good News' in Arabic, and is from a Semitic root found in the Old Testament Hebrew, and the Aramaic of the Christian Gospels as well as the Arabic of the Koran.[1] The word is reputed to have been used by the angel Gabriel to Mary mother of Jesus when he announced the coming of Christ, in that Beshara was his first word; 'Good News, a son is to be given'.[2]

Students of the Beshara School exhibit a complex and multifaceted understanding of what exactly Beshara means to them. In different interviews, the present Principal of the school at Chisholme has suggested some important interpretations:

> We who are involved with Beshara are still very much finding out what Beshara means because it isn't something that any of us have invented. It refers to a Reality, which is archetypal, and our role in this is to serve it. It's good news in that it is the perennial announcement from our interior,

---

1. From the Beshara brochure (2000), back page.
2. From an interview with the present Principal of the school, Peter Young, published in the *Beshara Magazine* 8 (1989), pp. 26-31 (26). Although this interview was not conducted very recently, it is still used as a standard outline of the aims, intentions and objectives of the courses at Chisholme and is now available in brochure form separate from the magazine. The interviewer was Angela Holroyd, a writer and editor who was at the time of the interview considering becoming a student at Chisholme.

from our essence, of its essential oneness to ourselves which is its exterior and if you think about it, this is the good news which perhaps frees us from ourselves if we are receptive to it.[3]

In another interview the Principal reiterated that he does not fully understand what Beshara is, but he does quote a recent definition that describes it as 'the opening from the Unseen (Unknowable) of the unlimited potentiality of Man to recognise and reflect the unlimited beauty of the One'.[4] There is still, though, an element of 'not-knowing' which is quite intentional because through the study participated in at the School the conclusion may be reached that Beshara is not something invented or brought into being by people. He described it as being a 'name for a movement from the One Reality to the individual man', and because it comes from the Divine side, a human understanding of exactly what it is could only be partial.[5] He suggested that what is happening now through Beshara is not new. 'Ever since there has been man capable of knowing himself, there has been an emergence of what might be called "the perennial tradition" which has been known to a few'. And this 'perennial tradition' has through the ages, emerged in such figures as, for example, Socrates and Lao-Tzu. What is new about Beshara, he explained, is that it is available to anyone from any tradition; the knowledge is accessible to all people. Furthermore, no previous knowledge is necessary for those taking the courses, only the incentive to learn.[6]

In his most recent interview, the Principal expanded upon the organisation's understanding of Beshara, bringing fresh insights to the general interpretation.[7] He explained that Beshara is a *new impulse*, a new divine inspiration, and the impact for those who are involved or aware of it could be compared to the birth of a baby. It occurs as a gradual change in the (collective) consciousness, in much the same way that Christianity took hold at its beginnings. It is from Reality (or God), like a revelation, but it is also something new. It is something that we know about in the depths of our being, but that we have forgotten at a conscious level. '*We are God manifesting Himself, and we can remember*'. The Principal then suggested that this interest, far from deriving from the seekers

---

3. From an unpublished interview with the Principal conducted by Cecilia Twinch, an early participant of Beshara, in the mid-1980s. This interview was actually intended for the *Beshara Magazine*.
4. From the Beshara brochure (2000), p. 1.
5. Interview with the Principal published in the *Beshara Magazine* 8 (1989), p. 26.
6. Ibid., p. 26.
7. Personal interview with the Principal at Chisholme, August 1999.

themselves, is actually coming from God or Reality. God is the impulse for a search for a new spirituality: He is influencing people to feel the need to seek a new expression. He explained that this impulse is what, deep within our consciousness, we want most, and that is 'Unity with God'. He qualifies his argument by conceding that the initial ideas of the 1960s lacked direction in that 'people saw an opportunity but the ideas became dissipated'. Another way of being was tasted, but the people involved had not learned to 'ride the wave' and most of the energy released was squandered. But there was enough to 'launch the ship that was Beshara'.[8] He further suggested that the universal realisation of the Unity in Diversity could become the 'hallmark of the age'. In answer to a question as to how to articulate these ineffable ideas, he replied that it is possible to express what is happening through the works of Ibn 'Arabi, and this is why the school uses them.

To highlight further the school's understanding of Beshara, the Principal provided an illustration from the words of Rûmî: 'Never does the lover seek without being sought by the Beloved', a point Rûmî illuminates with the analogy of straw (human beings) being invisibly attracted to amber (the Divine).

BESHARA AS A GLOBAL MANIFESTATION

As the Principal pointed out in our most recent interview, the school's operating assumption is that God is revealing Himself in an unprecedented way, manifested globally and as one Reality, which appears differently in every section of humanity, for example in every science. He suggested that the increase of the human population and advanced communications highlight unavoidably that there is a single Reality wherever one turns.[9] He proposed that there are models of this phenomenon occurring everywhere. For example, the Internet could be interpreted as an expression of Universal Unity. In the last ten years there has been a change of global landscape in areas such as communications, technology, and global economy (rather than independent economies), each economy being inextricably related to others. He cited Bulent Rauf's argument that the Beshara School's education is the best for promoting an experience, understanding and realisation of the principle of *tawhîd* or 'Unity with Reality'. What is needed, though, is a new vernacular, not just words but a new mind-set based on the principle of Unity-and-diversity, diversity being an intrinsic expression of Unity. Rauf had suggested that this

8. Interview with the Principal, August 1999.
9. Interview with the Principal, August 1999.

vernacular would find expression in such fields as science, physics and economics. It is therefore necessary to be aware of what is happening in those areas. The primary emphasis, though, is that there will be a 'whole, new different way of being'.[10]

In response to a question concerning the school's hopes for the outcome of a more widespread diffusion of the realisation of the knowledge of the Unity of Being, the Principal replied:

> Because we do not know the future, this is a difficult question to answer. We hope though that there will be recognition of who and what we are in our dealings with each other. Limits and boundaries would only exist in appearance; internally we would be united to the Real as though we had never left. There would be recognition of the Universal Reality of Love, that Love being identical with the movement of The Being. This is connected with the Second Coming of Christ. We, i.e. present humanity, are between the Seal of Muhammadan Sainthood who is Ibn 'Arabi and the Seal of Universal Sainthood who is Jesus in his Second Coming. Humanity is between the two. What was brought by the Seal of Muhammadan Sainthood is being expanded into universal flow and effect, so that it is recognised universally throughout mankind.[11]

He then went on to explain that whatever the 'Second Coming of Christ' is, it will have a global impact and will be in the form of a human being rather than an abstract 'energy' or realisation. 'He/she will not be another prophet, but will be a universal saint. And he/she will be recognised because he was not recognised last time. He/she *will* come, although perhaps not for several generations'.[12] The Principal again emphasised that this is what the school is about—it is 'for the preparation of a platform of knowledge for the Second Coming of Christ'.[13]

10. Interview with the Principal, August 1999.
11. Interview with the Principal, August 1999.
12. Interview with the Principal, August 1999. See Chapter 4 for more details on this subject.
13. Interview with the Principal, August 1999. Three decades ago, early participants of Beshara used a further analogy to try to explain what they understood Beshara to be: 'Beshara is likened to a bomb explosion. It incorporates the bomb thrower, the bombed and the whole of the extent of their mutual distance or space. The best historical and spiritual example of it was the annunciation made to Mary. The spirit blew into Mary the word of God—Jesus. The episode was known as Beshara—not only the act of blowing, nor the act of reception, nor only the gestation of Jesus in Mary, nor the announcement alone is Beshara. Beshara is the whole episode inclusive of all that happened with the coming of Christ. For us the word Beshara came by "accident" because the requisite was to find a name for the then "new" idea upon which we were to embark. What came out was the word Beshara!— And quite "accidentally" it fit the purpose of what was to happen: to prepare,

IBN 'ARABI AND THE 'SEAL OF SAINTHOOD' AS A 'MEANING' (SPIRITUAL REALITY)

In relation to what was just mentioned in the above section regarding Ibn 'Arabi's famous role as the 'Seal of Muhammadan Sainthood', Beshara's particular conception of Ibn 'Arabi as a living spiritual reality or 'meaning'[14] must be taken into account.

The suggestion that Ibn 'Arabi could be understood as a 'meaning' himself was explained by Bulent Rauf in the Foreword to what is known in Beshara circles as the *White Fusûs*.[15] Since this four-volume work was produced and published in the late 1980s, this concept has become more widespread in these circles. In the book's foreword, Rauf concludes his first paragraph by suggesting that '...Muhyiddin Ibn 'Arabi is not only a man of wisdom, the greatest Shaykh, Doctor Maximus, but a Meaning'. Further on he continues:

> An Iraqi friend of mine once said that it was easier to understand the Quran than Ibn 'Arabi. All this is because Ibn 'Arabi is a meaning to understand which one must have a receptivity of the heart pre-ordained where meaning will filter in until the receptacle is so attuned to this meaning that it will lay itself open and ready to receive the full impact of the weight the meaning represents. This condition is not obtainable either be it by resolve, application or fortitude. It is a gift, directly given by the giver of all gifts for whatever reason, He alone knows why.[16]

But what did this really mean to Rauf, and to the contemporary participants of Beshara? A passage in Stephen Hirtenstein's recent publication provides a possible interpretation or contribution to what it

---

through people attaining each their own "goal", the universal esoteric platform for the coming of Christ for the second time. To prepare in short: the second Beshara'. Manuscript produced by W., exact date unknown, but probably ca. 1972.

14. The wider underlying notion of the spiritual realities or 'meanings' (*ma'nâ*) of the prophets and saints (*awliyâ*) is central to both the popular and more learned expressions of Islamic spirituality. The most comprehensive and reliable expression of these fundamental ideas, based on Ibn 'Arabi's own discussions, is to be found throughout Michel Chodkiewicz's the *The Seal of the Saints: Prophethood and Sainthood in the Doctrine of Ibn 'Arabi* (Cambridge: Islamic Texts Society, 1993), which is also an authoritative treatment of Ibn 'Arabi's central self-conception as the 'Seal of Muhammadan sainthood'.

15. Which is Rauf's translation into English of Ismail Hakki Bursevi's Turkish translation and commentary of Ibn 'Arabi's *Fusûs al-Hikam* (also attributed to Abdullah Bosnevi). For details see Chapter 4 above.

16. Ibid., Foreword to Vol. 1 (Oxford: Ibn Arabi Society, 1986), p. v.

implies.¹⁷ He reminds the reader that it was Ibn 'Arabi who systematised five and a half centuries of Islamic spirituality which had been handed down through largely oral tradition into an all-encompassing written synthesis. Only eighteen years after Ibn 'Arabi's death in 1240 CE, the Mongols sacked Baghdad, changing the face of Islamic civilisation forever. When this civilisation finally rebuilt itself after the invasion, it was Ibn 'Arabi's work that eventually infused spiritual teaching and practice throughout the whole Muslim world, particularly in the Ottoman, Safavid and Mongol realms. His terminology became standard in most Sufi teaching and his philosophy an important reference point from then on in all the prominent Sufi orders, including the Naqshbandiyya, Qadiriyya and Mevlevi. He had arguably, more influence on Islamic spirituality than any other later spiritual teacher. Inscribed over the door of his tomb in Damascus is a remarkable couplet, which he himself composed, that shows his own awareness of his later historical significance as an ongoing spiritual master and guide:

> In every age there is one after whom it is named; for the remaining ages I am that one.¹⁸

This understanding of the accomplishments and significance of Ibn 'Arabi could provide one relatively tangible way of defining how he may be conceived of as a 'meaning', in that it shows how his writing has undoubtedly been instrumental in transmitting and communicating the understanding of the implicit spiritual interpretation of the Quran, following the devastation caused by the Mongol invasion.

In an article published in the first issue of the Muhyiddin Ibn 'Arabi Society's journal (1982), Peter Young provides a further perspective on the person of Ibn 'Arabi based on Ibn 'Arabi's complex discussions of the messengers, prophecy, sainthood and the 'Seals' in the *Fusûs* and other works.¹⁹ The article involves Ibn 'Arabi's understanding of himself as the 'Seal of Muhammadan Sainthood'. Young summarises this understanding in relation to Ibn 'Arabi's comprehension of his ongoing spiritual function. Referring to the notion of *nafas ar-Rahmân*, the creative 'Breath of divine Mercy', he interprets the famous divine saying (*hadîth qudsî*) 'I was a hidden treasure and I loved to be known' as an illustration of the 'hidden' divine essence (*al-bâtin*) coming into manifestation

---

17. Stephen Hirtenstein, *The Unlimited Mercifier: The Spiritual Life and Thought of Ibn 'Arabi* (Oxford: Anqa, 1999), pp. 5-6.

18. Ibid., p. 6. The author has recently pointed out that he prefers the following translation: 'In every age there is one *through* whom it is *elevated*; for the remaining ages, I am that one'. Written comments to me from Stephen Hirtenstein, May 2002.

19. Peter Young, 'Ibn 'Arabi', *JMIAS* I (1982), pp. 3-11.

(*zâhir*). Understood in this way, everything in the universe is in fact essentially *bâtin*. According to Young, Ibn 'Arabi's professed status as the Seal of Muhammadan Sainthood may be understood in the light of this explanation. For Ibn 'Arabi arguably stands historically between the Seal of the Prophets, who was Muhammad and the Seal of Universal Sainthood, who is Christ in his Second Coming. In Islamic spirituality, sainthood is the 'internal' aspect of prophecy,[20] because all prophets are also saints. Therefore, Ibn 'Arabi as Seal of Muhammadan Sainthood, manifested the internal reality, *bâtin*, of the Muhammadan message, his ongoing function being to make explicit what had been implicit in God's revelations through Muhammad. Following generations of commentators of Ibn 'Arabi, Young further proposes that although there will be no new 'legislating' divine Revelations (*sharî'*) or messenger (*rasûl*) following the Seal of the Prophets, there would be a 'prophecy of explanation' which would reveal the deeper spiritual truth in the earlier Muhammadan Revelation, and this was a function of Ibn 'Arabi.

In terms of global spiritual evolution, Young goes on to suggest that Ibn 'Arabi understands himself to be the preparation of the place and the 'Second Coming' of the divine Spirit, and he says '…this is none other than the actualisation of the aptitude which such a form possesses having already the predisposition for it, to receive the inexhaustible effusion of the essential revelation'.[21] The author concludes by explaining:

> The place must be prepared to receive the essential revelation of the Second Coming of Christ, and the preparation can only be in terms of knowledge. At the Second Coming the *Bâtin* is seen to be nothing other than *Zâhir*, and the external revelation is both the mirror image of and identical to, the internal revelation.[22]

A further distinctive quality of Ibn 'Arabi, which may suggest an understanding of how the adherents of Beshara perceive his person, function or meaning, is his association with the mysterious initiatic figure of 'Khidr' (*al-khâdir*).[23] Peter Young also refers to this association in his article.[24] Here the reader is reminded that Ibn 'Arabi was a companion of Khidr, and that Khidr himself is a spiritual guide for those who strive to

---

20. The author explained in a footnote: 'The Saint (*al-walî*) is he who knows without a doubt that God is One, Unique and Indivisible; i.e. he knows God in the same way that God knows himself. It is this that God names Himself *al-walî* in the Quran', ibid., p. 9.
21. Referring to the *Fusûs al-hikam*, chapter on Adam.
22. Young, 'Ibn 'Arabi', p. 11.
23. See Chodkiewicz, *Seal of the Saints*, pp. 93-97.
24. Young, 'Ibn 'Arabi', p. 11.

attain knowledge of the Reality without the mediation of a visible teacher. The author explains that a Khidr-like spiritual teacher is one who knows himself to be the essence and manifested consciousness of God, and that this awareness is possible for all humans. Consequently, inasmuch as the outward movement of the divine Breath is the 'Hidden' becoming manifest in an outward revelation, in time the need for outward teachers becomes unnecessary and the aspirant gains knowledge of Reality from its Source: this therefore becomes a direct transmission. This was the way in which Ibn 'Arabi offered guidance to his followers, pointing beyond himself to Reality, unlike some Sufi sheikhs. And this is the way that, following in Ibn 'Arabi's footsteps, Bulent Rauf provided guidance to his students.

So it seems that from the above perspectives the notion that the person of Ibn 'Arabi is himself a 'meaning' could be interpreted on many levels. He has a specific function in that he believes that he brings out what is implicit in the Quran and makes it explicit in this way, preparing that ultimate manifestation of the Spirit which is symbolised as the 'Second Coming' of Christ. In addition, his role as a 'meaning' could be inferred from the way in which he systematised, rescued and transmitted the intricacies of Islamic spirituality at the time of the Crusader and the Mongol invasions, with his interpretation of the esoteric aspect of God's revelation in the Quran becoming the dominant one in the Muslim world since then. More immediate is the understanding that Bulent Rauf appears to have of Ibn 'Arabi as a 'meaning', in that what he passes on is a gift to the individual human 'heart',[25] the knowledge of the superiority of spiritual intuition and revelation over reason. Thus it is only by 'opening up the heart' that the seeker will be able truly to receive the 'meanings' which are made manifest in and through Ibn 'Arabi.

THE AIMS OF THE BESHARA COURSES

Bulent Rauf's objective in creating the Beshara courses was to aim at what Ibn 'Arabi called the 'Completely Human Being' (*al-insân al-kamîl*), and Chisholme was designed as a place where one would be educated to begin to become a complete person. It offers a comprehensive, multifaceted education reflecting the multiple dimensions of Ibn 'Arabi's conception of the Completely Human Being.[26]

---

25. For Ibn 'Arabi's concept of the 'heart' as the place of knowledge of its own divinity, see the section in Chapter 4 on *The Twenty-Nine Pages*.

26. Interview with the Principal at Chisholme, August 1999. For references to Ibn 'Arabi's concept of the 'Perfect Man' see the section on *The Twenty-Nine Pages* and the *Blue Fusûs* in Chapter 4 above.

Consequently the courses at Chisholme centre on the development of that knowledge and awareness which is required for the students to align themselves with 'that which they actually are', so that they can come to know their inner connection to the Reality and all else with which they are in relationship. This approach is summed up in one of the most central hadiths in traditional Sufi teaching, 'whoever knows their self, knows their Lord'. This expanding awareness includes their fellow humanity, society and the cosmos as a whole, with all the consequent responsibilities 'and, fundamentally, appreciation'.[27]

In reply to the question why people enrolled on courses at Chisholme,[28] the Principal suggested that the students would all probably answer in different ways, each one arriving with a different need. But he proposed that the main reason that they enrol is for what they find when they come, 'which is the proper understanding of the possibility of self-knowledge'. Therefore, the main reason that people come is in order to understand themselves and their relationship to Reality.[29] He explained that today, people are brought up without a context to understand these things, but that Beshara demonstrates that there is a context and then shows an effective, adequate way to advance beyond it. This context is 'just a beginning, because beyond it there is a real integration in being'.[30]

The Principal was then asked whether this discovery was revealed to the students, or whether in fact the 'students reveal this to themselves'[31] whilst participating on the courses. His reply was that initially the courses at Chisholme provide the context for self-knowledge, and that in the case of some students this involves 'untying knots' within themselves which have been established over a large proportion of their lives. In the majority of cases, though, the students progress further and the knowledge that they attain and the realisations they achieve continue to strengthen and develop following the completion of their course.[32]

---

27. Unpublished interview with the Principal by Cecilia Twinch, late 1980s (for the *Beshara Magazine*).

28. Interview with Peter Young by Angela Holroyd, 'Courses at Chisholme', *Beshara Magazine* 8 (1989), pp. 26-29 (27).

29. Ibid.

30. Ibid.

31. This relates to a central emphasis of the course—the attainment of the knowledge and realisation that we as humans, and in fact all of creation, are self-manifestations (*tajalliyât*) of the Divine. See Chapter 6 below for students' experiences of the courses.

32. See the discussion of the courses' longer-term 'outcomes' in Chapter 6 below.

Regarding what it was exactly that students gained from the course, particularly as there is no 'piece of paper' presented to the successful students at the end of six months, the Principal replied:

> I hope that a certain connection becomes established for people, which is completely irrefutable for themselves—not for others, but for themselves—that they are in relationship to One Reality, and that they are the possible place of complete mirroring of that One Reality to itself. Even the certain awareness of that possibility is a source of constant growth. So one could say that it is not that the end result is expected at the end of the course, but that the effect will be felt at every moment of their life to follow; that they will go on in awareness and growing understanding and actualisation of that possibility.
>
> And of course they will be qualitatively different, in knowing how they stand in respect to One Reality, One God. They will inevitably be different, not in what they do—that may also be different, of course, but that isn't the point—but in the quality of their living. This will inevitably have effect on others, but again, the effect is not the point.[33]

The question then arose as to why people could not simply study Ibn 'Arabi on their own at home rather than having to attend a course to do so. Young cited part of the New Testament statement where Christ says: 'When two or three are gathered together in my name...',[34] explaining that it is easier to study with others where there is 'a reality to the situation and help from it' which is not always available to those studying alone. This applies also to reaching self-knowledge: it is possible to come to it alone, but most people need a great deal of help because of the risk of constant self-delusion. Being in a situation in which the students are mirrors to one another and where the situation is in itself a mirror, benefit is achieved because the student is shown his or her illusions very quickly. That situation also encourages the correctness of intention in a student and allows it to blossom. In short, the conditions need to be right, and although the potential is there, someone who hasn't taken the necessary conditions into consideration may not realise their actual potential.[35]

Young asserted that Beshara could act as a kind of catalyst through its courses and physical location, and that that function was especially essential now—first because there is an obvious need, and second in terms of global spiritual evolution. Humanity, he suggested, is at present in a state of transition and could be envisaged as having arrived at a

---

33. Interview with Peter Young, p. 27.
34. Matthew 18:20.
35. Interview with Peter Young, pp. 27-28.

transition point or in terms of maturity, like a teenager emerging into adulthood. But he proposes that at present we are behaving more like young children than even teenagers, in that we are almost entirely self-centred. To enable us to traverse that isthmus, we need to develop a fuller understanding of the self, or in fact of our selves. Humanity has to become aware of the fact that the totality of humanity and of nature is a reflection of One Reality and that it is humanity's honour to be of service to that Reality by looking after creation in an appropriate way. Young agreed that this human awareness will not happen immediately, but that on a spiritual level something is happening, indeed that something really big has to happen to make a substantial shift in the collective consciousness. He explained that initially the possibility has to become apparent, and he believes that this is what the courses can provide: 'making the possibility a possibility by letting people know that it is there'. But when the wider shift will actually occur, 'only God knows'.[36]

The above words are quoted from an interview with Peter Young which took place some time ago (1989), but he has recently stated that the shift has now begun and it is associated with the millennium and other factors such as planetary alignment.[37] He suggests that the following message from the American Elders (Hopi Indians), in the form of a poem entitled 'To My Fellow Swimmers', provides an appropriate illustration of the situation now:

> There is a river flowing now very fast. It is so
> great and swift that there are those who will be
> afraid. They will try to hang on to the shore.
> They will feel they are being torn apart
> and will suffer greatly.
>
> Know the river has its destination
>
> The Elders say we must let go of the shore,
> Push off into the middle of the stream, keep our
> eyes open and our heads above the water.
>
> And I say,
> See who is in there with you and celebrate.
> At this time in history we take nothing
> personally. Least of all ourselves. For the
> moment that we do, our spiritual growth
> and journey comes to a halt.
> The time of the lone wolf is over. Gather yourselves
> Banish the word 'struggle' from your attitude

36. Interview with Peter Young, pp. 28-29.
37. Discussion with Peter Young, April 2002.

and your vocabulary. All that we do now must
be done in a sacred manner and in celebration.
We are the ones we have been waiting for.[38]

A possible interpretation of this poem in relation to Beshara is that the river represents spiritual consciousness in relation to Reality. There is an irresistible impulse issuing from that Reality to surrender to the impulse. For those who surrender and 'go with the flow', pain and suffering of the psychological and spiritual kind ceases. This is because this type of pain is caused by resistance to the impulse from the Real. The destination of the river i.e., the impulse from Reality, is to bring humanity to knowledge of its own reality, i.e., knowledge of itself which is a reflection of the Real and the realisation that its destiny is to serve that Ultimate Reality. Those who have surrendered to this impulse should take joy in the companionship of their fellow travellers on the path (or river in this case). Of ultimate importance is to defeat the demands of the ego because by submitting to it, feelings of self-centeredness will arise resulting in the development of serious obstacles in the way of spiritual development. Submit to God/the Real and recognise the sanctity of all existence, rejoicing in the knowledge that we, as humans, are fully a part of it and potentially true reflections of it.

WHAT IS AN 'ESOTERIC EDUCATION'?

The full name of the Beshara School is the 'Beshara School of Intensive Esoteric Education'. The following discussion illustrates how the school defines the meaning of the term 'esoteric education' in the context of their current courses.

Another senior supervisor at the school described what the school understood by the term:[39] It concerns the process of discovering the inner meanings of words, that are not at first immediately apparent. There is nothing mysterious involved, but the student has to give attention to what is apparent in order to discover the inner meaning. She continued:

> Going on from the meaning, also when we say 'esoteric' we're talking about real meanings and those meanings are the truth of the person, what the person really means and so the education would be in drawing out the meaning of what is apparent in what is learnt. Since it is also the meaning of the person, that meaning acts as a mirror to what is in the person and,

---

38. Hopi Elders, 'To My Fellow Swimmers', *Beshara website*, www.beshara.org (Library Page, accessed February 2002, no longer accessible), p. 1.

39. From an unpublished interview conducted by Cecilia Twinch with WL., in the late 1980s.

> God willing, draws out that meaning for a person to see, and what they see is therefore nothing other than themselves. It's not putting anything in; it's drawing out what is already so, so that the person knows what is already so.[40]

This process therefore involves the subject matter, which is in fact the truth about oneself. This realisation is not, though, necessarily apparent; sometimes it appears to be outside of oneself in the form of texts, 'books that have been written from the truth, and from outside in that sense it is studying a completely universal perspective on the truth'.

> To say that the subject matter is the truth is not enough: it's the complete truth that is the meaning of what is apparent and the student, giving the proper attention to what he learns, comes to see and know through feeling and taste that what he is studying apparently outside is no other than the truth of himself.[41]

Although the school claims that the student will come to know through feeling and taste, the texts employed in this course are difficult, and it would seem necessary for students to have strong intellectual ability in order to understand them. However, the supervisor insists that what is required above all is attention or 'putting oneself under the education which is carried in the texts'. This involves a personal attitude which admits that one needs to learn, and this indispensable inner attitude is not dependent on what is outwardly known as intellect.

> So the meaning that is carried in these words cannot be dependent on a material ability to be understood. If the student puts himself under this education, and proposes that he be educated, this opens up or uncovers the mirror in himself for the meanings that are on the page. It doesn't need intellect, in that sense. It needs this opening up to uncover the mirror.[42]

Therefore, if a student is having difficulty grasping the concepts within the texts, then according to the interviewee he should:

> ...persist in using all his faculties of attention in it and the meaning of what he is studying has effect on all levels that he may not necessarily be aware of. His side of it is to persist in his efforts, and not be put off by perhaps not measuring up in the way that he thinks he should measure up, and that persisting with the right attitude will allow the possibility of the meaning to continue to have effect and he must trust that that will also become apparent to him.[43]

40. Ibid.
41. Ibid.
42. Ibid.
43. Reference as above.

This right attitude towards study arises when the student recognises that he or she needs knowledge and an education involving the realisation of the truth about him or herself. This involves the recognition that 'one doesn't know; then the recognition of not knowing is the beginning of knowing'. This recognition of not knowing is an essential part of this attitude that should continue throughout the education.

> Because if that attitude is present, if it's maintained in the student, then what is given actually deepens that attitude, strengthens it, so constantly the knowledge that one doesn't know deepens as one is given to know.[44]

CONCLUSION

The overall gist of this chapter explores the ways in which the participants of the Beshara School understand what they are doing and why they are doing it, i.e., what Beshara, Ibn 'Arabi, and Ibn 'Arabi's teachings mean to them. As already noted in the previous chapter, the eschatological and messianic ideas of some adherents (especially articulated around the year 2000) correspond to universal cross-religious expectations as well as Ibn 'Arabi's interpretation of Islamic eschatological themes. All the major world religions await with anticipation a similar figure. Each figure is expected to appear when the world is in a state of chaos, and each one will be heralded by signs and portents. What is particularly interesting about the understanding of some Beshara adherents is their belief that humanity is coming under the influence of a *'new impulse'* from the Real (God).

---

44. Reference as above.

6

STUDENT EXPERIENCES DURING AND FOLLOWING THE COURSES

This chapter begins with a brief discussion of student backgrounds and the reasons that are commonly given for their decision to enrol on one of the courses.[1] It then proceeds to an examination of some of the students' experiences of the courses, following which it concludes with a selection of case studies outlining how the experiences of these courses continue to affect the daily lives of the former students and those people with whom they have contact.

The information provided here is partly based on interviews and informal discussions with former students of Beshara during the first three years of research (1998–2000). Also included is some data from promotional interviews that the school has published in its own literature. The case studies used to illustrate how the Beshara education is manifested in the daily lives of the former students were obtained by ongoing interviews over the three years specified. In that section, people with a representative range of skills and talents have been selected in order to illustrate how the 'education experience' is not confined to any particular field. It was in dealing with this interview data that I have particularly applied the phenomenological methodological approach of the study of religion.

---

1. Although several different courses are offered by the school, including weekend, nine-day and an advanced six-month course, as well as retreats and courses presented by visiting speakers, the most important course and the one which is obligatory for serious students to take part in is the intensive six-month introductory course. The weekend and nine-day courses are based on the same format and the same texts and course structures are used as on the six-month course, although on these short courses, more emphasis is placed on the study of the texts than on work in the house and grounds. This discussion will therefore be focusing on the experience of students who have participated in the intensive six-month introductory course, and in some cases the nine-day course, which could be described as an abridged version of the intensive six-month introductory course.

An integral aspect of the introductory six-month course is the group pilgrimage to Turkey in December of each year. That important phase of the six-month course is discussed in Chapter 7. It is not included in this chapter because despite the fact that the trip is central to the experience of those students on the residential courses, it is also open to any other interested parties whether they are Beshara participants or not. The extensive volume of material concerning the trip also prohibits its accommodation in this chapter.

MOTIVATIONS FOR TAKING THE INTENSIVE SIX-MONTH INTRODUCTORY COURSE

Although many people interviewed had reached a crisis point in their lives which inspired them to enrol on the course, equally as many enrolled out of spiritual curiosity and a desire to know more about themselves, about the meaning of life, God and existence. Many had previously experimented with various spiritual paths and had come away unsatisfied. Yet when faced with the Beshara course, in spite of its sustained rigour, they generally decided that it was right for them and that at last they had found what they were searching for.[2]

On the whole, there is no single specific age range for the students who attend the courses, although there is a slight majority of younger students who are in their twenties and thirties, in comparison to those in middle age and older. When the courses began in the mid-seventies, the majority of students were in their twenties, with the oldest students being in their forties. Today students are usually either taking a break from their jobs for six months, or attending just before or just after college or university, or else they have reached retirement age. However, whatever their stage of life when they make the decision to take part in a course at Chisholme, their commitment has to be deep. This is because of the cost and required commitment, both in time and money.[3] There are also sometimes sacrifices to make involving family and other relationships. Students with children are able to bring them though, and educational facilities in the nearby towns are quite adequate.[4] For those who really

---

2. Adherents of Beshara almost all say that no one simply 'chooses' to attend a Beshara course, but that they are brought or guided to Beshara by Reality (God) itself.
3. Around £5885 which includes all meals and shared accommodation. The two-week trip to Turkey costs £850–900, and is discussed in Chapter 7 below.
4. I was told that when the courses were initially instituted in the mid-1970s, the wider situation concerning culture, society and lifestyles enabled people to be in a

cannot take six months out of their lives to be at Chisholme, there are the shorter nine-day and weekend courses.

The gender of the students appears to be more or less equally balanced, and most are from educated middle-class backgrounds. There is a significant proportion of 'creative' people, including artists, architects, writers, musicians, sculptors, and film and stage actors. Also of particular interest are those who approach cuisine as a serious form of spiritual discipline and artistic expression. Others include successful business people, doctors, psychologists and practitioners of alternative forms of healing. Many combine their professional skills with artistic accomplishments, such as painting or music. Those who come from non-professional backgrounds are likewise notable for enquiring minds and an abundance of curiosity and enterprise.

The majority of students come from the English-speaking world: Britain, the United States, Canada and Australia. Some come from other parts of Europe, including Germany, Spain, Holland and the Scandinavian countries. There are not so many participants from the Middle East, although there have been some. For example, one of the original adherents was from Saudi Arabia and taught Arabic on the early courses. There have also been some Turkish students, including a medical doctor and a Turkish friend of Bulent Rauf who taught Turkish on the early courses.

Interestingly, there is a significant number of Israelis who have taken part. One explanation for this is that Jews, Christians and Muslims are all, in the Quranic term, 'people of the Book', in that their religious roots are Abrahamic. The Hebrew and Arabic languages are also very similar on account of their Semitic roots. To quote an Israeli interviewee:[5]

> Jews have a spiritual streak, an idealism in which they fall in love with ideas and principles appertaining to this side of things. Although materialism is profound in Israel, many people are not happy about it so they end up here (on a Beshara course). There is a constant trickle.
>
> In Israel there is lots of spiritual searching, for example Buddhism, the ideas of Gurdjieff, Orthodox strains of Judaism, Hasidic movements and Kabala.[6] Israelis tend to find Kabala unsatisfactory, as it has become degenerate and there is too much paraphernalia involved.

position to attend the courses much more easily. For example, they could just work for a few months at any job and earn enough to attend a course, then go off again, do another probably menial job and then return for another course and so on. The way of life then was more relaxed with less competitive pressure to 'get on'.

5. Interview with V., February 2000, who was one of the first Beshara students.
6. Judaic mysticism.

The interviewee admitted that he had studied Kabala himself after having completed the first six-month Beshara course and was put off by the paraphernalia. In contrast he felt that Beshara has no such restrictive form and is beyond traditional religious structure.[7]

Another Israeli interviewee explained that 'what Ibn 'Arabi says is to do with man qualified only by Absoluteness. What is anyone's identity? Is it colour, genes, talents? It is none of this: the invitation which is Beshara goes beyond this'. She continued: 'Concerning Israelis and Beshara, in one sense at its most essential level, Beshara is what Judaism is about'. The interviewee explained that she was not personally interested in Judaism or any structured religion—what she was looking for was to know herself.[8] So it seems that to the understanding of such Israeli students, Beshara and the teachings of Ibn 'Arabi, as the school claims, involve a Truth which is not restricted to any particular religious structure and symbolism; and the central use of Islamic sources does not seem to generate any barriers to the experience.[9] Even in the light of such explanations, the fact that Israelis are comfortable using so many Islamic religious texts and practices at Beshara is striking.

'SECOND-GENERATION' STUDENTS

Another point of particular interest is that there are now an abundance of 'second-generation' students participating on the courses. Several of the offspring of the original participants are now in their late teens or early twenties and have completed one or both of the six-month courses. A selection of them were interviewed and asked what it was like growing up within the ethos and ambience of Beshara. Several explained that they had been infants at the time that their parents were students on the first courses run at Sherborne and were therefore taken care of in a large group of babies and toddlers in the nursery there. They all tend to remember vividly the intense cold of the place.[10] When they got older, some attended the local primary school in Hawick, the town in the Scottish Border region closest to Chisholme. A common recollection was the avoidance of mention of Beshara to anyone who was not involved, for fear of being labelled as members of a cult or commune.[11] Also some

---

7. Interview with V., February 2000.
8. Interview with G., February 2000.
9. The above opinions generally apply to other Israelis spoken to who are involved with the school.
10. Interview with A.B., and others, Chisholme, August 2000.
11. Interview with A.B., and others, Chisholme, August 2000.

reported a feeling of being 'different' from other people, but not necessarily in a negative way. An interviewee explained that: 'I did feel that I was different, but also very privileged that my parents made me see things that other friends at school did not see or know about'.[12] She felt that if her parents had not been involved she would have been quite a different person. Another interviewee described a blissful pre-teen childhood spent at Chisholme and attending the local school. This was followed, though, by total rebellion against all that the school stood for in his teens. However he explained, as did the other interviewees, that what Beshara did stand for had never been imposed upon him. Now in his late teens, he is no longer in rebellion, but feels no compulsion to do a course whilst he is at college studying music, his ambition being to be a full-time musician.[13] Some of the people interviewed admitted that they felt no compulsion to participate in a six-month course yet, but had attended special children's courses and the collective *zikrs* held each year on special occasions.[14] Others had completed the first six-month course and the advanced course.[15]

One interviewee, whose parents have been deeply involved with Beshara from the start, explained that after completing a degree in Arabic and Persian at university,

> I had no sense of where I was going. This brought up a lot of questions particularly involving the meaning of life, and there was a growing sense of needing to be more in tune with what it might be. The idea of dealing with the rigours of life and going straight into a job didn't feel right. I felt the need to confront fundamental questions, to be integrated (with whatever was the meaning of life) and find a balance. This was how it unfolded, a way was being shown, and by way of this, I knew that the right time had come to participate in the six-month course.[16]

This same student explained that he had completed a nine-day course when he was sixteen years old. This was when he had really begun to question the meaning of life and had sown the seeds for his later enquiry. He described his attitude on completion of the six- month course as:

12. Interview with A.C., Chisholme, August 2000.
13. Interview with B., Chisholme, August, 2000.
14. Such as 'The Night of Power' (*Laylat al-Qadar*), when the Prophet Muhammad received God's first revelation, celebrated during Ramadan; the Prophet's birthday; or 'The Night of ascent of Muhammad to Heaven' (*Laylat al-Mi'râj*).
15. Two 'second-generation' students interviewed were among my fellow travellers on the Turkey trip in December 2000; they were both half way through the advanced six-month course. One of these students had been interviewed in August 1999 (I.) and the other in August 2000 (R.I.).
16. Interview with R.I., Chisholme, August 2000.

> Like coming at life with a different point of view on perception, embracing all religions and affirming them with a deeper understanding—affirming, realising and experiencing 'things' to be true.[17]

The interview concluded with the student admitting that he was not yet clear what his next step would be. As it turned out, he proceeded to join the next advanced course, beginning later in the year of the interview.[18]

SOME STUDENTS' EXPERIENCES OF THE COURSES

Regarding the use of Ibn 'Arabi's teaching and philosophy as it is experienced by the students, an early participant of Beshara was asked, for example, how she thought the school made use of the works of Ibn 'Arabi. Her reply was that a more apt question to ask would be 'How does Ibn 'Arabi make use of the Beshara School and its students?'[19] This attitude to Ibn 'Arabi, fairly standard at the school, is typical of the wider traditional conception of the prophets and saints in Islamic spiritual tradition, that is, the perception that Ibn 'Arabi is still living and directly accessible to us on a higher level of existence, still in contact with our human level and trying to get a particular message across to those perceptive enough to receive it.[20] The discussion below will illustrate the range of general reactions from students to the whole of the course rather than just focusing on Ibn 'Arabi's teachings alone, bearing in mind that the whole structure of the course is based on Ibn 'Arabi's conception of our human place in reality and existence. This long quote from a former

---

17. Interview with R.I., Chisholme, August 2000.

18. It has been pointed out by several Beshara participants that the young students of today arrive at an understanding of the course study material significantly more quickly, on the whole, than did the original students.

19. From a discussion with N., one of the early adherents of Beshara, Oxford, November 1999.

20. Ibn 'Arabi was himself acutely conscious of other levels of being and spent a lot of time in the 'Imaginative World', which was quite as real to him as this one, as it was to most Sufis, meeting and talking to other Sufi sheikhs who were either still alive or were 'dead' but fully functional in this realm. For numerous and varied illustrations, see Claude Addas, *The Quest for the Red Sulphur: The Life of Ibn 'Arabi* (Cambridge: Islamic Texts Society, 1993); Ralph Austin, *Sufis of Andalusia (The Rûh al-quds and al-Durrat al-fâkhirah of Ibn 'Arabi)* (London: Alan & Unwin, 1971); Stephen Hirtenstein, *The Unlimited Mercifier: The Spiritual Life and Thought of Ibn 'Arabi* (Oxford: Anqa, 1999); and Michel Chodkiewicz, *The Seal of the Saints: Prophethood and Sainthood in the Doctrine of Ibn 'Arabi* (Cambridge: Islamic Texts Society, 1993).

student of the school who is now a supervisor is included here because those who have completed the school's courses would generally substantiate much of what he says:[21]

> One is not studying a book or books which are appendages to oneself or one's knowledge but one is studying meanings already present. Books clarify them: ... Blake said about his poetry that it was 10% inspiration and 90% hard work. Intellectual ability helps but study is not merely an intellectual thing... Sometimes the meaning is not clear through the words, but in reading them something is happening. There are intuitive ways within it. Otherwise there would be two worlds; one intellectual and one non-intellectual, but there is only One Existence. You have to have openness; you have to allow it to be effective. One's perception of oneself has changed in a way. The course is not a separate part of one's life. The whole thing is condensed and is about facing Truth in a moment, in an instant. All those things that you thought you were are illusions.
>
> The unity of perspective is to do with the nature of man. It's not to do with anyone having some ideology. It's to do with the nature of man as a cosmic reality, but it's His perspective as there is nothing but Him. Unity implies a synthesis; it's not about adopting a point of view.
>
> This is intense. One is put in the most terrible situations by oneself while one's here. It appears to be coming from outside but it's not. The structure of the course stops you from getting stuck in that! Also the Truth resides in every person. It's a way that Truth can operate, manifest and become effective. It's like a light shining in the darkness. The special thing about this course is it doesn't allow you to get trapped in your own psychological levels. There's always a way out and the only way is up. There's no way out except completing it... You put yourself in a light which is so powerful you have to deal with it or give in to it. The pleasurable side is in the meaning. It's not an emotional pleasure but in realising meaning. Joy is very deep. Joy is profundity and lies in the knowledge of that closeness—the complete presence. It's a pleasure and free in that respect: what have been compulsions become free acts, God willing.

The implication here is that although some degree of intellectual ability is required in order to study the texts, this is only part of a larger learning process. What is required in order to grasp their meaning is above all intuition and realisation. The interviewee also implies that certain aspects of the structure of the course are at times almost physically and psychologically intolerable, and that it is only through trust and submission to God or Reality that students are able to grow and thereby complete the course. However, the more practical aspects of the 'education' such as work on the estate, in the house, cooking, etc., are also an

21. He is now in his mid-30s and his mother was involved from the beginning. This quote is from an unpublished interview conducted for the *Beshara Magazine* in the late 1980s. This interviewee was S.S. and the interviewer Cecilia Twinch.

essential part of the course. Those are the times when what is being 'realised' through the texts is being put into practice, and they are also the times when the students may more fully manifest Ibn 'Arabi's central concept of human 'servanthood' (*ubûdiyya*). This means that whatever work is being partaken in, and whoever appears to be benefiting from it, all service is ultimately to God, because there is no other than God. In the following quote Ibn 'Arabi describes his interpretation of the Sufi concept of servanthood:

> Servitude is complete and pure submission in conformity with the very essence of the servant's nature (*dhâtiyya li'l-'abd*)... It is only realised by those who inhabit God's Vast Earth, which contains both the contingent (*hudûth*) and the eternal (*qidam*).[22] This is the Earth of God; whoever dwells there has realised full servitude with regard to God, and God joins that person to Himself...[23]

A common response to the experience of the course is the realisation that there is a way to live life from an alternative perspective which is far greater than the personalised, egocentric existence in which most people usually live. During the course, that mould gets broken and personal conditioning is undone, resulting in a clearer realisation of what is real. Levels within the self are awakened and contacted, levels of which the student was normally unaware.[24]

In an unpublished interview prepared for the *Beshara Magazine* in the late 1980s, a Turkish doctor who had lived in Germany for twenty-two years articulated his experience. What he says is also typical of the responses of most of the students whom I interviewed more recently:

> I tried to study by myself but I didn't understand a word. The concentration here is very fixed and condensed, but at home there are so many things to distract your concentration: you have to work, to earn money, to look after your family. I am very happy to have the chance to spend such a long time (which is not so long really) concentrating intensely on the study of Him. You feel His presence especially here very intensively. God is everywhere else as well, but this place is so...maybe He wants to show that He is present, He exists, He is the only existent, and this is the place where you can see it, feel it. What we learn here is constancy of

---

22. Ibn 'Arabi says of this: 'Every body in which spirits, angels and jinns clothe themselves and every form in which a man perceives himself while asleep is a subtle body belonging to that earth'. *Futûhât* I, p. 130, quoted in Addas, *Quest for the Red Sulphur*, p. 118.

23. *Futûhât* III, p. 224, quoted in Addas, *Quest for the Red Sulphur*, p. 118.

24. General response from an amalgamation of several student and former student accounts, 1998–2000.

awareness—this seems to be the most important point, remembering God, every single moment you have, and I notice that here, the more aware you are, the closer you feel to Him.[25]

The point that this interviewee makes about the constant awareness of God during the courses is commonly expressed by students and former students. But this awareness is really the central purpose of the course and its structure, and it manifests on different levels, as will be shown below. This awareness of God is closely related to the Quranic ideas of 'knowing' and 'remembering' of God (*'ilm*, *dhikr*), of 'attention' to God (*tawajjuh*) and confident abandonment to or trust in God (*tawakkul*).[26]

Other typical responses are that the course unfolds for the student in stages, usually being very enjoyable at the beginning, with the student feeling intense enthusiasm. Soon, though, the initial euphoria begins to wane and negative personality traits arise in the student's consciousness. Unresolved problems and psychological complexes have to be faced up to, acknowledged and resolved. The students often initially blame their discomfort on outside forces and circumstances, but as the course progresses they eventually arrive at the realisation that the problems faced are all in fact their own, coming from within themselves.

Many problematic mental states do surface; this is because of the unrelenting pressure to which the students are deliberately subjected. They are 'on the go' for sixteen hours a day everyday for six months with no break, apart from the Turkey trip. They are discouraged from leaving the school's premises, with the exception of medical emergencies, with the deliberate intention of isolating them from the outside world. They have no privacy, being in shared accommodation, so therefore they are never alone. They seldom have a moment to themselves, and even the three daily meditation sessions are done together as a group in a special meditation room. The physical work is usually performed with others, but even if the allocated job is solitary (for example, vacuuming the house), other people are never far away. Consequently the students have no time to reflect in solitude upon what is happening to them; they literally just 'live in the moment'. This description does not apply so much to the advanced six-month course, because on that course the days are not so minutely structured, and there is even a solitary one-week retreat.[27]

25. From an unpublished article by Cecilia Twinch, for the *Beshara Magazine*, late 1980s.

26. The latter is one of the 'five things' which new students of the intensive six-month introductory course are told about at the start.

27. This retreat used to take place during a separate one-month course, before the advanced six-month course was taken.

Nearly all the students go through a stage when they feel that they cannot cope anymore and are tempted to leave. Since the students have to face up to their own negative reactions to the course pressures, this is part of the education of getting to know themselves. When they get to the point of desperation and feel that they cannot go on, they eventually turn to a power beyond themselves in total submission and trust. They then report, almost unanimously, the feeling of being 'given' the strength and endurance coupled with a strong awareness of the presence of God or the Real, consequently enabling them to complete their training.[28]

This type of 'education' is reminiscent of Gurdjieff's methods as described by his pupil, J.G. Bennett, in his autobiography.[29] As noted above, Bennett lectured to the Beshara School in its early days. Gurdjieff structured a type of spiritual training which he called 'The Work', much of it based on his experience of diverse Sufi practices of the Caucasus and Central Asia.[30] Spiritual realisation was induced by making his students work so physically and mentally hard that they felt that they could endure no more. When they reached the point of desperation they frequently experienced an incredible breakthrough, feeling a rush of spiritual strength, energy and often a new awareness of the presence of God and a feeling of the certainty of His existence. Chisholme itself and its whole ambience can have a very peculiar effect on the psyche of a person, as illustrated in the case study below, detailed in the student's own words.

This student, Jane, had decided to attend the nine-day course (the same one that I attended as a participant-observer), an abridged, introductory version of the six-month course in that it follows exactly the same format with slightly more emphasis put on study than on work. She had been actively following an alternative spiritual path for many years, but was unprepared for the psychic impact that the experience at Chisholme would have on her. She described herself as being very 'open' to other levels of reality, perhaps due to her preceding activities on her own spiritual path.

---

28. General and typical response to the course from students and former students, derived from data collected 1998–2000. It is only in very exceptional circumstances that a student has not completed a course.

29. J.G. Bennett, *Witness: The Story of a Search* (New Mexico: Bennett Books, 1997), Chapter 10.

30. The Naqshbandi expression 'awareness of God in Society' (*Khalvat dar anjuman*), is closely connected to Ibn 'Arabi's spiritual ideal of the highest saints (the *afrad*, the solitaries), as being outwardly 'normal', active members of Society. See the articles by V.R. Holbrook, 'Ibn 'Arabi and the Ottoman Dervish Traditions: The Melamî Supra Order', Part 1, *JMIAS* IX (1991), pp. 18-35; Part 2, *JMIAS* XII (1992), pp. 15-33.

I arrived at Chisholme in the middle of an afternoon in November and having unpacked and had tea, I found myself drawn into helping where I could, particularly in the kitchen. There was a weekend course running concurrently with the nine-day course, which was to be attended by two students. There was only to be one other student with me on my course. The other weekend students all arrived that evening. The course began properly the following morning. The other students and myself had intended to attend the seven o'clock meditation session, but as a result of the alarm clock failing to go off, we missed it.

At nine o'clock, having finished clearing up breakfast, we attended our first study period. The two weekend students joined my fellow student and I throughout our daily schedule. The head of the school supervised this study period and we were surprised that although he was English, he was addressed by an Arabic name. The study text was *The Twenty-Nine Pages*. In retrospect, my fellow student and I must have appeared to be confrontational at the very least. We tended to be argumentative and challenging concerning the text and the school's interpretation of it. We were instructed to read and intellectualise it initially, but then let it 'speak to the heart'—using intuition, not reason to explore the various levels of meaning. By doing this, words would become living realities.

The first study session was followed by a coffee break and then a second study session supervised by another English person who had not yet been given an Arab name. He told us that this was because an appropriate name had not yet revealed itself. I was surprised because this supervisor had a good degree from a well-known university and could have landed well-paid employment—but had chosen to work here on a semi-voluntary basis. This situation, did though, seemed to support the school's claim that its teaching could revolutionise an individual's angle on his or her life, changing emphasis on ideals, values and priorities.

Following this study session was the mid-day meditation which students on all three courses attended. (There was a six-month course including five students in session at this time.) I did not feel that my meditation period bore much fruit as we had been instructed not to meditate on a theme or practice visualisation. My previous long experience of meditation had involved both of these methods. All we were told to do was to 'open up to God'.[31]

It was following this session—and also I believe, as a result of the study sessions as well—that during the lunch-time that followed I had my

---

31. We were told that the meditation session is a time put aside for 'taste of the awareness of God', without thought or distraction. Following the initial dedication, no technique or method is involved. If thoughts and images arise, we were advised to acknowledge them and then imagine blowing them away. This approach avoids any limits being imposed on the meditation, thus confining the meditation to that, because the communion that is the ultimate purpose of the meditation should not be qualified by limits.

first inexplicable experience. I began to feel that I was not part of this world at all, or that a pressure or presence from another level of existence was pressing down on me or even attempting to enter my psyche. The feeling could be equated to those of being under the influence of drugs and I later described it to myself as feeling 'other worldly'. Strangely, the feeling was not unfamiliar; I had experienced something similar in the same area of Scotland some twenty years previously. Characteristic of the experience then and now was the way in which it turned on and off. And when it was off it was difficult to remember or describe what it was like when it was on, almost like trying to recall a dream. But this was just the start and I was to undergo the experience periodically throughout the remains of the course.

I analysed this experience of 20 years ago and now as probably being due to 'the veil being thin' between this level of existence and the next here. Also the area was steeped in layers of history including Border battles and was not far from Hadrian's Wall. In addition I put the experiences at Chisholme down to the activities which were taking place there, drawing other levels of being to the area. I did consider that perhaps I was ill; this was until my fellow student on the nine-day course began to describe similar symptoms. He described feeling drugged, particularly following the study sessions. I agreed that this was my most 'other worldly' time as well. That this should happen most poignantly after reading text surprised us. If it had been after meditation it would be more explicable as meditation can result in a 'spacy' feeling. That it happened after studying text seemed to give weight to the school's claim that Ibn 'Arabi's words really did represent ultimate divine Truth and if having 'intellectualised' them you allowed them to 'speak to the heart' they would have a profound effect in the depths of your being. (We did though consider for a time, that perhaps we were victims of contagious hysteria, or suggestion.)

I was so powerfully affected, usually during or following study, meditation or *Zikr*, that on more than one occasion I nearly passed out; this even happened once while walking with my fellow student and a supervisor round the property.[32] At one stage I became quite distressed and discussed the situation with the head of the school. He told me that these experiences were normal and expected to a degree but usually happened with less intensity to the students taking part in the six-month courses and usually once they were well established into the routine. (He did though suggest that I had a medical check in case I had a faulty brain function, I

---

32. At the end of the course a senior supervisor admitted that he too often felt strange 'other worldly' feelings in some parts of the property. We two students rationalised that perhaps we were 'picking up' on underground water, in much the same way as water diviners, or sensing some kind of electro-magnetic fields. But in the light of the other experiences, i.e. during study and meditation, we certainly felt that these feelings belonged to something more spiritual.

said that that was unnecessary.) He told me that I was opening up to God, and that I should stop resisting, relax and let it happen. It was my resistance to the pressure, which was causing distress.[33]

Much less intense experiences were also produced as a result of the regime. Feelings of timelessness, loss of the track of time, awareness only of the moment and disorientation. There was also the chance to stand back from ordinary life and evaluate it—the effect of this could be positive or detrimental because the environment and schedule induced an original perspective on life and existence. I found the experience beneficial as it produced an original outlook for me. It must be admitted that adjusting to everyday life has not been easy even after only nine days. It must be a whole lot more difficult for the six-month students when they return to the 'normal' world.

The above description indicates how the student was advised to allow the 'opening up to God' by reducing that personal resistance which was the cause of distress.

The following passage from a student in the late 1980s, illustrates how students learn to establish dependency on God for everything, in this case for knowledge, as this particular student was worried because she had problems understanding the texts.

One must trust that one will be given everything that one needs. If it is knowledge that one needs, one can't determine what that is and in what way it will be given or when it will be given. It's to do with one's resolution and commitment and willingness to go on… There is no need to suffer anxiety… If you are trying your best to face Him…, that's all one can do… There is education in submission on the course, because if you are submitting to something limited, you are always being shown what that limitation is. There are tastes of the unlimited, even on the first visit, or some intimations of it…[34]

As a consequence of the intentional structure of the course, the students ultimately discover for themselves that the only way that they will get through it is through establishing a deeper connection to God, which involves utter dependency and trust.

One student analysed this typical discomfort experienced at stages during the courses as the battle of the lower ego against this total submission to God.[35] Having followed various spiritual paths over many

---

33. He did advise, though, eating apples or pears if necessary after study or meditation as this would help with the 'earthing' process. My fellow student noted that this was a well-known way of overcoming the effect of cannabis when necessary, as the fruits contain beneficial vitamin C.

34. From an unpublished article by Cecilia Twinch, late 1980s.

35. This 'battle' against the 'will' of the ego is common in most approaches to spiritual development from various traditions.

years and finding none of them to her full satisfaction, she had first begun regular study with a Beshara study group based in Cambridge at which *The Twenty-Nine Pages* were read. She explained:

> When I first read *The Twenty-Nine Pages*, I couldn't understand the teaching but I knew that it was real and that the words spoke the truth. I was drawn to the words in a way that I found inexplicable, but I wanted the education, I wanted to be led and there was submission in asking to be led or shown.[36]

That student attended the Cambridge study group for two years before participating in a weekend course at Sherborne. She found that during the weekend she did not 'respond' to the teaching and was not 'bowled over':

> I then came to Chisholme and joined a 'first study course'. I found it 'overpowering', though for no specific reason, it was not because I didn't get on with the other people on it, but I felt out of my depth, that I was not fitting in and was filled with anxiety. I left at coffee time, having only been there for two or three days, I just couldn't stay. I was very upset though because I felt that there was nowhere else to go for this type of 'inner dialogue'. After some time I knew that I had to go back and I booked on a nine-day course. This time the atmosphere was quite different and I felt welcome. I feel that what had been happening during my first visit to Chisholme when everything felt wrong, was that my ego was fighting the requirement to fit into an order, submitting to an order, submitting to His (God's) will.

The same interviewee made some more relevant points about the reaction of the ego to the structure and activities on the courses. She explained that when she started the first six-month course she worried about her own needs, for example, whether she would still be able to take a daily walk. She continued:

> It is about submitting to God's order, placing one's trust and well-being into His hands. One's habitual way of being clashes with what the structure of the course requires. Instead of reading there are periods of meditation, activities which bring attention to areas of conflict. There are weekly interviews with supervisors at which these areas can be discussed, examined and resolved...one can drop things, one's states can be dropped. One can also observe the reactions of others, because living at close quarters leads to a situation of interaction. People receive what they need in order to proceed on their path for their own good. One needs to be

---

36. Submission to the will of God is the literal meaning of the word '*islâm*' and is central to Ibn 'Arabi's thinking and Sufism in general. This interviewee (I.L.) has participated in both six-month courses and has joined the Turkey trip several times. Interview, Chisholme, 2000.

above egocentric needs and learn the lesson of compassion. One's thinking becomes refined as does one's belief system and attitudes leading to a calmer, happier kind of life.[37]

The advanced six-month course differs from the first six-month course in that it is centred around conversation or dialogue rather than texts to study. This conversation revolves around spiritual, philosophical, religious and existential issues as propounded by the great traditions and particularly Ibn 'Arabi. The desired outcome is a deeper realisation of the meaning of those approaches. However, the students often arrive at that realisation un-prompted, without depending on any particular tradition or reading.

Although it would seem that due to the lack of difficult study texts and its relative looseness of structure the course would be easier for the students, in fact those who were interviewed unanimously described the advanced course as being more challenging than the first.[38] This was, they deduced, partly due to the lack of structure and therefore the need for more self-discipline. Having no texts to refer to left room for conversation that at times flowed with ease and at others did not. Another commonly mentioned problem was the conflict between personalities that arose at times. One student described her experience thus:

> I found the second course more demanding than the first, it's more about getting to know oneself. On the first course one can just be carried along. On the second there is more time to oneself and there tends to be a clashing between people, friction. One has to learn to integrate what happened on the first course and this depends on how much has been realised, this kind of knowledge is not the same as ordinary learning. For me, the beauty of the first course was profound, the beauty of the language and poetry was so strong that one had to avoid being completely caught up in it. Sometimes during conversation on the second course silence is maintained in order to allow the spirit to speak through one. Then when conversation does flow it is beautiful, powerful, one is in a place that is unique and special because this is not usually known of throughout the world. Then afterwards one feels so grateful for the experience.[39]

Another student also explained that on the advanced course more responsibility was put onto the individual to put into practice what had been learnt on the first course. She explained the experience as being: 'Testing and supportive, like planting a tree loosely to allow it to be

---

37. Interview with I.L., Chisholme, August 2000.
38. Approximately ten former students of the advanced course mentioned this.
39. Interview with L.E., Ibn 'Arabi Symposium, Oxford 2001.

Student Experiences 157

buffeted by the wind'. She described both courses as being acts of submission: 'Thy will not my will be done'; 'I agree to expose my faults and will address them'.[40]

A senior supervisor was asked about the difference in emphasis between the first and the second courses. She explained that in the first course the student is put under an education which involves the mode of study in which guidelines have been put into place thereby providing the greatest support to the education. However,

> On the second course, the education takes the mode of drawing out from within the student himself, the meaning that has filtered through from this emphasis on the first course of study, so if you like, it's a taking in on the first course, and the second course is a drawing out of the meaning that has been allowed to open up, uncover this mirror that is in each person for the truth. The second course is to do with drawing out, helping the student to find expression for this meaning that has touched him... Now this drawing out, this finding expression for the meaning, is the beginning for the preparation for conversation. If this expression is developed and refined and clarified through the student undergoing and being willing to find expression, being willing to serve the meaning that he's been given, then the expression refines itself and so becomes the voice of the meaning, the student serves the meaning and becomes the voice of the meaning.[41]

The second course also involves a week-long solitary retreat in a room in the main house at Chisholme.[42] During the preparation for the retreat some texts are studied in private.[43] Throughout the retreat the appropriate *wazîfas* (devotional practices) are performed each day, food is placed outside the door and there is a daily visit from one of the supervisors.

Practical Service and Devotion

The students and visitors to Chisholme are generally struck by the way in which all that takes place there is executed with such love and care, from food preparation, housework or planting bulbs, to feeding the geese. This is all associated with the central spiritual theme of service (*'ibâda*) which was particularly emphasised by Ibn 'Arabi. As a supervisor explained: 'One of the great saints, Abû Yazîd al-Bastâmî asked "Lord, with what

---

40. Interview with I., Chisholme, August 2000.
41. Unpublished interview by Cecilia Twinch with W.L., late 1980s.
42. A shorter version of the central Sufi practice of meditation 'retreat' (*khalwa*)
43. It was explained that although the translations used are well known, they are not for public knowledge.

should I do to draw near to thee" and the answer came: "With that which does not belong to me, to wit servility and dependence". All service is to God, the Beloved'.[44]

The meditation sessions do not take any particular form, and this is intentional. As a student once described:

> It's to do with establishing a relationship between your self and your invisibility, which is Him; like opening doors, being present and willing at the doorway between worlds—if there are two worlds.[45]

The general response to the experiences of meditation and devotional practice is that they are both virtually impossible to describe, particularly to someone who has not participated in one of the courses, but that they involve remembrance of God at its highest level. They wholeheartedly affirm the 'existence of God, the Absolute, all otherness is annihilated so that only Beauty expressing itself remains'.[46]

So what is required on the courses is a balance between study, work, meditation and devotional practices. In order to achieve this balance, a student is required to apply five particular attitudes which are discussed at the beginning of the six-month courses; these attitudes are trust, certainty, patience, resolution and veracity.[47]

Submission and the 'Order of Things'

A central focus of the courses concerns submission and the order of things. The question of submission to God has been discussed above, that is, how a central purpose of the courses is to develop an understanding and practice of inner submission to and trust in God. This submission also manifests in the way certain things are done at Chisholme, and it can sometimes seem strange to an outsider. A very visible example is the way in which the great dining room table is set for meals. It is always set starting at the top end and working down, with all the patterns on the crockery facing in the right direction. Everything that is put on the table is put down in a certain order and position. Only the Principal actually has a fixed place at the top end of the table, but there is a natural tendency

---

44. The attainment of 'pure servanthood' (*ubûdiya*) is probably Ibn 'Arabi's central spiritual teaching. This answer was regularly quoted by Beshara adherents, 1998–2000.

45. From an unpublished article by Cecilia Twinch, late 1980s.

46. Ibid.

47. Refs.: discussion with a 'second generation' former student and qualified psychologist, August 1999. These were the words that Maryam, the first wife of Ibn 'Arabi, described to him, having heard them in a dream. Cited in Austin's *Sufi's of Andalusia*, pp. 22-23.

for all the supervisors to sit at the top as well and for the students to sit at the bottom; this is in spite of the assurance that there is no hierarchical system in place at the school. It was explained that everything has a place and position in God's Order—sometimes it is not appropriate to question why but just to accept this as fact even if something very negative has occurred. This concept derives from Ibn 'Arabi's teaching and coincides with the central idea of service and perfectibility. Everything that a student does whilst participating on a course at Chisholme has to be done perfectly: this ranges from putting one's best effort into study, to hammering a nail in a fence post correctly or finding the most perfect way to dig a flower bed.

Technical Vocabulary
The school has a very distinctive vocabulary that is evident in the way in which students and former students speak when referring to the teachings of the school and is also reflected in its publications. Integral to this is the way in which students come to understand the school's teaching and their own experiences whilst participating on the courses. The example below provides some typical illustrations of terminology used by Beshara students in order to articulate their experiences.

This particular student has been involved with the school since the early 1990s and has completed both the intensive six-month introductory course and the advanced six-month course in addition to other shorter courses, and retreats.[48] In this first short quote she uses the words 'desire' and 'invitation' in relation to her embarkation on the Beshara education and she explains how she did not seek out what Beshara is, but how it sought her out. She explains that Beshara came to her as a result of desire, but where and how did it arise?

> My understanding of Beshara is that it is 'good news' and it concerns getting to know reality and myself. It is innate in every human being, i.e., the invitation that awakens desire is universal, some follow it and some bury it. For some it comes more than once and in others it is a constant invitation in the heart. An invitation to desire, to want to know.

She explained that when she first read Ibn 'Arabi she did not understand any of his writing but she 'knew that it was the Real, speaking the Truth'. She was 'drawn to the words in a way that she found inexplicable'; she 'wanted the education and wanted to be led'. What was significant to her was that 'the desire manifested in an asking, through the submission of asking to be led or shown'. She was then asked if she applied this

---

48. Interview with I.L., Chisholme, August 2000.

understanding of what took place in these terms at the time or later on. She answered that the 'sentiment was present and active at the time', but she probably would not have used this terminology to interpret it then. Even her way of referring to the 'sentiment being present and active' is a typical phrase at the school.

Bestowal of Arabic Names
As with Sufism and other initiatic traditions, most of the staff and associates of the school were first given individual Arabic names by Bulent Rauf, usually familiar, spiritually significant expressions. Many of the students also become recipients of such names during the progression of the introductory six-month course. It was explained that this is common cross-culturally to most religious or spiritual orders. This bestowal functions as a type of initiation at the time that an 'acolyte' makes a decision to embark upon and dedicate him/herself to a new life. Beshara participants today emphasise that these names are not consciously chosen, but are revealed to the recipient or someone closely associated with them, for example, intuitively during meditation or whilst dreaming. The name will tend to describe the essence and character of, or to draw out a particular quality in, the person upon which it is to be bestowed.

LIFE AFTER A BESHARA COURSE:
APPLYING COURSE EXPERIENCE TO EVERYDAY LIFE

The lives of most people who have participated in a Beshara course are commonly transformed in that their understanding of life and existence is often radically altered. Their priorities change and they tend to put more value both on their own lives and on life in general, for example, through an increased emphasis on ecological or other global social issues. They have a tendency to live in accordance with what they have learned at the school. Many keep in close touch and participate, for example, on the advanced six-month course, retreats and other courses, lectures or functions being offered by the school. Here are a few representative cases of the way former students, from many different backgrounds and professions, see themselves as living their lives in consonance with what they have learned during their time at Chisholme.

The Reiki Practitioner
This student first came across Beshara whilst living in Cambridge in 1983. She had been searching for a suitable spiritual path and had just started 'T.M.' meditation. She joined the Cambridge Beshara study

group, and it was with this group that she experienced her first *zikr*. In 1984, she participated on the first six-month course held at Chisholme. Unlike many participants, she describes having 'loved it from the start', it was 'wonderful'. She stayed on to do the advanced course straightaway, and following that she remained at Chisholme, working in the office and the kitchen. After that she went to Sherborne, where she ran the administrative aspects of the school there for two years. She describes both courses as:

> ...completely changing my outlook on life. So that in daily life I was shown that I am a spiritual being and this informs everything that I do, for example, in my approach to work, my social situations and my knowledge of God. Reading the texts of Ibn 'Arabi provides an awareness that knowledge is being given when I get insights into what is being said. Understanding comes not from reading but from the Self...because there is only one God. Understanding occurs in a different way. Slowly knowledge of what unity means grows in one. What I need is given in whatever area I am working, e.g. whilst working in the garden I might be given knowledge of something I need to know while working in that environment.

This student now works as a Reiki healer and takes care of her ninety-year old mother. She maintains that she is helped in this work through knowledge of herself and openness to what is being asked of her. She notes that she is constantly asking to be brought to self-knowledge and this is what is given.[49]

The World of Fashion
This participant has a fashion business and creates her clothes as an expression of what she came to realise as truth about Being, existence and God during her education with Beshara. She is an Israeli who became involved with the school after having attended a local Beshara study group of former students in Tel Aviv. Following a traumatic personal upheaval, she left Israel for Britain and participated in the six-month course at Chisholme. This was in the mid-1980s, and she has been involved with the school ever since.

She specialises in creating clothes for modern women which, though unique, do exhibit an influence of Middle Eastern robes or caftans and classical medieval design. They are made of silk and are available in a wide range of subtle colours. These items of clothing have a unique feel to them and a special way of draping, and because they are made of silk they are exceedingly light but comfortably warm: 'they are like wearing

49. Interview with U., Ibn 'Arabi Symposium, Oxford 2001.

air, and quite unlike anything else ever worn, just by the action of wearing one can promote the feeling of an alteration in consciousness, an enhanced awareness of another reality'.[50]

Her prime objective in creating these clothes particularly for women is to enhance a woman's essential natural beauty. She has strongly developed ideas about this, because she believes that it is wrong that women should to be judged and evaluated by the shape of their bodies. Her approach reveals similarities to those of the social scientist and specialist on the subject of fashion and modernity, Elizabeth Wilson, who proposes that '…dress which is an extension of the body yet not quite part of it, not only links the body to the social world, but also more deeply separates the two. Dress is the frontier between self and the non-self'.[51] My interviewee believes that a woman's beauty is from within, which is in fact reality or God Himself. To quote from her own explanation:

> We fashion clothes for the woman whose beauty is determined not by the perfection or imperfection of one or a few attributes she may possess, but by the whole of her original purpose. What inspires our design is the vision of the New Millennium Woman as free, or freeing, from the condition of effecting attraction, equally, power or influence, by any means other than that which extends from her Being. Remember? Being is Beauty.[52]

In this participant's understanding, her clothes are an intentional expression of Reality, or ultimately in fact the Reality (God) expressing itself. They are particularised manifestations of the divine Beauty. She perceives herself as a channel or as a servant enabling this particularisation to occur. She believes that we in the West, particularly women, are 'naked by the way we wear clothes' in that the clothes are often tight and figure hugging. Thus, we define beauty by form, whereas beauty corresponds to Being. As Wilson suggests 'It is often said that dress enhances sexual attraction because it both reveals and conceals the body. Articles of dress even become for some individuals, essential to erotic arousal'.[53]

---

50. Jane (the student whose account of her participation in the nine-day course has just been detailed) explained that from her previous experience on an alternative spiritual path, putting on an item of this clothing had a similar effect on the psyche as robing had preceding various devotional practices when involved with her own approach, particularly in the way that a shift of consciousness seemed to occur.

51. Elizabeth Wilson, *Adorned in Dreams, Fashion and Modernity* (London: Virago, 1985), p. 2.

52. Ref.: a promotional leaflet for the student's business, 1999.

53. Wilson, *Adorned*, p. 91. Wilson also makes an interesting point, one that is often disregarded in the heat of debates involving fashion and gender—that it is not

Thus beauty is diminished wherever form is treated as deity, through the desire and constant attempts to be physically attractive. In that case a woman's beauty is limited to and identified with the body, but the body, though beautiful, is not the definition of beauty. Ideas about body shape is culturally defined, whilst what is truly beautiful is the woman's actual Being, her essential self. Through wearing clothes made by this student, women can come to realise and begin to know their essential self and feel content with themselves through that realisation.

This student suggested that she found a correlation with her ideas for creating these clothes in Ibn 'Arabi's *Fusûs al-Hikam*, where he describes the relationship between God and servant as, 'when my servant is apparent I become hidden in him, and when my servant becomes hidden I become apparent in him'.[54] She found inspiration concerning conduct and how women should dress and behave in the Sura of Light in the Quran. She felt invested with the question as to what was the deeper relationship between this Sura's elevated transcendental reference to 'light upon light' and the practical question of conduct. She believes that it was during the 1960s that women's dress became increasingly daring, and it was because of the counter-cultural ethics that women increasingly tried to look sexually attractive, though not attractive from their Being. For this latter attitude has to do not with social conventions, but with deeper spiritual 'taste'. Her clothes are not concerned with imposing ideas, but about a profound sense of spiritual taste (*adab*) that does not demean women.

For this student, every stage of the creation of an item of clothing is approached with reference to the 'Total' or Unity. This includes all

---

only women who are 'fashion victims', she says: 'Fashion has been a source of concern to feminists, both today and in an earlier period. Feminist theory is the theorization of gender, and in almost all societies the gender division assigns women to a subordinate position. Within feminism, fashionable dress and the beautification of the self are conventionally perceived as expressions of subordination, fashion and cosmetics visibly fixing women in their oppression. However, not only is it important to recognise that men have been much implicated in fashion, as much "fashion victims" as women; we must also recognise that to discuss fashion as simply a feminist and moral problem, is to miss the richness of its cultural and political meaning' (p. 13). Finally, Wilson argues that dress and ideas of beauty are culturally defined: 'Yet the attempts to explain fashion in purely or even in predominantly sexual terms is doomed to failure. In the first place, standards of beauty—what kinds of looks and appearance get defined as sexually alluring—vary so widely from one culture to another that objective judgements of whether dress heightens attraction or not become impossible' (p. 91).

54. *Fusûs al-Hikam*, chapter on Abraham.

details from cutting to sewing and working on the computer, 'then every part finds perfection in its rightful place'. Her whole approach and the spirit of her creation has roots in what she came to realise and know about herself and her relationship to reality through the school and its interpretation of Ibn 'Arabi.[55]

Visual Arts

The next example shows how the influence of Ibn 'Arabi's concepts as understood and realised by the Beshara School actively inspired the activity of a talented artist.[56] The interviewee was a former student of the nine-day course at Beshara. She was a talented artist who was sent to Turkey with the school by the 'British Arts Council', to draw the Mevlevi dervishes in action. She claims that Ibn 'Arabi guides all her work as an artist. And she explained that when she is working she tries to be in the 'place of Khidr' which has been interpreted as a 'timeless place', or as a place where timelessness meets our human and cosmic timeline.[57] She explained that 'in order to draw the dervishes, I have to be "in the moment" because they are moving; but in order to draw movement I have to bring discipline, knowledge and an understanding of the history of drawing'. She further explained that when she draws she has to let go of everything and 'meet the moment'. If she does not let go of everything, she cannot fully do this. A colleague who observed her working told her that when she drew the Mevlevi dervishes 'she was invited to join them'. She agrees that this was true because in that moment of drawing them she felt that she had 'become one with them, annihilated, lost in the action of drawing and connected with them at the same time'. She explained that even when drawing water, for example, she experiences unity with it. This experience is similar to her experience whilst drawing the dervishes, although water 'just is'. But when drawing the dervishes, she felt that she became consciously connected. This differed from the water because she believes that water is not conscious of what it is, but the dervishes were conscious, and she was conscious and reflecting and being at the same time. This is the result of the uniquely human possibility of conscious surrender to God, which water does not consciously do.

During the trip to Turkey she felt that she had to ask herself why she was really there. Explicitly it was to make art, but she realised that this

55. Interview with G., Oxford, December 1999.
56. Interview with A.I., Oxford, December 1999.
57. This idea was proposed at a lecture at the Ibn Arabi Society AGM, presented by Sara Sviri, lecturer in Hebrew and Jewish studies at University College, London. The informal interview took place with the student soon after the lecture.

was not the principal thing. She explained that she had to be there in a state of passivity, without activity, and that drawing was a secondary process. Having accepted that, she realised that her talent for drawing was coming from the 'right place'. Art can generally be understood as being from the outside looking in, but coming at it from the perspective of Ibn 'Arabi was the opposite. She had already realised this herself, but Ibn 'Arabi formalised it for her.

Psychotherapy and Counselling
A fourth example that goes to illustrate how the effect of the Beshara education can guide the daily and professional lives of former students may be seen in the following account by a psychotherapist.[58]

Before attending any courses at Chisholme, this participant taught physics at a Scottish High school and then became a counsellor at St. Andrews University. She had had some spiritual experience in the Kabalistic mystical tradition. She first heard about Beshara whilst attending a course run by Reshad Feild in Switzerland.[59] A year later she attended her first nine-day course at Chisholme, and recalled her initial resistance to the shared dormitory accommodation. This negative reaction is almost standard amongst new students at the school; most people clearly value their privacy. However, as is also customary at the school, she soon adjusted to the situation and learned to cope by 'submitting to the order of things'. She then participated in the six-month course but found that perhaps due to her former spiritual experience, her outlook had not changed markedly but in a subtle way.

She participated in the advanced six-month course two years later. This is the course in which textual study is replaced with conversation. She explained that although the focus of the course revolves around conversation, in preparation for the week-long retreat, which is now integral to the course, the students were given texts to read, such as some poems from Ibn 'Arabi's *Tarjumân al-Ashwâq*. The particular choice of texts chosen for the retreat usually arose out of the topics of conversation. The format for the retreat was that students would stay on their own in a single room in the main house for a week. They were instructed to say *wazîfas* (litanies of divine Names), as indicated by Ibn 'Arabi. Food was placed outside the door for them to pick up, and they were visited once a day by the head of the school or another course co-ordinator.

The result of this second course was that she became completely aware of God's impulse, and she described herself as 'like a camel being

---
58. Interview with H.A., Chisholme, August 2000.
59. For Reshad Feild, see Chapters 1 and 2 above.

directed by this impulse'. She quoted the following description of this state from the Quran: 'There is no power or strength except in God, the Most High the Most Mighty'.[60]

Having completed the courses, she continued in her line of work as a counsellor, but brought into her work what she had learnt at Chisholme. For example, she ran a course for the Exeter branch of the 'PCA', i.e. the 'Person-Centred Approach', which as the name suggests, involves an individual-focused approach to counselling. During that course she presented a paper entitled 'Ibn 'Arabi's Metaphysics'. She described the course participants as being very receptive to the paper, although she felt at the time that there was room for improvement in its contents and structure. Some time after this she presented the same paper in South Africa, at the *Sixth Forum of the Person Centred Approach*, to positive acclaim and then presented a modified version at a conference in Sheffield under the new title of *In You there is a Universe*,[61] subtitled *Psychotherapy as a Manifestation of the Breath of the All Merciful*. The focus of this paper was on the relief that a person undergoing therapy experiences in relation to the 'merciful Breath' or unfolding manifestation of God as understood by Ibn 'Arabi.

Since the presentation of those papers, this participant continues to bring the influence of Ibn 'Arabi into her work and teaching in her professional life. She is also actively involved with various activities at Chisholme.[62]

Because of the interest and success generated by this student's theories through her proposed correlations between the Person-Centred Approach to counselling and Ibn Arabi's teachings, there follows a more detailed exploration of these possible correspondences presented in a précis of her central arguments extracted from her paper.[63]

First, it is necessary to define of the Breath of the Merciful according to Ibn Arabi. The author explains:

60. Quran 18:13.
61. A quote from Ibn Arabi's *Kernel of the Kernel* (trans. into Turkish with a commentary by Ismail Hakki Bursevi and into English by Bulent Rauf; Gloucestershire: Beshara, 1979).
62. The use of Sufi ideas in contributing to various forms of psychotherapy is increasingly common, particularly in the USA. See the Introduction above.
63. This section has been added since the completion of the original thesis. The paper, by Mhairi Macmillan, is entitled: '"In You there is a Universe": Person-Centred Counselling as a Manifestation of the Breath of the Merciful', in *Women Writing in the Person Centred Approach* (ed. I. Fairhurst; Ross-on-Wye: PCCS, 1999), n.p.

> In the Unknowable station of complete Unity, the Reality is 'rich beyond need of the universes'. In this state of Absolute Transcendence, nothing can be said of Him. Why then should the universes be brought into existence? A *hadith qudsi* (extra-Koranic word of God) states: *'I was a hidden treasure and I loved to be known, so I created the world that I might be known'*. In the poetic language which is necessary to even approximate happenings at this level, another way of saying this is that God (Reality) wished to behold itself and created the cosmos as a mirror in which its own reflection might be seen. This desire first caused God to emerge from (but not leave) the Unity. Therefore, *Love* (or longing or desire) is the cause of creation, and knowledge ('to be known') is the purpose of creation.
>
> Concomitantly, the process of creation is one in which God's *Mercy* predominates. There is no essential separation between the organismic self, its valuing and its archetype or 'mentation in the mind of God', the '*ayn i thabita*' or 'fixed potentiality'. The myriad of created things (the 'ten thousand things' that the Tao refers to) demand, as the *a'yan i thabita*, to come into existence and God, in response to demand (which remember is from within Himself) releases them on the exhalation of the Breath of the Merciful, *nafs i rahman*.

The author then explains the Sufi (and Kabbalistic) theory that humanity is a 'microcosm' of the 'macrocosm' (the universe).

> Every human being is a 'microcosm' of the universe. Each and every individual is created from God's Self and, like a hologram, each fragment also contains the whole. One esoteric axiom is 'as above, so below'; this means that the processes described in 'universal', 'cosmic' or 'God-related' terms, are the same processes that we can observe occurring within ourselves.

In the light of the above definitions we will now explore in brief how the author relates Ibn 'Arabi's teachings to the Person-Centred Theory.

1. The Actualizing Tendency. The author starts by quoting the psychotherapist, Carl Rogers, who first set out the Person-Centred Approach to counselling: '...the substratum of all motivation is the organismic tendency towards fulfilment' and 'The individual has an inherent tendency towards actualizing his organism'.[64] And, the 'formative tendency' within the universe not only provides but *is* the motivational direction.[65] The author then relates these suggestions to those of Ibn 'Arabi:

---

64. C.R. Rogers, *A Way of Being* (Boston: Houghton Mifflin, 1980), p. 123.
65. Ibid., p. 114.

> The primary determining factor (or tendency) in our lives according to Ibn 'Arabi, is... the *a'yan i-thabita*, the latent potentialities, our images in the imagination of God (Truth). A person becomes closer and closer to the utmost that they can be. This does not mean being fatalistic: it is a question of receptivity and of aptitude. What we can become is essentially out of our hands, but we still have our part to play. The essential goal and direction is 'to be that self which one truly is'.[66]

2. 'The Fully Functioning Person' and the 'Gnostic'. Ibn 'Arabi says, according to the author, that:

> ...everything is tied in his aptitude, a man will do what he has to do accordingly... He finds things happening within himself, one after the other, each in its own time. If that man thinks his aptitude in this is short, then he suffers.[67]

The author suggests that this is reminiscent of what Rogers writes of the 'fully functioning person': 'What I will be in the next moment, and what I will do, grows out of that moment, and cannot be predicted in advance either by me or by others'.[68] Guy Claxton, commenting on Rogers' thought, remarks, 'the fully functioning person realizes that his organism can cope on its own'.[69] The author concludes, 'The person who thinks their aptitude is short—who is beset with doubts and worries—is not "fully functioning"'.[70]

3. Congruence. The author quotes Rogers: 'When self-experiences are accurately symbolized, and are included in the self concept in this accurately symbolized form, the state is one of congruence of self and experience'.[71] She explains that he used 'integral', 'whole' and 'genuine' as synonymous with 'congruence', but she suggests that this definition depends on what is meant by 'self' and experience. She asks, what happens to congruence when the idea of 'self' is extended (such as during meditation, when the meditator becomes aware of levels of being not usually accessible and can even experience the disappearance of the concept of 'self'? She explains that Ibn 'Arabi insisted that his disciples

---

66. In Macmillan, 'Universe', p. 9.
67. Ibn 'Arabi, *Kernel of the Kernel* (trans. Ismail Hakki Bursevi; trans. into English by Bulent Rauf; Gloucestershire: Beshara, n.d.).
68. Rogers, *On Becoming a Person*, p. 188.
69. G. Claxton, *Wholly Human* (London: RKP, 1981), p. 126.
70. Macmillan, 'Universe', p. 9.
71. C.R. Rogers, 'A Theory of Therapy, Personality and Interpersonal Relations, as Developed in the Client-Centred Framework', in *Psychology: A Study of Science*, vol. 3 (ed. S. Koch; New York: McGraw-Hill, 1959), pp. 184-256.

observe all aspects of themselves through the spiritual practice of *muhasaba* (examination of one's conscience), which involves not only recording all personal actions of the day but also examining all thoughts.

> This is because 'those who have arrived at closeness to God are responsible for untoward thoughts that come into their hearts'. By examining one's thoughts, a person can distinguish between that which is from God—or we might say, from the authentic self—and that which is from the 'lower self', the *nafs*, the ego. 'Even though God is the creator of all thoughts, all the same, the servant is subject to questioning due to his own unmindfulness'.[72]

4. Empathic Understanding. The author asks: How can it be possible for one person to understand another? What lies behind Rogers' experience (and more significantly, the experience of each of us) that at a deep level there is a 'resonance' between people?[73] She explains that from Ibn 'Arabi's teachings, we see, hear and understand each other within the Oneness of Being. We are only able to see each other through the reflection in the mirror of Ipseity, God the One and Unique (*wahid al- Ahad*), in a way analogous to the kind of mirror device that enables seeing round corners. She continues: 'Yet we are "unique" as well as "one". Thus the inner experience of "understanding", resonance or whatever that means—is unique or idiosyncratic, and "so is the expression of this experience, not a parroted formula".[74]

5. Unconditional Positive Regard. The author explains Rogers' suggestion that a therapist strives to engender a basic attitude of acceptance and respect.[75] The attitude is described as 'warm, positive, acceptant', meaning that the therapist 'prizes the client in a total rather than a conditional way'. Roger's terms this as 'unconditional positive regard'. According to the author, in the view of Bozarth, a foremost exponent of client-centred therapy, unconditional positive regard is the primary condition for constructive change to occur.[76] He explains, quoting Rogers, 'The experience

---

72. Macmillan, 'Universe', p. 10 citing Ibn 'Arabi, *Kernel*, p. 42.
73. Rogers, *On Becoming*, p. 26.
74. Macmillan, 'Universe', p. 10 citing J. Bozarth, 'Beyond Reflection: Emergent Modes of Empathy', in *Client-Centered Therapy and the Person Centered Approach* (ed. R.F. Levant and J.M. Shlien; New York: Praeger, 1984), pp. 59-75.
75. C.R. Rogers, *Client Centered Therapy* (London: Constable, 1951), p. 20.
76. J. Bozarth, 'A Theoretical Reconceptualization of the Necessary and Sufficient Conditions for Therapeutic Personality Change', paper presented at the *Fifth International Forum on the Person-Centred Approach*, Terschelling, Netherlands, 1992.

of threat is possible only because of the continued unconditional positive regard of the therapist, which is extended to incongruence as much as to congruence, to anxiety as much to absence of anxiety'.[77] In other words, suggests the author, the message that the therapist gives is, 'You are alright as you are'. The author suggests several parallels between this approach and that of Ibn 'Arabi, probably the most central, she proposes, being: 'when those aspects of the client that have been blocked, denied or distorted are enabled to become, the process is the intrapersonal equivalent of the original act of bringing the manifest world into existence on the Breath of the Merciful. Unconditional positive regard, then, is a manifestation of the Mercy that englobes and maintains the universe'.[78]

6. The Problem of Evil. The author provides a very interesting discussion about the problem of evil, therapy and Ibn 'Arabi which will be quoted in full here:

> Both good and evil have their origin in God; 'All things are manifestations of God and all actions are His actions, only we call some of them good and others bad'.[79] The Ipseity in the Absolute Unknowable is without quality or determination. But in the phenomenal world the polarities arise, each quality with its polar opposite. As part of the created world, this also holds for human beings. Not surprisingly, in this view, since it is also found in Kabbalistic thought, Ibn 'Arabi appears to be closer to the position of Martin Buber than to that of Carl Rogers—at least as far as Rogers expressed it in the 1957 dialogue with Buber. As the very basis of human nature, Rogers takes into account only one 'pole' namely a 'constructive' one.
>
> ROGERS:...my own experience, which is that when you get to what is deepest in the individual, that is the very aspect that can most be trusted to be constructive... Does that have meaning for you?
>
> BUBER:...I would put it in a somewhat different manner... And my experience is...if I come near to the reality of this person, I experience it as a *polar* reality... There is again and again in different manner a polarity, and the poles are not good and evil, but rather yes and no, rather acceptance and refusal...this polarity is very often directionless. It is a chaotic state. We could help bring a cosmic note into it. We can help put order, put a shape into this. Because I think the good, what we may call the good, is always only direction. Not a substance.[80]

77. Rogers, 'A Theory of Therapy'.
78. Macmillan, 'Universe', p. 10. Macmillan had several more correlations in this section but time and space prevents inclusion.
79. *The Twenty-Nine Pages*, p. 38.
80. H. Kirschenbaum and V. Henderson, eds., *Carl Rogers Dialogues* (London: Constable, 1990), pp. 58-59.

The author concludes by proposing that: The difference is a subtle one as all polarities perceived manifested in the phenomenal world, are ultimately resolved in the Essence (God).

As already mentioned above it is only possible here to provide a brief outline of this student's proposals regarding correlations between Ibn 'Arabi's teachings and the 'Person-Centred Approach' to Counselling. She offered many more parallels in her paper but what is summarized here seems to be the core argument.

Psychology and Ibn 'Arabi. Related to the above section which explores how Ibn 'Arabi's ideas may be applied within a psychotherapeutic context is the approach of an early participant of the Beshara School and lecturer in psychology, Peter Coates, who recently published a study of Ibn 'Arabi and modern thought.[81] In the book he considers some central ideas in modern social scientific thought, i.e., modern philosophy, social science and psychology in the light of Ibn 'Arabi's teaching on *Wahdat al-wujûd*, the Oneness of Being. He says of Ibn 'Arabi's attitude to the human self:

> We can fairly say that for Ibn 'Arabi the human self is to be properly viewed as essentially and unequivocally a point of vision (or locus of awareness) which acts as a mirror in the unitive divine act of self-expression. Ibn 'Arabi tells us that the human in its primordial universal condition is a point of vision which possesses 'no essential characteristics other than totality and absoluteness'.[82] Its very nature is to mirror the totality and absoluteness of the Unity of Being.[83]

Coates proceeds to compare Ibn 'Arabi's approach to that of the modern scientific psychological approach to the self[84] and concludes rather disparagingly that:

> Overall, the prevailing metaphysical picture of the self presented by the late twentieth century psychology might be one of the human self conceived as an intelligent adaptive organism. Whatever its merits (and it probably seems particularly meritorious if you are a cognitive scientist), itleaves so much off the metaphysical agenda that the picture it presents,

---

81. Peter Coates, *Ibn 'Arabi and Modern Thought: The History of Taking Metaphysics Seriously* (Oxford: Anqa, 2002).

82. Ibn 'Arabi, *Fusûs al-Hikam* (rendered into English by Bulent Rauf with the help of R. Brass and H. Tollemache, from the 1832 Boulaq Edition of a manuscript written in Turkish and Arabic c. 1700; 4 vols.; Oxford: Muhyiddin Ibn 'Arabi Society, 1986–91), vol. 1, p. 94.

83. Coates, *Ibn 'Arabi*, p. 124.

84. Ibid., p. 135f.

by comparison with the metaphysics of Ibn 'Arabi, it is a metaphysically impoverished, microcosmic landscape of the self.[85]

In the concluding pages of his book, Coates discusses what he refers to as the 'seismic changes in Western and global twentieth century human life'[86] and relates this to Ibn 'Arabi's concept of *Wahdat al-wujûd*. Coates's approach here briefly summarizes the way in which participants of the Beshara School understand the way in which Ibn 'Arabi's teachings integrate into some aspects of modern psychological approaches to questions regarding the human Self at the start of the new millennium.

> ...The question which stands on the immediate horizon of this new millennium and which faces each of us, collectively and separately, consciously and unconsciously, is the question of 'Who are we?' in the light of the Unity of Being. Ibn 'Arabi is categorical about the answer to this question: the era is no other, we are no other, there is no other. It is the existential realization of this state of affairs, which is for Ibn 'Arabi and his followers the fundamental human project and possibility. The *wahdat al-wujud* of Ibn 'Arabi requires that we go beyond the self-descriptions of modernity, beyond its individualisms, beyond its ideologies, beyond its divisions and its boundaries, and beyond its conceptual and theological categories. The metaphysics of the Unity of Being challenges citizens of the new millennium to reconceptualise its epistemological and theoretical co-ordinates and adopt as its axiomatic descriptor the very idea of the Unity of Existence...[87]

An Actor and Cabinet Maker[88]

The next example of how the teachings of Ibn 'Arabi are realized in the lives of some of the students of the Beshara School is the account given by an actor and a cabinet maker by profession who lives in the USA. He was involved with the Beshara School from its early days and is now active in the US branch of the Muhyiddin Ibn 'Arabi Society. He says of work that it is

> an education, and it is ongoing. There is a saying of Muhammad that 'work is prayer', and there is a piece of calligraphy, commonly displayed in places of work that means literally 'one who earns a living is the beloved of God'.

So this is the intention of this participant regarding work, and he finds that in both activities (as a self-employed cabinet maker and an actor), this applies:

85. Ibid., p. 163.
86. Ibid., p. 181.
87. Ibid., p. 182.
88. Interview with M., Turkey trip, December 2000.

Each job is different in every case and what this requires is to follow or submit to the order (God's order of things) which is both general and particular to each situation. On a practical level, this means that I have to get myself out of the way, put myself under the 'order of things', knowing that what work I do is from God, and therefore let God take over.

With regard to his work as an actor this participant found that he had to be in the 'place of compassion' in order to tell a person's story. He explains that what Ibn 'Arabi tells us is that in the primordial creative act, first God imposed His compassionate Self upon Himself, so therefore everything is the flowing of compassion:

So I have compassion over the character that I am playing and this is whether they display good or bad characteristics, because the aim of the play is to show the audience the story/character so that the audience recognise themselves in the character.

He then explained that he had a problem that he described as hiding, 'not letting the audience see'. The directors told him that he was not letting the audience see characteristics that he was ashamed of in himself. It was pointed out to him during the running of one production, that 'it was a gift to be able to play a particular part because he knew this character's inner life so well, so who better to play the part?' From then on he discovered that he could stand aside from the character and have compassion for him, so that the character's life, particularly his inner life, could be portrayed. The participant also connects this experience to not revealing things in his own self. He also spoke about the problems of revealing emotions as an actor and the necessity to allow the emotion to be real and not an act: 'to have an emotion and then act it out is dishonest, honesty is showing clearly what is happening'.

This is how you should want to live your life. Remove the mask/persona, so that what is revealed is the Real, so that you have not placed your sense of illusory self in between. This is what Ibn 'Arabi is referring to in the opening of the chapter on Adam in the *Fusûs* when he discusses the essence of the Names etc.

The participant concluded the discussion by describing that what is relevant to both his jobs is that he 'has to be willing to take direction'. That is, he cannot be an actor if he cannot take direction, or a cabinet maker either:

But *'this is the quality of submission, this is how one would want to live one's life as a servant'*. This is all a matter of love. This is what I was told when I started cabinet making; a contemporary said 'You *will* make a living, but you need to do this because you love it'.

Art Education, Therapy and Reflexology[89]

The account below was provided by an original student of Beshara who has a degree in fine art. She works in art education, therapy and reflexology. She describes her work as 'bringing people into the moment, for example, through art workshops requiring a completely holistic approach, not working for a mental goal but what is done must be done completely'. She quotes Ibn 'Arabi's discussion about his relationship with Nunah Fatimah Bint Ibn Al-Muthanna[90] in order to illustrate her point:

> I, together with two of my companions, built a hut of reeds for her to live in. She used to say, 'Of those who come to see me, I admire none more than Ibn Al-'Arabi'. On being asked the reason for this she replied, 'the rest of you come to me with part of yourselves, leaving the other part of you occupied with your other concerns, while Ibn Al-'Arabi is a consolation to me, for he comes to me with all of himself. When he rises up it is with all of himself and when he sits it is with his whole self, leaving nothing of himself elsewhere. That is how it should be on the Way'.

To this participant her work means:

> ...simplifying, letting go, not imposing any set of ideas, having to make the self vulnerable and being prepared to face the unknown which is the *ghayb* [the 'unseen' spiritual side of reality]. This is really our true condition, we are facing the unknown at every instant, we are just limited by the extent of our receptivity. Work is to do with 'becoming', allowing receptivity. By leaving the space to God through, for example, prayer, we do not react to the ego as we might and therefore we refrain from some reactions. This is really what we mean when we say 'God knows best', there is no judgement involved or imposition of opinions.

She explained that this could also be understood from the perspective of sainthood and the concentrated intention of the saint (like *himmah*); the help given by a saint through his *himmah* is from the Source of all *himmah*, which is God.

> One has to ask through the interior. The saints are there to bring people to this realisation, this is only possible because the saints are 'complete', they are His Names, they are there as helpers from the Single Source, everything returns to the Single Source.

She further explained that she teaches what she loves, and what she does gives what she teaches love. Her students understand with what they bring and those who have brought all of themselves learn a lot quicker.

---

89. N., Turkey trip, December 2000.
90. Cited in Austin, *Sufi's of Andalusia*, p. 143.

Finally, she uses an aspect of her work, etching, to illustrate how she understands what is happening when she is working:

> I see in terms of balancing the opposites, quite simple element aspects, oils and inks balancing acids and alkalis. This is His beauty in the tangible world. These elements are used to express an image (of Him) much as in the way of cooking. This is what one has been moved to work on, there is a dialogue between materials and ideas and this will inform as one goes along (the artist still has to learn the basic skills though), but this is so with any creative art, being open to what is present and drawing it out. This is not separate from spiritual work, it provides mutual nourishment (job satisfaction). The Buddhists express this as 'non-attachment', not being fooled into thinking that this is ones own expression. The Real [God] expresses itself in this way.

CONCLUSION

This chapter has offered a selection of various aspects of students' experiences of the Beshara courses applying the phenomenological methodological approach to their verbal accounts. It also provides an illustrative sample showing in some detail how the education provided by the school often has an active influence on the everyday lives of the former students and those people with whom they come into contact, thus spreading the seed of understanding of what Beshara means through a ripple effect. Many other important examples of the ways in which Beshara's philosophy is manifested in the outer world can be drawn from the fields of science, ecology, economy, architecture and culinary art, and some of these will be discussed below in Chapter 8.[91]

---

91. One particular publication, the *Beshara Magazine* tended to focus almost entirely on how different interpretations of what Beshara actually represented becomes manifest in all areas of life.

7

THE PILGRIMAGE THROUGH TURKEY

For participants in the Beshara courses, the two-week pilgrimage through a selection of shrines and sacred places in Turkey is the pivotal point of the courses. It is where what has been studied begins to become reality. Before I joined the journey in December 2000, it was made clear to me that the students were not to be approached for interviews because the trip is so intensive for them, as well as being a spiritual journey, and that my position must be solely in the role of a participant observer. However, when some of the travellers, particularly those who were not currently students, discovered my purpose in joining them and learned about my research, they offered to discuss some aspects of it with me and in a couple of cases agreed to be interviewed. The following account will draw on their descriptions and explanations, and on my own experiences as a participant observer.

The discussion of the pilgrimage to Turkey is presented in this separate chapter because this annual journey is open to any interested parties, including former students, Beshara participants and others with no connection with the school but purely an interest in spirituality.

As throughout this study, I have attempted to cover as accurately and fairly as possible the students' reactions at shrines and sacred places, and to the journey as a whole, leaving those experiences to 'stand on their own' without applying any value judgments.

THE PURPOSE OF THE PILGRIMAGE

Since 1973, The Beshara School has organised an annual trip to Turkey that takes place every December, and culminates with the celebration of the 'nuptial night' (*'urs*)[1] of the mystic and poet Jelâluddîn Rûmî and the

---

1. Throughout the Islamic world, Muslims normally celebrate not the birthday of the great saints, but the date of their death, the 'wedding' (*'urs*) of their soul with the divine Beloved.

Sema in Konya.² This pilgrimage was originally organised and led by Bulent Rauf. Although some aspects of it have altered—for example the standard of accommodation throughout the journey has become decidedly more sophisticated—the key shrines and sites visited have remained the same, though the route sometimes varies slightly as does the itinerary for visits to some of the less central key places. The participants on the trip include students who are studying on the six-month intensive course and also, as was the case on this journey, those taking part in the advanced six-month course. The trip is also open to people who have slight or no involvement with Beshara, but who have a general interest in spirituality. The school strongly emphasises that the trip must be consciously intended as a spiritual journey and is pivotal for the course students, as the following quote illustrates:³

> The trip to Turkey is not a holiday, a period of reprieve from study and work, a week of license; it is on the contrary a time for direction and devotion and pleading for the beneficence and *himmah* from the Source of all *Himmah*, so the intensive course can find its proper function and focus: that of advance towards, and approach to a state of non-being in Union (*tawhîd*).
>
> 'Only he who has the love of tawhîd branded in his heart brings light to the tomb of Ismail Hakki Bursevî'.
>
> Consequently it is necessary that all persons of this group of students going on this journey take great heed and care to comport themselves first of all in *adab* (good form), and more, in good taste, avoiding to give, even unwittingly, an impression of laxity to those among whom they will pass.
>
> This means care in dressing, in cleanliness, in comportment, in attitudes and conversation. Therefore, anything that would distract from full conscious attention being paid to these details, like alcohol for example, should not be indulged in on the journey except with moderation and modesty in the times of relaxation in the evenings, yet always paying

---

2. The Sema' is the form of *zikr* which is participated in by those who are commonly known as the Whirling Dervishes. They are correctly entitled the 'Mevlevi Dervishes' of the Mevlevi Order of Sufis, founded by Rûmî's son, Sultan Walad. (Mevlânâ [Rûmî] means 'our master', a title which was bestowed onto Rûmî in his lifetime.) The Mevlevi Dervishes only celebrate this occasion during one week in the year, the week that coincides with Rûmî's Nuptial Night on the 17 December. This is due to a state ruling that became enforced after the Ottoman Empire became the Republic of Turkey after World War One under Mastafa Kemil Ataturk.

3. Ref.: First page of the booklet given to all travellers on this trip. The booklet was originally compiled by Bulent Rauf but has been added to over successive years by various original participants and supervisors of the school. Information about the authorship of the booklet was gained from discussions with K. and T., Oxford, April 2001. The Arabic in the quote translate approximately as follows: *Himmah*—spiritual energy; *Tawhîd*—union with God; *Adab*—good form or right conduct.

absolute attention to the fact that people around them must not think of them as in any way lacking in the strictest good taste.

So it is clearly understood by the travellers that the trip was to be undertaken through the application of a spiritual approach. The particular emphasis on *adab* (good form) is not a universal requirement for all spiritual pilgrimages; for example, some pilgrimages are approached through a less solemn more light hearted but perhaps more taxing approach. For the thousands who walk or bicycle from all over Europe to the Christian shrine of Santiago de Compostella in Northern Spain, for example, this is a triumph over a physical challenge, a physical journey to God which can help the mind to focus. Or there is the flavour of the holiday spirit of the 'medieval package tours', some which actually included souvenirs and entertainment, a taste of which may be found in Chaucer's 'Canterbury Tales' (c. 1390 CE). As is noted in the work of Benjamin Beit-Hallahmi and Michael Argyle,[4] pilgrimages may be understood to be an elaborate form of ritual and sacrifice.

The trip to Turkey is, for the students and friends of the Beshara School, however, above all a pilgrimage, the purpose of which is to visit the shrines of certain saints, particularly those who have a special personal connection with Ibn 'Arabi's spiritual influence. Second, the broader purpose of the journey is to visit other sacred sites, including important mosques, the house of the Virgin Mary at Ephesus, ancient churches and other sites, which included the remains of Greco-Roman temples. The route and sequence of the visits during the journey had been planned initially by Bulent Rauf in a particular way and with a definite purpose that gradually became apparent to the travellers as the journey progressed.

THE INFLUENCE OF IBN 'ARABI AND ITS RELEVANCE TO THE JOURNEY

Since the period in which Ibn 'Arabi lived in Anatolia (now Turkey) up until the present day, his influence has been and continues to be tangible in this part of the world. This influence was propagated through a

---

4. Benjamin Beit-Hallahmi and Michael Argyle, *The Psychology of Religious Behaviour, Belief and Experience* (London: Routledge, 1997), p. 3. The authors also note that on the journey to Santiago de Compostella, which is immortalised in numerous works of art, pilgrims march for hundreds of miles hoping for spiritual salvation and regeneration. They also note that some pilgrimages around the world are initiated in the hope of finding miracle cures by visiting relics or tombs, while others are made to sites where apparitions have been reported or to areas that have been considered sacred for many millennia.

succession of his followers, many of whom became teachers and in some cases taught the sultans themselves.[5] Mahmud Erol Kiliç suggests[6] that it is firmly acknowledged that Ibn 'Arabi was adopted by many Ottomans as their patron saint. He claims that the majority of Ottoman Sufi saints and scholars, who were in fact the Ottoman intellectual class, were his sincere followers. He lists the following as among the most important figures of this transmission: Da'ûd al-Qaysarî (d. 1350), who was the disciple of Kamâl al-Dîn al-Kâshânî and who was, during the initial rise of the Ottomans, the highest religious authority, Shemsuddîn al-Fanârî (d. 1430), 'Abdullâh al-Bosnevî (1636), Niyâzî Misri (d. 1693), Ismaîl Hakkiî al-Bursevî (d.1724), 'Abdullâh Salahuddîn al-'Ushshâqî (d. 1782) and finally Nûru'l-'Arabî (d. 1887). Kiliç also suggests that at the very start of the Ottoman *shajara* (The Ottoman Imperial Tree—*al-Shajara al-Nu''mâniyya*) there was a spiritual seed, in that the founder of the Ottoman Empire, Othmân Gazî, had a spiritual father by the name of Sheikh Edebali. This sheikh was an unknown student of Ibn 'Arabi, and according to one account he actually met Ibn 'Arabi in Damascus. So therefore the 'breath of the Sheikh al-Akbar was behind the Ottomans through Sheikh Edebali'.[7] The second Ottoman sultan, Orhan, established his first religious academy or *madrasa* at Iznik and installed Da'ûd al-Qaysarî, who was a famous fourth-generation disciple of Ibn 'Arabi and commentator on the *Fusûs*, as its director.[8] It was an avid student of Ibn 'Arabi and collector of many copies of works for his private library, by the name of Molla Fenârî (d. 1430), who was to become the first Ottoman 'Sheikh of Islam', which was the highest position in the legal and educational establishment of the Empire. He was appointed to this position by Mehmet I, also known as the 'Chelebi Sultan', because he was a direct descendant of Jalâluddîn Rûmî.[9] Some of the sultans themselves were directly educated through the works of Ibn 'Arabi, for example Mehmet II, who conquered Istanbul in 1453, had an advisor who was an eminent student of Ibn 'Arabi's teachings, and he himself actually commissioned commentaries on al-Qûnawî's works.[10] He also

---

5. See related discussion in Chapter 1 above.
6. Mahmud Erol Kiliç, ' "The Ibn 'Arabi of the Ottomans", 'Abdullah Salâhaddîn al-'Ushshâqî', Life, Works and Thoughts of an Ottoman Akbarî', *JMIAS* XXVI (1999), pp. 110-20 (111).
7. Ibid.
8. Al-Qaysarî's commentary on the *Fusûs* became one of the most influential books in Iran and other areas of the Islamic east.
9. Stephen Hirtenstein, *The Unlimited Mercifier: The Spiritual Life and Thought of Ibn 'Arabi* (Oxford: Anqa, 1999), p. 241.
10. Ibid.

attempted to bring to his new capital the famous Persian poet and most influential transmitter of Ibn 'Arabi's thought, 'Abd al-Rahmân Jâmî. The connection between Ibn 'Arabi and the Ottoman sultans is brought into sharp focus in the case of Sultan Selim I. Having conquered Syria in 1516, he immediately ordered Ibn 'Arabi's grave to be found upon his entry into Damascus. Following its discovery he ordered a tomb to be built on top of it, with a mosque, *tekke* and *madrasa* beside it which symbolised the three dimensions of religious education and realisation.

In addition to the ongoing encouragement of Ibn 'Arabi's influence by the Ottoman sultans, his influence also permeated there in a different way, through an unusual Sufi approach explained in an important study by Victoria Holbrook.[11] Although Holbrook acknowledges that involvement with Ibn 'Arabi's thought was almost universal to the literate Ottomans (in an era when 'literacy' normally included at least Arabic and Persian, as well as Turkish) through his writings, commentary tradition and oral teaching, she points out that it was through the Turkish *Melâmî* sheikhs that Ibn 'Arabi's ideas were frequently put into practice. It is particularly noteworthy that *Melâmî* affiliates typically reject any attempts that have been made to categorise them as a Sufi order, for reasons which are reflected in Bulent Rauf's own actions and characteristic approach. As Holbrook describes here, the Turkish *Melâmî* teachers claim 'self-deprecation' (*malâmîyya*) as the purest practice of Ibn 'Arabi's teachings, without invoking any outward genealogy or chain of authority (*silsila*)[12] passed on by initiation originating with 'The Greatest Shaykh'.[13] She goes on to explain that the *Melâmî* association with Ibn 'Arabi is a result of their own claims as well as centuries of 'popular understanding' which attribute to the supra-order a radical observance of the philosophy of *vahdet-i vucûd* (unity of being), which is most commonly associated with Ibn 'Arabi.

So as may be understood through the brief summary above, Ibn 'Arabi and his spiritual influences have been closely associated with the Ottoman lands, including modern Turkey, since the rise of that great empire.

---

11. V.R. Holbrook, 'Ibn 'Arabi and the Ottoman Dervish Traditions: The Melamî Supra Order', Part 1, *JMIAS* IX (1991), pp. 18-35, part 2 XII (1992), pp. 15-33.

12. '*silsila*': The chain, in Sufism, the continuity of spiritual descent and transmission of wisdom from Shaykh to Shaykh from the Prophet. Aisha Bewly, *Glossary of Islamic Terms* (Norwich: Ta-Ha, 1998), p. 223.

13. Holbrooke, 'Ibn 'Arabi', Part 2, pp. 16-17.

THE SHRINES VISITED AND THEIR CONNECTION WITH IBN 'ARABI

Probably the most significant aspect of the whole journey is the visit to the shrines of the saints. The broad concept of sainthood and the power of saints and their ability to intercede between humanity and God in whatever way God may be perceived is common to most religions, including Islam. The shrines of the saints visited on this trip all had connections, directly or indirectly, with Ibn 'Arabi. Those saints whose connections were less direct could be included within the general influence of Ibn 'Arabi's spirituality in Turkey as discussed above. Those with a more intimate connection included such saints as Ismâ'îl Hakkî Bursevî, who translated Ibn 'Arabi's *Fusûs al-Hikam* from the Arabic into Turkish and also produced a very enlightening commentary on the *Fusûs*. In addition, he was the translator of Ibn Arabi's *Kernel of the Kernel*. Both of his works have been central to the study courses of the Beshara School.

Three saints who are very closely connected to Ibn 'Arabi have shrines in Konya, a city central to the visit.[14] The first is Sadr al-Din Qûnâwî, Ibn Arabi's stepson, close disciple and the initial propagator of Ibn Arabi's works following his death in 1240 CE. The other two saints in Konya who are indirectly connected to the Sheikh al-Akbar in the perspective of the later Ottoman tradition are Shams-i Tabrîz and Jelâluddîn Rûmî. Rûmî, who was to become probably the greatest and most influential Islamic poet mystic, was born in 1207, forty-two years after Ibn 'Arabi. From an early age, he showed great promise in spiritual matters. According to later legends this was attested to by Ibn 'Arabi himself who supposedly met him in Baghdad when he was still a boy. Apparently, Ibn 'Arabi's reaction to the young Rûmî indicates that he had already intuited how great Rûmî would one day become, because he was prompted to say when he saw him walking behind his father: 'How strange, there goes a sea followed by an ocean'. This meeting is said to be the only one that took place between Ibn 'Arabi and Rûmî.

Although they never met in Konya, there was a link made between them there through Sadr al-Dîn Qûnâwî, whom Ibn 'Arabi had adopted and had taught some of his closest disciples. Rûmî studied with Qûnâwî and became his intimate friend. His work, which was profoundly influenced by Ibn 'Arabi's ideas, is concerned with the beauty and love of God. The essence of his expression again as understood by later Islamic

---

14. See n. 2 above.

tradition, is the doctrine of the Unity of Existence as expounded by Ibn 'Arabi, and he illuminated this expression through colourful stories and analogies. It has been said that Rûmî is the 'Pole of Love' and Ibn 'Arabi is the 'Pole of Knowledge', but there is nothing other really than the one 'Perfect Human Being', and there cannot be real Love without Knowledge or Knowledge without Love.[15]

The third saint visited in Konya who had a particular connection with Ibn 'Arabi was Shams-i Tabrîz. There is a special connection between himself, Ibn 'Arabi, Qûnâwî and Rûmî in that if he and Rûmî had not met there is a strong possibility that Rûmî would not have been inspired to embark upon the spiritual path that he did. When they met they secluded themselves from other people for many months and then Shams mysteriously disappeared. The relationship between Shams and Rûmî has been described as follows:

> While in seclusion with Shams-i Tabrîz, Rûmî learned, and he became transformed like the one who has burned in the fire and found intuitive certainty, and after the disappearance of his friend he manifested most explicitly the intoxication of the Lover with the Beloved which has been described. If he loved Shams-i Tabrîz it was because he saw reflected there a perfected image of the Beloved. They were two of a single heart and what better friend can there be than another whose taste is also for the Beauty of the Beloved. Rûmî says in a poem, 'Oh for a friend to know the sign, and mingle all his soul with mine'. They were as 'two bodies with one soul'.[16]

OTHER ISLAMIC, CHRISTIAN AND HELLENISTIC SITES VISITED AND THEIR CONNECTION WITH IBN 'ARABI

The itinerary of the annual journey incorporates visits to numerous Islamic and Christian religious sites, some of them being shared by both traditions. The reason for this common heritage was first, because many Christian sites, particularly churches, became mosques following the Ottoman conquest of most of Anatolia and finally Istanbul in 1453 CE, just as many earlier Hellenistic sacred sites and temples had earlier transformed into churches. As will be shown below, the church/mosque/museum Hagia Sophia is a prime example of this.[17] A second important

---

15. As explained on p. 12 of the Beshara School Travel Booklet, reflecting a widespread traditional attitude in Turkey.
16. Travel Booklet, this passage written by John Brass, p. 11.
17. As described in the Beshara School Travel Booklet: 'The destruction of St. Eirene and St. Sophia after the Nika riots in 532 allowed Justinian to build a temple to the Holy Wisdom so splendid, enlarged and magnificent that, as legend would

reason for including these sites was their association with the Virgin Mary. Although Mary, the mother of Jesus, is a central figure in Christian faith, the Virgin is also highly revered by Muslims, as may be seen in her unique status among women in the Quran,[18] and exceptionally in the case of Ibn 'Arabi.[19]

The pilgrimage itinerary also included visits to several Greco-Roman temple sites. The essences of what these deities represented also related to the later faiths of Christianity and Islam in two principle ways which will be addressed in more detail below. Briefly, it was indicated to the travellers by the school's leader that first Mary was a continuation of what the pagan goddesses had stood for, i.e., the feminine, receptive principle which runs through all things in existence. Second, it was explained how the philosophical conception and metaphysical role of the Hellenistic gods were paralleled by Ibn 'Arabi's conceptions of the 'Names' of God.

The travellers also visited many other sites of interest which were connected with the history and the spirituality in this part of the world, such as the Karye church/mosque/museum[20], the Topkapi Palace[21] and the ruins of Constantinople.

THE TRAVELLERS

As mentioned above, a significant number of travellers on the trip were students on one of the two six-month Beshara courses that were running concurrently. There were about ten participants on each course. Students

have it, when he saw the finished splendour he cried out, "Solomon, I have beaten you"... The building took five years, eleven months and ten days to complete and in 537 CE, the temple was dedicated'.

18. For example: Sura 3:36-52; Sura 19; and Sura 23:50.

19. See the *Fusûs al-Hikam*, chapter on Jesus, and H. Corbin, *Creative Imagination in the Sufism of Ibn 'Arabi* (Princeton: Princeton University Press, 1969); now reprinted as *Alone with the Alone: Creative Imagination in the Sufism of Ibn 'Arabi* (Princeton: Princeton University Press, 1998).

20. A small church originally built in the fifth century and rebuilt between the eleventh and fourteenth centuries, it contains mosaics and frescoes which are masterpieces of Byzantine art. It was converted into a mosque in the sixteenth century and like most of Turkey's holy places, has been officially a museum since Ataturk's secularising reforms in the 1930s.

21. The oldest and largest of the remaining palaces in the world, it was the second palace built by Turks in Istanbul. After Sultan Mehmet II conquered the city in 1453, he built his first palace. Soon afterwards he ordered a new palace, and in 1479 the Topkapi Palace was ready as his place of residence and as centre of government.

on the intensive course included three women in their thirties. One of them was an artist and cartoonist from London; another was from California and worked for the immigration authority; and the third was a veterinary surgeon from Australia. The reactions from these women to the course and the trip will be discussed below. Other students from the first course included two Swiss psychotherapists in their thirties and two women in their late teens whose parents had been original adherents of Beshara; i.e., these girls were 'second- generation' participants. Another participant was a young English woman in her late teens who brought her eighteen-month-old baby on the trip. (Whilst at Chisholme her partner takes care of their child, allowing her to study).

Participants from the advanced course included three 'second-generation' students, one of whom had recently qualified as a clinical psychologist. Another in his twenties had recently gained a university degree in Arab and Islamic Studies, and the third was university educated and had a good job in London.

In addition to the students involved in current courses, other travellers included around twenty students of the school who had been involved with its activities since the 1970s. Some of these people were on the trip in the capacity of 'pilgrims' taking part in respectful visits to holy places, particularly the shrines of the saints. Many of them had been several times before. Others from this group were there to support the leader, (the Principal of the Beshara School, Peter Young), and to assist in co-ordinating aspects of the journey. There were also some children of present and former students of the school who were just attending the journey out of interest and as a pilgrimage, although they were not course participants. One of these children was the twelve-year-old son of the Australian veterinarian, who had accompanied her to England and was residing at Chisholme for the duration of the course. There was a girl of nine, who was gratifyingly interested in the activities of the journey. The remaining children were older, in their teens or twenties.

There was also a large group of Americans, mostly from California, including the secretary of the American branch of the Muhyiddin Ibn 'Arabi Society. Some were members of a Beshara study group that meets regularly in San Francisco. One woman, a Russian academic with medical qualifications and who was an occasional participant in the Beshara study group in San Francisco, had a major interest in Sufism. Since her arrival in the USA in the early 1990s, she turned to the study and teaching of comparative religion, with an emphasis on the psychology of the Kundalini process and contemplative psychology. She had joined the trip because she wanted to know more about what Beshara stood for as a contribution to her own study and teaching.[22]

In addition to several Australians who had been living at Chisholme for some time (amongst whom was the Australian vet who was a student on the first course and other long-standing participants) was a woman who had travelled from Australia solely to take part in the trip. Finally, there was a couple who had no connection with Beshara whatsoever but had learnt about it on the Internet. He was Hindu, a well-known musician with in-depth knowledge and experience of Hindu mysticism. She was English and an artist who used her artistic skills in her employment as a social worker.

ITINERARY OF THE JOURNEY

The journey began in Istanbul where the travellers were accommodated at the Pera Palace Hotel, a building whose interior and decor had not changed since the Victorian era when it was originally built as the final stopping place at the end of the Orient Express.[23] For the first two days of the journey the travellers visited various sites in Istanbul including the shrine of the saint Mahmud Hudai Effendi, as well as the famous Hagia Sophia and the basilica/mosque Topkapi Palace. The next city to be visited was Bursa; the group travelled there by coach visiting Iznik (Niceae) on the way.[24] During the two-night stop in Bursa, the Ottoman capital prior to the conquest of Constantinople, the group visited the shrines of the saints Hazreti Uftade and Ismâ'îl Hakkî Bursevî (famous translator and commentator of Ibn 'Arabi's *Fusûs*) and other related sites such as Uftade's house, the Green Mosque and the Grand Mosque.

---

22. She was my roommate throughout the trip, so I was able to have in-depth discussions with her about the trip and related subjects. She had been actively involved with Sufism and Hinduism both in Russia and America, and had a profound knowledge of religion and spirituality.

23. Its famous guests had included Agatha Christie, the well-known author of detective novels, who wrote one of her most famous works of fiction, *Murder on the Orient Express*, whilst staying at the hotel; Mata Hari, who was a spy for the Germans in the First World War; and Ataturk, the founder of modern Turkey, who proclaimed the country a Republic in 1923 when he became its first president.

24. Famous in, among other things, Church history as the meeting place for the First Ecumenical council, which laid down, in 325 CE, the first 'orthodox', governmentally enforced doctrines of Christianity.

The journey then continued for a three-night stopover in Selçuk, visiting Ayvalik, Pergamum and the Asklepieion (sanatorium) en route.[25] During the stay in Selçuk the party visited Mary's House and the Basilica of St. John. Also visited were the remains of the city of Ephesus, famous for St. Paul's associations with the early Church there.

The journey continued to Konya, a ten-hour coach drive away, where the party visited the shrines of the saints Sadr al-Dîn Qûnâwî, Shams-i-Tebrîz, Mevlana Jelâluddîn Rûmî and Atesbaz Veli. Here the group also attended the famous Sema, the ritual dancing celebration of Rûmî's 'nuptial night' by the Mevlevi Dervishes. Having completed the visits in Konya, the party moved on to Ankara where it visited the shrine of Haci Bayram Veli, the patron saint of that city, and the fascinating Anatolian Museum. The following day the party flew back to Istanbul where they were allowed a day and a half of free time. However, they all decided to visit the shrine of Hudai Effendi again on the last afternoon, and, at the *tekke*[26] adjoining the shrine, all fifty-eight travellers were provided with a wonderful meal. This meal was followed by interesting conversation between the travellers and people involved with the *tekke*.

VISITATION (*ZIYÂRA*) OF THE SHRINES OF MUSLIM SAINTS

As Valerie Hoffman explains in her recent book on *Sufism, Mystics and Saints in Modern Egypt,* saints both alive and dead play an important role in the lives of both Sufis and non-Sufis alike.[27] The tombs of saints that

---

25. Ayvalik is an attractive fishing town which is in sight of the Island of Lesbos best known for being featured in Homer's *Odyssey*. At Pergamum (*Bergama*) the party visited the remains of the acropolis of a Greco-Roman city which included the ruins of a Temple of Athena and an altar to Zeus. The Asklepieion (first established in the fourth century BCE) has been described as an ancient health centre which experimented in the healing powers of herbs and sacred waters. It was considered to be one of the finest centres of its kind in the world.

26. Buildings belonging to the Sufi order associated with a particular saint. These buildings can provide accommodation and meals for travellers, students, visitors and the poor. Hudai had founded this tekke. Our host here was a Turkish University lecturer who had been a student at Exeter University and Leeds University named Suleyman Derin. Concerning this final visit to Hudai, although it is not compulsory, it has almost become a standard feature of the journey that the travellers go to say 'goodbye' to him on the final day of their visit.

27. V.J. Hoffman, *Sufism, Mystics and Saints in Modern Egypt* (Columbia: University of South Carolina Press, 1995), pp. 101ff. Although this book focuses on Sufism in Egypt, much of the information in it concerning Muslim saints is widely applicable throughout the Islamic world, especially in Turkey, since present-day Egypt and Turkey shared a common Ottoman heritage for more than three centuries.

have become shrines are usually attached to mosques, sometimes mosques of very large proportions. Hoffman considers that the saints' shrines in Egypt are sacred places, and this is certainly so in Turkey. These shrines share many of the conventions of sacred space in the Muslim world, e.g., shoes should be removed before entering, ideally people should be in state of purity before they enter the shrine, just as they should before entering a mosque. Hoffman suggests that it is considered proper etiquette to pray two *rak'as* as a sign of respect to the saint within the shrine just as Muslims normally do when first entering a mosque.[28] Pilgrims believe that the saint is particularly 'present' in spirit and receptive to their pleas for help and intercession.

Hoffman explains how the architecture of the tomb also contributes to the sense of sanctity. For example, the tomb-cover (*tâbût*) is situated at the centre of the shrine and is covered with a thick green cloth that denotes again the spiritual relationship to the Prophet.[29] This cloth is decorated with the names of the Prophet and key religious figures and verses from the Quran, often in sparkling gold. On top of the cloth is often placed the saint's personal copy of the Quran and a turban; sometimes there are also other items left by visitors such as handkerchiefs or blossoms. The *tâbût* is usually surrounded by a wooden or brass enclosure resembling a grid-work cage. This is called a *maqsûra* and constitutes a barrier (and simultaneous connection) between the pilgrims and the tomb. It often has a plaque attached to it bearing the name and dates of the saint and some Quranic verses used as prayers and blessings. As everywhere in the Islamic world, there is normally a dome above the tomb.[30] As Hoffman argues:

> All these features converge to create an atmosphere that is, to use Rudolf Otto's expression, numinous. Indeed, many shrine visitors speak of their visitations as profoundly moving and satisfying, something quite distinct from their daily lives; it is clearly a liminal experience, and the shrines are places of spiritual power and holiness.[31]

---

28. '*Rak'a*': A cycle of prostration in *salat* (prayer), which consists of postures of standing, bowing at the hips, prostration with the forehead on the floor and a sequence of utterances. *The Encyclopaedia of Islam: New Edition, Glossary and Index of Terms*, vol. 1–9 (ed. P.J. Bearman et al.; Leiden: Brill, 2000), p. 238.

29. The *tâbût* is an oblong wooden structure over the vault in which the body of a saint is buried.

30. One striking exception being the actual shrine of Sadr al-Dîn Qûnâwî which is open to the sky according to his own instructions.

31. Hoffman, *Sufism*, p. 103.

The scholar Havina Pedaya who lectures in Jewish thought makes an interesting observation that goes some way to substantiate this insight:

> The essential factor in all types of relationship between the holy and the heavenly place is presence, providing as it does the sacred dimension. Mircea Eliade has argued that the sacred place is connected with the primal story, so that the process of arriving at the sacred place is tantamount to arriving at that place at which 'the hierophany repeats itself.' In this way, the place becomes an inexhaustible source of power and sacredness, enabling one, simply by entering it, to have a share in that power, to hold communion with sacredness.[32]

The scholar Mircea Eliade also wrote that 'a centre, a concentration of sanctity, a pole that links heaven and earth always mark sacred space'. He detailed his argument by suggesting that every religious 'cosmos' has possession of a 'centre', pre-eminently the zone of the sacred, of absolute reality, a point where the axis mundi penetrates the earthly sphere.[33] Hoffman agrees that this is how she would describe those shrines that she visited in Egypt, and it appears that this description is quite fitting for the shrines we visited in Turkey.[34] Hoffman concludes her argument by saying:

> ...it is the belief that prayers are more efficacious at the tombs of saints, that the saints function as conduits to God, that makes the tombs of saints shrines at all. The presence of the saints themselves confers sanctity on the shrines and constitutes a nexus of the earthly and the divine.[35]

The location of a shrine is also not arbitrary, the saint having often indicated its potential position during his lifetime. If he did not do this whilst alive, the place is often indicated through a dream after his death; or, as Hoffman points out, through the body itself pulling the pallbearers to the saint's preferred burial site.[36]

Visitors to the shrines may not be people who regularly attend the mosque or pray the standard daily prayer. The shrines seem to offer a feeling of sanctity which is more easily perceived there than at mosques or through ritual. Hoffman lists the reasons for visiting the shrines:

---

32. Pedaya Haviva ('The Divinity as Place and Time in Jewish Mysticism', in *Sacred Space: Shrine, City, Land* [ed. Z. Kedar Benjamen and R.J. Zwi Werblowsky; New York: New York University Press, 1998], pp. 84-111 (94) citing Mircea Eliade, *Patterns in Comparative Religion* (Londo: Sheed & Ward, 1958), p. 368.

33. Mircea Eliade, *The Myth of Eternal Return* (Princeton: Princeton University Press, 1971), p. 12.

34. Hoffman, *Sufism*, p. 103.

35. Ibid., p. 104.

36. Ibid.

[they] exude a sense of power and tranquillity, marks of being in touch with the Really Real (*al-Haqq*). While Sufis may go to shrines as a regular expression of their devotion, other visitors go to shrines in order to feel peace in their turbulent lives, to seek a place of refuge for their problems, and to appeal to the intervention of the saint. Saints' shrines are perceived as places of mercy for the oppressed, as much as they are places of power.[37]

The Visits to the Shrines by the Beshara Participants

Probably the prime purpose of the Beshara School's trip to Turkey was to visit the shrines of certain saints particularly those closely associated with Ibn 'Arabi. Prior to their pilgrimage the students on the Beshara courses would have been studying the principles of sainthood according to Ibn 'Arabi, through texts such as the translation of his *Rûh al-quds* and *al-Durrat al-fâkhirah*.[38] The visits then add real substance to their study and previous experience. The school's travel guide describes the abilities of the saints as such:

> There are *Walîs* (saints) who because they themselves are in the station of witnessing the beauty of Oneness through the witnessing of the plurality of the images of this world and the other world, serve the servants of God by order of the *Haqq* (Truth). They guide them and bring them to safety. Their service to those who want to approach God is to lift off the veils which prevent the witnessing, to ease the way for them to approach the station of Oneness. This they do through their *Himmah* (spiritual power) upon the servants of God by cleaning the hearts of these and removing the impediments on their way and polishing them and protecting them from all that may cause the distancing of the servant from God.[39]

It is important here to bear in mind the objective of the courses at the Beshara School, i.e., for the students to have a true taste of what Reality really is and to come to realise what is truly the essence of their own being. This is what is meant in the above quote that refers to being in the 'station of the witnessing of the Beauty of Oneness'.

The same booklet goes on to describe *Himmah* as:

> ...Spiritual Will and Spiritual Power which comes from the original *Mamad-al-Himmam* (The Place of Extension of all *Himmah*) through the agency and channel of the Archetypal Perfect Man which is the Reality of Realities, or the Reality of Muhammad.[40]

---

37. Ibid., p. 105.
38. R.W.J. Austin, *Sufis of Andalusia* (*The Rûh al-quds and al-Durrat al-fâkhirah of Ibn 'Arabi*) (London: Alan & Unwin, 1971).
39. Travel Booklet, p. 7.
40. Ibid.

Although it is not absolutely necessary to go in person to a shrine, since it is of course possible to encounter the saints in the spiritual realm, it is considered more appropriate and respectful to go in person if at all possible. As we have seen above, the saints, although outwardly dead in a historical sense, are known by pilgrims to still be alive, receptive and active in responding to their prayers and petitions. As the Beshara School booklet says:

> One does not have to go to the tombs of such people to plead for their *Himmah*; but to make the effort of fully abluting, going especially to visit them at their last worldly abode, since there is no other 'place' where they abide, is a sign of determination and of delicacy and of reverence, so as to put oneself at the mercy and compassion of the 'Friends' of God so that through your plea—which possibly they have provoked—they are moved to respond with clemency and compassion with the *Himmah* which they have derived from the Source of all Spiritual Will and Power, the *Mamad-al-Himmam*, and act in one's favour and help to cleanse one and bring one closer to God.[41]

The instructions in the booklet then advise the travellers to prepare themselves for the visits to the tombs by proceeding in a state of reverence, in a state of cleanliness, with a pure and trusting heart and to ask the saint for *Himmah*, and then repeat for and dedicate to the saint the *Fâtihah*[42] and then the *Ikhlâs*.[43] These instructions and what has been said about the saints in the booklet corresponds to much of what Hoffman had described at similar shrines in Egypt. As we shall see below, the behaviour of the visitors inside the tombs also corresponds to her impressions in most ways.

Before visiting a saint's shrine, the Beshara travellers were expected to have performed a complete ablution, which involves a full shower including washing the hair. This ablution is prescribed by Islamic religious law and is required of worshippers before participating in certain prayers or rituals (for other rituals, only partial ablution, i.e., washing of hands, feet, face and head is obligatory) or in preparation for a visit to a saint's tomb. This ensures bodily purity. But above all they are also expected to approach the shrine in a state of inner purity of intention. This was partly established by maintaining silence during the journey to

---

41. Ibid.
42. The *Fâtihah* is the opening sûra of the Quran. *The Encyclopaedia of Islam*, vols. 1–9, p. 107. The *Ikhlâs* involves dedicating, devoting or consecrating oneself and is pre-eminently an interior virtue of the faithful Muslim (p. 149). In Turkish culture particularly, these prayers are especially recited for the souls of the dead.
43. Travel Booklet, pp. 7-8.

the tomb. As the tombs were usually located some distance from the hotels in which they were staying, the party was usually transported at least part of the way by coach (and on the occasion of the visit to Hudai Effendi, by ferry also). Having boarded the coach, the leader would then instruct all the travellers to be quiet and maintain silence until after the visit to the saint. This period of silence allowed for the cleansing of thoughts and the reduction of negativity, in other words purifying the heart and mind. It also allowed for the thoughts to focus on the saint and his qualities, as well as generating an attitude of reverence and trust. Quite often the coach could not park very near to the tomb in question, and the travellers were dropped off and then had to walk a fair way, frequently through a bustling city street, whilst still in silence. As the travellers neared the tomb, the women covered their heads with scarves, an obligatory requirement for female pilgrims. On entry, everyone had to remove their shoes.[44]

Once inside, the travellers respectfully greeted the saint and offered their required prayers. Normally, the prayer, *al-Fâtihah*, is said for and in dedication to the saint. At several of the tombs there were large crowds of local visitors, many of them women. This led to difficulty at times in getting very close to the tomb. The inner architecture of most of the shrines visited was almost identical to the way in which Hoffman described the saint's tombs in Egypt and other Islamic countries. The shrines visited by the Beshara group usually had the main tomb of the saint along with other small tombs belonging to his family and followers surrounding his grave.

Having murmured the required prayers, the visitors would then try to get as close to the tomb as possible. (Ideally they would say their prayers very close to it.) Once beside the tomb, some of them held onto the bars of the grid-work enclosure (*maqsûra*), others held their hands out palms upwards, the normal gesture for petitionary prayers (*du'ât*). At this stage they are also asking for the saint's *Himmah* and the hands are out held as though to receive it. Their request for that blessing is in the hope that the saint would act in their favour, helping to cleanse them and to bring them closer to God.

Pilgrims might also ask a particular question or for help to solve some specific problem. These types of personal requests are usually responded to through dreams or apparent coincidences. The visitors then circumambulate the tomb whilst remaining in a receptive state and sometimes murmuring prayers and blessings. Having done this, some return to the

---

44. These are general Islamic requirements for worshippers entering into sacred space, whether shrine or mosque.

maqsûra, whilst others stand or sit around the outside wall of the shrine communing with the saint. The holiness and blessing (*baraka*) of the saint is believed to remain with objects brought back from the tomb, and attendants at some of the tombs hand out sweets and other blessed objects to visitors.[45] Finally, the visitors leave the tomb, carefully avoiding turning their backs on the saint. Once outside the sacred place, shoes are replaced and scarves removed if desired. Most of the Beshara group seemed subdued and introspective for some time after the visits, and silence was often spontaneously maintained for several minutes.

THE TRAVELLERS' REACTIONS TO THE VISITS

Reactions to the visits to the shrines tended to vary from those of extreme and visible emotion, through subdued introspection, to no reaction or response at all. A common thread that ran through all the various visits and was agreed upon by those group members to whom I spoke was the feeling of a quite tangible 'presence' or power in the tombs; a feeling of being in the palpable presence of a 'living' being.[46] Other descriptions included feelings of love and being loved, peace, calm, confidence, certainty. Someone described a burning/tingling sensation in her hands when she held them out to receive *Himmah*. Some group members described an experience in the shrines akin to prompting their memories and bringing to the fore of their consciousness knowledge about the reality of existence and of their own being which they already knew about intimately, but had buried below the level of their conscious awareness and had long forgotten.[47]

---

45. Some of the group visited the house of the saint Hazreti Uftade (b. 1487 CE) and were greeted there by a woman who is a direct descendent of his and also the caretaker of the house. When we had paid our respects and left a donation, she presented us all with sugar lumps representing the *Himmah* of Uftade. We were told to eat these in order to take in Uftade's 'sweetness'. We were also given salt at the shrine of Atesbaz Veli, Rûmî's cook for the first Mevlevi Dervishes, and instructed to put it with food when cooking, again in order to retain the *Himmah* of the saint. At the shrine of Hudai, some of the female Muslim pilgrims also handed out blessed sweets to members of our group.

46. I asked a large selection of the party about this, and this feeling was certainly a common one even if other aspects of their experiences varied. These descriptions tie in with those described by Hoffman above.

47. This experience happens frequently to students on the six-month courses during study periods. For example, a group may be reading a passage from Ibn 'Arabi and the meaning of the text falls into place like awakening a memory, as though the meaning is something innate, something which they have always known about.

As Hoffman also states, the strength of the feeling of presence can vary from shrine to shrine as can the 'flavour' of the presence.[48] The visitor's reaction to the saint can also be affected by the personal 'relationship' between the visitor and the saint.[49] Tears were also a common reaction at some of the tombs, sometimes silent but at other times somewhat overwhelming. For example, several members of the group were strongly overcome at the house of the Virgin Mary near Ephesus.[50] Although this is not a tomb but the traditional site of the 'Dormition' of the Virgin (the Assumption of her body at death), a shrine within it has become a place of pilgrimage for both Christians and Muslims; many miracles have been associated with it. A possible reason for such overwhelming reactions taking place as a result of this visit could be the associations related to the Virgin Mary. In addition to being the mother of Christ, and the central female sacred figure in the Quran, she is also associated in this area particularly with the feminine principle that is present in all levels of existence. This principle has manifested and been worshipped, particularly in the area of Ephesus, under many names including Cybele, Athena and Artemis. Mary could be understood as a manifestation of this principle, especially associated with an all-encompassing outpouring of divine compassion.[51] It was the feeling of an outpouring of unconditional compassion, acceptance and love from the presence of Mary that seemed to be responsible for the triggering of strong emotional reactions amongst many of the party at this place.

Similar experiences also occurred at some sites not 'officially' connected to any particular saint. For example, the party was taken to the tomb of Sultan Mehmet I in Bursa. His *maqsûra* was in the centre of a

48. Hoffman, *Sufism*, p. 107.
49. For example, one of the travellers felt a special connection with Sadr al-Dîn Qûnâwî because he was Ibn 'Arabî's stepson and direct spiritual heir, and at the time of the journey this traveller was engaged in writing about Ibn 'Arabî's works.
50. At the Third Ecumenical Council of 431 in Ephesus, it was claimed that Mary came to Ephesus with St. John between 37 and 48 CE and lived and died here. The site of her house and ascension (one of the major holy days of Catholicism) was for centuries a Muslim pilgrimage site before this recent 'rediscovery' in Catholic circles. The discovery of the work of Clemens Brentano of 1852, *The Life of the Young Woman, the Virgin Mary*, based on the revelations of Anne Catherine Emmerich, amazed everybody. The location of the house and its site were described in full detail. After the discovery of the house, the Archbishop of Izmir declared it a place of pilgrimage in 1892. On 26 July 1967, Pope Paul VI visited the place and prayed there. The house has been a place of pilgrimage since and there have been many miracles and cures associated with it.
51. See Chapter 4 (pp. 114-16) above and the discussion concerning Ibn 'Arabî's concepts of the feminine dimensions in the divine.

highly decorated mausoleum. He was not recognised as a saint. However, one of the party was overcome by a powerful spiritual presence in the tomb, quite as strong as any that she had felt in the shrines. She felt faint, her knees were weak and her heart was racing. She commented on this effect to the leader of the group who said that he had felt something similar on his first visit to the place many years before. And he explained that although this Mehmet I was not officially recognised as a saint, many Muslims recognised him as one.[52] Another in the party felt a strong presence in the tomb that made him feel very ill, the sensation passing as soon as he left the place.

In addition to providing *Himmah* to those who are worthy, the saints are also understood to solve problems and answer certain questions, as may be seen in the following personal example. This account is from one of the travellers on this trip who was an original student of Beshara and knew Bulent Rauf very well (actually living in Rauf's London house for some time). Although English born, he has lived in America for many years and is active there with Beshara and the Ibn 'Arabi Society.

The incident occurred when this pilgrim participated in the Turkey trip in the early 1990s. He had been suffering from headaches intermittently for several years and whilst standing at the 'wishing column' in Hagia Sophia he decided that he would request a cure from his headaches at all the sacred sites that the group would be visiting. Having completed nearly all the visits, he was conscious of no definite relief from the headaches but still had the sense that he was 'surrendering to something'. He then remembered that years before whilst meditating during a retreat at Chisholme, he had asked for the headaches to be removed, and had received an inner answer which was 'You wouldn't feel like this if you were in complete conformity'. It struck him then in Turkey when the relief did not occur that he could be asking the wrong question, and that what he needed to be shown was what it meant to be in 'complete conformity'. He still had one visit left to complete, and this was the final (non-compulsory) visit to Hudai on the last day of the trip. He decided that he would ask Hudai to show him what it meant to be in 'complete conformity'.

In order to get to the tomb of Hudai from the hotel that is annually used by the group in Istanbul, it is necessary to cross the Bosphorus by ferry. During the crossing, the pilgrim decided that he would take his father with him and introduce him to Hudai; his father had died when he himself was only three years old.[53] On entering the tomb and before he

52. Sultan Mehmet I was a direct descendent of Mevlana Rûmî.
53. Experiences like the following are common for people involved with any form of Sufism or cognate spiritual traditions and are at the heart of Ibn 'Arabi's

could ask anything, Hudai said 'I love you' and at the same time, simultaneously, the pilgrim was saying back to Hudai 'I love you'. Then Hudai said 'this is complete conformity'. For the pilgrim, this corresponded with what had happened at Chisholme many years before. It had not, therefore, been a matter of asking for a cure for the headaches, but he should have been asking what was meant by 'complete conformity'. He had been told this years before, so in retrospect he believed that that particular retreat at Chisholme was the beginning of true self-knowledge of what it means to love and be loved.

After this simultaneous exchange of words, the pilgrim said to Hudai 'I have brought my father, I want to introduce him to you', and Hudai's reply was, 'I am your father'. His perception then shifted away from his actual father to a true understanding of what one's father is, i.e., 'unconditional love, which is God acting through the saint'. He then pointed out the significance of the order of the saint's relationship to these experiences, i.e., what came first was 'I love you' which equalled 'complete conformity'; it included 'no parenthesis, no "with", just total Unity'. This simultaneous 'I love you' was unconditional, this realisation being followed by the knowledge and understanding of who his father really was.

The traveller said that he was 'broken down' by this response and also as a result of previously unresolved grief at his father's death. He was also 'heartbroken' to leave Turkey and Hudai the following day, and the last thing that he saw as the aeroplane circled Istanbul was Hudai's shrine directly below.

He describes that in the following years he was given the space, capacity and grace to deal with the grief of death. His headaches also vanished. He thinks that this was a gift from Hudai that was brought about through 'beautifully arranged delicacy'. This experience correlates to the experience that this participant had following Bulent Rauf's death. Having been devastated by Rauf's death he believed that Rauf eventually indicated to him that even in death there is no separation from the living.[54] He concluded that the appearance of Hudai's tomb below the aeroplane as it circled Istanbul was a gift of the same nature, i.e., 'there is no separation'.[55]

During conversation, another American traveller agreed that the powerful, tangible presence (*Himmah*) within the shrines reaches beyond

---

teachings. As we have seen above regarding the saints, they are understood to still be alive in a different level of existence, as indeed are ordinary people who have died to the material world.

54. For the full account see Chapter 1 above.
55. From discussions with M. on the Turkey trip, December, 2000.

rational explanation.[56] She had travelled widely and visited the shrines of saints of many religious traditions. She believes that the power and presence felt at these shrines is 'pure love', it is a 'comfort, reassurance and a blessing'. She suggests that if a person is 'open enough' they will feel this presence anywhere, but usually, in their daily lives, people are closed and unaware of it. The presence is more concentrated in the saints, and she proposed that if a person is 'opened up' to it through one of the saints, it is then possible to bring it back with them to their normal lives even, for example, if they live in a city. The result is that they can go about their daily lives with a more conscious awareness of what Reality really is.

Retrospective Accounts from Two Former Participants

This section will conclude with two accounts from former participants of Beshara.[57] The first involves a question-and-answer email interview that took place since the first round of data collection. The interviewee has been a participant of Beshara since the 1990s and was also interviewed when data was being gathered for the original thesis (at that time providing valuable data for Chapter 6, included in the section 'Life after a Beshara Course: Applying Course Experience to Everyday Life'). She very generously agreed to be interviewed for this chapter, and the questions and absorbing answers are as follows:

1. How did you feel/what was your reaction to the pilgrimage in general? How did you feel/ were affected at the shrines and sacred sites?

> Being on the pilgrimage raised my awareness of the changes in human spiritual consciousness, era following era, for example:
> - Didyma; the Oracle of Apollo, passing away at the start of the Christian era ('Apollo has left the building').
> - Ephesus; Diana/Artemis giving way to the consciousness represented by Mary, and the church of St. John.
> - The Chora, Istanbul, where the Byzantine mosaics were not destroyed in Islamic times, but covered, so that we can now see the iconography. And the survival of the Greek Orthodox church of Panaya. The magnificent Hagia Sofia, embodying Christian, Islamic and secular eras.
> - Iznik and the significance of the definition of the nature of Christ and the Council of Nicea.

---

56. A member of the Beshara Study Group in San Francisco and a psychoanalyst by profession.

57. These two accounts have been very generously provided for me since I submitted my original doctoral thesis: they were both provided in November 2008.

- Visits to the 'Saints' giving the sense of the chain of transmission, e.g., Haci Bayram to Sumuncu Baba to Uftade to Aziz Mahmud Hudai to Ismail Hakki Bursevi, all in the Akbarian line (line of Ibn 'Arabi). And the Beshara School has its place in this line. As we were told at Hudai's tomb: 'The friends of God, their hands are everywhere'.
- Also, the special relationship in Konya; Mevlana, Sadruddin and Ibn Arabi.

More generally, brought up as a Presbyterian, I had never been much aware of saints. Going on the pilgrimage gave me a sense of these people as very special examples of the human being; the 'perfect ones', confirmation for us of 'the perfectibility of man' (humankind).

2. Did your reactions vary at different sites/shrines?

Yes, my favourite place/visit is Mary's House at Ephesus. Probably some connection with my given name which is 'O Mary' in English. Visiting the different places is like going to different houses, the inhabitants of which you respect and enjoy, but each in their own way different. I am reluctant to suggest that I had strong, particular reactions but that is partly due, I'm sure, to my Presbyterian/rationalist background.

3. If you have been more than once, has your response altered since earlier trips?

On my last trip (2005), I was much more deeply aware of a sense of continuity through time of the message being brought out to humankind, through the different eras represented in the places visited; Didyma, Priene and Miletus, Ephesus and the 'Islamic' sites in Istanbul, Konya, Ankara. I was reading *'The Nightingale in the Garden of Love'* (Paul Ballanfat), which seemed to help tie it together.

I have been on the School pilgrimage four times altogether, but my first visits to Turkey were before I found Beshara. On the first I found myself staying at Robert College, where Bulent Rauf had been educated, and also became entranced by Hagia Sofia. On the second and third I visited Mary's House and Ephesus and loved the place. Visiting with the school deepened this feeling.

4. What does the journey mean to you?

It's hard to put into words. It's literally a 'grounding' or 'earthing' of ideas and/or what is read on the course (the first course in particular). 'Reading' the physical places, perhaps. What is travel all about anyway? The pilgrimage is a focussed and intensified 'travel'? An outer journey connected to the inner journey of the seeker/gravellier.[58]

---

58. AH November 2008.

The second very personal account below was provided by an original participant of Beshara. It offers an alternative approach to the Turkey pilgrimage to those reported above, as it relates not only to the participant's original journey but also details of events leading up to it. It concludes with an interpretation of events and how the participant understands them to relate to the 'unveiling' of Beshara.

> We first went to Turkey in 1970, the year that Hazel and I met at Cambridge University. We had both acquired a taste for travel and had separately visited Spain, where Hazel worked for 6 months as a governess and in North Africa—which I had hitchhiked through the previous summer.
>
> For the summer of 1970 I had targeted Iran and my passport boasted a heralded eagle—the insignia of Imperial Persia. Hazel's trip was less ambitious—to visit her friend Vivi in Crete. So we were heading in the same direction and joined forces for the early stages. But fate was not to take me to Iran, as Hazel and I were betrothed in the romantic city of Venice—she just 20 and I still 19!
>
> So our journey took us to Crete then Rhodes and then across to Marmara in the company of a large cheerful Italian man—who took a liking to us—especially Hazel whose Spanish was understandable—he was missing his Spanish wife.
>
> We had already acquired a taste for 'magic 'places' having been introduced to the mysteries of sacred sites through the work of John Michell, which rescued me in particular from the self destructive world of left wing student politics of that time. In Crete we visited the beach where Odysseus was said to have landed, and followed the lines of ancient pathways through the desolate scrub in the heat of the day, carrying overweight and badly designed backpacks! In Rhodes we met with Mir, a so called monk—who lived in an ancient cave and enticed wanderers in with his bongos made from Quaker oat tins—a remnant of the British Empire.
>
> So seeking strange places and sleeping in caves and ruins was already imbued in us, before we ever knew that this was a 'sufi practice'.
>
> Once in Turkey we travelled en-tourage in a hired mini-van with our Italian patron up the west coast of Turkey pausing at the great sites Priene probably and certainly Ephesus, little knowing that this was the first of many visits over the next 40 years. Our Italian returned whence he came, leaving me with an infected foot and us with no particular plans. Leafing through the brochures of Ephesus we learnt of the Cave of the Earth Goddess Cybele and the Cave of the Seven Sleepers and above all we learnt of Meriam Ana—the House of the Virgin perched high above the ancient city. So, returning to hitch hiking—we made our way to Seljuk where we left our burdensome bags in a café and set off across the fields where we were fed most hospitably by a family tending watermelons—and in return handed out antibiotic cream (which I had for the infected foot) and elastoplasts. The night was spent in a huge collapsed cave with copious quantities of ripe figs—more than we had learnt to digest.

> The following morning we set off up the long climb—but not before another helper appeared and brought us into the sweet presence of Our Lady—such a welcome and such joy. Beshara as such did not exist in 1970, but its invitation was already being felt, through the presence of one of the closest of God's friends.[59]

My interviewee continued by explaining that what was going on, i.e., the gradual revealing of what was to become known as Beshara, did not at that time, have a name. Its emergence he suggested, was analogous to the birth of a baby. When a baby is born, the parents will see what it is like and then decide on a suitable name. Similar was the situation with the naming of what was too become known as Beshara.

Other Sites Visited
The itinerary included visits to numerous beautiful mosques, churches that had become mosques following Ottoman supremacy, and churches that had become mosques and were now officially museums such as Hagia Sophia and the Kariye Museum (originally the church of St. Saviour in Chora monastery). These famous buildings offered stunning architecture, mosaics and fascinating history. Many travellers described feelings of awe and reverence within them. In Istanbul the group also visited the Ayazma which is a church dedicated to the Virgin Mary. Here all the party sampled pure water that bubbled up from a sacred spring over which the church had been built. This visit was to interconnect with the later visit to Mary's House near Ephesus, at which members of the party also collected water from a sacred spring at the site.[60]

The party visited several Greco-Roman sites around the region of Pergamum and Ephesus, where various deities had been worshipped up until the rise of Christianity. Worship of the feminine deity in many aspects had been particularly evident in this area before Christianity, for example as Athena, Hera and Demeter. The principle feminine deity in Anatolia, though, was the fertility Goddess 'Cybele', later known as Artemis, who had been worshipped throughout the region. As we have shown above, the house of the Virgin Mary is located in that same region of Ephesus and has become a wider centre of pilgrimage. Many would argue that this is not purely coincidence and that there is an association

---

59. This account about William and Hazel's earliest trip to Turkey was provided for me since completion of my original thesis in 2003, by William on 2nd November 2008. William and Hazel's names are lightly disguised.

60. Water and sacred springs have a long historic association in many spiritual traditions with female deities.

between or even an ongoing continuation between the former goddesses and Mary.[61]

The final Hellenistic site visited was the Temple of Apollo at Didyma. It was here that a question posed for the group early on in the journey was confronted and partly resolved. The group had been asked by the leader to mull over the question of why the itinerary was set in the way that it was. It was thought by some to concern ongoing and continuous revelation from the One God through various symbolising revelations i.e., pagan, Christian, Islamic, to where we are today—still part of an ever unfolding revelation, the One Truth emerging through different faces. This answer was partly correct but the leader interconnected it more with Ibn 'Arabi's mystical philosophy and discoursed about the successive eras of religion, particularly 'pagan' religion, arguing that the gods represented different forms of the One through the divine Names until the arrival of Christianity, when forms were no longer needed, and then to Islam where there is no form at all.

Although there were other tourists at these sites it was possible at times to explore them in solitude and several travellers reported experiencing feelings of sanctity, and reverence and some kind of trace of a divine presence even in these places.

Reactions to the Trip Overall

In spite of having been asked not to approach the pilgrims for interviews during this trip, some were prepared to offer their opinions on aspects of it anyway. This included a discussion about why people do not often want to speak about the trip. It was concluded that this was because, from their own point of view, the experience was personal, spiritual, involving the heart and it was difficult or impossible to describe. The 'big question' arose as to what the experience is really all about and how is it possible to talk about it anyway. Ibn 'Arabi and Rûmî both frequently acknowledge the difficulties involved in talking about this.

The overall impression received from those with whom I spoke was that the journey was inwardly 'turbulent' in much the same way that the six-month courses at Chisholme are. A traveller described being in a state of perplexity, disturbed in a way, at times in a state of elation but at others overwhelmed with emotion—a 'roller-coaster' of feelings, emotions and reactions. Another came and apologised on the last day for being unsociable during the journey, having been, she explained, so wrapped up in herself. She said that the journey had been full of 'ups and

---

61. The leader of the group supported this idea as did most of the other travellers to some extent.

downs' exactly like the course was at Chisholme. Someone else also described the journey as 'turbulent', sometimes good, sometimes not. She found that the only way to cope was to open up to and trust totally in God; let God lead.

One traveller who was an original student of Beshara offered me his analysis of the journey:[62]

> The trip is a spiritual journey much like the courses at Chisholme, the purpose being 'Union'. During the trip the travellers meet and absorb if possible, different Names of God, i.e. different aspects of the divine, including the Greek and Roman gods. These visits often cause the arousal of a 'realisation' or an 'awakening of knowing', knowing something that we already know. On the Chisholme courses this happens when something someone says in conversation or study may cause this meaningful effect—something that in our hearts, we know. This is also happening at the sites. Given space at the sites we could for example, walk down a hill and find a temple to some Goddess and feel a 'breeze' of that aspect of divinity (divine name) still at the site. This is a gift/grace from God, the One Divine.

He then commented on James Morris's use of films in a recent seminar at Chisholme, to illustrate Ibn 'Arabi's concept of 'hidden sainthood':

> Who are these people (in the films) who are like 'hidden saints', where do they come from? The same could be asked of saints and sultans on visits, although they lived long ago, their influence is still palpable. Ibn 'Arabi is a prime example of the 'word' as direct action of Reality. So God's grace is working through in all different ways. In some ways what has been said above is obvious and something we know, but in other respects it needs someone with a gift of articulation to describe it.

He continued:

> What we are doing is getting to know what we really are—but really know—not just talk/read about it, but really know. The journey feels like a great outpouring of compassion from God!

And concluded:

> This trip is unique in comparison to, perhaps, other organised spiritual journeys in that Bulent Rauf originally organised it, and this compounded with Bulent's Turkishness and his connection with Ibn 'Arabi contributes to its uniqueness.

On the final evening in Istanbul, the whole party was provided with a meal offering at the *tekke* of the saint Hudai. This meal was actually a breaking of the fast feast, as Ramadan was taking place at the time. It

---

62. Discussion with E.R., Turkey, December, 2002.

was followed by stimulating conversation about Sufism and Ibn 'Arabi with the organiser, travellers and some adherents of the *tekke* in a meeting room. All the travellers were deeply impressed with the extent of the generosity, kindness and hospitality shown them, particularly as they were foreign strangers.[63]

CONCLUSION

In this chapter I have, in accord with the whole study, applied the phenomenological methodological approach both to acquiring data during the pilgrimage and interpreting it afterwards, therefore allowing the personal spiritual experiences of the travellers to 'speak for themselves'. To provide an alternative interpretation and analysis of some of the experiences of the travellers during the trip, the methodological approach of the psychologist might also be beneficial, but such an approach would require a researcher with a thorough professional background in appropriate areas of psychology. I have though offered a brief alternative perspective on the reactions of the travellers at various shrines and sites during the pilgrimage from the discipline of the psychology of religion. I mention here some observations made by researchers in the field of psychology and neurology as well as the psychology of religion in order to provide their interpretations of similar experiences observed under comparable circumstances to those cited above. In an article by the psychiatrist Moshe Kalian and the professor of medicine Eliezer Witztum,[64] the authors explore the suggestion that certain places induce or exacerbate psychopathological states or breakdowns, particularly in individuals with pre-existing pathological complaints and that the environment tends to colour the disturbance.[65] The authors may have applied

---

63. The organiser of the meal was Suleyman Derin, as already stated above, n. 25.

64. Moshe Kalian and Eliezer Witztum, 'Facing a Holy Space: Psychiatric Hospitalization of Tourists in Jerusalem', in Kedar and Werblowsky, pp. 316-30 (317).

65. There is plentiful examples of different types of extreme behaviour at religious sites in many sources, an example here is one provided by the specialist in psychology of religion, Scott Atran, in his *In Gods We Trust* (Oxford: Oxford University Press, 2002), p. 157. Atran illustrates extreme behaviour at the culmination of ritual, pilgrimage and shrine visitation at the site of Reza's tomb (an important historic and religious figure) in Iraq. The behaviour included crying and sobbing as holy men recounted Reza's death. Atran also cites the behaviour of attendants at the annual festival of La Tirana de Tarapaca in Chile, at which thousands of frenetic dancers with elaborate, diabolical masks whirl until exhausted. Thousands more chant and wail in procession as they agonise their way on their knees through streets

this analysis to some of the reactions by travellers at shrines as described above. I would contradict this analysis though and argue that many pilgrims from various and unrelated backgrounds experienced marked responses at a number of the sites and that underlying psychopathological disturbances could not account for all or any of them. The authors do suggest though that feelings of unreality and detachment can occur with travellers and not only at sacred sites but even at places such as airports.[66] Frazer N. Watts and Mark Williams[67] would support this argument concluding that some apparently religious experiences happen to non-religious people who provide non-religious interpretations of them. They tend not to apply a pathological diagnosis to the experiences. Kalian and Witztum also concede that it is not only people with a history of psychosis who experience these feelings and they cite an experience described by the psychotherapist Sigmund Freud:

> Freud wrote about the experience of travel and the associated loss of a sense of reality, in connection with his visit to the Acropolis in 1904. Writing home, he related that his experience there had surpassed anything he had seen or could imagine.[68] More than thirty years later, in a letter to Romain Rolland,[69] Freud described in detail this curious psychological experience, which was essentially a peculiar disbelief in the reality of what was before his eyes. He had puzzled his brother by asking him if it were true that they were on the Acropolis. He felt himself being divided into two persons, one who was in fact on the Acropolis and another who could not believe that this was the case.

This quotation above clearly exhibits echoes of some of the experiences described by the travellers to Turkey above, therefore offering a possible correlation between travelling to an unfamiliar place particularly with strong historic and or religious overtones and psychological reactions as described above. I would argue though that for many travellers on our pilgrimage, the sites were not unfamiliar as some of the travellers partook of the pilgrimage annually and still experienced strong reactions. It

---

to the Virgin's blessed alter. From J.U. Echevarria, *Fiesta de la Tarapaca* (Valparaiso, Chile: Ediciones Universitaria de Valparaiso, 1963).

66. The psychotic breakdowns of travellers could be due to unfamiliar surroundings, the presence of strangers, inactivity, boredom, a sense of isolation and the shock of cultural transplantation.

67. Frazer N. Watts and Mark Williams, *The Psychology of Religious Knowing* (Cambridge: Cambridge University Press, 1988), pp. 18-23.

68. Ernest Jones, *The Life and Work of Sigmund Freud*, vol. 2 (New York: Basic Books, 1955), p. 24.

69. Sigmund Freud, 'A Disturbance of Memory on the Acropolis', *Standard Edition* XXII (London, 1962), p. 239.

appears also that Freud's account above seems to imply that something happened to him at this ancient, historic site that was beyond any purely psychological or neurological explanation. This explanation would support the suggestion of the neurophysiologist, Scott Atran who following a rigorous investigation into possible neuropsychological reasons for the occurrence of religious and mystical experiences, finally concluded that he could identify no physical causes or changes in the brain to account for them.[70]

---

70. Atran, *In Gods We Trust*, p. 195. Issues surrounding religious and mystical experience as well as the problems with the language of mysticism was discussed in detail in the Introductory chapter pp. 20-24.

8

OUTREACH

PUBLICATIONS AND PUBLICITY

This chapter outlines the ways in which the Beshara Trust has produced and expanded its outreach and publicity through a wide range of initiatives with the view of generating increased public awareness, both nationally and internationally, of the activities of its school and its wider aims. The chapter addresses the Trust's response to those challenges to the school during its early development and at its more established stages. In addition it provides a selective overview of some of the ways in which the school understands its principles to relate to concepts and projects exemplified across a range of creative, scientific and academic disciplines, communicated primarily through its newsletters, its magazine and its more recent website.

Soon after the inception of Beshara, the Trust began a procedure of positive communication and outreach, actively 'spreading the word' about Beshara and their understanding of what it means. Initially, when Beshara was based at Swyre Farm and in the London house in Highgate, most publicity took place by word of mouth or through leaflets.[1] Shortly after related study groups began to spring up in centres throughout Britain and the English-speaking world, particularly the USA, Canada and Australia. As early as 1972, whilst Reshad Feild was still actively involved, the Trust began publishing its own newsletter. In 1975 Beshara's own publishing house, Beshara Publications, was set up at Swyre Farm, later to be based at Sherborne House. In 1976, the Muhyiddin Ibn 'Arabi Society was established,[2] and between 1987 and 1991, the Trust produced a glossy journal issued three times a year entitled *The*

---

1. These single-page advertisements were circulated around people interested in spiritual matters or in such places as bookshops. There was also a directory of Sufi Groups available, in which the Beshara Centre at Swyre Farm was listed. (Discussion with H., December 1999.)
2. See Chapter 9 below.

Beshara Magazine. Between 1991 and 2000 the Trust returned to producing the newsletter. Since 2000, all communication and correspondence with the school takes place through its own website.

Books

In 1975, the Beshara Trust established its own publishing company, Beshara Publications, based at Swyre Farm,[3] to make available in English important works of esoteric knowledge, especially the works of Ibn 'Arabi and his followers.[4] A sample of the books produced by Beshara Publications includes predominantly works by, distillations of, or commentaries on Ibn 'Arabi under such titles as *Wisdom of the Prophets*, *Kernel of the Kernel*, *Sufis of Andalusia*, *The Twenty-Nine Pages*, and *Mystical Astrology According to Ibn 'Arabi*, to name a few. Examples of other works published by Beshara but not directly concerned with Ibn 'Arabi include such books as Dom Sylvester Houedard's *Commentaries on Meister Eckhart Sermons*, and J.G. Bennett's *Intimations*.[5]

These publications were sold largely through bookshops that specialised in Islamic issues or related spiritual subjects, and more rarely through general bookshops that had sections dealing with similar topics.[6] Other books were sold by mail, through direct enquiry to Sherborne and Chisholme. The Beshara Foundation in the United States also acted as a direct distributor. The other main outlet was through conferences and symposia.[7] At the time that Beshara Publications produced its first titles in 1975, these were the only works of Ibn 'Arabi available in English apart from R.A. Nicholson's translation of the *Tarjumân al-ashwâq* and Ralph Austin's *Sufis of Andalusia*. This was the case for many years before more scholars began translating Ibn 'Arabi's work in the 1980s.[8]

---

3. It was later operated from Oxford with a store at Sherborne House.

4. Two separate businesses were established at around the same time. One was Beshara Publications, and the other was the Beshara Press, a printing business the managing director of which was Ted Pawloff. When he started the business in 1975 it was a one-man operation, but a decade later it had expanded into a multi-million pound operation, employing more than sixty people. Early on, the business printed books for Beshara Publications, but now the only connection with Beshara is the name. (It does though make a small contribution to Trust funds.) From the *Beshara Magazine* 2 (Summer 1987), p. 32, and from a discussion with Robert Clark, manager of Beshara Publications, May 2002.

5. See Chapter 4 above, which discusses the texts used by the Beshara School.

6. Such as *Blackwells*.

7. Discussion with Robert Clark, Muhyiddin Ibn 'Arabi Society Symposium, Oxford 2001. Sadly, Robert Clark died 1 January 2003.

8. See Chapter 9, on the Muhyiddin Ibn 'Arabi Society below.

The main markets for these books at this time were the UK, the USA, Australia, the Indian sub-continent and Pakistan, where a lot of pirate copies were produced.[9]

When the *Blue Fusûs*[10] was first produced, too many copies were printed, but gradually, as the company developed a feel for the market, sales settled to a few hundred per year. For each title, the number of sales has always been fairly small and by 2001 sales of all titles were around one thousand books a year. The aim is not commercial—the hope is simply to raise enough money for the next project.[11]

Since Beshara Publications began producing its books, many mainstream and smaller publishers have started to publish an ever-increasing number of other translations and interpretations of the works of Ibn 'Arabi.[12]

The *Beshara* Magazine

Between spring 1987 and summer 1991, the Beshara Trust published a well-produced journal that was issued three times a year. Its full title was *Beshara, the Magazine of the Beshara Trust*. The following quote from the editorial of the first issue illustrates the Trust's intention to produce a journal of intellectual and visual sophistication featuring a wide range of subjects designed to stimulate the interest of people from a cross-section of backgrounds and intellectual and creative disciplines.

> This magazine has grown up out of the *Beshara News Bulletin*, which has been circulated for several years now to those associated with the Beshara Trust. The expansion into a magazine format has been prompted by the degree of interest shown in recent issues, which have included articles by a number of distinguished speakers, and by the fact that within the UK the forum for intelligent and informed discussion on matters which concern a spiritual perspective is virtually confined to publications pressing a particular point of view.
>
> Beshara is not associated with any particular political, social or religious group or stance. Rather it is the name of a spiritual emergence, and an inclination towards a universal perspective that lies behind so many movements in the world today. Beshara is no-one's exclusive domain but its reality carries its own order; like the 'yeast in the dough' it is discernible within all movements that aspire to a holistic understanding.

---

9. Discussion with Robert Clark, Oxford, April 2001.
10. The *Wisdom of the Prophets* translated from French to English by Angela Culme-Seymour. See Chapter 4 above.
11. Discussion with Robert Clark, Oxford, 2001
12. Amazon.com lists 21 translations and studies of Ibn 'Arabi published by a selection of different publishing houses.

The scope of the magazine is therefore wide. Movements within science have been already discussed in previous issues of the *News Bulletin* and will continue to be a major area of coverage. In this issue we will also look at movements within the major religions and the World Life Fund's initiative towards a global perspective on conservation. Future issues will be considering economics, psychology, art, education, literature and many other areas. Central always will be the theme of the real place of conscious man in a reality understood to be one and unique...

The magazines were attractively produced with a glossy cover that featured a colourful, imaginative design. Many of the issues included beautiful illustrations, with reproductions of prints and photographs providing reinforcement to the articles. The larger aesthetic focus was also evident in the advertisements and formats of the articles.[13] The overall impression was that the publication was an example of the Beshara Trust applying its own principles in practice, in that it was clearly produced and presented to the highest possible standard of aesthetic and intellectual quality.[14]

Noticeable in these publications was a relative absence of articles about Ibn 'Arabi and his works. This reflects the fact that by the time it came into production, the Muhyiddin Ibn 'Arabi Society had been established in order to provide translations, commentaries and interpretations of Ibn 'Arabi's works and those of later authors and traditions he influenced, and to make his works better known in the Western world. The common thread which runs through the various disciplines discussed in the magazine is that in some way or another they reflect the growing acknowledgement of the truth about the Unity of Existence or Reality which, according to the participants of Beshara, is evident in surprisingly diverse and expanding aspects of life, such as the sciences, the arts, religion, ecology and even economy. Some of the central types and recurrent themes of the articles are as follows:

---

13. The magazine provided ample advertising space which was taken up by individuals or organisations wanting to market something which had in any way an affinity with Beshara, including seminars, courses, functions, books, furniture, clothing, architectural designs etc.

14. Jane Clark, the former editor of the magazine and wife of the late Robert Clark, explained that Bulent Rauf required 'excellent presentation', 'a publication with lots of class like the quality American magazine "Harpers Bazaar"'. He did not want it to be classified as just another 'alternative' magazine, attracting 'barefoot vegans', as he was distinctly against this type of image and lifestyle. Jane Clark also explained that several other magazines have since been modelled on the format of this one, for example a publication entitled *Caduceus* which explores a variety of alternative healing methods.

World Religions. Dialogue and points of contact between Beshara's perspective and the world's religions have always been important to those involved. This was demonstrated frequently in the publication. For example, one of the early issues announced the opening of the Samye-Ling Temple, a traditional Tibetan Buddhist Temple in the Scottish Borders, only about twenty miles from Chisholme. The Temple was built as a resource for Buddhists and non-Buddhists alike to promote interfaith understanding. Along with the Temple itself was a study centre, including lecture, therapy and translations rooms and two libraries. The opening ceremony included a three-day inter-denominational symposium, with representatives from Christianity, Judaism, Islam and Hinduism meeting with teachers from the Buddhist Tradition. The speakers included The Khentin Tai Situpa, Patriarch of the Karma Kagyu; Dom Sylvester Houedard; and from Chisholme, Peter Young, Director of Studies. Because of the close proximity of Chisholme to Samye-Ling, contact has always been close between them.[15]

The Physical Sciences. The disciplines of the sciences provide a prime expression of what Beshara stands for, and therefore offer a further important medium for the communication of its principles. As a result, generous coverage for a range of scientific disciplines was provided in the magazine. For example, articles included the extract of a seminar given at Sherborne in 1986 by the biologist Rupert Sheldrake, entitled 'The Presence of the Past'.[16] Jane Clark's editorial introduction to Sheldrake's article is interesting because it emphasises the significance of this seminar to an earlier lecture by Professor Brian Goodwin (Department of Biology at the Open University) to Chisholme House, relating biology to mysticism. According to Jane Clark, it was seen as marking the 'start of what promises to be a long dialogue between the "scientific" and "mystic" views of Reality and Self, and pleasurable in that the perceived space between these points of view is smaller than any since Isaac Newton'.[17] Further articles by Professor Goodwin published in later editions of the magazine included one on Neo-Darwinism,[18] and another

---

15. As is further affirmed by the fact that one of the Temple's representatives presented a paper at the Muhyiddin Ibn 'Arabi Society Symposium held at Chisholme in August 2000.
16. Rupert Sheldrake, 'The Presence of the Past', Part 1, *Beshara Magazine* 1 (Spring 1987), pp. 15-20 (15).
17. Editorial, *Beshara Magazine* 1 (Spring 1987), p. 15. At this time, Rupert Sheldrake was consultant plant physiologist to the International Crops Research Institute in Hyberadad.
18. 'Rumbling the Replicator', *Beshara Magazine* 4 (Winter 1987/88), pp. 12-16.

entitled 'The Generative Order of Life',[19] which addresses the contrast of his own biological theories with those of the biologist Dr. Richard Dawkins. Dawkins is described as one of Darwin's 'most erudite modern interpreters', with his assertion that our 'selfish genes' are the prime movers in evolution.[20] Goodwin, in contrast, affirms 'the deep intelligibility of nature'.[21]

The Gaia hypothesis raised another ecological issue that was discussed in the magazine. In a paper entitled 'Gaia Comes of Age',[22] a participant of Beshara explained that the Gaia hypothesis suggests 'that the entire range of living matter on Earth might be regarded as an organism—a single, living being endowed with the capacity of homeostasis (or self-regulation)'. This idea is also explored in another article called 'Life in a Living World' in which he examines some of the implications of the concept increasingly accepted by science that the universe is 'alive'.[23]

A wide selection of other scientific issues was explored in the magazine, ranging from scientific cosmology to physiological problems associated with perception and the mind.[24]

Poetry, Literature and Music. Poetry, literature and music provide other examples of creative expression in which the principles which are Beshara may be demonstrated and expanded. An interesting recent example of the way in which expression of Ibn 'Arabi's teachings subtly takes place in literature and music is demonstrated in the award winning novel *The Bear Comes Home* by Rafi Zabor, who is a jazz critic and a long-time participant of Beshara.[25]

A friend and supporter of Beshara and a regular contributor to the magazine was the well-known Blake scholar and poet Kathleen Raine.

---

19. *Beshara Magazine* 12 (Autumn/Winter 1990), pp. 16-23.
20. Richard Dawkins, *The Selfish Gene* (Oxford: Oxford University Press, 1976).
21. Goodwin, 'The Generative Order of Life', p. 18.
22. Ted Pawloff (at that time managing director of Beshara Press), 'Gaia Comes of Age', *Beshara Magazine* 5 (Spring 1988), pp. 8-10.
23. 'Life in a Living World', *Beshara Magazine* 5 (Spring 1988), pp. 8-10 (8); see also Sheldrake, 'The Presence of the Past', Part 1, pp. 15-21.
24. See, for example, J.D. Barrow, 'The New Cosmology', *Beshara Magazine* 6 (Summer 1988), pp. 19-25, and Richard Twinch, 'Perception and the Mind', *Beshara Magazine* 2 (Summer 1987), pp. 17-18.
25. Rafi Zabor, *The Bear Comes Home* (London: Jonathan Cape, 1998), winner of the Pen-Faulkner Prize. Rafi Zabor discussed the central (non-explicit) role of Ibn 'Arabi's ideas throughout his work in his talk at the International Muhyiddin Ibn 'Arabi Society Symposium in Berkeley (November 1998).

She was also editor of *Temenos*,[26] which she describes as a 'review devoted to the arts of the imagination', and a long-time associate of Henry Corbin and other members of the Eranos circle of Jungian scholars and thinkers (see Introduction above).[27] In 1987, she led a seminar at Sherborne, entitled *Nature, House of the Soul*. A report of the seminar quotes a passage from her opening paper that shows how much her thinking corresponds to and complements Beshara's principles:

> We are mistaken when we think of 'nature poetry' as conferring meaning upon nature; rather, nature itself is the true poetry of the universe, to which the poet listens. Sun and stars, trees, clouds, birds, every creature, are words in the language which the universe itself speaks... Is it possible to remember back to the kind of knowledge we had of our world before inner and outer became separate? It is knowledge of being that the poet seeks, a knowledge not of something other, but a kind of self-knowledge, and this in fact is the vision of what is called poetry.[28]

Reference to dance and music as an expression of Beshara also played an important role in some of the magazines, particularly with regard to cultural events listed and discussed in later editions of the publication.

A recent example of music and singing as a manifestation of the meaning of Beshara is to be found in the recordings of long-time Beshara student Narda Dalgleish, who was inspired by the works of Ibn 'Arabi, particularly translations of the *Tarjumân*.[29] Her work follows an album previously released which applies the lyrics of the *Tarjumân* to a traditional flamenco setting.[30]

Architecture. Architecture provides a fundamental expression of what Beshara means to those involved with the school and its principles. The work of several architects involved with Beshara well illustrates its

---

26. The editorial position of *Temenos* is to reaffirm those spiritual values which must be the ground of any human culture.

27. Examples of Kathleen Raine's contributions include 'The Puer Eternus', *Beshara Magazine* 6 (Summer 1988), pp. 9-12 and 'W.B. Yeats and the New Age', *Beshara Magazine* 9 (n.d.), pp. 35-37. Dr. Raine was an acknowledged scholar of Blake and Yeats and author of several books.

28. Report of the seminar by Hillary Williams, *Beshara Magazine* 3 (Autumn 1987), p. 6.

29. See Narda Dalgleish, *Let Love Love Love* (Sherborne, Gloucestershire: Vast Earth Words and Music, 2001). Dalgleish uses translations of the *Tarjumân* translated as *Stations of Desire* by Michael Sells. Reported in 'Music Review', *Muhyiddin Ibn 'Arabi Society Newsletter* (Autumn 2001), pp. 6-7.

30. With the Piñana brothers, *De lo humano y lo divino* (1998). This group performed at the annual Muhyiddin Ibn 'Arabi Society Symposium in Oxford in 1998.

efforts to communicate its principles to the wider world. Architecture has historically been closely associated with the sacred, from the building of Solomon's Temple, through the shrines of Buddhism and Hinduism to the building of Christian cathedrals and Islamic mosques. This expression of Beshara's ideas is emphasised in the magazines: one issue includes a feature on the Ottoman architect Sinan who lived in the golden era of Ottoman achievement in the latter half of the sixteenth century during the rule of Sultan Suleyman the Magnificent.[31] Sinan Aga was the greatest architect of that era leaving several great mosques as a legacy to the age.[32] During his 50-year career he held the official title of 'Architect of the Abode of Felicity'. One of the joint authors of that article, Keith Critchlow, comments: 'Sinan can perhaps be called the "Builder of Unity". It has been said that his mosques are simply "reproductions" of the Hagia Sophia in Istanbul but this is to misunderstand his achievement. He was superlative in that he took the principle of Unity and perfected it...'[33] Critchlow, who is an architect with an international reputation for his analysis of Islamic geometry and pattern, and is founder and director of the VITA (Visual Islamic and Traditional Arts) School, a department of the Prince of Wales's Institute of Architecture,[34] has been involved with Beshara since its beginnings and inspired the building of a kind of temple complex through the conversion of an old cruciform barn at Swyre Farm based on the principles of sacred geometry.

Visual and Theatrical Arts. The arts occupy an elevated position as means of spiritual expression. Kathleen Raine described the arts as: '...at all times the channel by which knowledge is disseminated throughout society. Properly, they should be speaking in forms which reflect sacred knowledge, that is knowledge of reality...'.[35] The fine arts were another key means of communicating more widely what Beshara means to its students. An article by Simon Blackwood, an early participant of Beshara

31. Peter Yiangou and Keith Critchlow, 'A Tribute to Sinan', *Beshara Magazine* 7 (1988), pp. 24-29.
32. The Shehzade, the Mihrimah, the Atik Valide and the Sulemaniye in Istanbul as well as several others.
33. Yiangou and Critchlow, 'A Tribute to Sinan', p. 27.
34. Part of the 'Prince of Wales Foundation', a charitable organisation formed to unite and extend the Prince of Wales' initiatives in architectural design, building and urban regeneration through several organizations, including VITA.
35. Christopher Ryan quotes Kathleen Raine in a report of the second *Temenos* Conference entitled 'Art in the Service of the Sacred', *Beshara Magazine* 8 (1988/1989), p. 9.

and an artist who has had paintings in collections throughout the world, discussed painting as a means of expression. He finds a significant comparison between painting and cookery, describing it as follows:

> The relationship between painting and cookery is one that has interested me a lot. Both involve the transmutation of base ingredients from one state to another in what might be called an alchemical process. And just as a well-prepared meal will arouse the appetite of the guest, so a painting should arouse a kind of hunger for beauty in those who see it.[36]

In an article entitled 'Angelic Presences', Sister Wendy Beckett introduces the paintings of Margaret Neve.[37] These paintings tend to feature sheep in idyllic landscapes and angelic figures, at times almost imperceptibly small. In a painting called *The Garden of Eden*, there is a minuscule angel apparently herding Adam and Eve into Eden. Beckett's interpretation of Neve's art is that it seems to ponder the question: 'Have we ever truly left our Paradise, or would we still be living there, are we still living there, with the happy sheep, if only we understood our condition?'[38] This reflection is again very much in line with the teachings of Ibn 'Arabi and Beshara, involving self-knowledge and our ultimate origins, states and purpose as humans.

Theatre provides another visible means of expression for Beshara, an example being a feature about the Japanese actor and director Yoshi Oida, who started his training in Noh and Kabuki, the classical theatre of Japan. He spent some time in Japanese temples learning about movement techniques within the local religious tradition. He makes an interesting comment about this which ties in with Ibn 'Arabi's discussions of the superiority of knowledge of the heart over the rationality of the intellect, and which also corresponds to student's reactions to the study at the Beshara School: 'What I found through Noh theatre training and through the research at the temples, is that through action—not "acting" but *action*—it is possible to understand things which are very difficult to understand with the intellect or through reading books and discussion. And it was great pleasure for me, to find a means of understanding which is not limited to the intellect'.[39]

---

36. Simon Blackwood, 'Painting as a Means of Expression', from an interview with Cecilia Twinch, *Beshara Magazine* 8 (1988/89), pp. 32-34 (32).

37. Neve paints by using an infinitesimal series of dots and typically employs a mystical theme to her work.

38. Sister Wendy Beckett, 'Angelic Presences', *Beshara Magazine* 13 (Summer 1991), pp. 18-19.

39. Yoshi Oida, 'Means of Expression' (an interview by Kathy Tiernan), *Beshara Magazine* 13 (Summer 1991), pp. 33-35 (35).

Cuisine. The art of cuisine is of foremost importance to those involved with Beshara because of the process of transmutation, mentioned above in relation to painting, and as analogy for the process of human transformation and self-knowledge. Bulent Rauf was himself a first-class chef and author of works on Ottoman cuisine. In an article entitled 'Cooking as a Means of Expression', Martin Lam, head chef at the time of a London restaurant called *l'Escargot* and a former Beshara student, discusses these ideas of transformation. He first of all quotes the cookery writer Elizabeth Lambert Ortiz, who says that 'man's place is to glorify in the sense of giving praise, and man glorifies the raw ingredients he cooks by transforming them into something greater'. He continues by suggesting:

> This is why vegetarians are only partly right in what they think. In the Western world, vegetarianism is usually not a matter of necessity but moral choice, because people have a particular idea that eating meat is wrong. But they fail to understand that what is important is not the specific ingredients but the principle behind the cooking. Vegetables and all those parts of diet which don't include meat or fish, are just as important as those that do are. We have to understand the full spectrum of how foodstuffs provide more than just a physical sustenance. Through the enhancement of the ingredients during cooking, they themselves are heightened, and so the whole process provides nourishment on a different level.
>
> There is also a direct correlation between processing food from raw to cooked, and that same process in ourselves. We can live our lives quite happily as raw ingredients which are never appreciated fully for everything that they contain in potential, or we can live our lives expressing completely what we contain. It's up to us.[40]

Multidisciplinary Features. Some issues featured a combination of various intellectual and creative disciplines, such as a report on a symposium, entitled *Art meets Science and Spirituality in a Changing Economy*. This symposium which was held in Amsterdam in September 1990, included internationally influential thinkers from the fields of art, science, spirituality and economics, amongst them the Dalai Lama, David Bohm (physicist), Huston Smith and Raimondo Panikkar (spiritual thinkers), and Robert Rauschenberg (artist). The audience was made up almost entirely of European businessmen. The idea of the symposium had developed from meetings which the Dalai Lama had had with leading scientists and artists in the early eighties. The concept behind the

---

40. Martin Lam, 'Cooking as a Means of Expression' (an interview by Cecilia Twinch), *Beshara Magazine* 10 (Winter 1988/90), pp. 30-31 (31).

idea of bringing together these people was the belief that it could help with the formulation of new global and cultural paradigms, an idea that was integral to the meaning of Beshara and its founding conceptions.[41]

The above brief examples serve to illustrate the multifaceted expressions of the principles that constitute the meaning of Beshara for its participants, as they were presented in the diversity of disciplines explored in its magazine. It was a source of deep sadness to those involved that Bulent Rauf was not around to appreciate its success, as he died on 5 September 1987, only a few months after the first issue was published.

Distribution and Market of the *Beshara Magazine*. Approximately two thousand copies of each issue of the magazine were printed, although in retrospect it has been acknowledged by its editors that this was more than necessary, since it had only around fifteen hundred regular subscribers.[42] The market was primarily the UK, but it also sold in other English-speaking countries such as the USA, Australia and New Zealand, and even had subscribers in countries such as Singapore. It was not sold through bookshops but was promoted by word of mouth, via mailing lists, or through paying other publishers to include a leaflet advertising it inside one of their own publications.[43] Although it was printed by the Beshara Press and was therefore not published at commercial rates, it was an expensive magazine to produce and it never made a profit.

The Beshara Trust published the magazine until 1991, when an unexpected financial crisis occurred which momentarily threatened to result in the total destruction of the organisation.[44] That crisis was eventually successfully overcome, but finances did not then allow the continued production of the magazine, so in 1993 Beshara resumed publication of regular newsletters.

41. Report by Richard Gault, *Beshara Magazine* 12 (Autumn/Winter 1990), pp. 7-8.
42. It has been recently suggested by an early participant of Beshara that the circulation amongst friends was far wider than this.
43. Such as the Element Books catalogue.
44. In 1990, the Trust lost nearly all its income when it was revealed that the investment manager of the Beshara Company (which was a subsidiary fund-raising company), a prominent City figure, was a fraudster. Many people involved with Beshara and who had invested money for its benefit found that they had lost their investments. This caused considerable upset and the Trust was left with major moral, financial and legal burdens. Even selling such properties as Frilford Grange did not greatly reduce the debts, and there were many who questioned whether the Trust should even try to continue. But eventually against all odds, the Trust paid off its debts and overcame its difficulties. Ref.: Peter Yiangou (then Chairman of the Beshara Trust), *Beshara Newsletter* (1993), front page.

The newsletters have usually included a lead article reiterating an aspect of the principles of the school, in addition to other related shorter sections, articles and features. After 1993, these articles and features have been more in line with the contents of the *Beshara Magazine* than with the earlier newsletters, in that they have highlighted various ways in which Beshara expresses itself across a broad spectrum of academic and creative disciplines. They have frequently featured publications of talks delivered by visiting speakers, or papers written by the school's own participants.

Other means of Beshara outreach have included the organisation of open seminars led at venues other than the Beshara properties. Typical examples include two which took place at a venue called 'The Old George', Burford, in April and May of 1995, *The Unity of Being and its Direct and Practical Implications for Human Perfectibility* and *Beauty beholding Beauty*. Both seminars included well-known speakers who were participants of Beshara or visiting speakers who were sympathetic to Beshara's aims.[45]

Newsletters/Bulletins

The Beshara Trust began producing newsletters or bulletins, as they were sometimes called, soon after its establishment in 1971. The early editions were hardly more than leaflets, being only a page or so long and containing usually one news article about the development of Beshara at Swyre Farm under the 'leadership' of Reshad Feild. One of the earliest newsletters, for example, has on its front cover Pir Vilayat Khan's emblem of the 'Sufi Order in the West', a winged heart, indicating Reshad Feild's continuing involvement with Pir Vilayat at this time.[46] On the back cover is the *Hû* emblem that came into use at Beshara when Bulent Rauf became actively involved at Swyre Farm.[47]

From March 1973 onwards, the newsletters became more substantial and were produced quarterly.[48] Volume 1, Number 1 printed at this time

---

45. Anon., 'Seminars at The Old George', *Beshara Newsletter* (Spring 1995), p. 8.

46. For details about Feild's relationship with Pir Vilayat, see Chapter 2 above.

47. The Beshara Design Centre Ltd published these early newsletters at Swyre Farm.

48. The newsletters did not have a completely standard format or arrangement of presentation, although they tended to provide similar categories from one issue to the next. The usual content of the early newsletters offered, for example, updates of activities at each of the major centres, or news of the Design Centre, fund-raising ventures, useful addresses, dates of *zikrs*, news of national and international study centres, seminars, lectures and calendars of events. Then there would frequently be

had a very interesting feature, which was a prayer put together by Beshara, an amalgamation of the Christian 'Lord's Prayer' and the Islamic *Fâtiha*. This example shows how Beshara participants applied their argument in support of the unity of religious truth from an early stage. It was actually used at the wedding of two of the first participants of Beshara. It reads as follows:

> Praise unto God the Lord of the Universes,
> Our Father which art in Heaven,
> Hallowed be Thy name,
> The most merciful and the most compassionate,
> The king of the day of reckoning,
> Let Thy kingdom come and Thy Will be done,
> On earth as it is in heaven,
> For Thine is the kingdom, the power and the glory,
> For ever and ever,
> It is Thee that we adore and it is in Thee that we take refuge,
> Give us this day our daily bread, and forgive us our trespasses,
> As we forgive those that trespass against us,
> Lead us not into temptation,
> But deliver us from evil,
> Direct us in the straight way,
> Not of those from whom Thou hast turned Thy face,
> In the way of those to whom thou has been gracious,
> Nor of those who go astray,
> Amen.

COMMUNICATION AND OUTREACH

Most of the newsletters, from the first produced through Swyre to those produced today, which are available through the World-Wide-Web at www.Beshara.org. reassert the principles of Beshara one way or another. They also, then as now, announced teachings, courses and facilities available. An important emphasis in Beshara is that esoteric knowledge should take practical, effective, exoteric expression, and this was apparent from the start. A brochure produced to publicise Beshara at Swyre Farm, which was used for promotion in the mid- to late 1970s, made a point of asserting this, offering skills and aspects of creative expression which are traditionally associated with esoteric learning. These skills included pottery, involving all aspects, from the nature of the clay itself,

an article related to Ibn 'Arabi, for example, an aspect of his doctrine, a translation or commentary or just a discussion about his work. Occasionally there would be a particular theme that dominated the whole newsletter, such as in the July 1975 issue, where a large amount of space was given over to affirming the principles of Beshara.

through the process of handling, glaze techniques and firing. Other courses on offer of this type were wool working and oriental carpet making, which included spinning, natural dyeing and weaving.[49]

By 1975, the organisation had study centres in twelve locations throughout Britain and others in Holland, Canada and Mexico. As a result of this, the school decided that there was a necessity to reaffirm its principles and to examine areas in which problems or potential problems lay in the way of this expansion. These issues were addressed and published in a substantial newsletter produced for July 1975.

Consideration of the issues discussed in the newsletter led to meetings and debates over matters that might concern both non-participants and participants who might consider taking courses. As early as 1975, a question arose during a meeting at which the school's principles were reaffirmed, which is particularly interesting in that it is a question that does occur to many non-participants who are interested in what Beshara means to its participants and who might be considering doing a course themselves. The question involved Beshara being just another of many forms of belief:

> I think that one paradox is that things like 'I was a hidden treasure' one can to some limited degree perceive directly. When we talk about Beshara being the most effective channel on the revelation in that, I can't help thinking one is then involved in a belief. It is more relative than those absolute principles, if you know what I mean. And one cannot, at that stage of understanding avoid matters of belief. I think that's what I'm quibbling about, is Beshara a channel or *the* channel?[50]

The question received various responses but the pragmatic one that was most conclusive and inclusive and summed up Beshara's ethos was:

> If you or I go around saying Beshara is the only way, or it is the only possible truth, then we're crazy. And yet there is only one way eventually, if one's going all the way.[51]

An issue that had to be addressed at this stage involved the study centres and the problems that the participants of Beshara experienced in their early attempts to increase awareness of Beshara throughout Britain and internationally. The problem was that the local centres were having difficulty in generating significant interest and maintaining their existing support. The main reason seems to have been that there was quite a

49. Brochure promoting Beshara at Swyre Farm (date of publication unknown but probably between 1976 and 1978).
50. Question posed by a Beshara participant during a taped discussion, transcribed and published in the *Beshara Newsletter* (July 1975), p. 8.
51. Ibid.

concentrated programme of study demanding high commitment at some of the centres, involving attendance at meetings three or four evenings a week, and that this level of commitment was too much to expect. It was suggested that the programme become less rigorous.

It was also suggested that for some potential students, what Beshara stands for was possibly not perceived as 'exotic' and therefore not as attractive as some other spiritual paths:

> We've had two talks in recent months. One given by...(a Beshara participant) which I'm afraid was not well attended. That I think was the fault of publicity. We had another talk by Warren Kenton on the Kabala and 100 people came to this, and I think it was because the name Kabala was familiar yet mysterious, and this drew people in tremendous numbers.[52]

Another comment connected to this point suggests that in contrast to 'set' or established spiritual paths, such as the Kabalistic path referred to above, the experience of Beshara is ongoing and expansive and should therefore attract people who want to know more about it and experience it further:

> If a thing is crystallised and given to people, they just accept it and put it away. But if it is expanding and expansive, they will come back for more.[53]

Further early ideas as to why there were problems in attracting interest in Beshara included, for example, the suggestion that some of the discussions were too abstract, particularly for potential participants attending a meeting for the first time. There was also the question of hierarchy, as there seemed to be strong emphasis on heads and deputy heads of centres. This emphasis could be confusing and potentially off-putting, as the question of hierarchical order was of great importance within Beshara circles. This is because it is a central principle that there is no set human hierarchical function—all those involved are understood to be in a continuous state of learning and of service to the Real or God. It was argued, though, in response to this suggestion, that there has to be a basically *functional* hierarchy, but according to the nature of Beshara this hierarchy changes regularly.[54] Ultimately the responsibility lies with each individual so therefore the collective responsibility rests with the collection of individuals.[55]

52. Ibid., p. 18.
53. Ibid.
54. The question of hierarchy and leadership within the school is addressed in Chapter 3, pp. 86-87.
55. *Beshara Newsletter* (July 1975), p. 12.

In addition to trying to attract newcomers to the centres in order to expand knowledge of their organisation, the Beshara Trust also publicised itself through public seminars, such as a seminar held over a weekend in August 1975 at Swyre Farm, which offered talks morning and evening, and a film about Turkey and the Mevlevi Dervishes entitled *Turning*.[56] On the Sunday night a *zikr* took place.

OTHER METHODS OF OUTREACH AND COMMUNICATION CONTINUING INTO THE 1980S

Several other ingenious methods were embarked upon to increase knowledge of Beshara and its activities at that time. In Cambridge, a variety of creative ideas were instituted, for example, in a Beshara Centre, which included a shop that sold antiques and various craft items made by Beshara participants on the ground floor, and a large room above for meetings, meditation and study groups. Some time later, although the shop remained, the rest of the ground floor and outbuildings were converted into an award-winning restaurant, 'Strudels', that was managed and staffed solely by participants of Beshara. The building still continued, though, to provide adequate space for study and meditation.[57]

By 1980, the Beshara Trust was making a concerted effort in terms of increasing public knowledge of its activities and instigating more effective administrative policies. This was to take place through a new organisational structure that included the following areas of activity: short courses and centres, university extra mural courses and seminars, publicity and public relations. A secretary, a financial advisor and a fund raiser were to be appointed. By now the focus of study on the courses was increasingly the works of Ibn 'Arabi. Also the Muhyiddin Ibn 'Arabi Society, an academic organisation originally developed by Bulent Rauf and other adherents of Beshara in 1976, was becoming more and more active.

The Trust continued to hold regular seminars at Sherborne to which distinguished speakers contributed. For example, there was a series of seminars held in the summer of 1985. The speakers at Sherborne

---

56. This film, for which Bulent Rauf was advisor and commentator, had recently been completed by Diane Cilento, who was at that time a student of Beshara and is still involved, although she now lives in Australia and runs her own retreat establishment there.

57. From a letter from T., February 2000.

represented a variety of disciplines which 'offer a wide ranging perspective within the overall theme of the Unity of Existence'.[58]

By the winter of 1985, Beshara had launched a vigorous advertising campaign. Short courses were being advertised nationally in the *Guardian* newspaper, with regular insertions planned for that winter. Long courses were announced in various publications in the UK and abroad. There was a poster campaign in the London Underground running for a year, which inspired a steady response, and a new brochure was also produced at this time. The Trust found that the most effective way of publicising itself locally was through study groups and events. Events included 'Open Days' at Sherborne where the public could find out about what was happening at Chisholme and what Beshara was all about (there is still an annual public 'Open Day' at Chisholme). The school has also offered extra-mural lectures at some universities. Also, in April 1986, the school was invited to attend the Scottish Careers and Education Exhibition in Glasgow's Anderson Exhibition Centre, resulting in the official recognition of the school as being a 'bonafide educational institute'.

July 1986 witnessed another surge in the generation of publicity for Beshara; this coincided with the Trust's move from the main house at Sherborne into the newly converted stables of the house. Among the new initiatives was the establishment of the *Beshara Educational Security Trust* (*BEST*), which was a scheme formed on behalf of the Trust to fund the expansion of Beshara over the following years. The organisation also decided then that in recognition of the world-wide role of the Beshara Trust, a full-time administrative officer was to be appointed, and that it

---

58. The speakers included three who had as their foundation the works of Ibn 'Arabi. They were: Peter Coates, who was lecturing in philosophy in the Humberside College of Further Education; Adam Dupré, who had been a supervisor at the Chisholme Institute for a number of years; and Khalil Norland who was writing a book that looked at the disciplines of mathematics and physics from the point of view of the Real as expressed in the works of Ibn 'Arabi. A further three speakers who had their basis in Christian spirituality were Father Noel O'Donaghue, a Carmelite priest lecturing in the Department of Theology in the University of Edinburgh; Dom Sylvester Houedard, a Benedictine monk, scholar and poet; and the Reverend George Pattison, who was a well-respected student of philosophy before becoming a parish priest (he is now Dean of King's College Cambridge). The remaining seminars were to be conducted by Warren Kenton, an authority on the Kabbala, who has written many books under his Hebrew name Zev Ben Shimon Halevi; Henri Bortoff—a physicist and one-time student of G.I. Gurdjieff and J.G. Bennett—of the Claremont Academy for Continuous Education. Bortoff's main work had been on the Unity of Nature, with particular reference to light and colour. Ref.: Anon., 'Seminars at Sherborne', *Beshara News Bulletin* (Summer 1985), back page.

was advisable to appoint a public relations consultant to advise on the most effective presentation to a wider public. It was also resolved that the news bulletin be increased from three to four issues a year, and that Trust meetings were to be open to all people interested in the expansion of Beshara. Finally it was decided that a school of intensive education should be set up in Australia, and that efforts should be made to set up Beshara courses in the United States under the Beshara Foundation.[59]

The outcome of these discussions was that a 'Priority of Communications' was decided upon, as this was seen as essential at every level of Beshara. In the words of Bulent Rauf:

> The time seems over when Beshara sat down and waited. They came. Now Beshara cannot sit and wait. Beshara's role is to go out and express itself.[60]

The discussion then proceeded to quality of presentation, in accordance with Beshara's principles, i.e., the continuous striving towards perfection in effort and a universal perspective in perception:

> In line with this it was agreed that the Beshara we are seeking to communicate is not an organisation, school or a centre as such and that our presentation at all levels should be completely in line with its true qualities. It is not possible therefore for us to present ourselves as one way, school or centre, amongst many, or to develop a 'corporate image' but it must always be kept foremost that the true Beshara is universal and pertains to the heart of all ways, religions, science and all human activities. Nor must it be seen that it is concerned only with inner understanding.[61]

Rauf added to this last point as follows:

> The intention is to help man in this life, not only his transcendent inner understanding and satisfaction. It is necessary to recognise and promulgate that the inner understanding has value only in relation to the outer life. People should be made to understand clearly that a man who lives a solely esoteric life with no expression in this world is not of Beshara.[62]

It was agreed then that the objects of the communications exercise should be to disseminate knowledge of Beshara through general communication and dialogue; for example: circulating press releases; responding to material in the press; appearing in the media; organising exhibitions and sending speakers to conferences—and also through promotion of courses run by the Beshara School at Sherborne and Chisholme, as well

---

59. Anon., *Beshara News Bulletin* (July 1986), n.p.
60. Ibid.
61. Ibid.
62. Ibid.

as through the promotion of Beshara as a forum for general dialogue between the different aspects of human knowledge through exercises such as seminars at Sherborne. The message that the principles constituting Beshara are applicable to all aspects of human knowledge, including areas as diverse as science, the arts, ecology and economy, was addressed in the newsletters, but had a particularly central role in the *Beshara Magazine*, as will be discussed and demonstrated below.

INTERNATIONAL EXPANSION

Beshara has communicated itself in diverse ways internationally, as well as nationally. One instance was the attendance of representatives of the Beshara Foundation, which is based in the San Francisco Bay Area in California, at an annual conference of Sufi-related groups in the area held in 1995. A report explains that there had been debate about the appropriateness of Beshara participating in a Sufi conference, but it was decided that the purpose of this conference was to promote the spirit and not the form of Sufism and that it was a good opportunity to promote Beshara. The talk by the representative of Beshara was attended by over one hundred people, and the speaker explained that Beshara is not a Sufi order as it is not bound by any particular religion or dogma, a notion which many in attendance could relate to. A description and slides from Chisholme followed the talk, which resulted in a very receptive attendee reaction. The attendees also understood the value and significance of such things as the restoration of the estate and the care given to cookery. This is because these activities illustrated values of central importance to any Sufi order, the idea being that any task undertaken should be approached with the intention of performing it to the highest possible standard, with constant endeavour for perfection. Beshara also set up a bookstall for Beshara Publications, which generated a lot of interest.[63]

Two participants of Beshara who live in California have explained that the situation for Beshara there is significantly different compared with the way it is at Chisholme. The Beshara Foundation was established in California in 1979, and at that time many people attended its functions, which took place in a house in Berkeley. The majority of people who participated had already visited and attended courses at Chisholme. The Foundation initially ran weekend and nine-day courses, but it did not thrive. One of the participants suggested that in retrospect this was because everything has its place, and the British situation at Chisholme

---

63. Jane Carroll, 'Sufism Conference in California', *Beshara Newsletter* (Spring 1994), p. 3.

was not appropriate to the situation in America.[64] The house at Berkeley was eventually sold, and smaller premises were made available for study in the Bay Area. Here regular study of the *Fusûs* began and continues to this day, but the attendance figures are not high, averaging about five to six people per weekly session.

In September 1987, the Muhyiddin Ibn 'Arabi Society held its first annual symposium at Berkeley, which was a great success. A participant explained that at this time, the symposia in England were rather 'dry', whereas those in California were more like the actual Beshara courses.[65] For example, conversations involving the audience as well as speakers developed out of the papers delivered, and no one was particularly worried about whether the approach was strictly 'academic'. The attendees felt happy to ask 'direct' questions of professors. It was through these Berkeley symposia that many well-known academics became involved with the Ibn 'Arabi Society and Beshara.[66] It was also through the symposia there that participants enquired about Beshara, with the result that some began attending Beshara study groups, whilst others would visit Chisholme when in Britain. One participant explained that although the first symposia of the Muhyiddin Ibn 'Arabi Society in England had been 'seriously academic' and were still extremely scholarly, they have tended to 'lighten up' and are now less formal, more on the lines of the annual symposium at Berkeley. The participant explained that more scholars are beginning to allow into audience discussion personal spiritual attitudes, whilst maintaining objectivity in the delivery of their actual papers.

The same interviewee explained that in America there is not the problem which is apparent in England, of a rigid divide between the academic study of Ibn 'Arabi through the Muhyiddin Ibn 'Arabi Society and the practical approach to his work through Beshara. She then explained that it was also in America that the Internet first became useful

64. The physical and 'atmospheric' situation of Chisholme House provides a setting that is highly conducive for the education that is Beshara. Its remote, secluded but fiercely beautiful location, added to the tangible communal support provided by the fellow students and other personnel at the venue, create an ideal environment for this type of experience and education. The environment at Berkeley, on the other hand, not being able to provide such conducive circumstances in which to study, was less attractive to students, potential students and other participants. From a discussion with M., 2000.

65. This tends to highlight stereotypical cultural differences between English and Americans anyway, especially in an academic arena, Americans tending to be more open to new ideas and easy going than their more inflexible English counterparts.

66. See Chapter 9 below on the Muhyiddin Ibn 'Arabi Society.

to Beshara, and it was a priority to find a place for Beshara here, rather than a physical place. But it was in fact the Muhyiddin Ibn 'Arabi Society that was the first to launch its website in the United States, and within six months there were enquiries coming from all over the world.[67]

In addition to the meetings of the Beshara Foundation that took place in San Francisco, involving study and *zikr*, other smaller Beshara groups with similar intentions have met in San Leandro (in the East Bay area), New York City, Idaho and Austin, Texas.

Beshara Australia Incorporated (BAI), is a registered charity in Australia with the same aims as the Beshara Trust in the UK and the Beshara Foundation in the USA. It owns a property, Canonach, near the town of Yackanandah in New South Wales, described as a beautiful and tranquil environment, at which it runs courses and retreats. In June 1996, BAI produced a newsletter in which the leading article provides a flavour of what is on offer there. The writer's description of his experience there provides an interesting comparison to most descriptions of the Chisholme experience. This writer was a first-time visitor to Canonach, entirely unfamiliar with Beshara's principles and education. He reports that he undertook the visit with the intention of maintaining an open mind during his stay in order to derive full benefit from the experience, yet his account corresponds closely to those of students and visitors to Chisholme. He reports:

> Canonach is located in one of the most beautiful regions of Victoria and when I finally arrived at the homestead I simply liked what I saw. Upon reflection I feel I understand why. It is a special place. When I think of the required maintenance of the property and the various chores which needed to be performed it could all be described as a labour of love. People who might hold no affiliation to Canonach were asked to do their best, or what they could, and care about how they did it. It was never a demand but the study is put into practice through physical work. What I greatly appreciated was the time I perceived I was given to settle in. I felt no pressure and after being greeted and introduced I felt comfortable in the knowledge that my exchanges with others around me were not in any way contrived or thrust upon me. Placed within this framework I was able to appreciate those around me as themselves without judgement and if I did judge I was ripe to recognise and scrutinise its manifestation.
>
> What came through as 'Essential Truth' for me was the fact that people (collectively and individually) moved together responsibly, with respect for one another and with a structured discipline through *zikr*, study, work and meditation to acquire or be given a taste of grace and selfless action

---

67. Interviews with L. (Chisholme, August, 2000). A similar suggestion was made by M. (Turkey trip, 2000).

which may lead us to the path to Him. One appropriate way of describing our union at Canonach is as Jelâluddîn Rûmî puts it, 'the same wine in different bottles'...[68]

The Beshara Trust and its associates have also generated other intriguing forms of publicity, such as cards produced by the Beshara Design Company, which have gone on sale nationally and internationally through outlets such as Harrods and the National Trust. A report described the cards as beautiful, informative and worth keeping. The front of the cards offered detailed original artistic illustrations,[69] and on the reverse side were texts or recipes furthering the expression of each subject. Included in the first four series were trees in their natural seasonal settings; flowers with their characteristics and corresponding folklore; fruit and vegetables with additional recipes and seasonal recipes within the setting of inviting domestic scenes. The report concludes: 'Most of the recipes are taken from the tradition so integral to education at the Beshara School, and eventual profits from the sale of the cards will be put towards making the Beshara School better known'.[70]

BESHARA TODAY

In March 2000, the Beshara Trust announced that it would no longer be sending out newsletters through conventional mail, but that all its communication would be via its new website. The letter making the announcement also suggested that the Internet itself is a manifestation of the increasing evidence of the Unity of Existence apparent in all aspects of Being, and even a means through which Beshara can announce itself. The concluding paragraph suggested:

> The Internet is itself great good news as effortlessly we are afforded the means of maintaining contact with students and friends; but more importantly here is the way that has been put in place for reaching to anywhere in the world, to all those who are looking knowingly or not, for the news of the Unity of Existence, the boundless potential of man, for the School and a superlative education towards Union.[71]

---

68. Spiros Antionides, 'Easter 1996', *Beshara Australia, Newsletter* (June 1996), p. 1.

69. By Laura Blackwood, an early Beshara adherent, and Angela Culme-Seymour, wife of the late Bulent Rauf, artist, and translator of several books. See Chapters 2 and 4 above.

70. Anon., 'Cards from Beshara Design Company', *Beshara Newsletter* (Spring 1994), p. 4.

71. Letter sent by the Beshara Trust, March 2000.

Some students of Beshara had already suggested in earlier interviews that the Internet is an expression of what Beshara is about, i.e., a further expression of the continuing revelation about the Unity of Being through a 'new impulse' from the Real or God.[72] As the new millennium drew nearer, the focus of the Beshara website dwelt increasingly on the concept of newness and change, a new impulse or a new era. This was evident in the opening article by Peter Young entitled 'The New Covenant', which related some of Jeremiah's prophecies to the world today.[73]

The Millennium Forest project at Chisholme, which is frequently discussed on the website, is significant in that all the activities which take place at Chisholme, be they study, meditation, devotional practice or work, are aspects of an integral whole, or 'Unity'. In the late 1990s, this ambitious tree-planting project began at Chisholme, and anyone who happened to be staying there at certain times of the year would help with the project in some respect. The project involved replanting thousands of trees in areas in which original forest surrounding the house had been clear-felled in the late eighties. This reforestation project was made possible through various grants, including one from the 'Millennium Forest for Scotland Trust'.

The wider categories on the Beshara website originally included: Home, News, School, Courses, Beshara, Books and Contacts.[74] The magazine/library website section was of central importance as it included articles and papers connected with the principles involved with Beshara according to various expressions and points of view. There were, for example, reprints of articles written by participants of the school which

72. Interview with E., August 1999 and K., Winter 2000.
73. A quote from Jeremiah 31:31 is discussed in Chapter 3 above. Peter Young's article was published in the final published *Beshara Newsletter* (Spring 1998), pp. 1-2.
74. Since this study was completed in the early 2000s the Beshara website has been redesigned and is continually updated. The wider categories listed on the website in October 2011 now include: School, Ideas, Events, Worldwide, Home, About and Contact. The latest information on the Millennium Forest project, for example, is to be found on a list appearing under the School category entitled Millennium Forest: http:// www.beshara.org/school/chisholmehouse/chisholme_ estate/millennium_forest/html. Although some of the names of the categories have changed, the contents still correspond reasonably closely to the previous categories; for example, information that has been placed under the library section now appears within the wider category 'Ideas' under the subtitle 'Readings' (beshara.org/ essentials/readings.html, accessed October 2011) and the previous 'News' section now appears under the subtitle 'Events', again in the wider category 'Ideas' (beshara.org/events.html, accessed October 2011). For other changes and updates visit the Beshara website: http://www.beshara.org.

had previously been published in newsletters. Also included were original articles, including those from other religious standpoints which could be described as expressing what students of the school understand Beshara to mean. For example, this category included a poem by the famous Bengali poet Rabindranath Tagore, entitled 'Heaven of Freedom':

> Where the mind is without fear and the head is held high;
> Where knowledge is free;
> Where the world has not been broken up into fragments by narrow domestic walls;
> Where the words come out from the depths of Truth;
> Where tireless striving stretches its arms towards perfection;
> Where the clear stream of reason has not lost its way into the dreary desert sand of dead habit;
> Where the mind is led forward by Thee to ever-widening thought and action—
> Into that heaven of freedom, my father, let my country awake.[75]

The website also offered the latest international news involving Beshara. For example, it reported on a paper presented by Principal of the school, Peter Young, in Sidney and Melbourne in June 2000, entitled 'United by Oneness: Global Considerations for the Present'. This feature was particularly interesting as it restated the history of Beshara and its key premises from its perspective at the start of the new millennium. More importantly, it showed how the school's perception of itself had not altered much in the nearly thirty years since its beginnings with Bulent Rauf's production of *The Twenty-Nine Pages* at Swyre Farm. It also argued that what Beshara is was becoming increasingly evident in varying global manifestations:

> Beshara is concerned with the establishment in this world of the knowledge of the Unity of Existence. Since the foundation of the school an establishment has been taking place in three inter-related ways. Firstly in the hearts and minds of the students of the Beshara School—all those who have attended courses over the years and who now live in various places throughout the world. Secondly, during this time we have seen unprecedented growth of interest in esoteric matters, and all sorts of sometimes bizarre New Age manifestations, together with interests which are altogether quite new, concerns particular to this present time. In the last quarter of a century we have all come to realise that we inhabit one world, each part of which is related to every other part. Everyone now has some notion of there being an ecological whole. We also know that the global economy is a single reality, no part of which is independent of any

---

75. Taken from www.beshara.org (Magazine Page, accessed March 2000, no longer accessible), p. 1.

other part. Unity is making itself known from many different sides. This has been the preparation of the fertile ground ready to receive the 'seed' of the knowledge of Union. And thirdly the Beshara School, which in its essential reality has no definite location, has been established at Chisholme House in Scotland. Since its foundation a clarification and unfolding from the Interior has been taking place without interruption, such that the focus of Unity and Union becomes ever clearer, and established in the place with the reverberations of the Real. This can now extend geographically beyond the confines of place. It is a move of enormous and literally far-reaching significance.[76]

The Australian meetings were a considerable success, and among other foci of discussion was the place of Australia in the global unfolding of the 'Knowledge of the Unity of Existence'. They led to the holding of new nine-day courses in January and February 2001.

The website regularly offers news of upcoming courses. One important recent development was a nine-day course which took place in June 2000, in Jakarta. This was the first of its kind in Indonesia. News of the course was found on the Internet by two future participants who told their family and friends about it, which resulted in there being enough interest to justify running a course in Jakarta. Through exchange of emails the arrangements were made, with the Indonesians guaranteeing to undertake preparations, such as gathering participants and managing the venue, catering and financial details, and the school arranging study materials, the programme and supervisors. The course itself took place in a private house on the outskirts of Jakarta. Twenty-three people attended the first weekend, and sixteen participated for the whole nine days. The course began at 7.30am when the participants arrived for twelve to thirteen hours of study, meditation, contemplation and conversation. Because of the circumstances, it was not possible to assign time to work, which is integral to other Beshara courses; instead participants and supervisors went for an early evening walk. The report concludes that the course was remarkable for students and supervisors alike: 'All were moved to a new place of vision, as if without effort, without difficulty…' By the end of the period the group had a 'strong intention' to meet for study and conversation and two of the participants voiced their intention to join the next six-month course at Chisholme. This course was highly significant for the Beshara School, as it was the first time that a course had been 'taken out' of Chisholme and held elsewhere.[77]

76. Taken from www.beshara.org (News Page, accessed Autumn 2000, no longer accessible), p. 3.
77. The Principal has recently mentioned that although this was true in the way that he meant it, there needs to be mention of the fact that some six-month courses

230   *Ibn Arabi and the Contemporary West*

Although this chapter has placed more emphasis on the Beshara School than Ibn 'Arabi himself, this has been necessary in order to illuminate the extended history and creative activities of this organisation in providing further contexts within which to express and communicate Ibn 'Arabi's ideas. And as mentioned above, following the establishment of the Muhyiddin Ibn 'Arabi Society in the mid-1970s, the focus of the work of translating Ibn 'Arabi's writings and those of his followers was taken over primarily by the Society instead of the school. This resulted in the works of Ibn 'Arabi receiving less direct mention in the Beshara periodicals, although his ideas were always central to the school's ethos.[78]

were held under the name of Beshara at a place belonging to Diane Cilento, named Karnak, in North Queensland, Australia from the late 1970s to the mid-1980s. Supervisors were sent from Chisholme and Sherborne to help with these courses, during which they used some of the Beshara material together with techniques received by Cilento from Mr. Bennett's course which she attended at Sherborne. From a discussion with the Principal, April 2002.

78. Since completion of this work for my doctoral thesis in 2003, there have obviously been plentiful updates to the 'outreach' information for both the Beshara School and the Muhyiddin Ibn 'Arabi Society. I have only mentioned updates that are of obvious significance to recently contacted participants of the school. These include a book recently published about the school by Suhar Taji Farouki (one of my PhD examiners), *Beshara and Ibn 'Arabi: A Movement of Sufi Spirituality in the Modern World* (Oxford: Anqa, 2007); a programme promoting alternative holiday locations, which featured the school, made for Israeli television by an Israeli film company *Sha. maim* in 2008; also, the school is in the process of becoming an accredited educational establishment and I am told that there are now regular courses run in Jakarta, Indonesia.

9

THE MUHYIDDIN IBN 'ARABI SOCIETY

INTRODUCTION

In 1976, Bulent Rauf, with the assistance of other associates of Beshara, formed the Muhyiddin Ibn 'Arabi Society. The Society's aim was to promote knowledge and understanding of the works of Ibn 'Arabi and his followers, particularly in the English-speaking world, through translations, interpretations and commentaries of his works and those of his followers. Until the Society's inception, the few works by Ibn 'Arabi readily available in English were, by and large, those published by Beshara Publications such as *The Wisdom of the Prophets*.[1] Although the Society was established by Rauf and other associates of Beshara, the intention was that the Beshara School and the Muhyiddin Ibn 'Arabi Society should be entirely separate entities, i.e., the Beshara School would concentrate on developing the experiential aspects of Ibn 'Arabi's teachings, whilst the Society would focus on the academic discussion and dissemination of Ibn 'Arabi's teachings. This was pursued initially through encouraging translations and interpretations by scholars from the Western world, and later from the Islamic world as well. These studies were to be presented at annual international symposia and published in the Society's journal. In addition, collections of Ibn 'Arabi's works and related material were to be housed in the Society's new library.[2] Today, the Society has over three hundred official members throughout the world, and a rapidly expanding network of national 'Branches'.

Until the beginning of the twentieth century, the works of Ibn 'Arabi were little known in the West, although his influence had been widespread and sometimes controversial in the Muslim world since his lifetime. But in the early part of the last century, Western scholars began the work of translating and interpreting his writings. These scholars

---

1. For texts published by Beshara Publications, and for those studied on Beshara courses, see Chapter 4. Also see below for some earlier translations into English.
2. First housed at the Beshara Centre in Charlwood Street in Pimlico, London.

included: Nyberg,[3] Asin Palacios,[4] Nicholson,[5] Affifi,[6] Corbin,[7] Burckhardt,[8] Landau,[9] Nasr,[10] Izutsu,[11] and more recently Austin,[12] Chittick,[13]

3. Henrik S. Nyberg, a German scholar whose works included a pioneering edition and translation of three difficult cosmological works: *Kleinere Schriften des Ibn al-'Arabi nach Handschriften in Uppsala und Berlin zum ersten Mal hrsg. Und mit Einleitung und Kommentar von H.S. Nyberg* (Leiden: E.J. Brill, 1919).

4. M. Asin Palacios, a Spanish scholar whose work included: *Islam Cristianizado* (Madrid: Plutarco, 1931) and *La escatologia musulmana en la Divina Comedia* (Madrid: Granada, 1943). The first book focused on Ibn 'Arabi's life and the Spanish period of his youth.

5. R.A. Nicholson, a British scholar whose works included a translation of the *Tarjumân al-Ashwâq* (London: Royal Asiatic Society, 1911); a translation and commentary on *The Mathnawî of Jâlâl 'uddin Rûmî, Books 1–VI* (London: E.J.W. Gibb Memorial Trust, 1926, 1930, 1934; latest repr. 1982) and *Studies in Islamic Mysticism* (Cambridge: Cambridge University Press, 1921).

6. A.A. Affifi, an Egyptian Scholar and student of R.A. Nicholson, who wrote *The Mystical Philosophy of Muhyid-dîn Ibnul 'Arabî* (Cambridge: Cambridge University Press, 1964) and was responsible for a scientific edition of the *Futûhât al-Makkiyya*.

7. H. Corbin, a French scholar who wrote *Creative Imagination in the Sufism of Ibn 'Arabi* (trans. from the French by Ralph Manheim; Princeton: Princeton University Press, 1998), now renamed *Alone with the Alone*; and *Spiritual Body and Celestial Earth: From Mazdean Iran to Shi'ite Iran* (trans. Nancy Pearson; London: I.B. Tauris & Co., 1990), which include important translations of Ibn 'Arabi and al-Jîlî. See in the Introduction above for his wider role in the spread of Ibn 'Arabi's ideas.

8. See Chapters 2 and 4 for details of his texts used by the early Beshara School. Burckhardt was one of the key successors of Rene Guénon (see the Introduction above).

9. Rom Landau, *The Philosophy of Ibn 'Arabi* (London: Allen & Unwin, 1959).

10. S.H. Nasr wrote 'Ibn 'Arabi in the Persian Speaking World', in *Al-Kitâb al-tidhkâri: muhyî Ibn Arabî fî dhikrâ al-mi'awiyya al-thâmina li-mîlâdih 1165–1240* (Cairo: alHay'a al-Misriyya al-'Amma li 'L-kitâb, 1969), pp. 257-63 and a multitude of other works highly influenced by Ibn 'Arabi's ideas. See also the Introduction above.

11. T. Izutsu, a Japanese scholar who wrote *Sufism and Taoism: A Comparative Study of Key Philosophical Concepts* (Berkeley: University of California Press, 1983).

12. See Chapter 4 above, regarding his translations used by the Beshara School: *The Bezels of Wisdom* (The complete translation of the *Fusûs al-Hikam*) (New York: Paulist, 1980) and *Sufis of Andalusia (The Rûh al-quds and al-Durrat al-fâkhirah of Ibn 'Arabi)* (London: Alan & Unwin, 1971).

13. W. Chittick, an American scholar who wrote *The Sufi Path of Knowledge: Ibn 'Arabi's Metaphysics of Imagination* (Albany: SUNY Press, 1989); *Imaginal Worlds* (Albany: SUNY Press, 1994); *The Self-Disclosure of God* (Albany: SUNY Press, 1997); and *Ibn Arabi Heir to the Prophets* (Oxford: Oneworld, 2005).

Chodkiewicz,[14] Morris,[15] Addas,[16] Knysh[17] and Beneito.[18] An important influence on many of Ibn 'Arabi's earlier interpreters writing in French was a school of thought rooted in the thinking of Rene Guénon[19] whose objective was a return to what he understood to be a perennial spiritual 'Tradition'. Guénon's emphasis on 'Tradition' and strict adherence to the historical forms of a particular revealed tradition, however, was somewhat different from the more open approach of Bulent Rauf.[20]

The only early twentieth-century translation in English was Nicholson's version of Ibn 'Arabi's poetry, the *Tarjumân al-ashwâq*, Before Beshara Publications produced the *Blue Fusûs*, a translation of Titus Burckhardt's French translation of *The Wisdom of the Prophets* (twelve abridged chapters of Ibn 'Arabi's *Fusûs al-Hikam*) in 1975, the only recent English translation of Ibn 'Arabi's work was Ralph Austin's *Sufis of Andalusia*, published first in 1971. Austin's work was republished by Beshara Publications in 1987, and Beshara continued to publish translations of Ibn 'Arabi and related works for use as study texts in the school

---

14. Michel Chodkiewicz, a French scholar who wrote recently key French studies translated as *An Ocean Without Shore: Ibn 'Arabi and the Law* (Albany: SUNY Press, 1993) and *The Seal of the Saints: Prophethood and Sainthood in the Doctrine of Ibn 'Arabi* (Cambridge: Islamic Texts Society, 1993).

15. James Morris, an American scholar currently at the University of Exeter. His most recent works include: *Orientations: Islamic Thought in a World Civilisation* (Sarajevo: El-Kalem, 2001); *The Master and the Disciple: An early Islamic Spiritual Dialogue* (London: I.B. Tauris, 2001); and *Ibn 'Arabi: The Meccan Revelations* (New York: Pir Press, 2002).

16. Claude Addas, a French scholar and daughter of M. Chodkiewicz, who wrote *The Quest for the Red Sulphur: The Life of Ibn 'Arabi* (Cambridge: Islamic Texts Society, 1993).

17. Alexander Knysh, a Russian scholar, Professor of Islamic Studies at the University of Michigan, whose works include *Ibn 'Arabi in the Later Islamic Tradition: The Making of a Polemical Image in Medieval Islam* (Albany: SUNY Press, 1999).

18. Pablo Beneito, a Spanish scholar who has recently edited and co-translated two of Ibn 'Arabi's works, the English editions of which are (with Cecilia Twinch): *Contemplation of the Holy Mysteries and the Rising of the Divine Lights (Mashâhid al-asrâr)* (Oxford: Anqa, 2001); and (with Stephen Hirtenstein): *The Seven Days of the Heart (Awrâd al-usbû)* (Oxford: Anqa, 2000).

19. For Burckhardt and Guénon, see Chapter 2, and, for example, Robin Waterfield, *René Guénon and the Future of the West* (London: Crucible, 1987).

20. This difference is *vividly* illustrated in the interaction (in 1985) between Bulent Rauf and a vocal French disciple of Guénon discussed in Chapter 9 (pp. 246-48).

and in order to make Ibn 'Arabi more widely known.[21] One of the aims of the Muhyiddin Ibn 'Arabi Society was to encourage the production of more translations and to make Ibn 'Arabi's works generally more accessible in the English-speaking world.

FOUNDATION PERIOD

The dominating presence of Bulent Rauf was at the centre of the inception of the Society as indicated by the following quotes from members of the Society active at that time:

> In 1977, while staying at Swyre Farm, I was descending the staircase into the dining room, when Bulent, Angela [Culme-Seymour], Grenville Collins[22] and Hugh Tollemache appeared at the foot of the stairs. Bulent called to me: '...(name), we have just formed a Muhyiddin Ibn 'Arabi Society! We would like you to become a member if you will'. Of course I signed on the spot, and later, over lunch he explained to me the nature of the Society, its involvement with the search for and translations of 'Arabi's works and the formation of an international library. It was an exciting new venture.[23]

Another version of the incident that took place on that day was offered by the editor of the Society's journal and another close witness:[24]

> One day, the idea about a Muhyiddin Ibn 'Arabi Society came into Grenville Collins' mind, the objectives of which would be to encourage the translation of books by Ibn 'Arabi, as there was nothing available and that which had been available was out of print. His idea was to make Ibn 'Arabi's work more accessible. What was needed was more study material for the Beshara School's courses and for other people who were interested in Ibn 'Arabi. Although Grenville had had this idea he said nothing about it to anyone else at the time. One morning two or three days later, he was invited to have a cup of coffee with Abdullah Binzagr in his room.[25] During the course of conversation Abdullah commented that he had an idea for the founding of an Ibn 'Arabi Society. What he said to Grenville repeated almost word for word the idea that had

21. See Chapter 4, above.
22. Involved with Beshara from the beginning, and current chairman of the Muhyiddin Ibn 'Arabi Society.
23. From a letter including memoirs about Beshara and the Society by an original member who wishes to remain anonymous (February 2000). (The Society was actually formed in 1976, so the date here is not quite accurate.)
24. Who wishes to remain anonymous.
25. An early participant of Beshara from Saudi Arabia, who taught Arabic on some of the courses.

previously entered into Grenville's mind. ('It was almost as if arrangements for the establishment of the Society had already been made'.) They looked at each other in surprise and then immediately sought out Bulent Rauf who on being told what had happened, thought for a moment and then said 'you had better do it'. They agreed and Grenville asked Bulent there and then if he would become President of the Society and Bulent was delighted to take on the role.[26]

The implication here is that there was something deeper happening than just the idea to translate and make available more of Ibn 'Arabi's work, and that Bulent and his associates were in fact being guided to make these decisions on a more esoteric, intuitive level.

> Discussion then took place as to how this was to be done, and a group was nominated/volunteered, which heralded the birth of the Society. The main idea at the very beginning was to get in touch with the publishers of any work connected with Ibn 'Arabi in English, such as R.A. Nicholson's translation of the *Tarjumân al-ashwâq*, and get them republished in order to build up a library. Grenville Collins wrote to the publishers to ask whether they were prepared to republish or whether Beshara Publications could do it. Beshara Publications already existed and had published the *Blue Fusûs*.[27] This became course material—the process was like 'building blocks'—not like an institution then—more in the way that a 'good idea' comes up, this is acted upon, and then another 'good idea' arises.
>
> In 1974 the ideas of courses was just beginning—Swyre Farm had already developed a daily routine of meditation, study, work and *zikr* so therefore a gradual evolution had been taking place. From then on progress continued, and with the establishment of the Society, pressure began to be exerted on publishers to reprint relevant material and people were encouraged to translate. At this time, William Chittick had just started to publish and a connected journal *Sophia Perennis* was being produced in Iran—production ceased with the Revolution.[28]

The library was the first amenity of the Society to be set up in order to collect and preserve the works of Ibn 'Arabi and to make them more widely known. The initial collection of books and manuscripts was kept

---

26. Other members on the founding board were Christopher Shelley, Angela Culme-Seymour, Abdullah Binzagr (treasurer), Grenville Collins (Chairman), Peter Young and slightly later Lady Elizabeth Hornsby and her two sons.

27. My interviewee explained that the *Blue Fusûs* had been set up with something special in mind and that there had been lots of energy from those involved but no experience. That work was translated over 1973–74 and came out in 1975. For details see Chapter 4 above.

28. Interview with S. Hirtenstein; phone discussion, April 2002, supported by W., phone discussion, April 2002.

at the Beshara Centre in Charlwood Street in Pimlico, London, before it was moved to a large rented building in Oxford in 1980. The collection was moved again in 1981 to first one and then finally to another private house belonging to original students of Beshara in Oxford, where it has remained ever since.

In 1982, the first issue of the *Journal of the Muhyiddin Ibn 'Arabi Society* was published. The second appeared in 1984 in connection with the first Ibn 'Arabi Society international symposium which was held at Durham University. The journal then appeared annually until 1991, after which it has been published twice a year. The symposia have since become annual events in England, usually held each spring in Oxford. In 1987 the Society held its first symposium in the USA at the University of California, Berkeley, and this too has become a regular annual event.[29] The contributors to the journal and the speakers at the symposia include long-term associates of Beshara, scholars who are specialists in Islamic and Arabic Studies, and others with expertise in related disciplines including psychology, philosophy, mysticism and the arts. Participants have been drawn from an ever-widening circle, originally largely from the UK and Beshara associates, and subsequently those from other English-speaking countries and European scholars. More recently, scholars and related artists and intellectuals from throughout the Islamic world have contributed. The journal includes new translations of texts, commentaries and interpretations of Ibn 'Arabi's works, and studies of his later interpreters and of scholars from his own era to the present day who have been influenced by his thought. There are also extracts from the symposia and reviews of related works. The Society has also produced several special thematic editions of the journal and published its own books.[30]

The Society currently has a membership of at least three hundred registered members. In addition it also has world-wide contacts through the thirty-five university libraries that subscribe to its journal and through the forty countries that order its books. The majority of contacts reside in the English-speaking world, but there is an increasing interest from other countries, particularly in the Islamic world.

---

29. In 2001, the US Symposium was held at the University of California in Santa Barbara.
30. See Bibliography for details.

EARLY DAYS: THE LIBRARY AT CONCORDIA HOUSE

The first function of the newly formed Society was to establish premises for its headquarters and library. To this end, the Beshara Trust rented a large building, called Concordia House.[31] The Trust was able to rent the whole building at a reasonable price because it was in need of restoration. A room on the first floor was used as an office and library for the Society. Associates of Beshara also used other parts of the building for various enterprises connected with it, such as a restaurant offering 'Chisholme' cooking, and an artists' studio/gallery.[32]

Although the Society was only in residence for six months at Concordia House (late 1980–April 1981), it did firmly establish itself at this time. An organising committee was formed comprising early associates of Beshara, with a President, Honorary Fellows, Fellows and members. Even at this relatively early stage of its evolution, it could boast an impressive list of well-known scholars who had accepted the invitation to become Honorary Fellows. These included Mr. Abdullah Binzagr, Mme. A. Ayashli, William Chittick, Keith Critchlow, Prof. H.A. Hourani,[33] Prof. T. Izutsu, Prof. S.H. Nasr and Dr. Osman Yahia.[34] Thus, the Society membership at this time included a healthy cross-section of academics and lay scholars, including some with an excellent working knowledge of Arabic, enabling them to translate relevant works, and others who were interested in works and subjects related to Ibn 'Arabi. Many of the earliest contributors to the journals and symposia tended to be people closely associated with Beshara, such as course supervisors and former students. However, as the Society evolved, an increasing number of specialist scholars from ever-widening circles became more actively involved.

---

31. Before the Trust rented Concordia House, a small library collection was actually housed at the Beshara Centre in Charlwood Street in London from 1977–1980.

32. The artists' studio was managed by Simon Blackwood.

33. Writer of two classic books on the Middle East: *Arab Thought in the Liberal Age* (Cambridge: Cambridge University Press, 1962) and *A History of the Arab Peoples* (London: Faber & Faber, 1991). He was director of the Middle East Centre in Oxford and lectured on the modern history of the Middle East from 1958 to 1980. He attended most of the Oxford symposia prior to his death in 1992.

34. Author of *Histoire et classifications de l'oeuvre d' Ibn 'Arabi* (Damascus: Institut Français de Damas, 1964), the standard bibliographical work in this field. He worked for more than 20 years on the first critical edition of the *Futûhât al-Makkiyya*. He also spoke at the Oxford symposia, and greatly aided younger scholars working on Ibn 'Arabi. He died in 1997.

Whilst at Concordia House, the Society devoted much time and effort to making Ibn 'Arabi's work more accessible. For instance, a transliteration of the *Wird of Ibn 'Arabi*, Ibn 'Arabi's prayers for the morning and evening of each day of the week, was undertaken by A. Abadi and S. Hirtenstein, who also worked concurrently on a companion volume of prayers of protection set down by Ibn 'Arabi for recitative purposes. Both were published in Arabic text and transliteration.[35] Also at this time, two related books were reissued following the Society's recommendation to the publishers.[36]

The minutes of the Annual General Meeting for 1980, during the time of the Society's brief residence at Concordia House, record other circumstances that were of central relevance and concern to the Society at that formative moment. The two paragraphs are quoted in full below because they provide evidence of the importance of the Society not in only diffusing Ibn 'Arabi's works in the West, but also in helping to preserve them in the face of political disturbances in the Middle East. The first quote relates to the revolution that took place in Iran in 1979.

> Consequent to the revolution in Iran, the Imperial Iranian Academy of Philosophy was closed and its scholars dispersed. Prof. Nasr has taken up an appointment at Temple University, Pennsylvania and Peter Lamborn Wilson in London. Prof. Izutsu has retired to his home in Japan. Dr. Chittick continued his researches in Cairo and Istanbul, finding a wealth of new material on Sadruddin Qûnâwî, and has now returned to the United States to collate and translate. He hopes to publish his book on Qûnâwî[37] shortly, the first ever to be published in the West.[38]

Second, on 15 February 1979, the Egyptian People's Assembly, advised by its Committee for Social and Religious Affairs and Endowments, recommended a ban on publishing the writings of Ibn 'Arabi, particularly the *Futûhât al-Makkiyya*, which was then being actually edited for the first time with government support, by Osman Yahya. In addition to underlining the problems of political unrest in this part of the world and the need to preserve Ibn 'Arabi's works, the circumstances of

---

35. The work itself was actually undertaken at Chisholme House from 1978–79, and then published by the Muhyiddin Ibn 'Arabi Society.

36. These were the *Lawâ'ih*, by Jâmî (a famous Persian poet and interpreter of Ibn 'Arabi), originally published by the Theosophical Publishing House; and Nicholson's *Studies in Islamic Mysticism*, which incorporates a section on Ibn 'Arabi.

37. The book was *Faith and Practice in Islam* but by the time he had finished it, Chittick had decided that the three works were not by Sadr al-dîn, but by a Nasîr al-dîn Qûnâwî. Ref.: Telephone interview/discussion with S. Hirtenstein, April 2002.

38. *MIAS, AGM* minutes, 1980.

the ban also provide another contemporary example of the controversy which has surrounded Ibn 'Arabi and his ideas from his lifetime to the present day.[39]

> The ban on the study of Ibn 'Arabi in Egypt early in 1979 which so outraged both Egyptians and more general world opinion, was happily of short duration. The ban was lifted within a week. Dr. Osman Yahya is reported to be well and continuing his work on an edition of the *al-Futûhât al-Makkiyyah*.[40]
>
> The events in Iran and Egypt showed it to be imperative to establish a proper comprehensive collection of Ibn 'Arabi's works, free from the political uncertainties of the Middle East. The Society entered into correspondence with the Arab League in February 1979 with a view to getting copies of all those works of Ibn 'Arabi which are on film in their archives department. They have kindly agreed to send these...[41]

At this time the library was also developing through the generosity of such people as Sheikh Muzaffer Hoja of Istanbul,[42] who gave several copies of manuscript texts of Ibn 'Arabi, and Abdullah Binzagr, whose donation brought the initial collection up to 150 volumes. It also provided a venue for relevant talks, lectures and study groups and was used on a weekly basis by the Beshara Oxford Group for reading from the works of Ibn 'Arabi.[43]

At this early stage, the Society determined to promote its existence through advertisement in appropriate journals and periodicals.

A branch of the Society was established in Turkey in 1980. Madame Ayashli, an Honorary Fellow of the Society, offered her house in Istanbul as a venue for the Society. This was singularly appropriate in the light of Ibn 'Arabi's connection with Turkey and the abundance of relevant

---

39. For details, see T.E. Homerin, 'Ibn 'Arabi in the People's Assembly: Religion, Press and Politics in Sadat's Egypt', *The Middle East Journal* 40 (Summer 1986), pp. 462-77.

40. Osman Yahia ultimately had to move from Egypt to Damascus in order to continue his work.

41. *MIAS, AGM*, minutes 1980.

42. Muzaffer Hoja was the head of the Helveti Sufi Order in Istanbul, and he was also a book dealer from whom many books were purchased for the library. One early adherent remembers entering his bookshop with Bulent Rauf and Abdullah Binzagr, whereupon he produced an eighteenth-century manuscript copy of Ibn 'Arabi's work. They left the shop having paid £70 for the work, which was a substantial sum in the early seventies. Muzaffer Hoja introduced the Khalwati-Jerrahi Order to the USA in the 1980s.

43. Examples of talks provided by Beshara at the library in 1980/81 included: 'Mystical Astrology', by Abraham Abadi; 'Aspects of Modern Philosophy', by Peter Coates; and 'Prayer, Meditation and Mysticism', by Hilary Williams.

manuscript material available there.[44] Other members of the Society were working actively throughout the world, particularly in Australia, Canada and the USA, in making the existence of the Society and its aims more widely known.[45]

Two other projects that developed during these early days at Concordia House were, first, the sending of micro-fiche copies of the *Fusûs al-Hikam* and the *Treatise on Being*[46] in English translation to one hundred selected libraries all over the world. The second project was the planned production of the Society's annual journal.

In the spring of 1981, the Society, having used the premises at Concordia House for only six months, had to vacate that locale when the company owning the building went into liquidation. The library and headquarters were then moved to temporary accommodation in a private house. However, by this time a firm foundation for the future of the Society had been established.

THE DEVELOPMENT OF THE *JOURNAL*

At the Society's general meeting of 1980 held at Concordia House, the proposal for establishing a journal was first put forward by Bulent Rauf. The Society would hold annual symposia at which papers would be presented, and those papers, along with reprints of texts of Ibn 'Arabi that had passed out of print and other relevant material, would form the basis of the publication. After discussion, the Society asked Stephen Hirtenstein and Martin Notcutt to collaborate in producing such an annual journal to coincide with the first annual symposium. As it happened the first journal was published in 1982, two years before the first symposium, which was held in 1984; it was only after 1984 that the journal and symposia papers were able to coincide.

The first two editions of the journal included re-published articles from the Iranian journal *Sophia Perennis*, publication of which had terminated following the Revolution in Iran in 1979. Both these articles were by William Chittick, one of the foremost Western scholars to translate the works of Ibn 'Arabi into English.[47] Volume 1 of the journal was published in 1982, and in addition to Chittick's articles, contained papers by

   44. *MIAS, AGM*, minutes, 1980.
   45. *MIAS, AGM*, minutes, 1980.
   46. Also known as the *Treatise on Unity* (trans. T.H. Weir, 1901) and reprinted as *Whoso Knoweth Himself* (Gloucestershire: Beshara, 1976).
   47. William Chittick, 'Ibn 'Arabi's Own Summary of the *Fusûs*: The Imprint of the Bezels of Wisdom', *JMIAS* I (1982), pp. 30-93; 'The Chapter Headings of the Fusûs', *JMIAS* II (1984), pp. 41-95.

contributors who were all early students of Beshara. As already noted, it was only as the Society expanded that the contribution of outside scholarship rapidly increased.

The following quotation from the introductory page of the first journal of the Society (Volume 1, 1982), illustrates the intention of the Society and its motivation to produce a journal in the first place:

> ...As the late Henry Corbin has pointed out, 'Ibn 'Arabi is one of those rare spiritual individuals who are the norm of their own orthodoxy and their own time, because they belong neither to what is commonly called "their" time, nor to the orthodoxy of "their" time'. It is this universal element in his teaching that is constantly applicable and particularly appropriate to the present need, not for materia nor for facts, but for the Real itself. The writings of Ibn 'Arabi and his followers are undoubtedly of incalculable value in this age of uncertainty and confusion when rival systems of thought are not brought into completion in a single Truth—for he always demonstrates the Unity of Being as the matrix of all knowledge and stresses the supreme privilege of Man as moulded with both hands, transcendent and immanent, of God.
>
> Within the traditions of esoteric knowledge Ibn 'Arabi's influence has been both enormous and unique. The list of his followers and students is impressive indeed: Sadruddin Qunawi, Jelaluddin Rumi, Fakhruddin al-Iraqi, 'Abd al-Karim al-Jili and 'Abd ar-Rahman Jami, to name a few. His influence has also been extended, as Professor Asin Palacios observed, to men like Dante Alighieri and Thierry of Chartres and to a whole tradition of Courtly love amongst the troubadours of Provence. And yet, of all Ibn 'Arabi's vast literary output, only a handful of works have been translated into European languages and most of these only partially.
>
> This journal which will appear annually, is one of the first fruits of the Society's commitment to make these writings available in the West. It is our sincere hope that this may encourage not only translations and critical editions, but also expositions and discussions of the central themes of these writers. This will naturally include an evaluation and establishment of the very best criteria for translation and study, since the problems in this field are notorious and manifold...[48]

The second volume of the journal was produced in 1984. It is interesting to note that this early issue addressed a question which is of great significance to participants of Beshara and their approach to studying Ibn 'Arabi in the school. This issue involves their experiential approach to his work in relation to the academic and scholarly approach of the Society. This question arises in the editorial, and is then addressed in detail in the first article by Peter Young, entitled 'Between the Yea and the Nay'. This title refers to the youthful Ibn 'Arabi's meeting with the

---

48. Anon., introductory page, *JMIAS* I (1982).

famous philosopher, Ibn Rushd (Averroes), and their remarkable discussion about the superiority of either the mystic way or that of reason and philosophy in attaining to the Truth about Reality.[49] The question put forward by Young in the article is whether there is an unbridgeable gap between the way of the mystic and that of the academic. He tries to show that the two positions are not irreconcilable, but that both approaches to the Truth have similar ends.

These questions were being brought forward at this stage of the Society's development, not simply because they were crucial in Ibn 'Arabi's lifetime, but also because they continued to be of extreme importance to Beshara students. This was because the proposition that these two approaches could be reconciled was not universally accepted in academic circles or by those academic scholars who were invited to contribute to early issues of the journals and to the early symposia in the UK. Interestingly, in contrast to the British symposia, the US branch was able to blend the two positions from early on, because the attendees were prepared to ask personal spiritual questions of the speakers, and the speakers, whether academic, or lay scholars, felt comfortable in replying to questions and in entering into discussions of a personal and spiritual nature.[50] This 'loosening up' and 'breaking down the barrier between the personal mystical approach (speaking from the heart) and the purely speculative' is now becoming more common even in British symposia.[51]

As Peter Young explains in his article, in the journal's second issue (1984), an academic is obliged to remain in a state of objectivity and detachment with regards to his subject matter, whereas in contrast the mystic is required to immerse himself in the subject matter, to 'surrender himself to the subject until identification of objective and subjective Truth is perfect, henceforth any judgement made through him proceeds from that same subjective and objective Truth in his own individual expression.'[52] He argues that in all academic disciplines this detachment

---

49. The quote is "Ibn Rushd put to me the following question, "What solution have you found as a result of mystical illumination and divine inspiration? Does it coincide with what is arrived at by speculative thought?" I replied "Yes and no. Between the Yea and the Nay spirits take their flight beyond matter, and their necks detach themselves from their bodies".' *Futûhât* I, p. 153, quoted in R.W.J. Austin, *Sufis of Andalusia* (London: Allen & Unwin, 1971). See Young's article, 'Between the Yea and the Nay', *JMIAS* II (1984), p. 4.

50. Interviews with L., Chisholme, August 2000, and M., Turkey trip, December 2000.

51. Interviews with L., Chisholme, August 2000, and M., Turkey trip, December 2000.

52. Young, 'Between the Yea and the Nay', p. 2.

is not always required to maintain academic integrity and gives the example of logic and how a logician does not lose this integrity by subordinating himself to the established rules of logic. He is in fact a servant of the discipline, which itself pronounces whether a conclusion is true or false. Young suggests that if this follows with such disciplines as logic, then why not with the academic study of mysticism?[53] He says 'whether the servant of this...discipline is to be considered a mystic or an academic student of mysticism depends entirely on what portion of himself he offers as servant of the discipline...'[54]

In support of this question, the Editorial also addresses the question of the quality of translation of Ibn 'Arabi and tends to affirm Young's point that academic submission to an immersion in the subject is more likely to 'reap rewards'. The discussion provides examples to illustrate '...the complete relationship between that which is studied, and how it should be studied and realised between the works of the great mystics and the quality of translation'. In this regard Ralph Austin is cited: 'every aspiring student of [Ibn 'Arabi's] work must proceed with caution and humility';[55] as is Professor Arberry: 'I am an academic scholar, but I have come to realise that pure reason is unqualified to penetrate the mystery of God's Light and may indeed, if too fondly indulged, interpose an impenetrable veil between the heart and God'.[56]

As already noted, these first two volumes of the journal both contained articles by William Chittick that had previously been published in *Sophia Perennis*. Volume II also included an article by Ralph Austin. Both of these academic scholars were working on new translations of Ibn 'Arabi into English at about the time Beshara and the Ibn 'Arabi Society had begun work on their own translations. Volume II also introduced a section for the review of books on Ibn 'Arabi or related to his work and its wider influences, which has also grown in importance in recent decades.

1984 ONWARDS: THE FIRST ANNUAL SYMPOSIUM

In 1984, the Society increased and expanded its activities even further with the organisation of its first annual symposium, which was held at Collingwood College at the University of Durham. Apart from Professor

---

53. Ibid., p. 3.
54. Ibid., p. 4.
55. R.J.W. Austin, 'The Feminine Dimensions in Ibn al-'Arabi's Thought', *JMIAS* II (1984), pp. 5-14.
56. Prof. Arberry: translator of Arabic and Persian writings. Ref.: 'Editorial', *JMIAS* II (1984), n.p..

Ralph Austin,[57] the speakers were all early participants of Beshara. Austin was, at that time, a senior lecturer in Arab and Islamic Studies at the University of Durham

The date of this symposium coincided with the date of publication of Volume II of the journal. In Volume III, published the following year, the Benedictine monk, Dom Sylvester Houedard, offered his impressions of this first annual symposium. He reminds readers at that time that it seems incredible that although Ibn 'Arabi had written over five hundred works, only two hundred had been printed, twenty-five of which had been translated and only half of these into English. He remarks of Ibn 'Arabi that of all spiritual writers he is the one who seems to reflect most completely that catholic tradition of Scripture, of the original desert contemplatives and the Rule of St. Benedict.[58]

In another enthusiastic summary of this first symposium, Richard MacEwan contemplates the Arabic root *Hubb* (usually translated as 'love' but also related in meaning to 'seed') and he relates the idea of 'seed' to the Ibn 'Arabi Society and its activities in relation to Ibn 'Arabi's ideas:

> Firstly, I would like to thank Dr. Austin and the Symposium Committee for making this Symposium possible, and bringing about this truly international and inter-disciplinary gathering of people all with a united interest in Ibn 'Arabi. A gathering symbolised in a certain way by the Arabic word *Hubb* described for us yesterday by Dr. Austin as having a dual meaning of love and seed: 'the seed that is bursting with potential for multiple and universal manifestation in a seminally predisposed way as also the urge to return that potential to seed form'. Here we have a beautiful cyclic image drawn from the world of Nature, Nature which 'Arabi says is the same as *Nafas ar-Rahman*—the Compassionate Ipseity or the Breath of the Merciful. A meditation on this word *Hubb* and its meaning and symbolism could itself be the subject of a lengthy dissertation, each insight of its meaning leading to proliferation of further possibilities just as the seeds give rise to flowers which give rise to seeds ad infinitum and in constant unique display. So through contemplation and analysis of the subject, Union and Ibn 'Arabi, that we have chosen, we are drawn into an unceasing movement around and towards the heart of the matter—an epectasy which is the expression of the other more usual meaning of *Hubb* as love, which however understood, implies our motivation for being here today and our action in coming here this morning. So I see this gathering as a fertile occasion, like the seed bursting with potential for expression...[59]

57. Who presented a paper entitled 'Union in Ibn 'Arabi'.
58. 'First Annual Symposium of the Ibn 'Arabi Society', *JMIAS* III (1984), p. 3.
59. Summary of Proceedings of the 1984 Symposium.

The second annual symposium was held at the University College of Wales, Aberystwyth, in April 1985. Its title was *Universality and Ibn 'Arabi*. All the speakers here were again associates of Beshara and at this symposium, in contrast to those that were to follow, the programme included small group seminar sessions in addition to main presentations. This was a particularly interesting symposium in that its very theme raised a question that frequently arises in relation to the study of Ibn 'Arabi by the Beshara School and some members of the Ibn 'Arabi Society. This is the question of whether non-Muslims could properly study and apply the teaching of Ibn 'Arabi. In this regard it is helpful to quote from the symposium's summing-up paper by Richard MacEwan, who begins by quoting the question which arose in the plenary session:

> Are the teachings of Ibn 'Arabi applicable or equally accessible to anyone, from whatever religious background—or are they of immediate interest only to a Muslim, or one who speaks Arabic? Are they universal or not?

MacEwan then quoted a passage from John Dunne, which Stephen Hirtenstein had used in his lecture:

> We have a choice, if we wish to know God, between learning from the friends of God and learning from the common notion. I would choose to learn from the friends of God. The common notion is a way of interpreting whatever happens but it does not seem to arise out of any actual communication between God and Man. The friends of God, on the contrary, walk and speak with God, experience a love that is 'from God and of God and towards God'. To actually know God we will have to enter into the to and fro. From that vantage point we may be able to see the common notion from a new light.[60]

MacEwan then suggested a rendering of Ibn 'Arabi's approach which could be said to represent the way in which adherents of Beshara and the Society understand and interpret his teachings:

> Arabi certainly was a friend of God, a *Waliyy*, one who knew God from God and in God, without any separation in being, i.e. having no being in himself. As he describes—it was only when there was no vestige of Lordship within him that Jesus invited him to sit on the chair of Mohammedian Sainthood. 'Arabi is one of those rare individuations who have divested themselves of the notion of otherness and have reached a union with God their beloved and can truly say 'My heart is capable of every form', so that his heart is given over completely to contemplation of the

---

60. John S. Dunne, *The Reasons of the Heart: A Journey into Solitude and Back again into the Human Circle* (Notre Dame, Ind.: University of Notre Dame Press, 1978), p. 2, quoted in Stephen Hirtenstein, 'Universal and Divine Sainthood', *JMIAS* IV (1985), p. 8.

infinite and absolute beauty of the One and Unique in whatever manner that One reveals itself to him. And from that degree of union it is the being itself, reflected in the supreme passion of Man, that compassionately gives consequent expressions through the pen of 'Arabi, expressions which are always universal in their meanings. So that Man, *Insân*, the intimate of God is at the station of completeness. He is *Kâmil* and through him, as 'Arabi says, 'God contemplates his creation and dispenses his mercy'.[61]

The controversy over the question of whether Ibn 'Arabi's work is 'accessible' to non-Muslims continued that year and rose forcibly at the Society's Annual General Meeting, when the guest speaker, the French Sufi teacher, Charles André Gilis, confronted the question.[62] Gilis' remarks were openly directed against Bulent Rauf and Beshara participants—since the distinct identity and scholarly aims of the Ibn 'Arabi Society were not yet publicly evident at that time (only a year after its first Oxford symposium) and were rooted in his own controversial personal claims to be the only authoritative representative of the 'true' school of Rene Guénon.[63] He concluded his presentation of a paper which appeared to implicitly accuse supporters of the Ibn 'Arabi Society of distorting the meaning of Ibn 'Arabi's works by stating that:

> ...there can be no doubt that there is, between the universal metaphysical Doctrine as expressed by Ibn 'Arabi and the Islamic tradition, an indissoluble link. Chiekh al Akbar is neither a thinker, in the profane meaning of the word, nor a philanthropist trying to promote some sort of ideals for the welfare of mankind. He is a traditional author, commissioned to advise Allah's faithful, deriving his inspiration from the same transcendent source as the Prophet Muhammad's, constantly referring to the very traditional precepts of Islam or those confirmed by Islam, scrupulously abiding by the slightest prescriptions of the Sacred Law, speaking the name and in favour of Allah's Religion. His teaching represents a sacred character in view of its origin, expressive modes and aims. Therefore, one cannot underestimate the link between this teaching and Islamic tradition without taking the risk of totally distorting its meaning and significance, and even in some way, violating it.

Responding to Gilis' criticism regarding the question of whether non-Muslims should study Ibn 'Arabi, particularly in translations without full conversion to Islam, Rauf pointed out that anyone who has read the Quran knows that the key expression 'muslim' has a wider application

61. R. MacEwan, from the 'Summing Up' of the 1985 Symposium.
62. Presentation: 'An Approach to the Function of Islam in the Teaching of Ibn 'Arabi', printed in the report of the *MIAS, AGM* (1985), n.p. (26 October 1985).
63. See below, p. 247.

than purely to the historical followers of Muhammad, citing the examples in the Quran of Pharaoh's wife and sister who brought up Moses, as being referred to as 'muslims',[64] as are the twelve apostles of Jesus. He remarked:

> For Monsieur Gilis to confine Islam to his co-religionaries today is to say the least, surprising.[65] To castigate the Ibn 'Arabi Society on this account was out of place and smacked of the zeal of a neophyte, whereas Monsieur Gilis has been a Moslem since 17 years... The Muhyiddin Ibn 'Arabi Society is and will continue to represent...a body of people who are devoted to the promulgation and diffusion of knowledge of Ibn 'Arabi and his exposition of the Realities, no matter from what creed or belief the membership of the Society originates... In the Quran it is said: 'Had we wished we would have made you all one religion...' [*umma*, 5:48] This definitely confirms the intentional diversity, as again God may say: 'I conform to the idea my servant has of me'. The latitude and majesty of this saying is beyond any attempt man can make at relegating God to a form, a form of belief, or a supposition other than that which is in accordance with what the Greatest Shaykh Muhyiddin Ibn 'Arabi, brings the 'Arif or the Gnostic to see and believe.[66]

The disparity between Gilis' and Rauf's remarks provides stark illustration of their contrasting points of view regarding not only the interpretations of the metaphysical concepts of Ibn 'Arabi but also some Quranic passages as well. In the early years of the Ibn 'Arabi Society when its independent identity and scholarly aims were not always understood by

---

64. Suras 66:11 and 28:11

65. It should be stressed that Mr. Gilis, in 1985, was involved in heated polemics concerning the rightful spiritual heir of René Guénon and other Sufi teachers, but in fact represented only one small, highly controversial Parisian branch among a vast spectrum of Western spiritual groups, teachings and teachers partially inspired in various ways by Guénon's 'traditionalist' writings and understanding of Ibn'Arabi's teachings. Equally importantly, it should be particularly noted, for readers unfamiliar with the broad range of Guéonian movements, that 'Islamic tradition' in his remarks, as in most Guénonian contexts, refers not to the immense range of actual historic forms of Islamic religious life and expression (as it would in modern religious and Islamic studies), but to an idiosyncratic, avowedly partisan and polemical, personal vision of 'true' Islam which is expressed, in Mr. Gilis' own writings, in a distinctive admixture of Ibn 'Arabi's ideas with complex 'esoteric' Masonic, astrological, numerological and other symbolisms drawn primarily from Guénon's works. Readers without access to Mr. Gilis' writings in the original French can refer to the summaries and wider contexts provided in Morris, 'Ibn 'Arabi and His Interpreters', Part I, *Journal of the American Oriental Society* 106 (1986), pp. 539-51; Part II, 106 (1986), pp. 733-56; Part III, 107 (1987), pp. 101-19.

66. Note from Mr. Bulent Rauf in addition to the Minutes of the Annual General Meeting, printed in the report of the *MIAS, AGM* (1985), n.p.

outsiders, this type of disagreement tended to surface on occasions, but today it is much less of a problem. This is because, as may be clearly witnessed in the contents of the journal and symposium papers over two decades, no scholar, translator or interpreter of Ibn 'Arabi anywhere denies that his thought is firmly grounded in traditional Islamic sources.[67]

THE EVOLUTION OF THE SOCIETY THROUGH THE 1980S TO THE EARLY 1990S

In 1985, the Society published the first volume of the *Fusûs al-Hikam*, translated with an extended commentary and introduction into Turkish by Ismael Hakki Bursevi and into English by Bulent Rauf.[68] This first volume contained Ismael Hakki's Introduction and the opening chapters of Adam and Seth. It was noted in the announcement that Ismael Hakki's commentary is regarded as an extremely important work because it is 'perhaps the summum and summaton of all the commentaries which the *Fusûs al-Hikam* inspired'.[69] A later announcement explains the importance of the book to the Society through the way in which it was a partial fulfilment of the Society's original intentions:[70]

> From the coming together of all the aims of the Society in this book, its publication is of paramount importance to it, and while the Society itself neither commissioned nor undertook its publication, it has been given the honour of having the book in the name of the Society. And so in this instance the objectives of the Society for the translation, publication and promulgation of the works of Muhyiddin Ibn 'Arabi, are fulfilled, not by desert but by grace.

Later in the same year (1985), a symposium on the work of Ibn 'Arabi was held in Australia at the University of Melbourne. It was not organised by the Society but by Diane Cilento, who had strong involvement with Beshara in its early days and had made the film *Turning* about the Mevlevi Dervishes, featuring the commentary of Bulent Rauf. The Society was invited to send a guest speaker, and Dr. Peter Coates agreed to speak and represent the Society. The symposium, entitled *The Sufi Legacy of Muhyiddin Ibn 'Arabi*, was attended by over one hundred people.

---

67. Although Gilis's address seemed to attack the Ibn 'Arabi Society, it was probably intended to be directed at the Beshara School, as the Society has always had an academic, scholarly approach to Ibn 'Arabi. The school applied the experiential approach and this was from the start controversial to some Muslims.
68. With the assistance of R. Brass and H. Tollemache. For details see Chapter 4.
69. *Newsletter* (1985), n.p.
70. *Minutes of the AGM* (1985).

Also in 1986, the Society established a branch in Australia, and this coincided with a second international symposium that was held there that year. It was intended that in the future, events concerning Ibn 'Arabi in Australia would be run under the auspices of the Society there and that awareness of the Society would be increased through such media as bookshops and universities.[71] Another interesting result of the early activities of the Society which demonstrates how, even in 1986, it was being heard of in unexpected places, was recorded in the *AGM Minutes* of that year. It described an enquiry from an Alexander Knysh, who was then a junior researcher in the Institute for Oriental Studies at the University of Leningrad. Knysh asked for copies of the journal and agreed to send to the Society articles of his on Ibn 'Arabi appearing in Soviet periodicals.

Of course, the spread of knowledge and influence of Ibn 'Arabi in the English-speaking world was by no means confined to the activities of the Muhyiddin Ibn 'Arabi Society. In 1984, for example, there was a panel entirely devoted to Ibn 'Arabi by scholars and students at the annual conference of the American Academy of Religion in Chicago. That panel accentuated the historical, intellectual and spiritual importance of Ibn 'Arabi's legacy. The speakers, who were professors of Islamic Studies and translators of Ibn 'Arabi's works, included William Chittick and Michael Sells, who have since participated frequently in symposia, publications and other activities of the Muhyiddin Ibn 'Arabi Society.[72]

During this time the Society continued to evolve, drawing on an increasing network of academic and lay scholars from the English-speaking world and France and increasingly from the Muslim world, both through its international symposia (in the UK and Berkeley), and especially in the range of the translation, reviews and other studies included in its journal.

Despite Bulent Rauf's insistence that his role in the emergence of Beshara and the Ibn 'Arabi Society was minor and that he was just a 'consultant' to the school, it is clear that his inspiration was anything but insignificant. When he died on the 5 September 1987, many people thought that interest in the Beshara School and the Society would decline significantly. Especially in wider Sufi circles, many observers had concluded that he was actually a sheikh to the Beshara School, and that

---

71. *Newsletter* (September 1987), p. 3.
72. Professor of Comparative Religion at Haverford College in Pennsylvania. His books include *Mystical Languages of Unsaying* (Chicago: University of Chicago Press, 1994); translator and editor of *Early Islamic Mysticism* (New York: Paulist Press, 1996) and *Stations of Desire*, translations from the *Tarjumân al-Ashwâq* into modern poetic English (Jerusalem: Ibis Editions, 2000).

the school was actually another Sufi order.[73] Rauf himself always vigorously denied this assumption, insisting that those he helped should 'look at what I am pointing at, not at me'.[74] And in any case, both organisations continued to flourish and expand in the years following his death.

An appreciation of his enormous contribution to the knowledge and understanding of Ibn 'Arabi was published in the journal after his death:[75]

> At the Annual General Meeting of the Society, the Chairman expressed the Society's indebtedness to Mr. Rauf in the following terms: His passing, though a great loss to the Society has at the same time left a vast legacy for the future.
>
> Bulent was the inspiration for the founding of the Society. In 1976, it became clear, since there were so many people who had developed an interest in the writings of Ibn 'Arabi and the body of translated work was so meagre, an organised attempt should be made to co-ordinate this interest, and thus provide a forum for discussion and a support for those who wish to translate or expound on the matters written about the Sheikh and his successors. It is from this very small beginning, that the Society has grown into what it is today.
>
> From the first Bulent encouraged, advised and pointed the way, thus ensuring that the fledgling Society could become established in time as an influential and respected organisation. Publishers were encouraged to reissue works long out of print; world-wide contacts were established with academics writing in the field and many of them generously consented to become Honorary Fellows. In 1982 the first journal was published and the Society Library founded which today contains some 500-specialist books and many microfilms of original manuscripts.
>
> It was Bulent who made contact with the Suleymaniye Library in Istanbul, a library which is rich in manuscripts by Ibn 'Arabi. As a result, we continue to receive works on microfilm from them. All this treasure sits in the Society Library and it is hoped that more people will avail themselves of this facility.
>
> In 1980, it was proposed to Bulent Rauf that he translate Hakki Bursevi's translation of and commentary on the *Fusûs al-Hikam*, a vast undertaking that involved having to translate from two languages into a third and at the same time being completely at one with the author so that the meaning was correct also. There was a small sigh of agreement and the work began. It continued until his death without interruption...'[76]

Shortly after Bulent's death in late 1987, the Society held its first Annual International Symposium at the University of California, Berkeley (in 1987), under the title of *Universality and Ibn 'Arabi*. The

73. Early participants of Beshara generally shared this understanding.
74. See Chapter 1 above.
75. *JMIAS* VI (1987), pp. 2-3.
76. Ibid. Grenville Collins, Chairman.

US branch of the Society, based in San Francisco, invited distinguished guest speakers from Europe as well as America. A report described the symposium as having been well attended and suggested that the promulgation of the works and ideals of Ibn 'Arabi in the US was 'in response to an urgent and pressing demand'.[77] It is further suggested in the report that the 'recognition of the immense stature of Ibn 'Arabi is long overdue in America; but that this recognition would become more prevalent through the symposium and its proceedings which would be published for wider circulation. The speakers included several Beshara associates[78] as well as professors Elton Hall,[79] and Michael Sells. Since 1987, the annual Berkeley Symposium has become a key occasion for the worldwide gathering of distinguished scholars, writers, artists and others involved in creatively applying and interpreting Ibn 'Arabi's ideas in many fields of activity.

1990 marked a very important year for those interested in Ibn 'Arabi's thought and works, since it coincided with the 750th anniversary of the death (the *'urs* or 'nuptial night') of Ibn 'Arabi.[80] This anniversary was widely celebrated in several countries around the world. In Spain, the country of his birth, the regional government of Murcia arranged a major three-day conference.[81] The Vatican mounted an exhibition of his manuscripts. In Istanbul, a related symposium was held at Marmara University's Theological Faculty. In England and America, the Society hosted international symposia, lectures and special publications that brought together students and scholars from all around the world.[82] The title in 1990 was *Muhyiddin Ibn 'Arabi—1165–1240: His Life and Times*. The UK symposium was the first to draw on such a wide variety of internationally renowned speakers from a wide range of cultural backgrounds extending from Murcia, where he was born, to Damascus, where he died. In addition to scholars were other speakers more

---

77. David Hornsby, 'Communications: American Symposium', *JMIAS* VI (1987), pp. 55-61.

78. Peter Young, Peter Coates, Dom Sylvester Houedard and Peter Lamborne Wilson.

79. Professor in the Department of Philosophy, Moorpark College, California who spoke on 'The Real and the Universal Man According to Ibn 'Arabi'.

80. In Islamic spiritual tradition, when a saint or true 'friend of God' dies, they are understood to achieve complete intimacy with God, in the same way that a couple achieves intimacy on their wedding night.

81. After exchanges with the Muhyiddin Ibn 'Arabi Society, Dr. Francisco Gimenez came from Murcia as a speaker at that year's Symposium.

82. 'Notices: Commemorative Volume', *JMIAS* VIII (1989), pp. 71-72.

interested with the practical perspective of Ibn 'Arabi's teaching, 'seeing him as a spiritual teacher of immense importance and significance for our times'.[83]

> In many ways this Symposium made significant steps towards the fulfilment of the Society's intention to emulate the universality of the Shaykh himself, and to provide a forum for all who are attracted to and by the Shaykh to meet and share insights, understandings and the result of research. It seems fitting that a gathering to celebrate the 750th anniversary of the Shaykh's nuptial night should involve such a disparate group whose central concern is in reality, not so much with the Shaykh himself, but with that which the Shaykh loved, knew and expressed so fully throughout his life and writings.[84]

The 1990 annual symposium in the USA was part of this 'global event' celebrating Ibn 'Arabi's nuptial night. The Spanish conference on his life, works and thought was part of a week-long programme of events. The speakers came from a variety of backgrounds and included such respected scholarly authorities as Osman Yahya and Michael Chodkiewicz.[85] Further activity took place in Algeria, where there was an international scholarly conference held at the University of Oran, entitled *L'Heritage Mystique d'Ibn 'Arabi*. M. Chodkiewicz reported for the Muhyiddin Ibn 'Arabi Society:

> The importance of the fundamentalist or reformist movements in Algeria (which have in common an acute hostility to Sufism in general and Ibn 'Arabi in particular) might have made one fear that the envisaged Conference would take place in less than calm atmosphere. In fact, it went off under excellent circumstances in front of a large attentive audience, and benefited from surprising coverage in the Algerian media.[86]

Chodkiewicz also reported from a conference in Moscow, *The Concept of Man in the Traditional Cultures of the East*, organised by the Oriental Department of the Institute of Philosophy of the Scientific Academy. A young Russian researcher, Andre Smirnov, presented one of the papers,

---

83. The speakers at this special Symposium included a proliferation of international scholars, including Dr. Claude Addas; Dr. Ralph Austin; M. Michael Chodkiewicz; Dr. Francisco Gimenez; Dr. Souad Hakim; Dom Sylvester Houedard; Prof. Elton Hall; Dr. Alexander Knysh; Sama Z. el Mahassini; Prof. Frithjof Rundgren; Alison Yiangou; and Peter Young.
84. Adam Dupré, 'Report of the Seventh Annual Symposium of the Muhyiddin Ibn 'Arabi Society, 1990', *Newsletter* (Summer 1990), p. 3.
85. Cecilia Twinch, 'Conference in Murcia, 12–14 November 1990', *JMIAS* IX (1991), pp. 65-66.
86. Ibid., p. 67.

entitled 'Nicholas of Cusa and Ibn 'Arabi: Two Types of Rationalisation of Mysticism'. At this time, Smirnov had just finished the first translation into Russian of the *Fusûs al-Hikam*.

Also in this year Ibn 'Arabi featured prominently at a further conference, *The Legacy of Medieval Sufism*, this time in London at the Centre of Near and Middle Eastern Studies, SOAS (The School of Oriental and African Studies, University of London).

To mark this unique year, the Society had also decided to produce a special commemorative volume to replace the 1990 journal.[87] A wide range of people who had written about Ibn 'Arabi in the past was invited to contribute. It was produced in two parts, the first devoted to new translations of several of Ibn 'Arabi's works, whilst the second part was a collection of specially written studies of Ibn 'Arabi's teachings, the ways in which they have influenced succeeding generations and their implications for our era.

One of the earliest adherents of Beshara wrote an appreciation of the commemorative volume which is quoted here because it shows how those original members of the Society and Beshara felt then about the activities and the accomplishments of the Society in relation to its original intentions.[88] She begins by reminding the reader that twenty years before the appearance of this volume, there were very few publications by Ibn 'Arabi available in English, which is mysterious in the light of the fact that Ibn 'Arabi is a 'towering giant in the world's mystical literature'. The few translations into English that did exist stood out prominently, and most students of Ibn 'Arabi in the West were of necessity readers of Arabic. By the early 1990s, the situation had already changed significantly, with prolific English and French translations and studies and a wealth of students who studied Ibn 'Arabi in their own languages. The writer then discusses the question of why this activity has happened recently:

> Was the interest in Ibn 'Arabi so small because so few works had been translated, and so no one knew about him? Is the proliferation of translations and studies a response to an increasing demand, or the cause of it? I think anyone who studies Ibn 'Arabi would consider this question to be fruitless: as Being is single, that which appears as a need and that which appears to fulfil that need are both aspects of a single situation. The relationship between them cannot be encapsulated by causality.

---

87. S. Hirtenstein and M. Tiernan, eds., *Muhyiddin Ibn 'Arabi: A Commemorative Volume* (Shaftesbury: Element Books, 1993).
88. Alison Yiangou, 'An Appreciation', *JMIAS* XIII (1993), pp. 79-81.

Finally, she approaches the subject of the actual study of Ibn 'Arabi and how many people who study him for the first time encounter grave difficulties. And here she cites words which are in fact entirely relevant to those studying Ibn 'Arabi on Beshara courses:

> The Shaykh intentionally forces his readers to situate themselves—in relation to the text—in at least two ordinary separate dimensions at the same time: the intellectual, discursive, ostensibly 'objective' dimension... and the inner experiential, inevitably highly personal, spiritual dimension... But as Ibn 'Arabi stresses throughout his Introduction, the tension carefully generated by the constantly varied confrontation of these two dimensions is actually meant to move the properly prepared reader through a spiral of higher and higher levels of participation and engagement, from conceptual understanding and analysis to the very different plane of spiritual knowing, returning to those mysterious 'Openings' which were the source and aim of all his writings.[89]

THE SOCIETY THROUGH THE 1990S TO THE NEW MILLENNIUM

Within the final decade of the twentieth century, the international symposia continued as an annual event in both England (usually at Oxford University) and at Berkeley, whilst the journal continued to be published biannually. Both the symposia and the journal saw an increase in numbers of international scholars and writers from related fields, particularly from the Islamic world, such as the novelist and literary critic Gamal al-Ghitani from Egypt who spoke at the 1998 symposium in Oxford.[90]

The Society newsletters also expanded in their content and sophistication, always with the central intent of expanding knowledge of Ibn 'Arabi and his works as widely as possible. They have now become an international forum for members around the world and part of their appeal is that their content provides attraction for the less academically inclined reader as opposed to the more scholarly journal.

In 1995, the BBC World Service broadcast *The Treasure of Compassion*, a programme about Ibn 'Arabi for which some of the members of the Society were interviewed. Also in 1995, a highly successful symposium was held at Chisholme House, home of the Beshara School, and a second equally successful symposium was held there in 2000. And

---

89. Yiangou, 'An Appreciation', p. 81, citing J.W. Morris, 'How to Study the Futûhât: Ibn 'Arabi's own Advice', in Hirtenstein and Tiernan, eds., *Muhyiddin Ibn 'Arabi*, pp. 73-89.

90. He had been a war reporter in the Middle East and is now a highly regarded novelist and short story writer, as well as being editor of the influential Cairo journal *Akhbâr al-Adab* ('Literary News').

throughout the 1990s, other events at Chisholme allowed students to work with scholarly specialists and translators of Ibn 'Arabi associated with the Society.[91]

By the end of the decade, in addition to the regular biannual journal, the Society itself had published or had been closely connected with several publications including: *Muhyiddin Ibn 'Arabi: A Commemorative Volume*;[92] *Fusûs al-Hikam* (4 vols.);[93] *Prayer and Contemplation* (a volume of papers first presented at the 10th Annual Symposium of the Society in the UK, University of Durham, 1993);[94] *The Journey of the Heart* (a volume of papers first presented at the 8th Annual Symposium of the Society in the USA, Berkeley, 1994);[95] and *Praise* (a volume of papers first presented at the 14th Annual Symposium of the Society in the UK, Oxford, 1997).[96] These final three on this list were special editions of the journal, presented as separate books because the articles had a common theme.

Closely connected to these publications was the founding by the journal's original editor, Stephen Hirtenstein, of a specialised publishing house, Anqa Publishing, devoted to the translation of Ibn 'Arabi and related studies. That service began with the first introduction to Ibn 'Arabi's life and teaching originally intended for general English-language audiences: *The Unlimited Mercifier: The Spiritual Life and Thought of Ibn 'Arabi* by Stephen Hirtenstein.[97] Other recent publications by Anqa include: *Contemplation of the Holy Mysteries* (*Mashâhid al-asrâr al-qudsiyya*), one of Ibn 'Arabi's first works, consisting of fourteen contemplations in the form of dialogues with God and epiphanic

---

91. In 1993, James Morris led a highly successful five-day seminar at Chisholme entitled *Spiritual Mysteries and Spiritual Life: Exploring Ibn 'Arabi's Futûhât al-Makkiyya*. The following year a further seminar was led at Chisholme by Ralph Austin entitled *The Language and Rhythms of Ibn 'Arabi*. In 1996 Michael Sells led another seminar there on Ibn 'Arabi's *Tarjuman al-Ashwaq*, and most recently in 1999 James Morris again led a seminar entitled *Climbing: Ibn 'Arabi on Spirituality in Everyday Life*.

92. Hirtenstein and Tiernan, eds., *Muhyiddin Ibn 'Arabi*.

93. See Chapter 4 above.

94. S. Hirtenstein, ed., *Prayer and Contemplation* (Oxford: Muhyiddin Ibn 'Arabi Society, 1993).

95. J. Mercer, ed., *The Journey of the Heart* (Oxford: Muhyiddin Ibn 'Arabi Society, 1996).

96. S. Hirtenstein, ed., *Praise* (Hirtenstein; Oxford: Muhyiddin Ibn 'Arabi Society, 1997).

97. Stephen Hirtenstein, *The Unlimited Mercifier: The Spiritual Life and Thought of Ibn 'Arabi* (Oxford: Anqa, 1999).

visions;[98] *The Seven Days of the Heart* (*Wird*), fourteen prayers for the days and nights of the week;[99] and the *Niche of Lights* (*Mishkât al-anwâr*), a collection of one hundred and one *hadîth qudsî* composed during Ibn 'Arabi's stay in Mecca in 1202/3.[100]

Since its establishment in 1977, the Society's library had accumulated a substantial collection of works. A significant number were due to generous donations from a variety of quarters.[101] By 1998, it had been reorganised and the contents catalogued on a computer database.

In 2001, a proposal was submitted to the Turkish government to instigate a co-operative project to preserve some rare manuscripts held in Turkey. This proposal was rejected. Later, however, the Turkish Department of Culture granted permission for certain members of the Society to study in the Turkish libraries. The permission came as a result of acknowledgment by the Turkish Department of Culture of the role played by the Society in the discovery of stolen manuscripts. The theft included 110 books and 65 letters including manuscripts of Ibn Arabi from the Yusuf Agha Library in Konya in June 2000. The theft was noticed by the Society when a collection of four Konya manuscripts in Ibn 'Arabi's hand appeared in Christie's Auction House in London in early 2001. Altogether twenty works by Ibn 'Arabi and Sadr al-Qûnâwî (Ibn 'Arabi's step-son) had been stolen, along with the works of other famous Sufis and philosophers such as Ibn Sîna and al-Ghazâli. Fortunately, some of the works had archive copies on microfilm, so not all were lost. The Society, which had long been interested on setting up a microfilm archive of the important manuscripts of Ibn 'Arabi, discussed the idea with the Turkish Cultural Attaché in London. The outcome of this was an invitation to submit a proposal of how an archive could be established and maintained which was sent to the Ministry of Culture.[102]

---

98. *Contemplation of the Holy Mysteries* (*Mashâhid al-asrâr al-qudsiyya*) (trans. Pablo Beneito and Cecilia Twinch; Oxford: Anqa, 2001).

99. *The Seven Days of the Heart* (*Wird*) (trans. Pablo Beneito and S. Hirtenstein; Oxford, 2000).

100. Published as *Divine Sayings: The Mishkat al-anwar of Ibn Arabi* (trans. Martin Notcutt and Daniel Hirtenstein; Oxford: Anqa, 2004).

101. For example the newsletter of 1985 reported that M. Patrice Brecq of Saumur had made gifts to the Society of several works published recently in France. In 1987 the Society received a copy of a manuscript from the Suleymaniyye, *Kitâb al-Yaqîn* (MS no. RG 832) which was an outstanding manuscript because it carried a *samâ'* certificate, which is a verification by the author of the correctness of the copy. It was dated 621AH at Damascus (*Newsletter*, September 1987).

102. Details in Jane Clark, 'News and Events World Wide: UK', *Newsletter* (Autumn 2001), pp. 2-3.

This project was approved in 2002, and having raised money from the Society's Fellows and members, Jane Clark and Stephen Hirtenstein were in a position to make some visits to Turkey to carry out research. During these visits digital copies of relevant manuscripts of Ibn 'Arabi's work were applied for through the Turkish library system, again financed with money raised by the Society. The importance of this project lies in the fact that most of the rare historic manuscripts pertaining to Ibn 'Arabi's legacy which have survived to this day are actually in Turkey. The project has been extended to libraries in other countries that may be custodians of relevant work. The project will continue until every original manuscript of Ibn 'Arabi has been accounted for. Ultimately, the Society's archive is a completely independent facility available to Society members for the purposes of research.

World Wide Web
Finally, in 1996, the Society created its own computer website, 'The Muhyiddin Ibn 'Arabi Society' (http://www.ibnarabisociety.org).

The Society's Support for Scholars of Ibn 'Arabi
The Society also provides a supportive environment for scholars of Ibn 'Arabi, as was recently attested by a well-known Spanish academic.[103] He described how, when he was starting his studies in 1991, he was asked to present a paper in Tehran. Here he met members of the Society who 'all knew more than him', but they soon became a permanent support in his developing ability. He described the Society as being different from other similar groups because it was not 'closed', the members being communicative towards outsiders. Since then he has found that the Muhyiddin Ibn Arabi Society has become a place of reference, for example, through consulting a member for advice as to how to explain the intention of an article. He suggests that the Society seems to be very conscious of its function as a centre of communication, providing intellectual, emotional and friendly support for scholars and that he has been personally inspired by his experience of it. Since his first meeting with some of its members, he has completed his PhD and is translating and editing works of Ibn 'Arabi and lecturing at the University of Seville.

---

103. Pablo Beneito, who is Professor at the Department of Arabic and Islamic Studies, Faculty of Philosophy, University of Seville. He has worked on translations of Ibn 'Arabi with Cecilia Twinch and Stephen Hirtenstein of the Muhyiddin Ibn 'Arabi Society.

THE GLOBAL EXPANSION OF KNOWLEDGE OF IBN 'ARABI

In recent years, the Society's activities have not only expanded in the English speaking world, but have also reflected the increasing interest in Ibn 'Arabi's teachings in many Islamic countries. This expansion of wider Islamic interest in Ibn 'Arabi is reflected not only in the increasingly global participation in the Society's international symposia and journal, but also in the variety of other organisations with which the Society has been connected.[104] These include, for example, the 1989 symposium in Noto in Sicily. This was an international event organised by Princess Vittoria Alliatta de Villa and the French Ibn 'Arabi specialist Michael Chodkiewicz. Its aims were to: 'bring together for the first time, scholars from round the world to discuss the future of studies on Ibn 'Arabi in general and more specifically to discuss the possible setting up of some sort of centre for the promotion and co-ordination of studies of the Sheikh al-Akbar'.[105] The speakers included noted scholars of Ibn 'Arabi from France, USA, Turkey, Lebanon, Egypt, Italy and Britain. In Algeria, after the Oran Conference (1990), already mentioned, a new Arabic edition of the *Fusûs al-Hikam* was published in Arabic in 1991, the first popular edition in Algeria or the Maghrib as a whole. And at the 11th Annual Symposium of the Muhyiddin Ibn 'Arabi Society in Oxford, 1994, the weekend concluded with an address by the cultural Attaché of the Bangladeshi Embassy in London, who was a representative for groups in Bangladesh who were interested in Ibn 'Arabi and had for some time been in contact with the Society. His primary message was appreciation from the community in Bangladesh for their contact with the Society, and an expression of their wish to deepen this contact.[106]

The same year witnessed a particular surge of expansion in activity related to Ibn 'Arabi and his works, including the Third International Congress on Ibn 'Arabi held in Murcia. This same year, the Society announced a significant increase in membership, with twenty-eight new members bringing the total to one hundred and seventy-nine, fifteen of the new members being from overseas, including Europe, Brazil, Indonesia, Tunisia, Saudi Arabia and Israel. By this time, contacts were also

---

104. As already briefly shown above, through the example of the group that organised a symposium on Ibn 'Arabi's works in Australia in 1985.
105. Ralph Austin, 'Reports: Eleventh Annual UK Symposium' *JMIAS* VIII (1989), p. 73.
106. Report by Adam Dupré, 'The Perfectibility of Man', *Newsletter* (1994), p. 2.

growing world-wide through such places as universities and bookshops that subscribed to the journal. When the editor of the journal, Stephen Hirtenstein, was working in Brazil, he was invited to give several talks on Ibn 'Arabi and he met many people interested in Ibn 'Arabi's works there. In response, the editor put these people in touch with the Society. This type of response also occurred when he visited Malaysia.[107]

In 1996, the Indonesian religious foundation, Paramadina, organised a course of study entitled *The Mystical Philosophy of Ibn 'Arabi*. The foundation also suggested that the Society held an annual symposium there. Although there has not yet been a formal symposium, the growing Indonesian interest in Ibn 'Arabi has led to several publications about him in Indonesian. In addition, other courses have been conducted more recently by Islamic foundations and organisations. For example, in April and May 2000, *Youth Islamic Study Club* (YISC), organised a series of meetings in philosophical Sufism, especially Ibn 'Arabi, and a similar course was arranged April–June of that year.[108] Also in June 2000, interested people in Jakarta co-operated with the Beshara School to organise a nine-day course on Ibn 'Arabi's *Oneness of Being*.[109]

In 1996, at a conference in Kuala Lumpa, Malaysia, entitled *Art and Cosmology*, the late Layla Shamash[110] of the Ibn 'Arabi Society, spoke on the 'Unity of Existence according to the Metaphysics of Ibn 'Arabi', and Khalil Norland, also of the Society, spoke on the 'Art of Cosmology—Creation, Human or Divine?'[111] 1996 also saw an International Seminar in Murcia, *The Legacy of Ibn 'Arabi: Thought Without Frontiers*. Besides papers delivered by the international delegates, who included a representative of the Society from Oxford, there was a round table discussion concerning future collaboration on the diffusion of Ibn 'Arabi's works, not only in Spain but as widely as possible. There was also great interest in the Muhyiddin Ibn 'Arabi Society itself, with a member of the Society based in Madrid being announced as representative of a new branch of the Society in Spain.[112]

---

107. Caroline Notcutt, 'Society News: The Society in the UK', *Newsletter* (1994), pp. 5-6 (5).
108. Organised by the students of Iain Shyarif Hidayatullah.
109. Directed by Peter Young and Peter Yiangou: see Chapter 8 above.
110. Senior lecturer in architecture at Oxford Brookes University and original student of Beshara.
111. Layla Shamash and Khalil Norland, 'Other Events: Art and Cosmology', *Newsletter* (Spring 1997), pp. 6-8 (6).
112. Laura Puy.

In 1997, the annual *Mawsimiyyât* Symposium of Marrakech was devoted to *The Intellectual and Spiritual Legacy of Ibn 'Arabi*.[113] The city of Damascus also played host to a conference on Ibn 'Arabi later that same year, also entitled *The Legacy of Ibn 'Arabi*. This was under the patronage of the Syrian Minister for Culture and organised in collaboration with the Cervantes Institute of Damascus (The Spanish Cultural Centre). As a result of this, a link was forged between the places of Ibn 'Arabi's birth and his death. The author of the report suggested:

> The movement of Ibn 'Arabi from the West to the East during his lifetime and the present resurgence of interest in the West 800 years later—which Dom Sylvester Houedard called 'his effective return home to Spain or Europe'—seems again moved East with this conference. This oscillation between East and West forms a striking image, and the irrelevance of the so-called East/West division is summed up in the lines from Ibn 'Arabi's *Tarjumân al-Ashwâq*: 'He saw the lightening flash in the East and he longed for the East, but had it flashed in the West he would have longed for the West. My desire is for the lightening and its gleam, not for places and the earth'.[114]

Following the success of this conference, an international symposium was held in Beirut (1997), entitled *Man in the thought of Ibn 'Arabi*.

In 2000, conferences took place in Chile and Argentina on al-Andalus and its history and the arts of the Arabs in the Mediterranean, at which Claude Addas gave talks within the context of the spiritual journey according to Ibn 'Arabi, the poetic function according to Ibn 'Arabi and the spiritual elite in the *Malâmiyya* (the invisible Sanctity).[115] That same year, an announcement was made of a new book-shop having been opened in Kuala Lumpar, Malaysia, which stocks the works of Ibn 'Arabi. The author of the article, Mohammed Nasseri Ali, who is also a joint proprietor of the shop, comments:

> As to why Ibn 'Arabi is of interest in this country, there are many reasons. Mainly these kinds of knowledge [*sic*] are usually kept within the confines of 'libraries and hallowed halls'. What we are trying to do is to present knowledge and doctrines that extend beyond mere rituals, and Ibn 'Arabi fits into this perfectly. Also no one else in the country and for thatmatter in this region, stocks books on Ibn 'Arabi and those of his

---

113. Cecilia Twinch, 'Events and Reports: Marrakech Festival—The Intellectual and Spiritual Legacy of Ibn Arabi', *Newsletter* (Spring 1998), pp. 3-8 (6).

114. Twinch, 'Events and Reports', pp. 6-7.

115. Stuart Kenner, 'Society Matters: News and Events—Chile and Argentina', *Newsletter* (Spring 2000), pp. 2-3 (2).

school, or the equivalent. Therefore we are breaking new ground and many have found this very refreshing.[116]

At the same time, an feature in the Society's *Newsletter*[117] outlined two historical overviews of Ibn 'Arabi's influence in Indonesia. The first was an article on the development of Ibn 'Arabi's teaching in Indonesia, researched by Tri Wibowo, Researcher at Circle of Perennial Wisdom Studies, Yogyakarta, entitled 'Historical Overview of Ibn 'Arabi's influence in Indonesia'. The second article, by Dr. Kautsar Azhari Noer, 'Recent Development of Interest in the Sufism of Ibn 'Arabi in Indonesia', lists all recent research, translations, publications and courses associated with Ibn 'Arabi there.[118] A number of Indonesians are now actually forming a local branch of the Ibn 'Arabi Society in Jakarta.

The growing interest in Ibn 'Arabi's thought and influence among the Muslims of Bosnia was reflected both in the participation in the 2001 Oxford Symposium by the distinguished Bosnian scholar Reshid Hafizovic[119] and by the ongoing efforts by Bosnian scholars to open a Sarajevo branch of the Muhyiddin Ibn 'Arabi Society.

CONCLUSION

This chapter has provided only a brief overview of the Muhyiddin Ibn 'Arabi Society and its activities since 1976. Even a summary development of the actual contents of the Society's journal and the proceedings of its two annual symposia (in the UK and California) throughout that period would require at least a separate volume. Hopefully these concise indications are enough to show that the Society has made a substantial ongoing contribution to its intentions of making Ibn 'Arabi more widely known, not only in the English-speaking world but also through encouraging and supporting study of his works throughout the Islamic world.[120]

---

116. Mohammed Nasseri Ali, 'News from Members Round the World: From Kuala Lumpa, Malaysia', *Newsletter* (Spring 2000), pp. 5-8 (7).

117. Editor, 'Articles and Translations: Historical Overview of Ibn Arabi's Influence in Indonesia', *Newsletter* (Autumn 2000), pp. 11-13 (11).

118. Editor, 'Articles and Translations', p. 13.

119. Translated the *Fusûs al-Hikam* into Bosnian for part of his doctoral thesis.

120. Reflecting the situation in Chapter 8 concerning the 'Outreach' of the Beshara School, the Muhyiddin Ibn 'Arabi Society has had obvious updates in the years since I completed my original study. I will not list and examine them here but mention only that the core focus of the Society, i.e., the publication of its biannual journal and annual symposia in the UK and USA, continues as before.

Conclusion

The prolific writings of the Spanish Muslim mystical philosopher, poet, theologian and spiritual teacher Muhyiddin Ibn 'Arabi (1165–1240 CE) point to a common spiritual 'Reality' which he understands as both the source and the ultimate aim of all the revealed religious paths, and indeed of human existence more generally. This unifying and self-consciously universal spiritual focus helps to explain the key intellectual and spiritual role of his works, ever since his death, in facilitating the spread and often highly creative transmutation of Islamic teachings, artistic forms and spiritual institutions in new cultural settings throughout the Muslim world. This was particularly evident in the creatively expansive centuries following the Mongol invasion of the Middle East in the thirteenth century. During the twentieth century, many of the same universalist intellectual and spiritual aspects of his teaching have increasingly inspired Western scholars, artists, creative thinkers and spiritual teachers from many countries. And as I have shown in this study, the wider phenomena of 'globalisation' in intellectual exchange and communication have meant that this particular approach to his teachings has in turn begun to have more widespread influences within the contemporary Muslim world.

The study has focused on one important and illustrative dimension of Ibn 'Arabi's teaching in the contemporary world, which is the development and activities of the Beshara Trust and the Muhyiddin Ibn 'Arabi Society from the late 1960s to the present. Whilst its initial organisational base was in the UK, the participants, activities and intentions of Beshara have always been explicitly international in nature, and the gradually widening circle of their influences is one of the connecting themes of this exposition. Thus the study has begun with the decisive initial creative influence of the little-known, intentionally self-effacing but highly inspiring figure of Bulent Rauf (1911–1987), and then followed historically the remarkable process by which his younger colleagues and dedicated 'fellow-students' have gradually developed a truly collective, multi-faceted, inter-confessional and globally active organisation, and an even wider creative network of international participants.

The study has demonstrated that neither the Beshara School nor the Ibn 'Arabi Society would have been established, let alone thrived, without the inspiring and cohesive figure of Bulent Rauf. That both organisations continue to thrive more than two decades after his passing supports Rauf's own insistence that he was 'only a fellow student' rather than a 'teacher' or spiritual master, and that the other participants should not look to him but to what he pointed to, which was ultimate Reality, and its approach and realisation through the teachings of Ibn 'Arabi.

This work has also revealed that in addition to the central objective of Beshara, which is to bring students to a deeper knowledge and realisation of their place within and relationship to that Reality itself, the courses do not lead to furthering a particular self-contained local group, but rather to forming active, creative individuals who continue to work to become transforming influences in the wider contexts of their own lives and professions throughout the world. These activities and influences range from the individual skills and endeavours of such people as artists, actors, fashion designers and psychotherapists, to the more broadly encompassing disciplines of science, ecology, architecture and economics. These disciplines, in the context of the Beshara education, become proactive living expressions of Ibn 'Arabi's key thematic teachings, such as the Unity of existence, the necessary diversity of paths within that Unity and the potential perfectibility of human beings as reflections of the Real (God).

Although the Muhyiddin Ibn 'Arabi Society was founded by many of the same individuals who had earlier established the Beshara Trust, it has always remained an entirely separate, more specifically focused effort, devoted to supporting the world-wide presentation, translation and interpretation of Ibn 'Arabi's works, along with wider awareness of his many historically influential interpreters. Throughout its widely read journal, newsletter and annual international symposia in the UK, Berkeley and elsewhere, the Society has come to involve the collaboration of an ever-expanding network of internationally recognised scholars, writers, artists and teachers not only from Western countries, but increasingly from throughout Muslim nations as well. Whereas the Beshara School has tended to approach the communication of Ibn 'Arabi's teachings from an experiential, necessarily individual perspective, the Society's activities have all remained focused on the necessary academic tasks of manuscript preservation, critical editions, translations and interpretative and contextual studies of his works and influences.

In some respects the activities of the Beshara School and the Muhyiddin Ibn 'Arabi Society reflect other examples, cited in the Introduction, of the wider ways in which Ibn 'Arabi's influence has expanded in the contemporary West. A significant example is Bulent Rauf's central role in introducing Ibn 'Arabi's ideas into the Western context, because his role reflects those of other influential contemporary Muslim teachers (some converts like Guénon and Schuon) or persons with a deep knowledge and experience of the Middle East, such as Henry Corbin. The closest comparable figure to Rauf, particularly with respect to the range of subsequent activities of his Western followers, is Shaykh Muzaffer Ozak, also from Turkey. All these figures were active as teachers or guides in various ways and it was through their lasting influences upon small intimate groups of followers, whose own various creative activities continue to effect ever-expanding circles of people around them, that the wider influence of Ibn 'Arabi's teaching continues to increase. Of course, this phenomena is not unique to those interested in the Sufism or Ibn 'Arabi alone, but is a common feature of the recent Western adaptation of traditional Eastern religious forms as was established in the introductory chapter.

Although the Beshara School corresponds in some ways to other Westernised Sufi movements in general, especially in areas where Ibn 'Arabi's influence is already being felt in the West, it is more difficult to relate the Muhyiddin Ibn 'Arabi Society to that wider context because its explicit academic focus on Ibn 'Arabi's works is more unique. Although some countries and organisations have at various times made profound efforts to promote Ibn 'Arabi's ideas, they do not have a specific organisation such as the Muhyiddin Ibn 'Arabi Society exclusively working towards this end.[1]

The study provides a contribution to the consideration of the recent expansion of the influence of the teachings of Ibn 'Arabi in the West, because by focusing on one particular area of his influence, possible explanations for the ready adoption of his ideas can be concretely examined. Of the many conceivable reasons for this influence, a primary suggestion is that his central metaphysical idea of one unifying Reality as the foundation of all being contributes to the ability of diverse religious traditions to relate to each other and to understand other perspectives without great conflict and resistance.[2] For the same reason, it is apparent

---

1. See Chapter 9 and discussions on the scholarly activities surrounding the works of Ibn 'Arabi in Spain, Algeria, Morocco, Sicily, Syria, Malaysia and Indonesia.

2. Historically, as briefly noted in the Introduction, Ibn 'Arabi's ideas have been most important in encouraging the cooperation and consistence of highly diverse forms and interpretations of Islam, especially in new multi-cultural historical

that his ideas are particularly attractive today in the face of increasing globalisation and dissatisfaction with other traditional or nationalist, politicised forms of institutionalised religion. It follows, therefore, that his metaphysical concepts offer a persuasive spiritual understanding and articulation of the super-cultural and religious dimensions of the wider phenomenon of globalisation, in all areas of life. In addition, his metaphysics provide a potential contribution to both interfaith and intrafaith dialogue, exploring points of potential communication in the actual spiritual phenomena and teachings in all religious traditions. This latter point corresponds with the wider phenomena of the spread and assimilation of Islamic ideas and religious practice (as well as of other spiritual traditions) in the West recently.

This study is the first to focus closely on one influential contemporary group who are actively involved with promoting and communicating Ibn 'Arabi's teachings and philosophy in the UK and throughout the world. As indicated at the outset, the activities of Beshara are in fact only one of several at least equally wide-ranging recent intellectual and spiritual movements, throughout Europe and North America, which have collectively helped bring the ideas of Ibn 'Arabi to the contemporary fields of the study of religions, psychology, ecology and practical spirituality.

Despite some of the intrinsic limitations of the phenomenological methodological approach, this method of modern religious studies and anthropology has been the most appropriate here because of the substantial amount of data involving personal descriptions of individual spiritual experiences. However, as Richard C. Martin has suggested, the phenomenological approach on its own is often inadequate and requires a pluralistic methodology adapted appropriately to each particular object of study.[3] In particular, this type of study could be complemented by a psychological interpretation or analysis of some of the acquired data, especially when discussing, for example, the reactions of some of the travellers at the sacred sites during the Beshara School's annual pilgrimage to Turkey or the effects of some aspects of the intensive courses on the students at Chisholme. Or alternatively, the approaches of sociology and political theory could also be applied to this study.

---

contexts. Many Muslim participants in the activities of the Ibn 'Arabi Society are particularly conscious of the heightened relevance of that 'inter-Islamic' context today.

3. Richard C. Martin, 'Islam and Religious Studies', in *Approaches to Islam in Religious Studies* (ed. Richard C. Martin; Tempe: University of California Press, 1980), pp. 7-8.

At the heart of Ibn 'Arabi's teaching is his vision of each authentic religious tradition—and of each human being's uniquely individual ethical and spiritual life—as an invaluable and necessary expression of the One Ultimate Reality underlying all existence. Those involved with the organisation of the Beshara School and the Muhyiddin Ibn 'Arabi Society have devoted their lives to realising this vision, in the hope that its spread will contribute to a more spiritually unified, co-operative and tolerant world. It is therefore an encouraging sign that such organisations continue to motivate and attract an ever-increasing circle of active participants and collaborators from around the world. Equally encouraging is the fact that those involved continue to come from such a broad, ever-widening cross-section of society, from different nationalities and religious and intellectual backgrounds, since they can provide ideal participants for the first steps in constructive inter-religious and inter-civilisational dialogue.

It seems appropriate to conclude this work by citing one of Ibn 'Arabi's most frequently quoted and beautiful poems, which illustrates better than any his concept of religious unity within the Oneness of Being:

> O marvel! A garden amidst the flames!
> My heart has become capable of every form:
> It is a pasture for gazelles, and a convent for Christian monks,
> And a temple for idols, and the pilgrim's Ka'ba,
> and the tables of the Tora and the book of the Quran.
> I follow the religion of Love: whatever way
> Love's camels take, that's my religion and my faith.

BIBLIOGRAPHY

TRANSLATIONS AND EDITIONS OF IBN 'ARABI CITED

Contemplation of the Holy Mysteries and the Rising of the Divine Lights (Mashâhid al-asrâr) (trans. Pablo Beneito and Cecilia Twinch; Oxford: Anqa, 2001).
The Bezels of Wisdom (The complete translation of the *Fusûs al-Hikam*) (New York: Paulist, 1980).
Divine Sayings: The Mishkat al-anwar of Ibn Arabi (trans. Martin Notcutt and Daniel Hirtenstein; Oxford: Anqa, 2004).
'Excerpts from the Epistle on the Spirit of Holiness (*Risâlah Rûh al-Quds*)' (trans. Roger Boase and Farid Sahnoun), in *Muhyiddin Ibn 'Arabi: A Commemorative Volume* (ed. S. Hirtenstein and M. Tiernan; Shaftesbury: Element Books, 1993), pp. 44-72.
Fusûs al-Hikam (rendered into English by Bulent Rauf with the help of R. Brass and H. Tollemache, from the 1832 Boulaq Edition of a manuscript written in Turkish and Arabic c. 1700; 4 vols.; Oxford: Muhyiddin Ibn 'Arabi Society, 1986–91).
Journey to the Lord of Power: A Sufi Manual on Retreat by Muhyiddin Ibn 'Arabi (trans. R.T. Harris; Rochester, Vt.: Inter Traditions International, 1990).
Kernel of the Kernel (trans. into Turkish with a commentary by Ismail Hakki Bursevi and into English by Bulent Rauf; Gloucestershire: Beshara, 1979).
The Seven Days of the Heart (Awrâd al-usbû) (trans Pablo Beneito and Stephen Hirtenstein; Oxford: Anqa, 2000).
Sufis of Andalusia (The Rûh al-quds and al-Durrat al-fâkhirah of Ibn 'Arabi) (London: Alan & Unwin, 1971).
The Wisdom of the Prophets (trans. from Arabic to French by Titus Burckhardt and French to English by Angela Culme-Seymour; Gloucestershire: Beshara, 1975).

OTHER REFERENCES

Addas, Claude, *Quest for the Red Sulphur: The Life of Ibn 'Arabi* (trans. Peter Kingsley; Cambridge: The Islamic Text Society, 1993).
Affifi, A.A., *The Mystical Philosophy of Muhyid Dîn Ibnul Arabî* (Cambridge: Cambridge University Press, 1964).
Algar, Hamid, 'Reflections of Ibn 'Arabi in Early Naqshbandî Tradition', *JMIAS* X (1991), pp. 45-56.
Ali, Mohammed Nasseri, 'News from Members Round the World: From Kuala Lumpa, Malaysia', *Newsletter* (Spring 2000), pp. 5-8.

Anderson, William, *Green Man: The Archetype of Our Oneness with the Earth* (London: HarperCollins, 1990).
Anon., 'Cards from Beshara Design Company', *Beshara Newsletter* (Spring 1994), p. 4.
———. 'Memorial For Bulent Rauf', *Beshara Magazine* 7 (1988), p. 43.
———. 'Seminars at The Old George', *Beshara Newsletter* (Spring 1995), p. 8.
Antionides, Spiros, 'Easter 1996', *Beshara Australia, Newsletter* (June 1996), p. 1.
Atran, Scott, *In Gods we Trust: The Evolutionary Landscape of Religion* (Oxford: Oxford University Press, 2002).
Austin, R.W.J., 'The Feminine Dimensions in Ibn 'Arabi's Thought', *JMIAS* II (1984), pp. 5-14.
———. 'Reports: Eleventh Annual UK Symposium' *JMIAS* VIII (1989), p. 73.
Baba, Meher, *Discourses* (London: Victor Gillancz, 1955). *God Speaks* (New York: Dodd Mead, 1976).
Baghavad Gita (trans. Juan Mascaro; Harmondsworth: Penguin, 1962).
Balyânî, Awhad al-Dîn, *Whoso Knoweth Himself* (Gloucestershire: Beshara, 1976). French trans., *Épître sur L'unicité Absolue* (trans. Michel Chodkiewicz; Paris: Les Deux Océans, 1982).
Barrow, J.D., 'The New Cosmology', *Beshara Magazine* 6 (Summer 1988), pp. 19-25.
Bearman, P.J., T. Bianquis, C.E. Bosworth, E. Van Donzel and W.P. Heinrichs, eds., *The Encyclopaedia of Islam: New Edition, Glossary and Index of Terms*, vol. 1–9 (Leiden: Brill, 2000).
Beckett, Sister Wendy 'Angelic Presences', *Beshara Magazine* 13 (Summer 1991), pp. 18-19.
Beit-Hallahmi, Benjamin, and Michael Argyle, *The Psychology of Religious Behaviour, Belief and Experience* (London: Routledge, 1997), pp. 74-75.
Benäissa, Omar, 'The Diffusian of Akbarian Teaching in Iran During the 13th and 14th Centuries', *JMIAS* XXVI (1999), pp. 89-109.
Bennett, John G., *Christian Mysticism and Subud* (London: Institute for the Comparative Study of History, Philosophy and the Sciences, 1961).
———. *Intimations: Talks with J.G. Bennett at Beshara* (Gloucestershire: Beshara, 1975).
———. *Witness: The Story of a Search* (New Mexico: Bennett Books, 1997).
Bewly, Aisha, *Glossary of Islamic Terms* (Norwich: Ta-Ha, 1998).
Simon Blackwood, 'Painting as a Means of Expression', *Beshara Magazine* 8 (1988/89), pp. 32-34.
Brenner, Louis, *West African Sufi: The Religious Heritage and Spiritual Search of Cerno Boker Saalif Taal* (Berkeley: University of California Press, 1984).
Bozarth, J., 'Beyond Reflection: Emergent Modes of Empathy', in *Client-Centered Therapy and the Person Centered Approach* (ed. R.F. Levant and J.M. Shlien; New York: Praeger, 1984), pp. 59-75.
———. 'A Theoretical Reconceptualization of the Necessary and Sufficient Conditions for Therapeutic Personality Change', paper presented at the *Fifth International Forum on the Person-Centred Approach*, Terschelling, Netherlands, 1992.

Burckhardt, Titus, *Alchémie: Sinn und Weltbild* (trans. from English edn by Madame J.P. Gervy; Basle: Foundation Keimer, 1974; Milan: Archè, 1979).
———. *Introduction aux Doctrines Esoteriques de L'Islam* (Paris: Dervy-Livres, 1969).
———. *Mystical Astrology According to Ibn 'Arabi* (Eng. trans.; Gloucestershire: Beshara, 1977).
———. *Principes et methodes de L'art Sacré* (Lyons: Derain, 1958).
Cantwell-Smith, Wilfred, 'Comparative Religion: Whither—and Why?', in *The History of Religions: Essays in Methodology* (ed. Mircea Eliade and Joseph Kitagawa; Chicago: University of Chicago Press, 1959), pp. 31-58.
Carroll, Jane, 'Sufism Conference in California', *Beshara Newsletter* (Spring 1994), p. 3.
Chittick, W.C. *Ibn 'Arabi Heir to the Prophets* (Oxford: Oneworld, 2005).
———. 'Ibn 'Arabi's Own Summary of the *Fusûs*: The Imprint of the Bezels of Wisdom', *JMIAS* I (1982), pp. 30-93.
———. 'The Chapter Headings of the Fusûs', *JMIAS* II (1984), pp. 41-95.
———. *Imaginal Worlds* (Albany: SUNY Press, 1994).
———. *The Self-Disclosure of God* (Albany: SUNY Press, 1997).
———. *The Sufi Path of Knowledge: Ibn 'Arabi's Metaphysics of Imagination* (Albany: SUNY Press, 1989).
Chodkiewicz, Michel, *An Ocean Without Shore: Ibn 'Arabi, the Book and the Law* (trans. David Streight; Albany: SUNY Press, 1989).
———. *Awhad al-dîn Balyânî, Épître sur L'unicité Absolue* (Paris: Les Deux Océans, 1982).
———. 'The Diffusion of Ibn 'Arabi's Doctrine', *JMIAS* IX (1991), pp. 36-57.
———. *The Seal of the Saints: Prophethood and Sainthood in the Doctrine of Ibn 'Arabi* (Cambridge: Islamic Texts Society, 1993).
Claridge, G. *Origins of Mental Illness* (Oxford: Blackwell, 1985).
Clark, Jane, 'News and Events World Wide: UK', *Newsletter* (Autumn 2001), pp. 2-3.
Claxton, G., *Wholly Human* (London: RKP, 1981).
Coates, Peter, *Ibn 'Arabi and Modern Thought: The History of Taking Metaphysics Seriously* (Oxford: Anqa, 2002).
Corbin, Henry, *Alone with the Alone: Creative Imagination in the Sufism of Ibn 'Arabi* (trans. from the French by Ralph Manheim; Princeton: Princeton University Press, 1998).
———. *Creative Imagination in the Sufism of Ibn 'Arabi* (London: Routledge & Kegan Paul 1969).
———. 'Sophiology and Devotio Sympathetica', in *Creative Imagination in the Sufism of Ibn 'Arabi* (Princeton: Princeton University Press, 1969), Chapter 2. Reprinted as *Alone with the Alone*.
———. *Spiritual Body and Celestial Earth: From Mazdean Iran to Shi'ite Iran* (trans. Nancy Pearson; London: I.B. Tauris & Co., 1990).
Cornell, Vincent, *The Realm of the Saint: Power and Authority in Moroccan Sufism* (Texas: University of Texas Press, 1998).
Dalgleish, Narda, *Let Love Love Love* (Sherborne, Gloucestershire: Vast Earth Words and Music, 2001).

Daner, Francine Jeanne, *The American Children of Krishna: A Study of the Hare Krishna Movement* (New York: Holt, Rinehart & Winston, 1976).
Dawkins, Richard, *The Selfish Gene* (Oxford: Oxford University Press, 1976).
Dunne, John S., *The Reasons of the Heart: A Journey into Solitude and Back again into the Human Circle* (Notre Dame, Ind.: University of Notre Dame Press, 1978).
Dupré, Adam, 'The Perfectibility of Man', *Newsletter* (1994), p. 2.
———. 'Report of the Seventh Annual Symposium of the Muhyiddin Ibn 'Arabi Society, 1990', *Newsletter* (Summer 1990), p. 3.
Echevarria, J.U., *Fiesta de la Tarapaca* (Valparaiso, Chile: Ediciones Universitaria de Valparaiso, 1963).
Eickelman, Dale F., *The Middle East: An Anthropological Approach* (New Jersey: New York University Press, 1989).
Eliade, Mircea, *The Myth of Eternal Return* (Princeton: Princeton University Press, 1971).
———. *Patterns in Comparative Religion* (Londo: Sheed & Ward, 1958),
Ernst, Carl, *Eternal Garden: Mysticism, History, and Politics at a South Asian Sufi Center* (Albany: SUNY Press, 1992).
Ewing, Katherine Pratt, *Arguing Sainthood: Modernity, Psychoanalysis and Islam* (Durham: Duke University Press, 1997).
Farouki, Suhar Taji, *Beshara and Ibn 'Arabi: A Movement of Sufi Spirituality in the Modern World* (Oxford: Anqa, 2007).
Feild, Reshad, *Going Home* (Shaftesbury: Element Books, 1996).
———. *The Last Barrier: The Universal Search for Self-discovery* (Shaftesbury: Element Books, 1976).
Feng, Gia-fu, *Tao Te Ching* (trans. Jane English; Hampshire: Wildwood House, 1973).
Frager, R., and J. Fadiman, eds, *Essential Sufism* (San Francisco: Harper San Francisco, 1997).
Freud, Sigmund, 'A Disturbance of Memory on the Acropolis', *Standard Edition* XXII (London, 1962),
Geaves, Ron, *The Sufis of Britain: An Exploration of Muslim Identity* (Cardiff: Cardiff Academic Press, 2000).
Geertz, Clifford, *Islam Observed: Religious Development in Morocco and Indonesia* (Chicago: University of Chicago Press, 1968).
Goodwin, Brian, 'Rumbling the Replicator', *Beshara Magazine* 4 (Winter 1987/88), pp. 12-16.
Gurdjieff, Georgei Ivanovitch, *Beelzebub's Tales to His Grandson: An Objectively Impartial Criticism of the Life of Man* (New York: Dutton, 1978).
———. *Life is Real Only Then, When 'I Am'* (New York: Dutton, 1982).
———. *Meetings with Remarkable Men* (New York: Dutton, 1969).
Haviva, Pedaya, 'The Divinity as Place and Time in Jewish Mysticism', in *Sacred Space: Shrine, City, Land* (ed. Z. Kedar Benjamen and R.J. Zwi Werblowsky; New York: New York University Press, 1998), pp. 84-111.
Hermansen, Marcia, 'Hybrid Identity Formations in Muslim America: The Case for American Sufi Movements', *The Muslim World* 90 (2000), pp. 158-97.

———. 'In the Garden of American Sufi Movements: Hybrids and Perennials', in *New Trends and Developments in the World of Islam* (ed. Peter B. Clark; London: Luzac, 1997), pp. 155-78.
Hick, John, 'Copernican Revolution of Theology' in *God and the Universe of Faiths: Essays in the Philosophy of Religion* (New York: St Martin's Press, 1973), pp. 120-32.
Hirtenstein, Stephen, 'Universal and Divine Sainthood', *JMIAS* IV (1985), p. 8.
———. *The Unlimited Mercifier: The Spiritual Life and Thought of Ibn 'Arabi* (Oxford: Anqa, 1999).
Hirtenstein, Stephen, ed., *Praise* (Hirtenstein; Oxford: Muhyiddin Ibn 'Arabi Society, 1997).
———. *Prayer and Contemplation* (Oxford: Muhyiddin Ibn 'Arabi Society, 1993).
Hirtenstein, S., and M. Tiernan, eds., *Muhyiddin Ibn 'Arabi: A Commemorative Volume* (Shaftesbury: Element Books, 1993).
Hoffmann, Valerie J., *Sufism, Mystics, and Saints in Modern Egypt* (Colombia: University of South Carolina Press, 1995).
Holbrook, Victoria, 'Ibn 'Arabi and the Ottoman Dervish Traditions: The Melamî Supra Order', Part 1, *JMIAS* IX (1991), pp. 18-35
———. 'Ibn 'Arabi and the Ottoman Dervish Traditions: The Melamî Supra Order', Part 2, *JMIAS* XII (1992), pp. 15-33.
Holroyd, Angela 'Courses at Chisholme: Interview with Peter Young', *Beshara Magazine* 8 (1989), pp. 26-29 (27).
Homerin, T.E., 'Ibn 'Arabi in the People's Assembly: Religion, Press and Politics in Sadat's Egypt', *The Middle East Journal* 40 (Summer 1986), pp. 462-77.
Hornsby, David, 'Communications: American Symposium', *JMIAS* VI (1987), pp. 55-61.
Hornsby, Richard, 'Rememoration for Bulent Rauf', *Beshara Magazine* 4 (Winter 1987/88), pp. 10-11.
Houedard, Dom Sylvester, 'First Annual Symposium of the Ibn 'Arabi Society', *JMIAS* III (1984), p. 3.
Hourani, H.A., *Arab Thought in the Liberal Age* (Cambridge: Cambridge University Press, 1962).
———. *A History of the Arab Peoples* (London: Faber & Faber, 1991).
Iraqi, Fakhruddin, *Divine Flashes* (trans. Peter Lamborne Wilson, J. Morris and William Chittick; New York: Paulist, 1982).
———. 'The Continuing Relevance of Qaysari's Thought: Divine Imagination and the Foundation of Natural Spirituality', in *Papers of the International Symposium on Islamic Thought in the XIIIth and XIVth Centuries and Daud al-Qaysari* (ed. T. Koç; Ankara, 1998), pp. 161-71.
Izutzu, Toshihiko, *Sufism and Taoism: A Comparative Study of Key Philosophical Concepts* (Berkeley: University of California Press, 1983).
James, William, *The Varieties of Religious Experience: A Study in Human Nature* (2nd ed.; New York: Longmans Green, 1902).
al-Jîlî, 'Abd al-Karîm, *Universal Man* (extracts from his work *al-insân al-kamîl*; trans. from Arabic to French by Titus Burckhardt and French to English by Angela Culme-Seymour; Gloucestershire: Beshara, 1983).

Jones, Ernsest, *The Life and Work of Sigmund Freud*, vol. 2 (New York: Basic Books, 1955).

Kalian, Moshe, and Eliezer Witztum, 'Facing a Holy Space: Psychiatric Hospitalization of Tourists in Jerusalem', in *Sacred Space: Shrine, City, Land* (ed. Benjamen Z. Kedar and R.J. Zwi Werblowsky; New York: New York University Press, 1998), pp. 316-30.

Katz, Steven, 'Language, Epistemology and Mysticism', in *Mysticism and Philosophical Analysis* (ed. Steven T. Katz; New York: Oxford University Press, 1978), pp. 22-75.

Kelly, Bernard, 'The Light of the Eastern Religions', in *Religion of the Heart: Essays Presented to Frithjof Schuon on His Eightieth Birthday* (ed. Seyyed Hossein Nasr and William Stoddart; Indiana: Foundation for Traditional Studies, 1991), pp. 159-61.

Kenner, Stuart, 'Society Matters: News and Events—Chile and Argentina', *Newsletter* (Spring 2000), pp. 2-3.

Khan, Pir Vilayat Inayat, *That Which Transpires Behind that Which Appears: The Experience of Sufism* (New York: Omega, 1994).

Kiliç, Mahmud Erol, ' "The Ibn 'Arabi of the Ottomans": 'Abdullah Salâhaddîn al-'Ushshâqî (1705–82)', *JMIAS* XXVI (1999), pp. 110-20.

Kirschenbaum, H., and V. Henderson, eds., *Carl Rogers Dialogues* (London: Constable, 1990).

Knysh, Alexander, *Ibn 'Arabi in the Later Islamic Tradition: The Making of a Polemical Image in Medieval Islam* (Albany: SUNY Press, 1999).

———. 'Ibn 'Arabi in Yemen: His Admirers and Detractors', *JMIAS* XI (1992), pp. 38-61.

———. *Islamic Mysticism: A Short History* (Boston: Brill, 1999).

Kugle, Scott Alan, *Rebel Between Spirit and Law: Almad Zarruq, Sainthood and Authority in Islam* (Indiana: Indiana University Press, 2006).

Lam, Martin, 'Cooking as a Means of Expression', *Beshara Magazine* 10 (Winter 1988/90), pp. 30-31.

Landau, Rom, *The Philosophy of Ibn 'Arabi* (London: Allen & Unwin, 1959).

Lewisohn, Leonard, *Classical Persian Sufism from its Origins to Rumi* (New York: Khaniqahi Nimatullahi, 1994).

———. *The Heritage of Sufism*, vol. 2 (Oxford: One World, 1999).

Lings, Martin, *The Book of Certainty* (London: Rider & Co., 1952).

———. *A Sufi Saint of the Twentieth Century: Shaykh Ahmad al-'Alawî* (London: Allen & Unwin, 1971).

———. *Symbol and Archetype: A Study of the Meaning of Existence* (Cambridge: Quinta Essentia, 1991)

———. . *What is Sufism?* (London: Allen & Unwin, 1975).

Loeffler, Reinhold, *Islam in Practice: Religious Beliefs in a Persian Village* (Albany: SUNY Press, 1988).

Macmillan, Mhairi, ' "In You there is a Universe": Person-Centred Counselling as a Manifestation of the Breath of the Merciful', in *Women Writing in the Person Centred Approach* (ed. I. Fairhurst; Ross-on-Wye: PCCS, 1999).

Martin, Richard C., 'Islam and Religious Studies', in *Approaches to Islam in Religious Studies* (ed. Richard C. Martin; Tempe: University of California Press, 1980), pp. 7-8.

The Mathnawî of Jâlâl 'uddin Rûmî, Books I–VI (London: E.J.W. Gibb Memorial Trust, 1926, 1930, 1934; latest repr. 1982).

Mercer, J., ed., *The Journey of the Heart* (Oxford: Muhyiddin Ibn 'Arabi Society, 1996).

Momen, Moojan, *The Phenomenon of Religion: A Thematic Approach* (Oxford: Oneworld, 1999).

Moore, Peter, 'Mystical Experience, Mystical Doctrine, Mystical Technique', in *Mysticism and Philosophical Analysis* (ed. Steven T. Katz; New York: Oxford University Press, 1978), pp. 101-33.

Morris, James W., ' "...Except His Face": The Political and Aesthetic Dimensions of Ibn 'Arabi's Legacy', *JMIAS* XXIII (1998), pp. 19-31.

———. 'How to Study the Futûhât: Ibn 'Arabi's own Advice', in *Muhyiddin Ibn 'Arabi: A Commemorative Volume* (ed. S. Hirtenstein and M. Tiernan; Shaftesbury: Element Books, 1993).

———. 'Ibn 'Arabi and His Interpreters', Part I, *Journal of the American Oriental Society* 106 (1986), pp. 539-51; Part II, 106 (1986), pp. 733-56; Part III, 107 (1987), pp. 101-19.

———. 'Ibn 'Arabi in the "Far West"', *JMIAS* XXIX (2001), pp. 87-121.

———. *Ibn 'Arabi: The Meccan Revelations* (New York: Pir Press, 2002).

———. *The Master and the Disciple: An early Islamic Spiritual Dialogue* (London: I.B. Tauris, 2001).

———. *Orientations: Islamic Thought in a World Civilisation* (Sarajevo: El-Kalem, 2001).

———. 'Theophany or "Pantheism?": The Importance of Balyânî's Risâlat al-Ahadîya; and Jâmî's Description of Abû 'Abdallâh Balyânî', in 'La Walâya, étude sur le soufisme de l'école d'ibn 'Arabî', *Horizons Maghrébins* 30 (1995), pp. 43-54.

Muhaiyaddeen, Bawa, *A Book of God's Love* (Pennsylvania: Fellowship Press, 1976) and *Islam and World Peace: Explanations of a Sufi* (Pennsylvania: Bawa Muhaiyaddeen Fellowship, 1987).

Murata, Sachiko, *Chinese Gleams of Sufi Light: Wang Tai-yü's Great Learning of the Pure and Real and Liu Chih's Displaying the Concealment of the Real Realm* (Albany: SUNY Press, 2000).

Nasr, S.H., 'Ibn 'Arabi in the Persian Speaking World', in *Al-Kitâb al-tidhkâri: muhyî Ibn Arabî fî dhikrâ al-mi'awiyya al-thâmina li-mîlâdih 1165–1240* (Cairo: alHay'a al-Misriyya al-'Amma li 'L-kitâb, 1969), pp. 257-63.

Nicholson, R.A., *Tarjumân al-ashwâq* (London: Royal Asiatic Society, 1911).

———. *Studies in Islamic Mysticism* (Cambridge: Cambridge University Press, 1921)

———. 'The Lives of Umar Ibnul Farid and Muhyiddin Ibn 'Arabi', *Journal of the Royal Asiatic Society* NS 38.4 (1906), pp. 797-824.

———. *The Mystics of Islam* (London, 1914)

———. *The Mathnawî of Jâlâl 'uddin Rûmî, Books I–VI* (London: E.J.W. Gibb Memorial Trust, 1926, 1930, 1934; latest repr. 1982)

Notcutt, Caroline, 'Society News: The Society in the UK', *Newsletter* (1994), pp. 5-6.
Nyberg, H.S., *Kleinere Schriftendes Ibn 'Arabi nach Handschriften in Uppsala und Berlin zum ersten Mal hrsg. Und mit Einleitung und Kommentar von H.S. Nyberg* (Leiden: E.J. Brill, 1919).
Oida, Yoshi, 'Means of Expression', *Beshara Magazine* 13 (Summer 1991), pp. 33-35.
Otto, Rudolf, *The Idea of the Holy* (trans. J.W. Harvey; London: Oxford University Press, 1923; original German ed. 1917).
Palacios, Miguel Asín, *El Islam cristianzado* and *La escatologia musulmana en la Divina Comedia* (Madrid: Granada, 1923).
———. *El Islam Cristianizado* (Madrid: Plutarco, 1931).
———. *Islam and the Divine Comedy* (trans. Harold Sunderland; London: J. Murray, 1926).
Pannenburg, Wolfgang, 'Religious Pluralism and Conflicting Truth Claims: The Problem of a Theology of the World Religions' in *Christian Uniqueness Reconsidered: The Myth of a Pluralistic Theology of Religions* (ed. Gavin D'Costa; Maryknoll, N.Y.: Orbis, 1990), pp. 96-106.
Pannikka, Raimundo, 'The Jordan, the Tiber, and the Ganges: Three Kairological Moments of Christian Self Consciousness' in *The Myth of Christian Uniqueness* (ed. John Hick and Paul Knitter; Maryknoll, N.Y.: Orbis, 1987), pp. 89-116.
Pawloff, Ted, 'Gaia Comes of Age', *Beshara Magazine* 5 (Spring 1988), pp. 8-10.
Persinger, Michael, *The Neuropsychological Bases of God Beliefs* (New York: Praeger, 1987).
Peter, Ouspensky, *In Search of the Miraculous: Fragments of an Unknown Teaching* (New York: Harcourt, Brace, 1949).
———. *A New Model of the Universe* (New York: Random House, 1971).
Raine, Kathleen, 'The Puer Eternus', *Beshara Magazine* 6 (Summer 1988), pp. 9-12.
———. 'W.B. Yeats and the New Age', *Beshara Magazine* 9 (n.d.), pp. 35-37.
Rauf, Bulent, *Addresses* (Gloucestershire: Beshara, 1987).
———. *Addresses II* (Gloucestershire: Beshara, 2001).
———. *The Last Sultans* (n.p.: Meral Arim, 1995).
———. *The Twenty-Nine Pages: An Introduction to Ibn 'Arabi's Metaphysics of Unity*, consisting of edited highlights from A.A. Affifi, *The Mystical Philosophy of Muhid Dîn Ibnul Arabî* (Cambridge, 1939 and 1964), compiled by Bulent Rauf (Gloucestershire: Beshara, 1998).
Rogers, C.R., *Client Centered Therapy* (London: Constable, 1951).
———. 'A Theory of Therapy, Personality and Interpersonal Relations, as Developed in the Client-Centred Framework', in *Psychology: A Study of Science*, vol. 3 (ed. S. Koch; New York: McGraw-Hill, 1959), pp. 184-256.
———. *A Way of Being* (Boston: Houghton Mifflin, 1980).
Ryan, Christopher, 'Art in the Service of the Sacred', *Beshara Magazine* 8 (1988/1989), p. 9.
———. 'Conversion to the Essence', in *Papers of the International Symposium on Islamic Thought in the XIIIth and XIVth Centuries and Daud al-Qaysari* (ed. T. Koç; Ankara, 1998), pp. 335-43.

———. 'Bulent Rauf: A Mystic in the Kitchen', paper presented at the *Fourth International Food Congress*, Istanbul, September 1992). Published in *Beshara Newsletter* (Autumn 1996), pp. 3-4.
Sedgwick, Mark, *Against the Modern World: Traditionalism and the Secret Intellectual History of the Twentieth Century* (Oxford: Oxford University Press, 2004).
Schimmel, Annemarie, *Mystical Dimensions of Islam* (Chapel Hill: University of North Carolina Press, 1975).
Schuon, Frithjof, *From the Divine to the Human: Survey of Metaphysics and Epistemology* (Bloomington, Ind.: The Library of Traditional Wisdom, 1983).
———. *The Play of Masks* (Bloomington, Ind.: The Library of Traditional Wisdom, 1992).
———. *The Transcendent Unity of Religion* (London: Faber & Faber, 1965).
Sells, Michael, *Mystical Languages of Unsaying* (Chicago: University of Chicago Press, 1994).
———. trans. and ed., *Early Islamic Mysticism* (New York: Paulist Press, 1996).
———. trans., *Stations of Desire*, translations from the *Tarjumân al-Ashwâq* into modern poetic English (Jerusalem: Ibis Editions, 2000).
Shamash, Layla, and Khalil Norland, 'Other Events: Art and Cosmology', *Newsletter* (Spring 1997), pp. 6-8.
Shaykh Nâzim, *Don't Waste* (Sri Lanka: Zero, 1989).
———. *The Fruit of Perfect Practising and Real Belief is Peace* (Birmingham: Zero, 1988).
———. *Power Oceans of Love* (London: Zero, 1993).
Sheldrake, Rupert, 'The Presence of the Past', Part 1, *Beshara Magazine* 1 (Spring 1987), pp. 15-20.
Smart, Ninian, *Concept and Empathy* (London: Macmillan, 1986).
———. *The Philosophy of Religion* (Oxford: Oxford University Press, 1979).
Smith, C.B., and S. Ghose, 'Religious Experience', *Encylopedia Britannica* 26 (1989),
pp. 624-37.
Smith, Huston, The *World's Religions: Our Great Wisdom Traditions* (San Francisco: Harper, 1991).
Stace, W.T., *Mysticism and Philosophy* (Philadelphia: P.A. Lippincott, 1960), p. 79.
Tahrali, Mustafa. 'A General Outline of the Influence of Ibn 'Arabi on the Ottoman Era', *JMIAS* XXVI (1999), pp. 43-54.
Thomas, Mansura, 'A Unique Message for Our Time: An Introduction to Beshara', *Beshara Newsletter* (Spring 1979), pp. 1-2.
Tollemache, Hugh, 'An Obituary of Bulent Rauf', *Beshara Magazine* 3 (Autumn 1987), p. 3.
Trimingham, S., *The Sufi Orders of Islam* (Oxford: Clarendon, 1971).
Twinch, Cecilia, 'Conference in Murcia, 12–14 November 1990', *JMIAS* IX (1991), pp. 65-66.
———. 'Events and Reports: Marrakech Festival—The Intellectual and Spiritual Legacy of Ibn Arabi', *Newsletter* (Spring 1998), pp. 3-8.
Twinch, Richard, 'Perception and the Mind', *Beshara Magazine* 2 (Summer 1987), pp. 17-18.

Van Donzel, E., ed., *The Islamic Desk Reference: Compiled from the Encyclopaedia of Islam* (Leiden: Brill, 1994).
Wasserstrom, S.M., *Religion after Religion: Gershom Scholem, Mircea Eliade, and Henry Corbin at Eranos* (Princeton: Princeton University Press, 1999).
Weber, Max, *On Charisma and Institution Building* (Chicago: University of Chicago Press, 1968).
Waterfield, Robin, *René Guénon and the Future of the West* (London: Crucible, 1987).
Watts, Frazer N., and Mark Williams, *The Psychology of Religious Knowing* (Cambridge: Cambridge University Press, 1988).
Wilson, Elizabeth, *Adorned in Dreams, Fashion and Modernity* (London: Virago, 1985).
Yahia, Osman, *Histoire et classification de l'oeuvre d'Ibn 'Arabi* (2 vols.; Damascus: Institut Français de Damas, 1964).
Yiangou, Alison, 'An Appreciation', *JMIAS* XIII (1993), pp. 79-81.
Yiangou, Peter, Review of *Fusûs al-Hikam*, *JMIAS* VII (1988), pp. 85-86.
Yiangou, Peter, and Keith Critchlow, 'A Tribute to Sinan', *Beshara Magazine* 7 (1988), pp. 24-29.
Young, Peter, Between the Yea and the Nay', *JMIAS* II (1984), p. 4.
———. 'Ibn 'Arabi', *JMIAS* I (1982), pp. 3-11.
———. 'The New Covenant', *Beshara Newsletter* (Spring 1998), pp. 1-2.
———. 'United by Oneness: Global Considerations for the Present' (paper presented at the Ibn 'Arabi Symposium, Chisholme, August 2000).
Zabor, Rafi, *The Bear Comes Home* (London: Jonathan Cape, 1998).

INDEX

Abadi, A. 238-39
Absolute Being 92-93, 101
Absolute Existence 124
Absolute Transcendence 107, 167
Absolute Unknowable 170
Actor 172-73
Adab, (spiritual taste) 47-48, 50, 86, 163, 177-78
Adam 91-92, 101, 106, 113-14, 134, 173, 213, 248
Addas, Claude 38, 147, 149, 233, 252, 260
Ad-Dîn Muzaffar 4
Addresses (Bulent Ruaf) 46, 124-25
Affifi, A.A. 43, 61, 89-90, 92, 98, 232
Al-Afrâd (saints, solitaries) 38, 47, 50, 151
Al-Alawî 8
Al-asmâs al-husnâ (Most Beautiful Divine Names) 83
Al-Balyânî 7, 121
Al-Bastâmî, Abu Yazid 103, 157
Al-Bâtin (Hidden Divine Essence) 133-34
Al-Bosnevî, Abdullah 132, 179
Al-Bursevî, Ismail Hakki (translation to Turkish of Fusus al-Hikam) 117-18, 166, 177, 179, 181, 185, 197, 248
Al-Din (religion) 108
Al-Fanârî, Shemsuddin 179
Al-Fârid 6, 10
Al-hadara al-dhâtiyya (Essential Presence) 105
Al-Haqq (the Real, Truth) 40, 79, 92, 94, 99-101, 189

Al-insân al-Kâmil (perfect man, complete human being) 67, 78, 82, 83, 91, 99, 100, 122
Al-Irâqî, Fakhr al-Din 6
Al-Jîlî, Abd al-Karim 67, 83, 122, 232, 241
Al-Kâshânî, Kamâl al-Dîn 179
Al-Khalîl (the intimate friend of God) 94
Al-Kawn al-jâmi' 100
Al-Mahdawî, 'Abd al-'Azîz b. Abû Bakr Al-Qurayshî 119
Al-Qaysarî, Da'ud 37, 179
Al-Qûnâwi 4-6, 34, 36-37, 124, 179, 181-82, 186-87, 193, 238, 241, 256
Al-Shadili, Abu Al-Hasan, 6
Al-Shîrâzîand, Qutb al-Dîn 6
Al-'Ushshâqî, 'Abdullâh Salahuddîn 7, 179
Algar, Hamid 9
Ali, Mohammed Nasseri 260-61
Antionides, Spiros 226
Aquinas, Thomas 123
Arberry, Professor 243
Architecture 112-12, 85, 122-23, 175, 187, 191, 199, 211-12, 259, 263
Argyle, Michael 21-22, 178
Arim, Meral 35
Aristotelianism 123
Art Education 174, 208
Arwâh (spirits) 105
Asin Palacious, M. 2, 6-7, 232, 241
Ataturk, Mustafa, Kemil 41, 177, 185
Atran, Scott 22-23, 202, 204

Index

Austin, R.W.J. 1, 3, 5, 50, 95, 101, 114-16, 119, 147, 174, 189, 225, 232, 242-44, 252, 255, 258
Averroes (Ibn Rushd) 3, 242
Awareness (of God) (taste of, attention to God) 150-52
Awliyâ (Saints) 38, 102, 132
A'yân Thâbita (fixed prototypes, fixed potentialities) 98, 167-68
A'yan al-muwjdûddât (pure essence of things) 109
Ayashli, Hatice, Munevver (Madame) 40, 41, 55, 237, 239
Az-Zahir, Malik 4

Baba, Sumuncu 197
Baghavad Gita 126
Baqâ' (subsistence or remaining in God) 106-107, 125
Baraka 54, 72, 192
Barks, Coleman 13-14
Barrow, J.D. 210
Barzakh (intermediary) 100
Basharic soul (lower animal soul) 103
Bawa, Muhaiyaddeen 13-14
Bayrak, T. 12
Bayram, Haci 139, 186, 197
Beautiful Divine Names 83
Beauty, Beauty of Oneness 40, 83, 109, 116, 124, 129, 156, 158, 162-63, 175, 181-82, 189, 213, 216, 246
Beckett, Sister Wendy 213
Being 13, 43-44, 78, 92-97, 101, 106, 108, 119, 122, 125, 131, 135, 137, 161-63, 167, 169, 171-72, 196, 216, 226-27, 241, 253, 259, 266
Beit-Hallahmi, Benjamen 21-22, 178
Benaissa, Omar 9
Beneito, Pablo 233, 256-57
Bennett, J.G. 14, 17, 32, 54, 59, 68-72, 151, 221
Beshara Trust 14, 26, 32, 35, 44-46, 54-77, 87, 124, 205-208, 215-16, 220-21, 225-26, 237, 262-63

Bewly, Aisha 83, 180
Binzagr, Abdullah 234-35, 237, 239
Blackwood, Laura 226
Blackwood, Simon 212-13, 237
Blake, W. 148, 210-11
Bly, Robert 14
Boase, Roger 119
Bohm, David (physicist) 214
Bortoff, Henri 221
Bozarth, J.A. 169
Breath of Mercy, All Merciful, Merciful Breath (ar-nafas ar-rahmani) 95, 99, 114-15, 133, 135, 166-67, 170, 244
Brass, Rosemary 46, 117, 171, 248
Brecq, M. Patrice 256
Brenner, Louis 31
Buber, Martin 170
Buddhism/Buddhists 15, 83, 85, 126, 144, 209 212
Burckhardt, Titus 9, 32, 46, 54, 66-67, 83, 91, 122-23, 232-33

Cantwell-Smith, Wilfred 20
Carroll, Jane 223
Charisma 47
China 1
Chittick, William 89, 93, 94, 96-98, 103-105, 232, 235, 237-38, 240, 243, 249
Chishti Sufi Order 12
Christ 58, 112-14, 123, 128, 131, 132, 134-35, 137, 193, 196
Chodkiewicz, Michel 7, 9, 37-38, 50, 111-12, 134, 147, 233, 252, 258
Cilento, Diane 46, 220, 230, 248
Clark, Jane 208-209, 256-57
Clark, Robert 206-208
Claxton, Guy 168
Coates, Peter 171-72, 221, 239, 248, 251
Collins, Grenville (Chairman of the Muhyiddin Ibn Arabi Society) 61-62, 234-35, 250
Comparative Religion 10, 18, 20, 184, 188, 249

Compassion, (Place of) 86, 156, 173, 190, 193, 201, 254
Complete human being - Perfect man, al-insân al-Kâmil 61, 67, 78, 83, 91, 99-101, 106, 110, 122, 135, 189
Congruence 168, 170
Cooking 45, 59, 71, 82, 84, 148, 175, 192, 214, 237
Coomaraswamy, Ananda 68
Corbin, Henry 10, 115, 124, 183, 211, 232, 241, 264
Cornell, Vincent 38
Cosmology 4, 33, 67, 92-99, 210, 259
Counselling (psychotherapy) 12, 119, 165, 166-67, 171
Critchlow, Keith 123, 212, 237
Culme-Seymore, Angela 32, 35, 43, 57, 60, 66-67, 83, 91, 122, 207, 226, 234-35

Dalai Lama 214
Dalgleish, Narda 211
Daner, Francine Jeanne 30
Dante 3, 6, 241
Dawkins, Richard 210
Dede, Sheikh 55, 66
Dependence (on God) 21, 123, 125, 158
Derin, Suleyman 186, 202
Desire 143, 159, 163, 167, 211, 249, 260
Devotion (to God) 59, 80, 157, 177, 189
Dhawq (intuition) 107
Dhat (personality) 103, 107
Dhikr (also see Zikr) 34, 39, 59, 83, 120, 150
Divine Breath 95, 115, 135
Divine Knowledge 99, 105, 118, 119
Dreams (also dreaming) 41, 50, 52, 105, 106, 162, 191
Dunne, John 245
Dupré, Adam 221, 252, 258

Eckhart, Meister 6, 126, 206
Effendi, Aziz Mumud Hudayi 40, 44, 50-51, 117, 185-86, 191
Ego 38, 71, 85, 124-25, 139, 154-55, 169, 174
Eickelman, Dale 31
Eliade, Mircea 10, 19-20, 188
Emphatic understanding 19
Ephesus 33, 85, 178, 186, 193, 196-99
Epistemology 24-25, 102-104
Eranos 10, 211
Ernst, Carl 31
Eschatology 111-12
Essence (of God, Divine, of things (a'yan al-muwjûddât), of Being 41, 81, 83-84, 93-94, 96-99, 101, 103, 105, 107-12, 115, 118, 119, 123-24, 129, 133, 135, 149, 160, 171, 173, 181, 189
Essential Realities 106, 122
Essential Truth 225
Eternal/Divine Youth 3
Evil (the problem of) 109, 170, 217

Fadiman 12
Fanâ' (annihilation or passing away in God) 106-107, 125, 179
Farouk, King of Egypt 36
Fashion 161-64
Fâtihah 190-91
Fatima of Cordova (Nunah Fatimah Bint Ibn al Muthanna) 3, 35, 55, 174
Fayza, Princess 36, 42
Feild, Reshad 42-43, 56-62, 66, 165, 205, 216
Feminine in the Divine 114
Fenârî, Molla 179
Firâsa (spiritual insight) 49
Food, Beshara and Bulent Rauf 45, 71, 84, 157, 165, 192, 214
Frager, R. 12
Freud, Sigmund 203-204

Gabriel 57, 114, 128
Gaia hypothesis 210
Gault, Richard 215
Geaves, Ron 10-11, 16-17
Geertz, Clifford 31
Ghazi, Orhan Gazi Othman 37
Ghayb (unseen spiritual side of Reality) 174
Ghitani, Gamel 254
Gilsenan, Michael 31
Gilis, Charles André 246-48
Gimenez, Dr. Francisco 251-52
God, the One and Unique (Wahid al-ahad) 169, 246
Goodwin, Professor Brian (Science) 209-10
Gnostics, gnostic (spiritual knowledge, see also knower and 'ârif) 3, 6, 19, 93, 103, 110, 116, 119, 168, 247
Guénon, René 8-9, 11, 16, 67, 232-33, 246-47, 264
Gurdjieff, Georgi Ivanovitch 13, 17, 59, 68, 70, 72, 144, 151, 221

Hadith qudsi (Divine saying) 3, 91-92, 95-96, 133, 167, 256
Hafizovic, Reshid (Bosnia) 261
Hakim, Dr. Souad 252
Halevi, Zev ben Shimon (Warren Kenton, Kabala, Jewish mysticism) 59, 221
Hall, Prof. Hall 251-52
Hardy, Alister (Research Centre) 21
Harris, R.T. 12
Haqq (Truth) (see al-haqq)
Haqq fi Zuhûr (Reality in Appearance)
Heart (qalb) 103-104
Helveti Sufi Order (Helvet - retreat from the world) 40, 117, 239
Hermansen, Marcia 11, 16
Hick, John 25-26
Hidayatullah, Iain Shyarif 259
Himmah (creative power of the intention of the saints - mystical knowers) 174, 177, 189-92, 194-95

Hirtenstein, Daniel 256
Hirtenstein, Stephen 37-38, 113, 133, 147, 179, 233, 235, 238, 240, 245, 253-56
History of Religions 18, 20
Holbrook, Victoria 7, 9, 17, 38-39, 151, 180
'hybrid' Sufi movements 11, 15-17
Husserl, Edmund 18-19
Hoffman, Valerie 186-88, 190-93
Hoja, Sheikh Muzaffer 239
Holroyd, Angela 79, 128, 136
Homerin, T.E. 239
Hornsby, David 251
Hornsby, Lady Elizabeth 235
Hornsby, Richard/Rashid 47, 69, 71, 112
Houedard Dom Sylvester (Benedictine Monk) 59, 126, 209, 221, 244, 251, 252, 260
Hourani, Professor H.A. 237
Hû (Divine spirit or breath of God underlying all creation) 56, 71-72, 81, 216

Ibâda (Divine service) 82, 110, 157
Ibn Arabi (as Pole of Knowledge) 124, 182
Ibn al-Jamî 4
Ibn Rushd (also see Averroes) 3, 242
Ibn Sawdakîn 6
Ibn Sîna (Avacena) 256
Ikhlâs (dedicating Oneself) 190
Imagination 10-11, 72, 99, 105-106, 115, 124, 168, 183, 211, 232
Immanence (of God) 96-97, 108
Immanent 21, 93, 96, 100, 110, 241
Impulse (Divine) 51, 69, 96, 112, 129-30, 139, 141, 165, 166, 227
Indonesia 1, 29, 31, 33-34, 87, 229, 230, 258, 261, 264
Insân (man/human) 78, 100-101
Insan al-Kâmil (Perfect servant/man/universal man/complete human being) (see al-insan) 67, 78, 82-83, 91, 99, 106, 122, 135

Interfaith/inter-religious Dialogue (understanding etc.) 209, 265-66
International Academy for Continuous Education (Bennett) 14, 69-70
Ipseity 72, 119, 169-70, 244
Islam (as in 'submission to God') 88
Ismaël 111
Israelis and Beshara 144-45
Izutzu, Toshihiko 10

James, William 20-21, 23, 25, 37
Jâmî, Abd al- Rahmân 180, 238, 241
Jelveti Sufi Order (Jelvet - open to the world) 7, 40, 44, 45, 48, 50, 55, 117,
Jesus 3, 95, 102, 111-14, 128, 131, 183, 245, 247
Joseph 106
Jungian psychologists/Jungian scholars 10, 211

Kabala 59, 144-45, 219
Kalian, Moshe 202-203
Khalîfa (Vice regent of God) 100, 102
Khalq (creation) 94, 97, 100
Karâma 50
Katz, Stevenv 24-25
Kay Kaus 4
Kedar, Benjamen Z. 188, 202
Kelly, Bernard 67
Kenner, Stuart 260
Kenton, Warren (also see Halevi) 59, 219, 221
Kernel of the Kernel 46, 118-19, 166, 168, 181, 206
Khalwah (retreat) 117
Khalwati-Jerrahi Sufi Order 7, 12, 239
Khan, Hazrat Inayat 12, 17
Khan, Hidayat 12
Khan, Pir Vilayat 12, 42, 57, 60, 216
Khayâl (Divine imagination) 105-106
Khidr 4, 72, 96, 134-35, 164
Khirka 39

Kingsley, Peter (translator of Claude Addas) 2
Knowable/unknowable 108, 129, 167, 170
Knowing and remembering God (ilm Dhikr) 150
Knowledge (spiritual gnosis), knower (*ârif*) 98-99, 102-103, 105, 108, 118-19, 124, 182, 229, 232, 247
Kiliç, Mahmud Erol 9, 179
Knysh, Alexander 8-9, 13, 90, 233, 249, 252
Koç, T. 11, 42
Konya 4, 6, 35-36, 66, 85, 177, 181-82, 186, 197, 256
Kugle, Scott Alan 38

Lam, Martin (chef) 214
Lambert Ortiz, Elizabeth 214
Lamborne Wilson, Peter 11, 251
Landau, Rom 232
Language of Mysticism 20, 23-25, 204
Lewisohn, Leonard 9
Library (of the Muhyiddin Ibn Arabi Society) 227, 231, 235, 237-40, 250, 256
Lings, Martin 8, 9, 68
Loeffler, Reinhold 31
Logos 78, 91, 99-103, 122
Lord (rabb) 111
Lordship (rubûbiyya) 110-12, 245
Love (hubb, seed) 244
Love and Hudai 195
Love (Divine) 96, 108-10

MacEwan, Richard 244-46
Macmillan, Mhairi 166, 168-70
Macrocosm (universe, God) 101, 106, 167
Mahdi 112
Mahassini, Sama, Z. 252
Majd ad-Din Ishaq 4
Malamati School of Mysticism 39
Malâmiyya (self deprecation) 38-39, 47, 180, 260
Martin, Richard, C. 20, 265

Ma'rifa (spiritual gnosis) 102
Maryam (wife of Ibn Arabi) 120, 158
Massignon, Louis 41
Mawlid (Prophet Muhammad's birthday - the Night of Power 83
Meanings (spiritual realities) 1, 69, 132
Mecca 3, 4, 57-58, 256
Meher Baba 13
Mehmet I (Chelebi Sultan) 179, 193-94
Mehmet II (Sultan) 179, 183
Melamî Sufi Order of Turkey 7, 39, 151, 180
Merciful Breath 166
Mercer, J. 255
Messianic 141
Metaphysics of the Imagination 10
Mevlevi Dervishes 45-46, 85, 124, 164, 177, 186, 192, 220, 248
Microcosm (Adam, humanity) 100-101, 167
Mirror (humanity as reflection of God) 84, 96, 100, 171
Misri, Niyâzî 179
Mistri, Kjosh (Zoroastrian) 59
Momen, Moojan 15, 18-19
Moore, Peter 24
Morris, James, W. 9-12, 121, 233, 247, 254, 255
Morocco 1, 31, 264
Moses 4, 96, 106, 113, 247
Muhammadan Sainthood 3, 102, 112-13, 131-34
Mudabbirûn (directors) 38
Muhammadan Reality 102
Muhammadan Spirit (and logos) 78, 91, 99-103, 122
Muhasaba (examination of ones conscience) 169
Multiplicity 16, 92, 94, 108
Murata, Sachiko 9
Mystical Astrology (according to Ibn Arabi) 123-24, 206

Nabî (Apostle) 102
Nafas (Divine breath) 95, 115

Nafas ar-Rahmân (Breath of Divine Mercy) 133, 244
Nafs (soul, ego) 104, 167, 169
Names (Divine), Names of God 59, 83, 97, 183, 201
Nasr, Seyyad Hossein 8, 67, 232, 237, 238
Naqshbandiyya Sufi Order/Naqshbandi 9, 13, 17, 56, 133, 151
Neurology/neuropsychology 22-23, 202, 204
Neve, Margaret 213
New Impulse 129, 141, 227
New Religious Movements 15
Newton, Isaac 209
Nicholson, R.A. 1, 90, 232
Ni'matullahi Sufi Order 14
Nizam 3, 116
Noer, Dr. Kautsar Azhari 261
Noh and Kabuki (Japanese theatre) 213
Norland, Khalil 221, 259
Notcutt, Martin and Caroline 240, 256, 259
Nurbakhsh, Dr. Javad 14

O'Donaghue, N. 221
Oida, Yoshi 213
One God, One Truth, One Divine, One and Unique 137, 161, 169, 200-201, 208, 246
One Reality/Oneness of Being/One Universal (ultimate) Reality/Oneness of God (wahyat al-Wahad) 13, 33, 39, 43, 94-97, 108, 129, 130, 137-38, 169, 171, 259, 266
Ontology 92-99
Order (God's order in the cosmos) 48, 110, 155, 159, 173
Orhan (second sultan of the Ottoman Empire) 179
Otto, Rudolf 19, 21
Ouspensky, Peter 13, 17, 59, 68
Ozak, Shaykh Muzaffer 7, 12, 264

Pahlevi, Riza (Shah of Persia) 36
Panikkar, Raimondo 214
Pattison, George 221
Pawloff, Ted 206, 210
Pedaya, Havina 188
Perennial Sufi Movements 16-17
Perennial tradition 129
Perennial Wisdom Studies 261
Perennialist School (Also see traditionalist school) 9
Perfection 17, 49, 61, 69, 83-84, 101, 116-17, 162, 164, 222, 223, 228
Perfectibility of Man/Perfect Man/Complete Human Being (archetypal) (see al-Insân al-Kâmil) 43, 61, 67, 78, 99-101, 106, 110, 122, 135, 189, 197
Person-Centred Approach (to counselling) 166-67, 169, 171
Persinger, Michael 22
Phenomena 18-20, 22, 94, 107, 116, 262, 264-65
Phenomenal world 98, 100, 105, 170-71
Phenomenology (of religion) 18-20, 27
Piñana Brothers 211
Plato 123
Polarity 101, 111, 170
Pole of Knowledge (Rumi) 124, 182
Pole of Love (Ibn Arabi) 124, 182
Pratt Ewing, Katherine 30
Prince of Wales (Institute of Architecture) 212
Psyche (see nafs/soul) 82, 104, 151, 153, 162
Psychology/psychologist/psychotherapist/psychiatrist 1, 4, 10, 12, 13, 18, 20-23, 28, 30, 33, 49, 64, 104-105, 110, 122, 139, 144, 148, 150, 158, 165, 167-68, 171-72, 178, 184, 202-204, 208, 236, 263, 265
Psychotherapy (see counselling) 165-66
Puy, Laura 259

Qadiriyya 133
Qalb (heart) 103
Qaysari, Duard al 37, 179
Qûnâwi, Sadr al-Din al (Sadruddîn) 4-6, 34, 36-37, 124, 181, 186-87, 193, 238, 241, 256
Qûstâni, Kamâl al-Din 37

Raine, Kathleen 10, 210-12
Rahma (Rahmet) - Turkish for Divine Mercy 84
Rasûl (prophetic messenger) 102, 134
Rauf, Mahmud 55
Rauschenburg, Robert C. 214
Razi, Fakhr ad-Din 103
Real/Truth (see Al-Haqq)
Reality (God) 94
Reality (Absolute) 188
Reality (Divine) 4, 102
Reality in Appearance 107
Reality of Muhammad 99-100, 189
Reality of Realities 99-100, 189
Reality (Ultimate) 20, 25, 53, 70, 139, 263, 266
Reiki (Practitioner) 160-61
Religious Experience (REs) 19-23, 27, 37, 203
Remembrance of God (see also Zikr/dhikr) 53, 59, 83, 158
Rogers, Carl 167-70
Rolling Stones 61
Ruh (spirit) 104
Rukkâb al-a'mâl 38
Rukkâb alhimam 38
Rumi, Jâlludîn 124
Rumi as the 'Pole of Love' 124, 182
Russell, The Hon. Rosemary (radionics) 59
Ryan, Christopher 42, 45, 84, 212

Sahnoun, Farid 119
Sainthood (see also Wali, walâya etc.) 3, 30, 37-38, 47, 102, 111-14, 117, 124, 131-34, 147, 174, 181, 189, 201, 233, 245
Samâ 39, 252, 256

Samye-Ling (Tibetan Buddhist Temple) 209
Schimmel, Annemarie 10
School for Continuous Education (see International Academy for Continuous Education) (Bennett) 14, 69-70, 221
Science (physical) 5, 19, 95, 130-31, 171, 175, 208, 210, 214, 222-23, 263
Schoun, Fritchjof 8
Seal of Muhammadan Sainthood (Ibn Arabi) 3, 102, 112, 113, 131-34
Seal of Saints 102
Seal of Universal Sainthood (Jesus) 112, 113, 131, 134
Second Coming of Christ 113, 131, 134-35
Sedgwick, Mark 8
Self (human and Divine) 13, 21, 26, 40, 49, 53, 56, 69, 73, 78, 84, 86, 88, 90, 93, 95, 98-99, 102, 104-105, 107, 110, 115, 122, 125, 132, 136-39, 149, 156, 158, 161-63, 167-69, 171-74, 180, 195, 198, 209, 211, 213-14, 232, 262-63
Self-knowledge 136-37, 141, 211, 213, 214
Self-revelation 99, 122
Sells, Michael 24, 211, 249, 251, 255
Sema (death [birth] when Mevlevi dervishes 'throw off the cloak of physical existence') 85, 124, 177, 186
Service (ihsân)/servanthood/servantship (to God) (ubûdiyya); true Divine service (ibâda) 38, 49, 59, 71-72, 82-83, 110, 117, 125, 138, 149, 157-59, 189, 212, 219, 254, 255
Seth 92, 102, 248
Shadhili Sufi Order 8, 34
Shah, Idries 16 56
Shamesh, Layla 259
Shams of Marchena 3

Sharî (shariah) 'legislating' Divine revelations 134
Sheldrake, Rupert (biologist) 209-10
Shelley, Christopher 235
Silsile/silsila (initiatic chain/chain of authority) 39, 180
Sinan (Architect) 212
Sirrhu Baba 40-41, 44
Situpa, Khentin Tai 209
Smirnov, Andre 252-53
Smart, Ninian 19
Smith, Huston 8, 214
Sophia Perennis (Journal edited by William Chittick) 235, 240, 243
Sorayya, Princess (Shah of Persia [Iran's] wife) 36
Soul (self) 81, 103-105, 113, 118-19, 176, 182, 211
Springfield, Dusty 56
Spiritual meaning of Ibn Arabi 32
Stace, W.T. 21, 24
Stoddart, William 67
Submission to God 88, 148, 154, 158
Submitting to the Order of things 165
Subud 68
Subuh, Mohammad 68
Sufi Movement 3-18, 31, 34, 38-42, 44, 46, 48, 52-60, 66-68, 72, 83, 85, 88-89, 93, 104, 116, 118, 120-21, 125, 133, 135-36, 147, 149, 151, 157, 166-67, 179-80, 186, 198, 205, 216, 223, 230, 232, 239, 246-50
Sufi Order of the West 15, 26, 88, 264
Sufis of Andalusia 1-3, 119-20
Suhba (companionship)
Sultan Selim I 180
Sultan Suleyman, (the Magnificent) 186, 202, 212
Sultan Walad 177
Sura 96, 100, 163, 183, 190
Surrender to God 164
Symposia (of the Muhyiddin Ibn Arabi Society) 2, 27-28, 33-34,

206, 224, 231, 236-37, 240, 242, 249, 251, 254, 258, 261, 263

Tao Te Ching 125, 167
Tabriz, Shams-i 124, 181-82
Tadbîr (government) 38
Tagore, Rabindranath 228
Tahrali, Mustafa 9, 37
Tajalliyât (self-manifestations of the Divine) 99, 136
Taji Farouki, Suhar 230
Tajrid (detachment) 113
Taste (spiritual, Adab) 25, 45, 47-48, 50, 86, 140, 163, 177-78, 182, 189
Tawakkul (trust) 139, 150
Tawhîd (union with God) 130, 177
Tayyer, Caferi 41
Temenos 10, 211-12
Thierry of Chartres 241
Thomas, Mansura 65
Tiernan, Kathy 213
Tiernan, M. 120, 253-55
Timelessness 123, 154, 164
Tollemache, Hugh 45-47, 55, 117, 171, 234, 248
Traditionalist School (see also Perennial School) 16, 67
Traditionalist writings (as in Rene Guénon) 8-9, 11, 16, 67, 232-33, 246-47, 264
Transcendence/Transcendent 24, 96, 97, 107-108, 167
Trimingham, Spencer 39
Trust in God 150, 158
Truth/Truth of Reality (Haqq) 94, 97, 100, 108, 189
'Turning' (film) 46, 220, 248
Twinch, Cecilia 78, 129, 136, 139, 148, 150, 154, 157-58, 213-14, 233, 252, 256-57, 260
Twinch, Richard 210

Ubûdiyya (see also Service to God) 38, 149
Uftade, Hazreti 185, 192
Uftade, Mahmud Muhyiddin 117

Ultimate Reality 20, 25, 53, 70, 139, 263, 266
Unconditional positive regard 169-70
Unity 1, 6, 8, 16, 21-22, 43, 45, 49, 65, 67-68, 70, 79, 90-92, 94, 100, 106-108, 110, 111, 119, 122-25, 130-31, 148, 161, 163-64, 167, 170-72, 180, 182, 195, 208, 212, 216-17, 221, 226-29, 240-41, 259, 263, 266
Unity in Diversity 130
Unity of Being 49, 106, 131, 171-72, 180, 216, 227, 241
Unity of Existence 43, 45, 65, 79, 91, 100, 119, 125, 172, 182, 208, 221, 226, 228, 229, 259, 263
Unity of Nature 221
Unity with God 20, 100, 107, 130
Unity with Reality/Union (tawhid) 130, 177
Universal Man/human (see also Al-insân al-Kâmil) 63, 83, 106, 122-23, 251
Universal Reality of Love 131
Universal Sufism 10, 16
Universal Unity 130
'Urs (Death -nuptial night, union with God) 176, 251

Veli. Atesbaz 186, 192
Villa, Princess Vittoria Allaitta de 258
Virgin Mary (or Mother of Jesus)/Our Lady 8, 33, 57, 85, 128, 178, 183, 193, 199
Virgin Mary at Ephesus 33, 178, 193, 197, 199
Visual Arts 33, 164
VITA (Visual Islamic and Traditional Arts) 123, 212
Vocabulary (technical) 159

Wahdat al-wujûd (Unity of Existence/Oneness of Being) 13, 39, 171, 172
Wajhu Illâh (those who see His love in everything etc.) 38

Walî, Walâya (saint/friend of God), awliyâ (pl.) 37-38, 40, 47, 51-53, 102, 132, 134, 189, 245
Wasserstrom, S. 10
Waterfield, Robin 233
Watts, Frazer, N. 203
Wazîfas (devotional practices, litanies of Divine Names) 59, 83, 157, 165
Weber, Max 47
Weir, T.H. 7, 121, 240
White Fusûs 62, 116, 132
Whoso Knoweth Himself 7, 121, 240
Wibowo, Tri 261
Williams, Hilary 211, 239
Williams, Mark 203
Wilson, Elizabeth 162-63
Witztum, Eliezer 202-203
Wujûd (Being/Existence) 6, 13, 39, 92-93, 96, 98, 103, 171, 172
Wujûd al-Kullî (Entire Being) 93
Wujûd al-mutlaq (absolute Being) 92

Yahia, Osman 3, 5, 237, 239
Yeats, W.B. 211
Yiangou, Alison 252-54
Yiangou, Peter 118, 212, 215, 259
Young, Peter (Principal of the Beshara School) 15, 29, 65, 78-79, 113, 126, 128, 133-34, 136-38, 184, 193, 209, 227-28, 235, 241-43, 251-52, 259

Zabor, Rafi 210
Zahir (divine essence coming into manifestation) 134
Zikr (see also dhikr) (remembrance of God) 26, 30, 34, 53, 59, 72, 76, 80, 83, 104, 146, 153, 161, 177, 216, 220, 225, 235
Zuhd (Renunciation) 113
Zwi Werblowsky, R.J. 188

www.ingramcontent.com/pod-product-compliance
Lightning Source LLC
Chambersburg PA
CBHW060945230426
43665CB00015B/2066